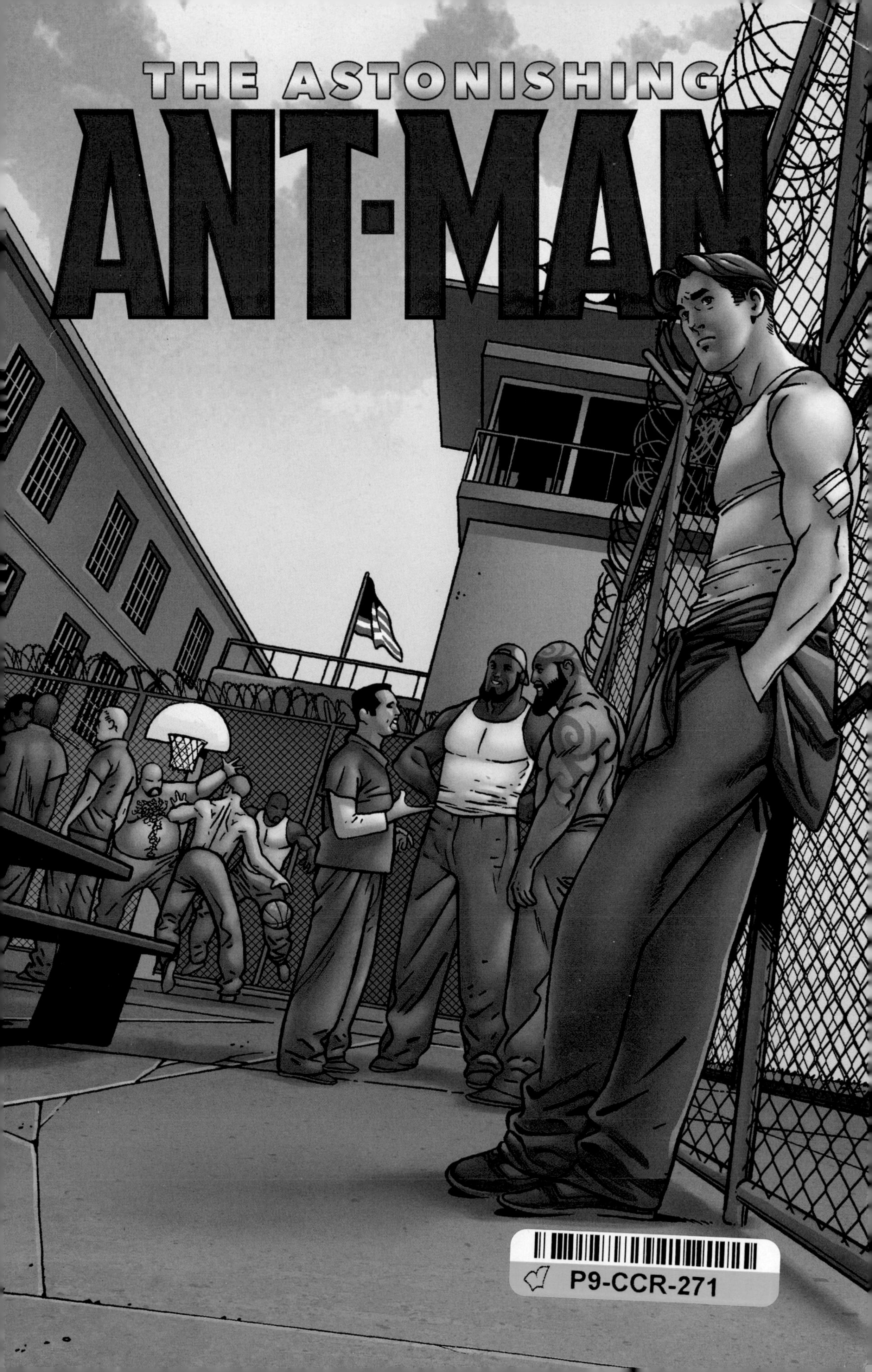
THE ASTONISHING
ANT-MAN

THE ASTONISHING ANT-MAN

EVERYBODY LOVES TEAM-UPS

WRITER: NICK SPENCER

ANNUAL

ARTISTS:
BRENT SCHOONOVER (FLASHBACK)
& RAMON ROSANAS (PRESENT DAY)

COLOR ARTIST: JORDAN BOYD

COVER ART: DAVID MARQUEZ
& JUSTIN PONSOR

LAST DAYS

ARTIST: RAMON ROSANAS

COLOR ARTIST: JORDAN BOYD

COVER ART: MARK BROOKS

1-4

ARTIST: RAMON ROSANAS

COLOR ARTISTS: JORDAN BOYD (#1-3) & WIL QUINTANA (#4)

COVER ART: MARK BROOKS (#1-3) & DAVID NAKAYAMA (#4)

VC's Travis Lanham
LETTERER

Chris Robinson
& Jon Moisan
ASSISTANT EDITORS

Wil Moss
EDITOR

ANT-MAN CREATED BY **STAN LEE**, **LARRY LIEBER** & **JACK KIRBY**

COLLECTION EDITOR:
ALEX STARBUCK

ASSOCIATE EDITOR:
SARAH BRUNSTAD

EDITORS, SPECIAL PROJECTS:
JENNIFER GRÜNWALD & **MARK D. BEAZLEY**

VP, PRODUCTION & SPECIAL PROJECTS:
JEFF YOUNGQUIST

SVP PRINT, SALES & MARKETING:
DAVID GABRIEL

BOOK DESIGNER
JAY BOWEN

EDITOR IN CHIEF:
AXEL ALONSO

CHIEF CREATIVE OFFICER:
JOE QUESADA

PUBLISHER:
DAN BUCKLEY

EXECUTIVE PRODUCER
ALAN FINE

THE ASTONISHING ANT-MAN VOL. 1: EVERYBODY LOVES TEAM-UPS. Contains material originally published in magazine form as THE ASTONISHING ANT-MAN #1-4, ANT-MAN: LAST DAYS #1 and ANT-MAN ANNUAL #1. First printing 2016. ISBN# 978-0-7851-9948-9. Published by MARVEL WORLDWIDE, INC., a subsidiary of MARVEL ENTERTAINMENT, LLC. OFFICE OF PUBLICATION: 135 West 50th Street, New York, NY 10020. Copyright © 2016 MARVEL No similarity between any of the names, characters, persons, and/or institutions in this magazine with those of any living or dead person or institution is intended, and any such similarity which may exist is purely coincidental. **Printed in the U.S.A.** ALAN FINE, President, Marvel Entertainment; DAN BUCKLEY, President, TV, Publishing & Brand Management; JOE QUESADA, Chief Creative Officer; TOM BREVOORT, SVP of Publishing; DAVID BOGART, SVP of Business Affairs & Operations, Publishing & Partnership; C.B. CEBULSKI, VP of Brand Management & Development, Asia; DAVID GABRIEL, SVP of Sales & Marketing, Publishing; JEFF YOUNGQUIST, VP of Production & Special Projects; DAN CARR, Executive Director of Publishing Technology; ALEX MORALES, Director of Publishing Operations; SUSAN CRESPI, Production Manager; STAN LEE, Chairman Emeritus. For information regarding advertising in Marvel Comics or on Marvel.com, please contact Vit DeBellis, Integrated Sales Manager, at vdebellis@marvel.com. For Marvel subscription inquiries, please call 888-511-5480. **Manufactured between 3/4/2016 and 4/11/2016 by R.R. DONNELLEY, INC., SALEM, VA, USA.**

10 9 8 7 6 5 4 3 2 1

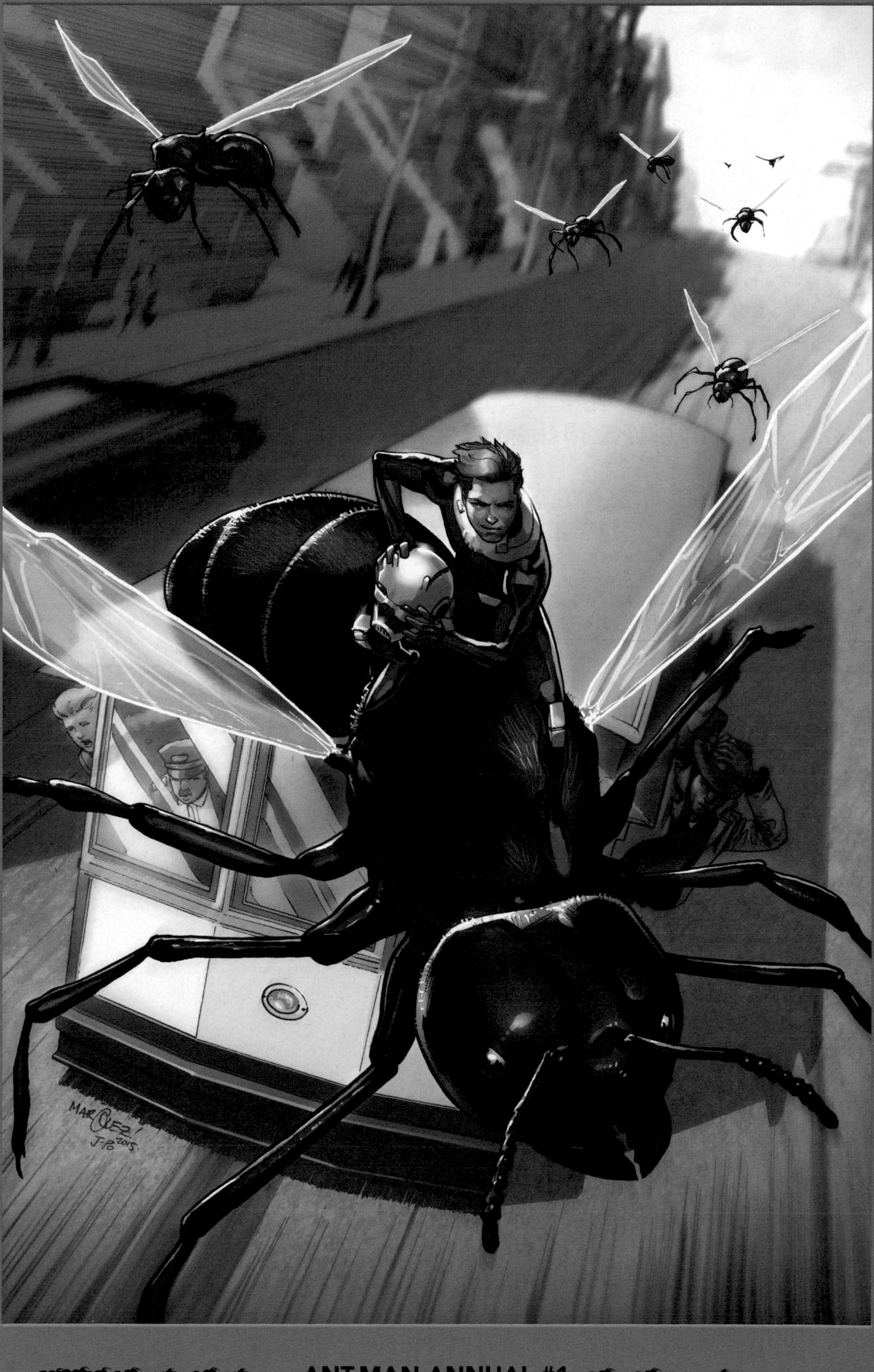
MARQUEZ!
J-Po 2015.

ANT-MAN ANNUAL #1

ANT-MAN

HANK PYM WAS A PIONEER WHEN IT CAME TO BEING A SUPER HERO. AS THE SIZE-CHANGING ANT-MAN, HE WAS A FOUNDING MEMBER OF THE AVENGERS. HE HELPED TO CHANGE THE WORLD FOR THE BETTER!

WHEN HANK DECIDED TO DON THE NEW HEROIC PERSONA OF GIANT-MAN AND LEAVE ANT-MAN BEHIND, ANOTHER MAN ROSE/SHRANK TO THE OCCASION (ERR, STOLE THE COSTUME) – SCOTT LANG! WITH HIS SOMEWHAT SORDID PAST SOMEWHAT BEHIND HIM, SCOTT TOOK ON THE SIZE-CHANGING, ANT-COMMUNICATING ABILITIES OF ANT-MAN!

RECENTLY, SCOTT MOVED TO MIAMI SO HE COULD BE PART OF HIS DAUGHTER CASSIE'S LIFE. HE'S OPENED A SECURITY FIRM CALLED ANT-MAN SECURITY SOLUTIONS, AND HIRED A FEW EMPLOYEES—GRIZZLY, A FORMERLY VENGEFUL EX-CON IN A BEAR SUIT, AND MACHINESMITH, AN ARROGANT CYBORG. TOGETHER, THEY'RE TRYING TO CHANGE THE WORLD -- AND MAYBE EVEN EACH OTHER -- FOR THE BETTER.

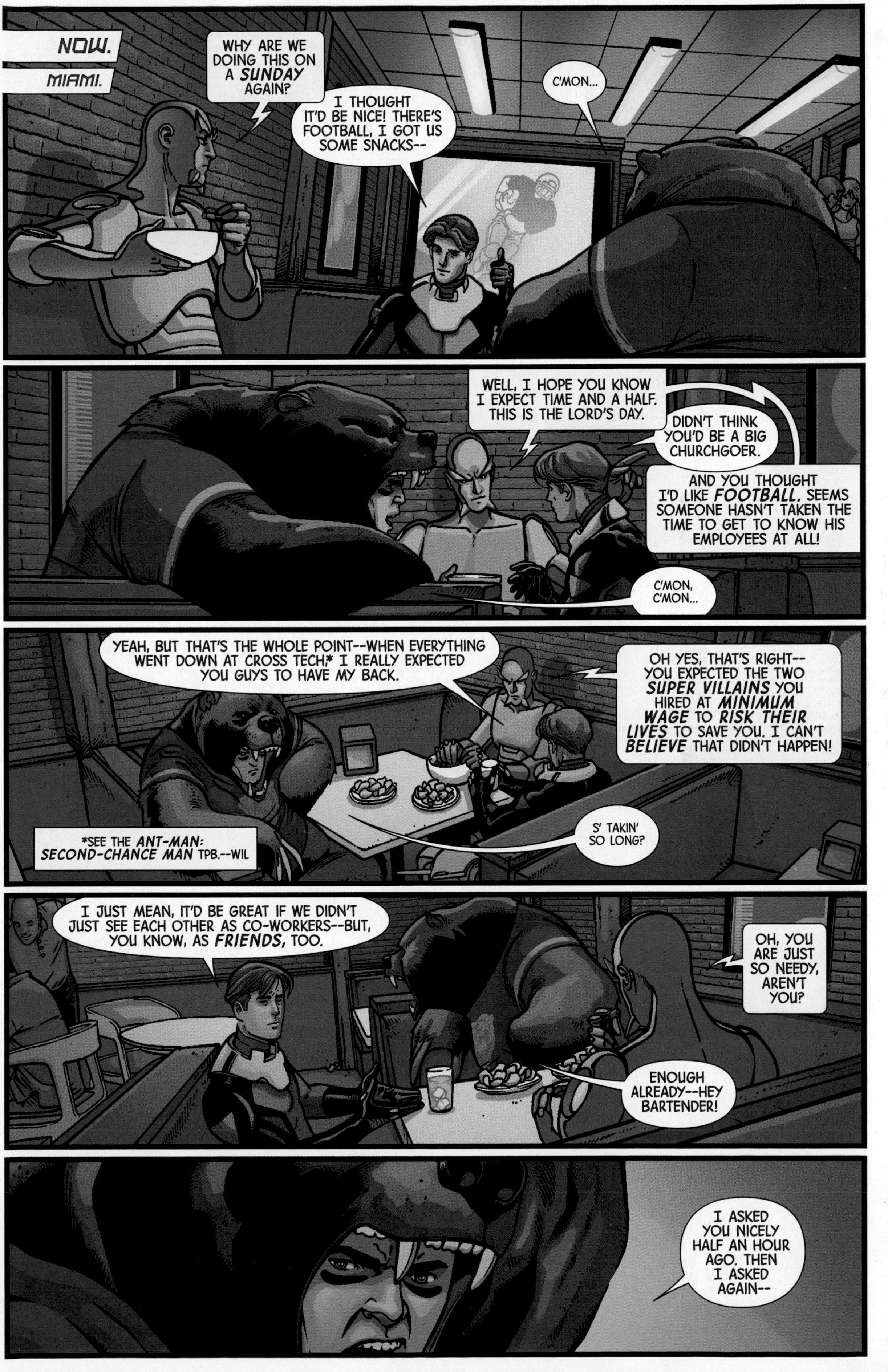
NOW.
MIAMI.
WHY ARE WE DOING THIS ON A SUNDAY AGAIN?
I THOUGHT IT'D BE NICE! THERE'S FOOTBALL, I GOT US SOME SNACKS--
C'MON...
WELL, I HOPE YOU KNOW I EXPECT TIME AND A HALF. THIS IS THE LORD'S DAY.
DIDN'T THINK YOU'D BE A BIG CHURCHGOER.
AND YOU THOUGHT I'D LIKE FOOTBALL. SEEMS SOMEONE HASN'T TAKEN THE TIME TO GET TO KNOW HIS EMPLOYEES AT ALL!
C'MON, C'MON...
YEAH, BUT THAT'S THE WHOLE POINT--WHEN EVERYTHING WENT DOWN AT CROSS TECH* I REALLY EXPECTED YOU GUYS TO HAVE MY BACK.
OH YES, THAT'S RIGHT--YOU EXPECTED THE TWO SUPER VILLAINS YOU HIRED AT MINIMUM WAGE TO RISK THEIR LIVES TO SAVE YOU. I CAN'T BELIEVE THAT DIDN'T HAPPEN!
*SEE THE ANT-MAN: SECOND-CHANCE MAN TPB.--WIL
S' TAKIN' SO LONG?
I JUST MEAN, IT'D BE GREAT IF WE DIDN'T JUST SEE EACH OTHER AS CO-WORKERS--BUT, YOU KNOW, AS FRIENDS, TOO.
OH, YOU ARE JUST SO NEEDY, AREN'T YOU?
ENOUGH ALREADY--HEY BARTENDER!
I ASKED YOU NICELY HALF AN HOUR AGO. THEN I ASKED AGAIN--

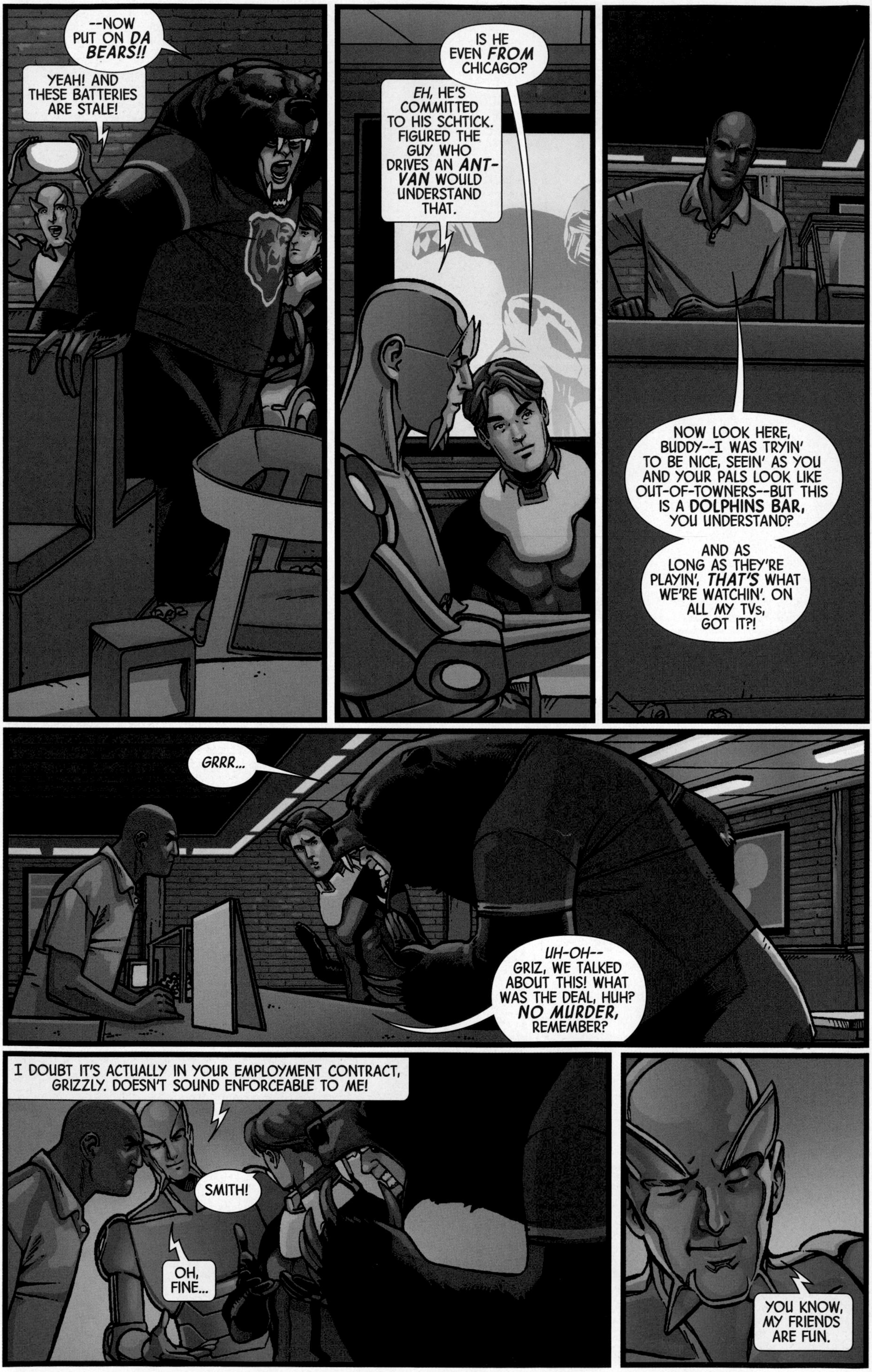
--NOW PUT ON DA BEARS!!
YEAH! AND THESE BATTERIES ARE STALE!
IS HE EVEN FROM CHICAGO?
EH, HE'S COMMITTED TO HIS SCHTICK. FIGURED THE GUY WHO DRIVES AN ANT-VAN WOULD UNDERSTAND THAT.
NOW LOOK HERE, BUDDY--I WAS TRYIN' TO BE NICE, SEEIN' AS YOU AND YOUR PALS LOOK LIKE OUT-OF-TOWNERS--BUT THIS IS A DOLPHINS BAR, YOU UNDERSTAND?
AND AS LONG AS THEY'RE PLAYIN', THAT'S WHAT WE'RE WATCHIN'. ON ALL MY TVs, GOT IT?!
GRRR...
UH-OH-- GRIZ, WE TALKED ABOUT THIS! WHAT WAS THE DEAL, HUH? NO MURDER, REMEMBER?
I DOUBT IT'S ACTUALLY IN YOUR EMPLOYMENT CONTRACT, GRIZZLY. DOESN'T SOUND ENFORCEABLE TO ME!
SMITH!
OH, FINE...
YOU KNOW, MY FRIENDS ARE FUN.

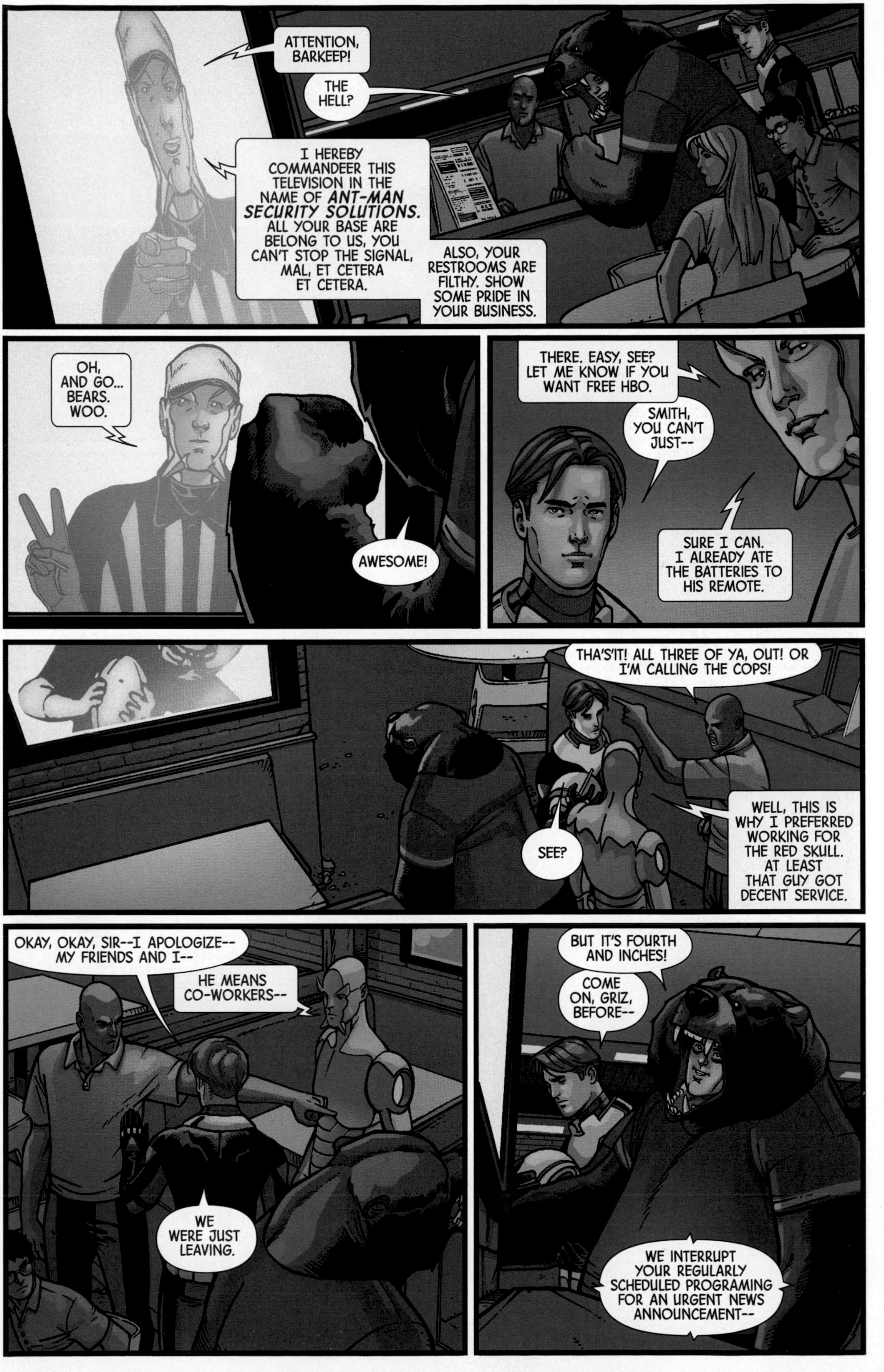
ATTENTION, BARKEEP!
THE HELL?
I HEREBY COMMANDEER THIS TELEVISION IN THE NAME OF ANT-MAN SECURITY SOLUTIONS. ALL YOUR BASE ARE BELONG TO US, YOU CAN'T STOP THE SIGNAL, MAL, ET CETERA ET CETERA.
ALSO, YOUR RESTROOMS ARE FILTHY. SHOW SOME PRIDE IN YOUR BUSINESS.
OH, AND GO... BEARS. WOO.
AWESOME!
THERE. EASY, SEE? LET ME KNOW IF YOU WANT FREE HBO.
SMITH, YOU CAN'T JUST--
SURE I CAN. I ALREADY ATE THE BATTERIES TO HIS REMOTE.
THA'S'IT! ALL THREE OF YA, OUT! OR I'M CALLING THE COPS!
SEE?
WELL, THIS IS WHY I PREFERRED WORKING FOR THE RED SKULL. AT LEAST THAT GUY GOT DECENT SERVICE.
OKAY, OKAY, SIR--I APOLOGIZE-- MY FRIENDS AND I--
HE MEANS CO-WORKERS--
WE WERE JUST LEAVING.
BUT IT'S FOURTH AND INCHES!
COME ON, GRIZ, BEFORE--
WE INTERRUPT YOUR REGULARLY SCHEDULED PROGRAMING FOR AN URGENT NEWS ANNOUNCEMENT--

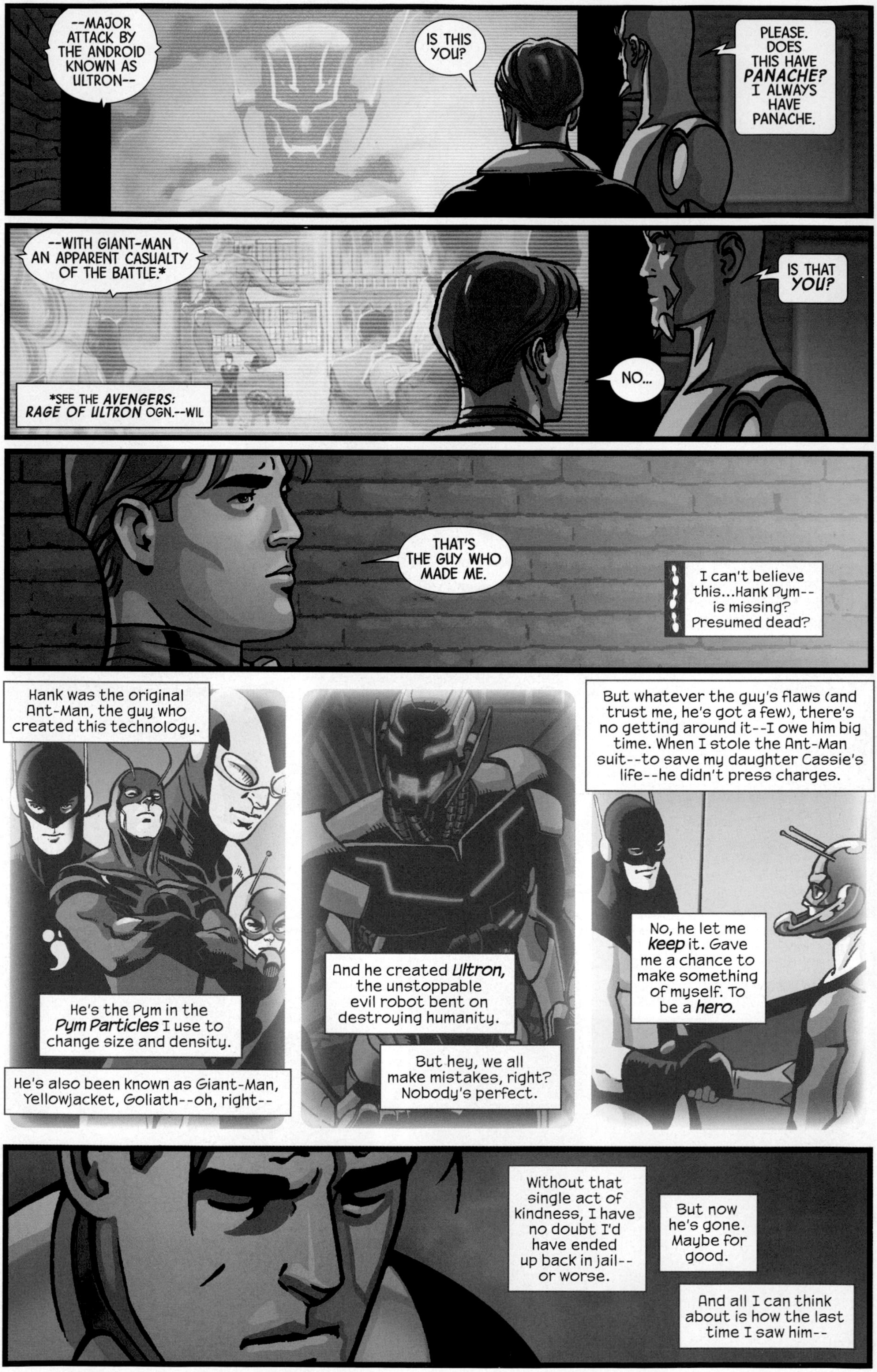
--MAJOR ATTACK BY THE ANDROID KNOWN AS ULTRON--
IS THIS YOU?
PLEASE. DOES THIS HAVE PANACHE? I ALWAYS HAVE PANACHE.
--WITH GIANT-MAN AN APPARENT CASUALTY OF THE BATTLE.*
*SEE THE AVENGERS: RAGE OF ULTRON OGN.--WIL
IS THAT YOU?
NO...
THAT'S THE GUY WHO MADE ME.
I can't believe this...Hank Pym--is missing? Presumed dead?
Hank was the original Ant-Man, the guy who created this technology.
He's the Pym in the Pym Particles I use to change size and density.
He's also been known as Giant-Man, Yellowjacket, Goliath--oh, right--
And he created Ultron, the unstoppable evil robot bent on destroying humanity.
But hey, we all make mistakes, right? Nobody's perfect.
But whatever the guy's flaws (and trust me, he's got a few), there's no getting around it--I owe him big time. When I stole the Ant-Man suit--to save my daughter Cassie's life--he didn't press charges.
No, he let me keep it. Gave me a chance to make something of myself. To be a hero.
Without that single act of kindness, I have no doubt I'd have ended up back in jail--or worse.
But now he's gone. Maybe for good.
And all I can think about is how the last time I saw him--

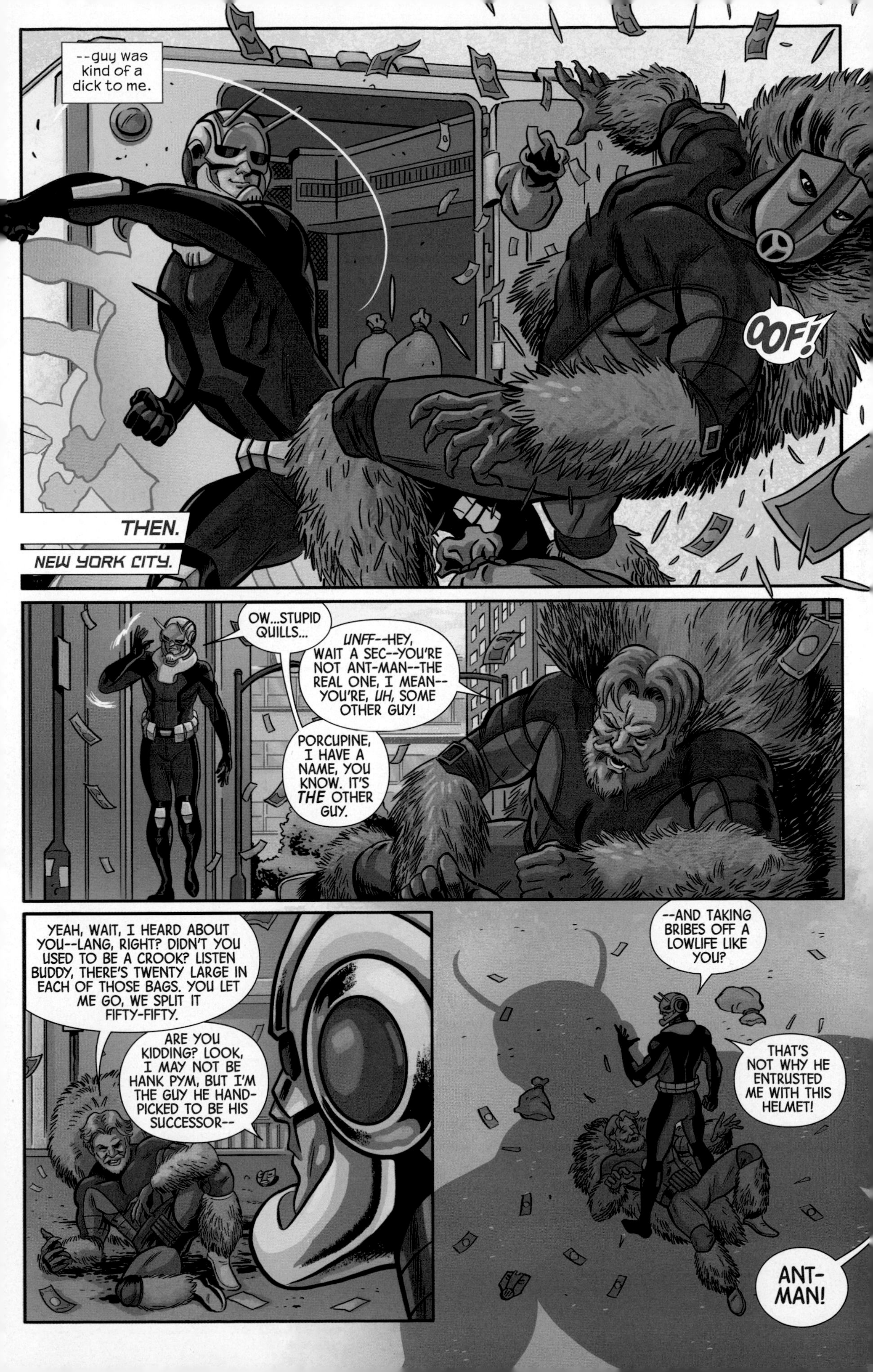
--guy was kind of a dick to me.
OOF!
THEN.
NEW YORK CITY.
OW...STUPID QUILLS...
UNFF--HEY, WAIT A SEC--YOU'RE NOT ANT-MAN--THE REAL ONE, I MEAN--YOU'RE, UH, SOME OTHER GUY!
PORCUPINE, I HAVE A NAME, YOU KNOW. IT'S THE OTHER GUY.
YEAH, WAIT, I HEARD ABOUT YOU--LANG, RIGHT? DIDN'T YOU USED TO BE A CROOK? LISTEN BUDDY, THERE'S TWENTY LARGE IN EACH OF THOSE BAGS. YOU LET ME GO, WE SPLIT IT FIFTY-FIFTY.
ARE YOU KIDDING? LOOK, I MAY NOT BE HANK PYM, BUT I'M THE GUY HE HAND-PICKED TO BE HIS SUCCESSOR--
--AND TAKING BRIBES OFF A LOWLIFE LIKE YOU?
THAT'S NOT WHY HE ENTRUSTED ME WITH THIS HELMET!
ANT-MAN!

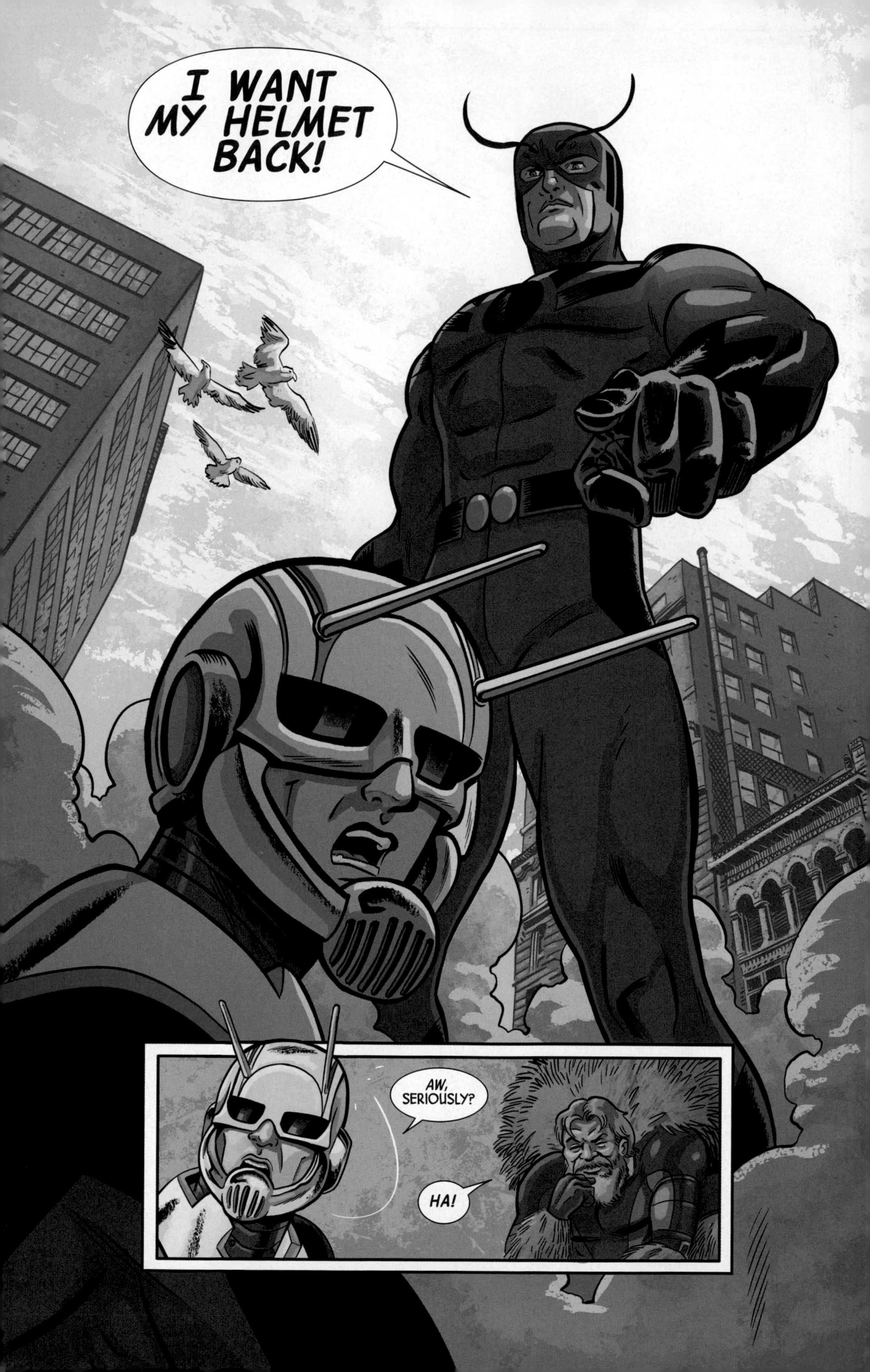
I WANT MY HELMET BACK!
AW, SERIOUSLY?
HA!

WHAT THE HECK, MAN?

JUST FOR A FEW MINUTES, THEN YOU CAN HAVE IT BACK.

OH, AND YOU COULDN'T SAY *THAT* IN FRONT OF THE SUPER VILLAIN?

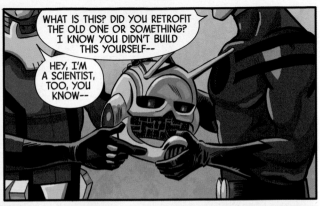

WHAT IS THIS? DID YOU RETROFIT THE OLD ONE OR SOMETHING? I KNOW YOU DIDN'T BUILD THIS YOURSELF--

HEY, I'M A SCIENTIST, TOO, YOU KNOW--

OKAY, YEAH, NO, IT'S A RETROFIT.

EVERYTHING'S IN THE WRONG PLACE--WHY WOULD YOU EVEN DO THIS?

UM, TO MAKE IT LOOK COOLER?

OH, RIGHT, YOU'RE THE *COOL* ANT-MAN. I FORGOT.

SHRINK WITH ME.

WHAT DO YOU EVEN NEED IT FOR?

I...SORT OF LEFT SOMETHING IN HERE.

LEFT WHAT?

THERE IT IS--HERE--

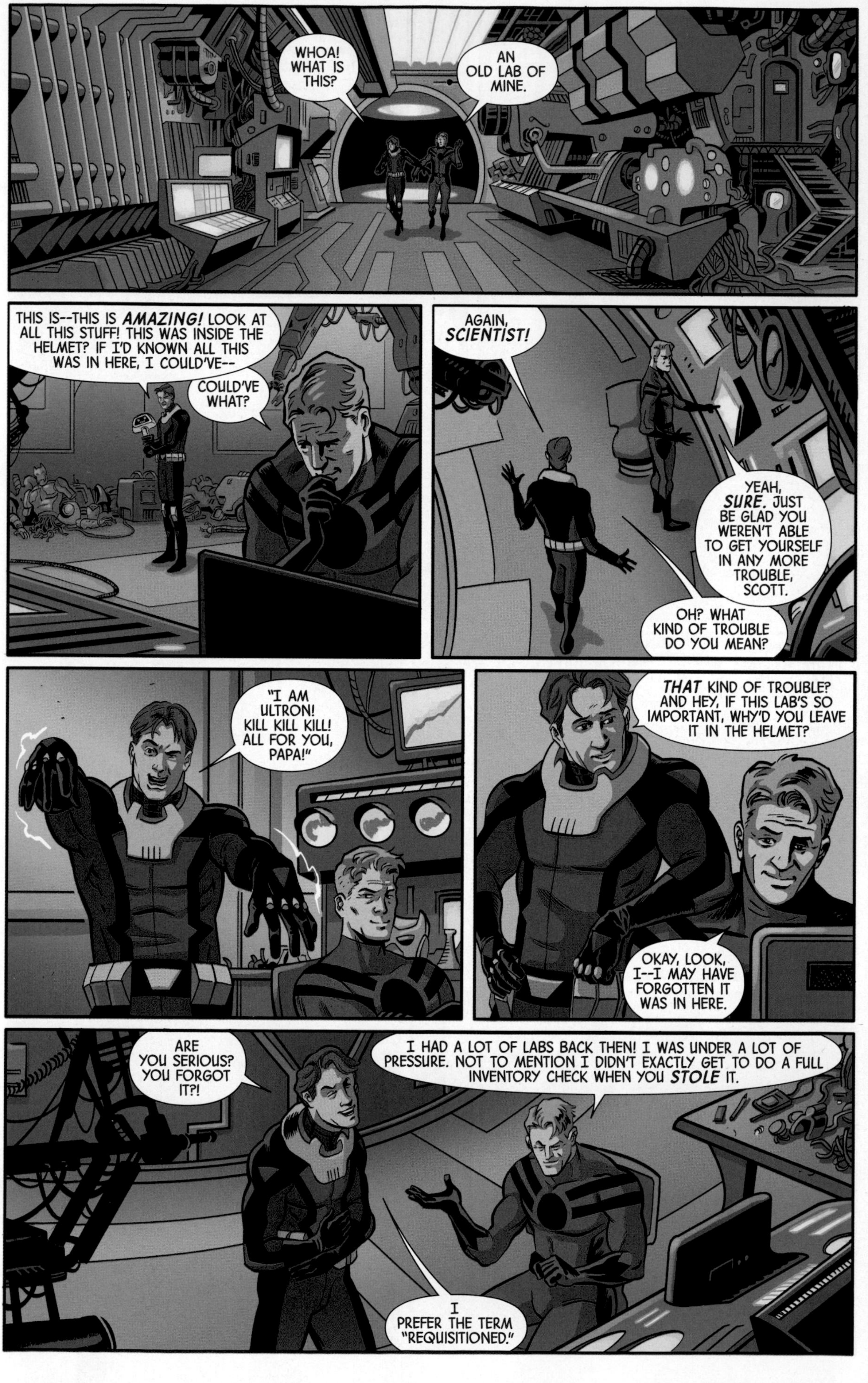
WHOA! WHAT IS THIS?
AN OLD LAB OF MINE.
THIS IS--THIS IS AMAZING! LOOK AT ALL THIS STUFF! THIS WAS INSIDE THE HELMET? IF I'D KNOWN ALL THIS WAS IN HERE, I COULD'VE--
COULD'VE WHAT?
AGAIN, SCIENTIST!
YEAH, SURE. JUST BE GLAD YOU WEREN'T ABLE TO GET YOURSELF IN ANY MORE TROUBLE, SCOTT.
OH? WHAT KIND OF TROUBLE DO YOU MEAN?
"I AM ULTRON! KILL KILL KILL! ALL FOR YOU, PAPA!"
THAT KIND OF TROUBLE? AND HEY, IF THIS LAB'S SO IMPORTANT, WHY'D YOU LEAVE IT IN THE HELMET?
OKAY, LOOK, I--I MAY HAVE FORGOTTEN IT WAS IN HERE.
ARE YOU SERIOUS? YOU FORGOT IT?!
I HAD A LOT OF LABS BACK THEN! I WAS UNDER A LOT OF PRESSURE. NOT TO MENTION I DIDN'T EXACTLY GET TO DO A FULL INVENTORY CHECK WHEN YOU STOLE IT.
I PREFER THE TERM "REQUISITIONED."

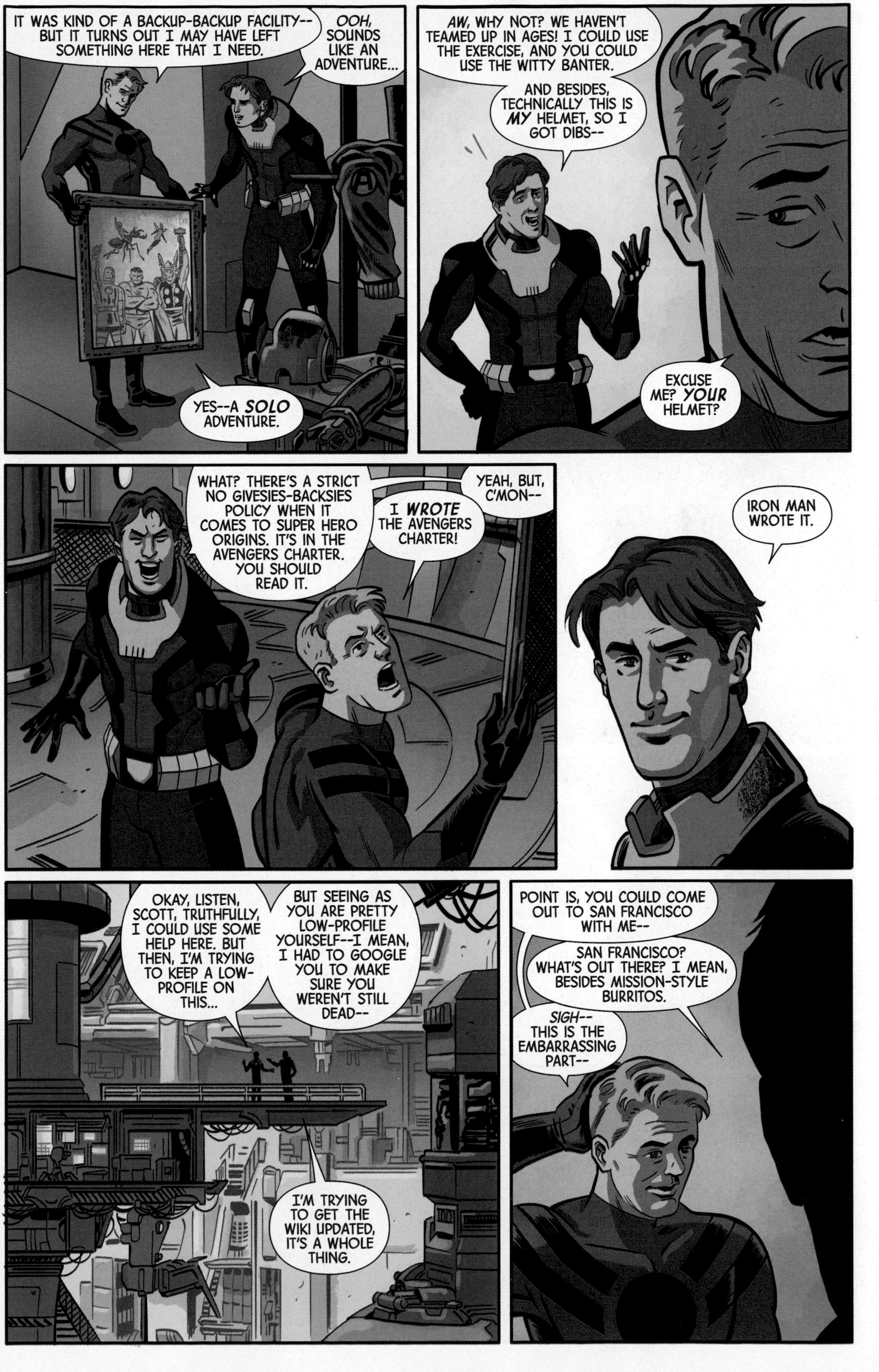
IT WAS KIND OF A BACKUP-BACKUP FACILITY-- BUT IT TURNS OUT I MAY HAVE LEFT SOMETHING HERE THAT I NEED.
OOH, SOUNDS LIKE AN ADVENTURE...
YES--A SOLO ADVENTURE.
AW, WHY NOT? WE HAVEN'T TEAMED UP IN AGES! I COULD USE THE EXERCISE, AND YOU COULD USE THE WITTY BANTER.
AND BESIDES, TECHNICALLY THIS IS MY HELMET, SO I GOT DIBS--
EXCUSE ME? YOUR HELMET?
WHAT? THERE'S A STRICT NO GIVESIES-BACKSIES POLICY WHEN IT COMES TO SUPER HERO ORIGINS. IT'S IN THE AVENGERS CHARTER. YOU SHOULD READ IT.
YEAH, BUT, C'MON--
I WROTE THE AVENGERS CHARTER!
IRON MAN WROTE IT.
OKAY, LISTEN, SCOTT, TRUTHFULLY, I COULD USE SOME HELP HERE. BUT THEN, I'M TRYING TO KEEP A LOW-PROFILE ON THIS...
BUT SEEING AS YOU ARE PRETTY LOW-PROFILE YOURSELF--I MEAN, I HAD TO GOOGLE YOU TO MAKE SURE YOU WEREN'T STILL DEAD--
I'M TRYING TO GET THE WIKI UPDATED, IT'S A WHOLE THING.
POINT IS, YOU COULD COME OUT TO SAN FRANCISCO WITH ME--
SAN FRANCISCO? WHAT'S OUT THERE? I MEAN, BESIDES MISSION-STYLE BURRITOS.
SIGH-- THIS IS THE EMBARRASSING PART--

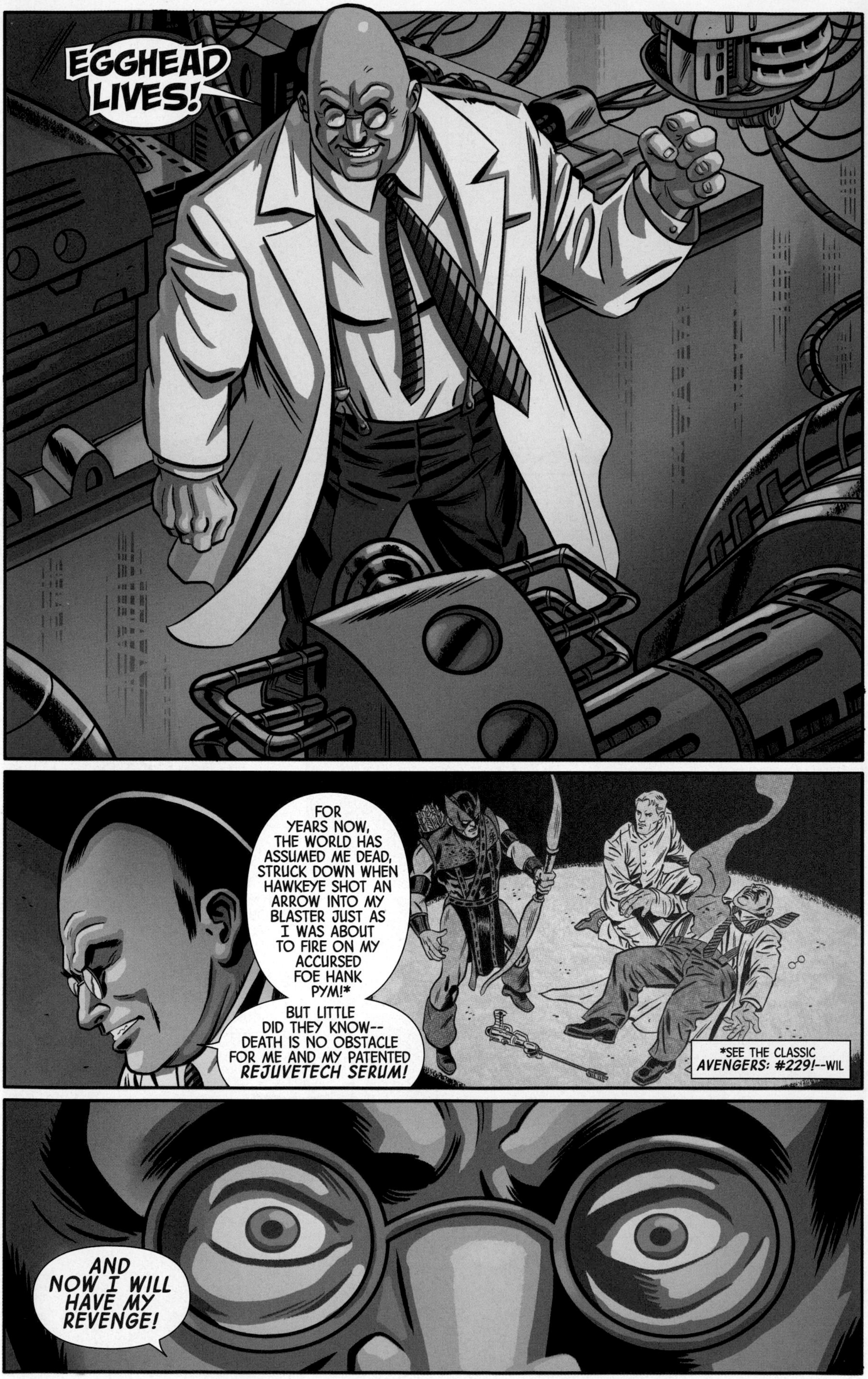
EGGHEAD LIVES!
FOR YEARS NOW, THE WORLD HAS ASSUMED ME DEAD, STRUCK DOWN WHEN HAWKEYE SHOT AN ARROW INTO MY BLASTER JUST AS I WAS ABOUT TO FIRE ON MY ACCURSED FOE HANK PYM!*
BUT LITTLE DID THEY KNOW-- DEATH IS NO OBSTACLE FOR ME AND MY PATENTED REJUVETECH SERUM!
*SEE THE CLASSIC AVENGERS: #229!--WIL
AND NOW I WILL HAVE MY REVENGE!

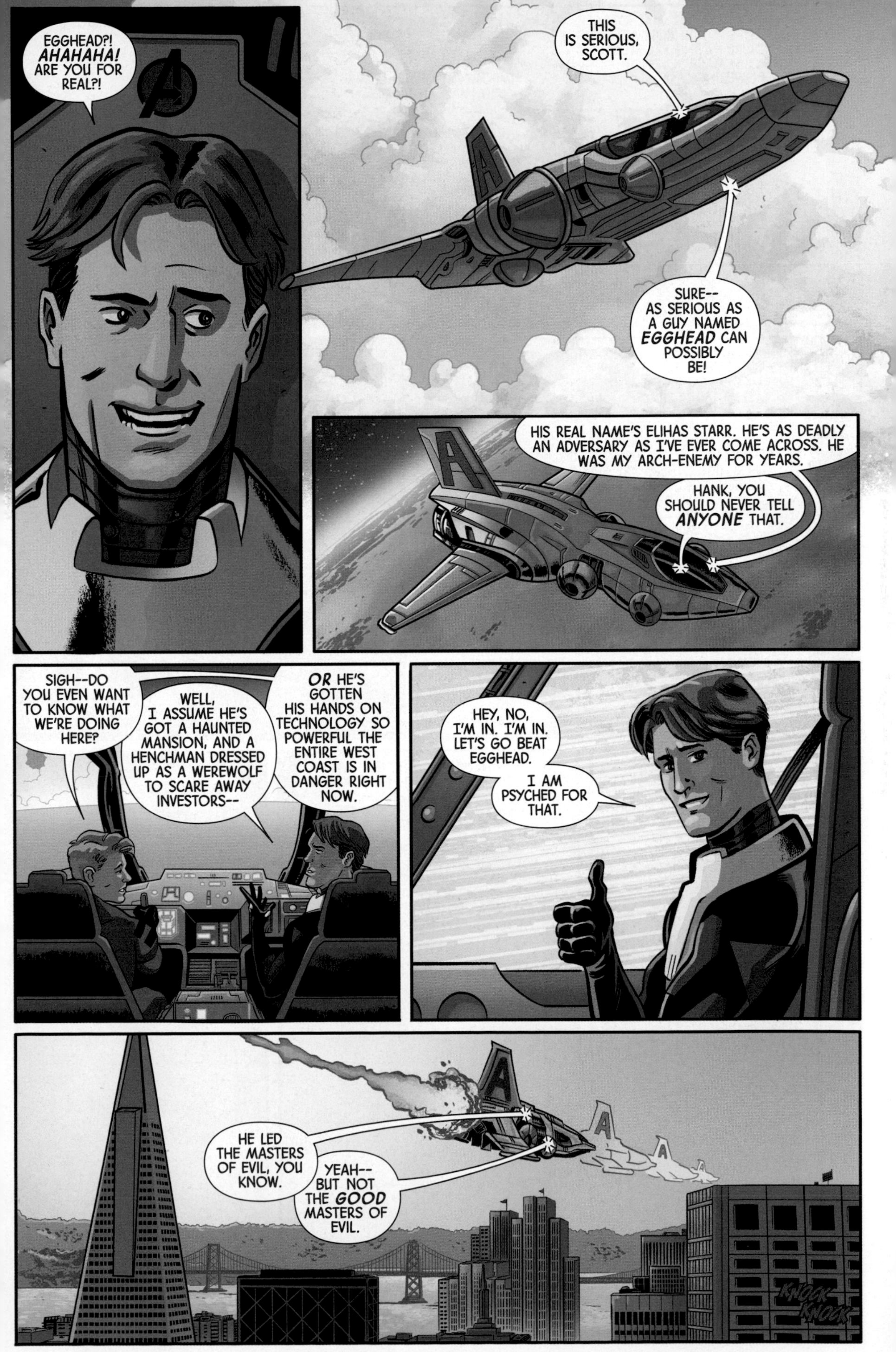
EGGHEAD?! AHAHAHA! ARE YOU FOR REAL?!
THIS IS SERIOUS, SCOTT.
SURE-- AS SERIOUS AS A GUY NAMED EGGHEAD CAN POSSIBLY BE!
HIS REAL NAME'S ELIHAS STARR. HE'S AS DEADLY AN ADVERSARY AS I'VE EVER COME ACROSS. HE WAS MY ARCH-ENEMY FOR YEARS.
HANK, YOU SHOULD NEVER TELL ANYONE THAT.
SIGH--DO YOU EVEN WANT TO KNOW WHAT WE'RE DOING HERE?
WELL, I ASSUME HE'S GOT A HAUNTED MANSION, AND A HENCHMAN DRESSED UP AS A WEREWOLF TO SCARE AWAY INVESTORS--
OR HE'S GOTTEN HIS HANDS ON TECHNOLOGY SO POWERFUL THE ENTIRE WEST COAST IS IN DANGER RIGHT NOW.
HEY, NO, I'M IN. I'M IN. LET'S GO BEAT EGGHEAD.
I AM PSYCHED FOR THAT.
HE LED THE MASTERS OF EVIL, YOU KNOW.
YEAH-- BUT NOT THE GOOD MASTERS OF EVIL.
KNOCK KNOCK

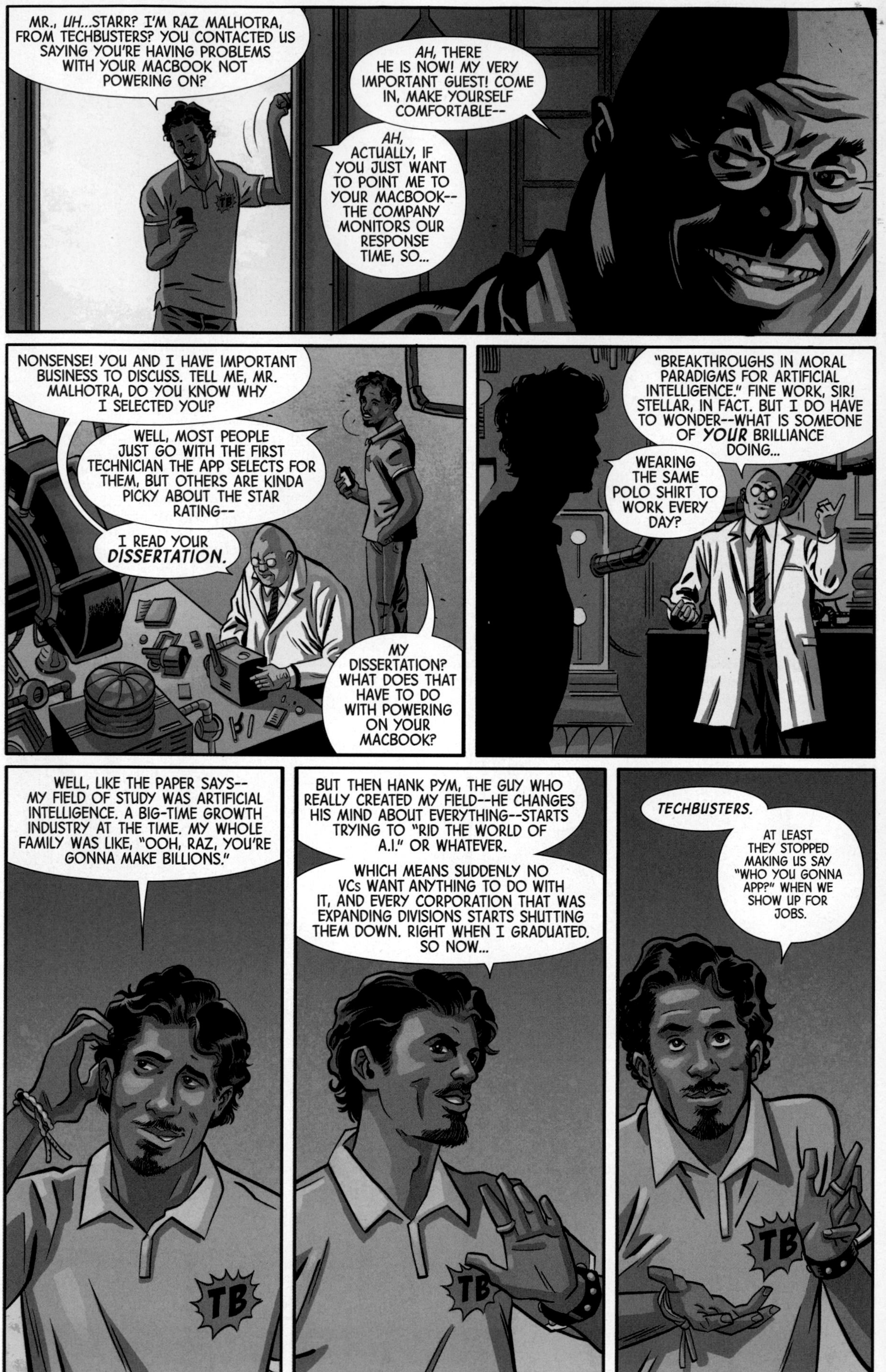
MR., UH...STARR? I'M RAZ MALHOTRA, FROM TECHBUSTERS? YOU CONTACTED US SAYING YOU'RE HAVING PROBLEMS WITH YOUR MACBOOK NOT POWERING ON?
AH, THERE HE IS NOW! MY VERY IMPORTANT GUEST! COME IN, MAKE YOURSELF COMFORTABLE--
AH, ACTUALLY, IF YOU JUST WANT TO POINT ME TO YOUR MACBOOK-- THE COMPANY MONITORS OUR RESPONSE TIME, SO...
NONSENSE! YOU AND I HAVE IMPORTANT BUSINESS TO DISCUSS. TELL ME, MR. MALHOTRA, DO YOU KNOW WHY I SELECTED YOU?
WELL, MOST PEOPLE JUST GO WITH THE FIRST TECHNICIAN THE APP SELECTS FOR THEM, BUT OTHERS ARE KINDA PICKY ABOUT THE STAR RATING--
I READ YOUR DISSERTATION.
MY DISSERTATION? WHAT DOES THAT HAVE TO DO WITH POWERING ON YOUR MACBOOK?
"BREAKTHROUGHS IN MORAL PARADIGMS FOR ARTIFICIAL INTELLIGENCE." FINE WORK, SIR! STELLAR, IN FACT. BUT I DO HAVE TO WONDER--WHAT IS SOMEONE OF YOUR BRILLIANCE DOING...
WEARING THE SAME POLO SHIRT TO WORK EVERY DAY?
WELL, LIKE THE PAPER SAYS-- MY FIELD OF STUDY WAS ARTIFICIAL INTELLIGENCE. A BIG-TIME GROWTH INDUSTRY AT THE TIME. MY WHOLE FAMILY WAS LIKE, "OOH, RAZ, YOU'RE GONNA MAKE BILLIONS."
BUT THEN HANK PYM, THE GUY WHO REALLY CREATED MY FIELD--HE CHANGES HIS MIND ABOUT EVERYTHING--STARTS TRYING TO "RID THE WORLD OF A.I." OR WHATEVER.
WHICH MEANS SUDDENLY NO VCs WANT ANYTHING TO DO WITH IT, AND EVERY CORPORATION THAT WAS EXPANDING DIVISIONS STARTS SHUTTING THEM DOWN. RIGHT WHEN I GRADUATED. SO NOW...
TECHBUSTERS.
AT LEAST THEY STOPPED MAKING US SAY "WHO YOU GONNA APP?" WHEN WE SHOW UP FOR JOBS.

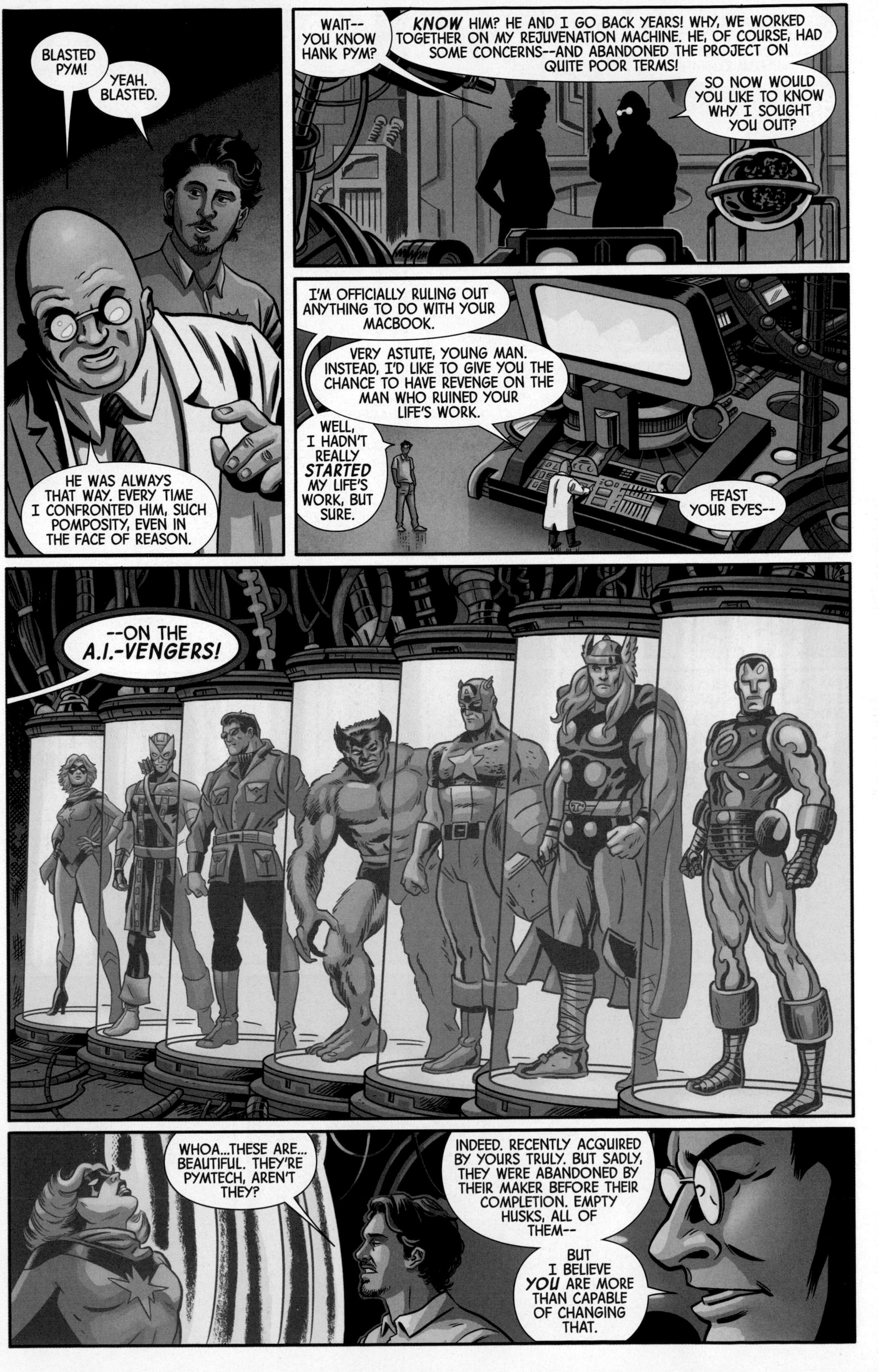
BLASTED PYM!
YEAH. BLASTED.
HE WAS ALWAYS THAT WAY. EVERY TIME I CONFRONTED HIM, SUCH POMPOSITY, EVEN IN THE FACE OF REASON.
WAIT-- YOU KNOW HANK PYM?
KNOW HIM? HE AND I GO BACK YEARS! WHY, WE WORKED TOGETHER ON MY REJUVENATION MACHINE. HE, OF COURSE, HAD SOME CONCERNS--AND ABANDONED THE PROJECT ON QUITE POOR TERMS!
SO NOW WOULD YOU LIKE TO KNOW WHY I SOUGHT YOU OUT?
I'M OFFICIALLY RULING OUT ANYTHING TO DO WITH YOUR MACBOOK.
VERY ASTUTE, YOUNG MAN. INSTEAD, I'D LIKE TO GIVE YOU THE CHANCE TO HAVE REVENGE ON THE MAN WHO RUINED YOUR LIFE'S WORK.
WELL, I HADN'T REALLY STARTED MY LIFE'S WORK, BUT SURE.
FEAST YOUR EYES--
--ON THE A.I.-VENGERS!
WHOA...THESE ARE... BEAUTIFUL. THEY'RE PYMTECH, AREN'T THEY?
INDEED. RECENTLY ACQUIRED BY YOURS TRULY. BUT SADLY, THEY WERE ABANDONED BY THEIR MAKER BEFORE THEIR COMPLETION. EMPTY HUSKS, ALL OF THEM--
BUT I BELIEVE YOU ARE MORE THAN CAPABLE OF CHANGING THAT.

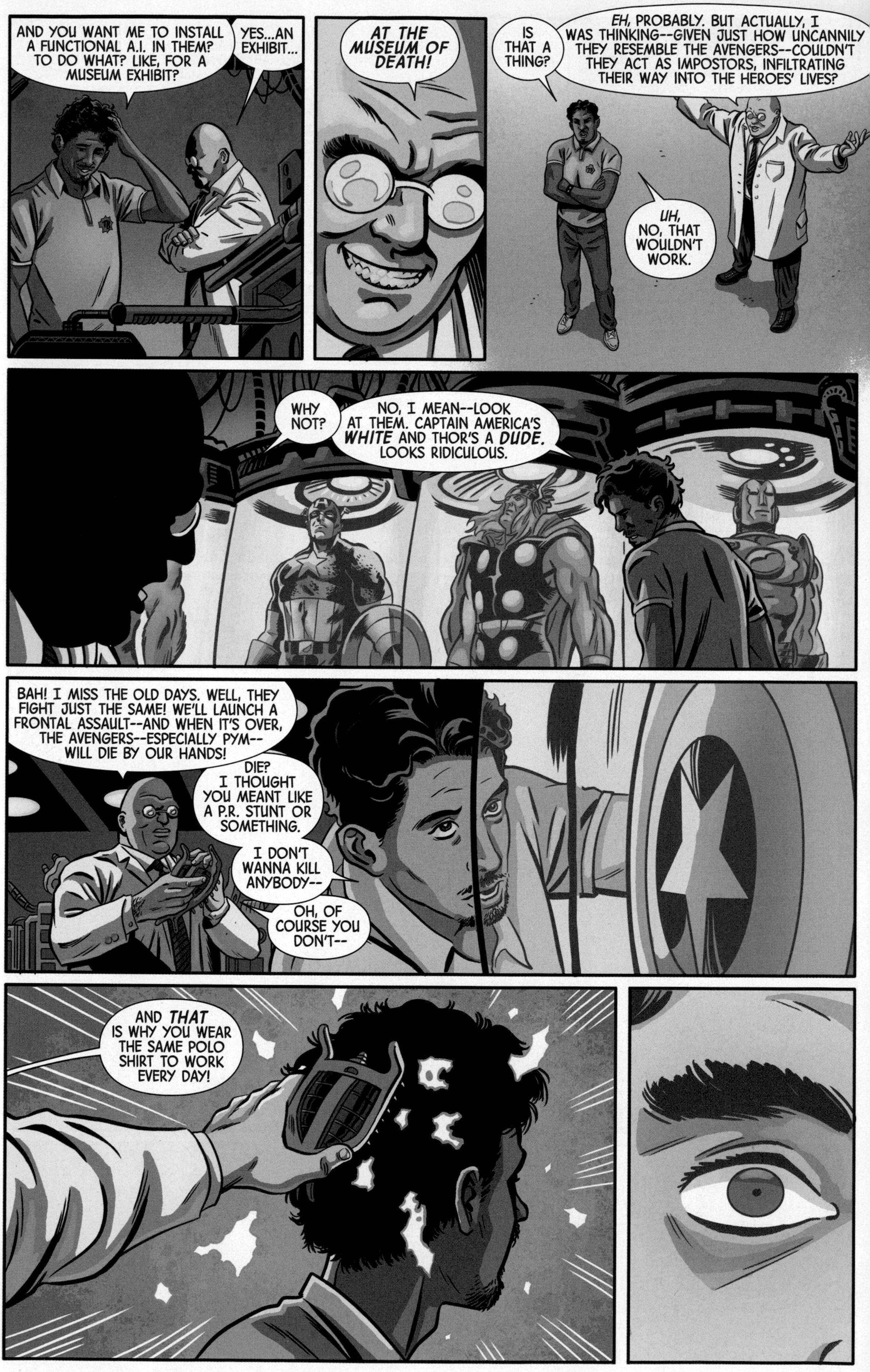
AND YOU WANT ME TO INSTALL A FUNCTIONAL A.I. IN THEM? TO DO WHAT? LIKE, FOR A MUSEUM EXHIBIT?
YES...AN EXHIBIT...
AT THE MUSEUM OF DEATH!
IS THAT A THING?
EH, PROBABLY. BUT ACTUALLY, I WAS THINKING--GIVEN JUST HOW UNCANNILY THEY RESEMBLE THE AVENGERS--COULDN'T THEY ACT AS IMPOSTORS, INFILTRATING THEIR WAY INTO THE HEROES' LIVES?
UH, NO, THAT WOULDN'T WORK.
WHY NOT?
NO, I MEAN--LOOK AT THEM. CAPTAIN AMERICA'S WHITE AND THOR'S A DUDE. LOOKS RIDICULOUS.
BAH! I MISS THE OLD DAYS. WELL, THEY FIGHT JUST THE SAME! WE'LL LAUNCH A FRONTAL ASSAULT--AND WHEN IT'S OVER, THE AVENGERS--ESPECIALLY PYM--WILL DIE BY OUR HANDS!
DIE? I THOUGHT YOU MEANT LIKE A P.R. STUNT OR SOMETHING.
I DON'T WANNA KILL ANYBODY--
OH, OF COURSE YOU DON'T--
AND THAT IS WHY YOU WEAR THE SAME POLO SHIRT TO WORK EVERY DAY!

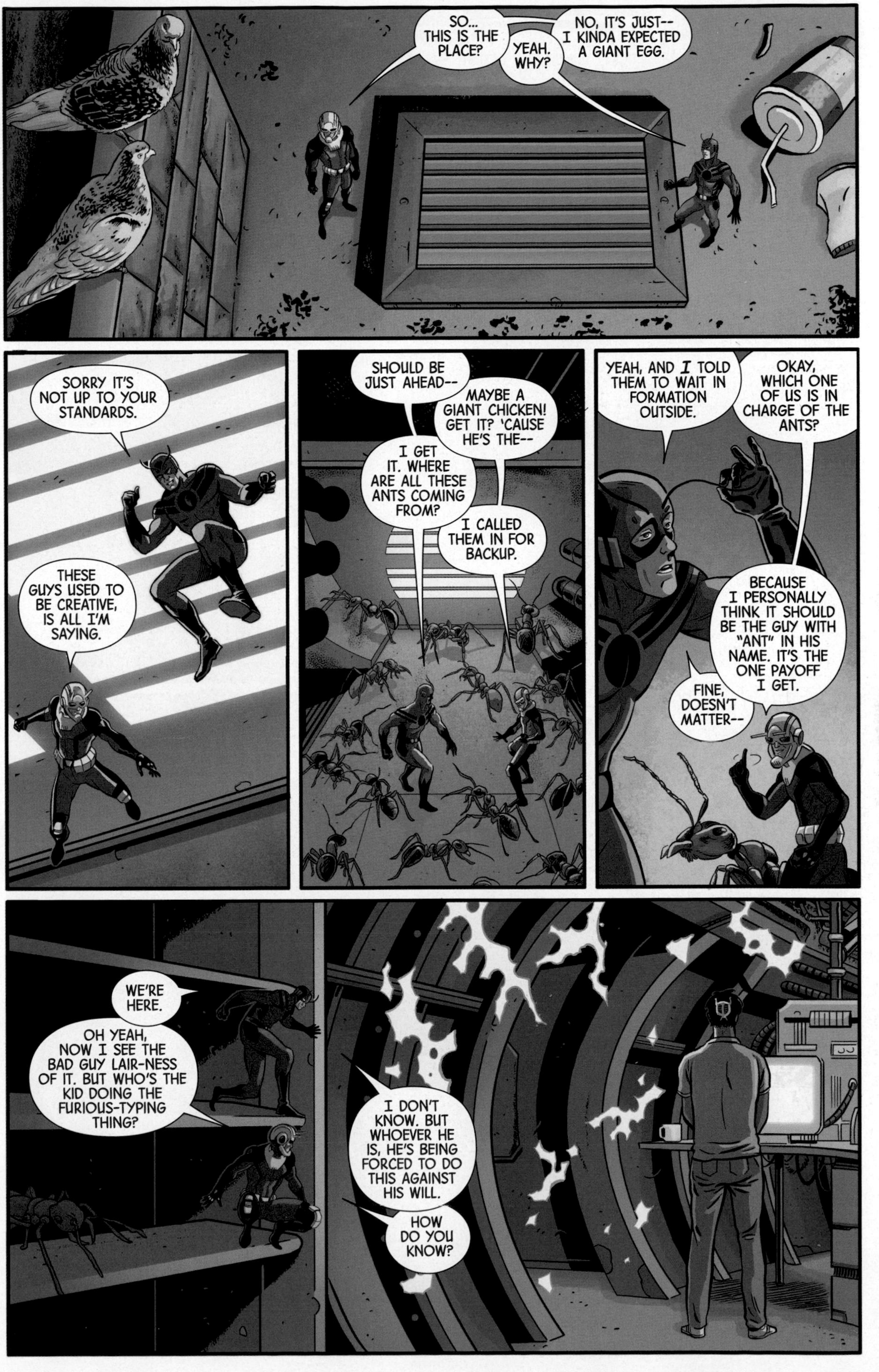
SO... THIS IS THE PLACE?
YEAH. WHY?
NO, IT'S JUST-- I KINDA EXPECTED A GIANT EGG.
SORRY IT'S NOT UP TO YOUR STANDARDS.
THESE GUYS USED TO BE CREATIVE, IS ALL I'M SAYING.
SHOULD BE JUST AHEAD--
MAYBE A GIANT CHICKEN! GET IT? 'CAUSE HE'S THE--
I GET IT. WHERE ARE ALL THESE ANTS COMING FROM?
I CALLED THEM IN FOR BACKUP.
YEAH, AND I TOLD THEM TO WAIT IN FORMATION OUTSIDE.
OKAY, WHICH ONE OF US IS IN CHARGE OF THE ANTS?
BECAUSE I PERSONALLY THINK IT SHOULD BE THE GUY WITH "ANT" IN HIS NAME. IT'S THE ONE PAYOFF I GET.
FINE, DOESN'T MATTER--
WE'RE HERE.
OH YEAH, NOW I SEE THE BAD GUY LAIR-NESS OF IT. BUT WHO'S THE KID DOING THE FURIOUS-TYPING THING?
I DON'T KNOW. BUT WHOEVER HE IS, HE'S BEING FORCED TO DO THIS AGAINST HIS WILL.
HOW DO YOU KNOW?

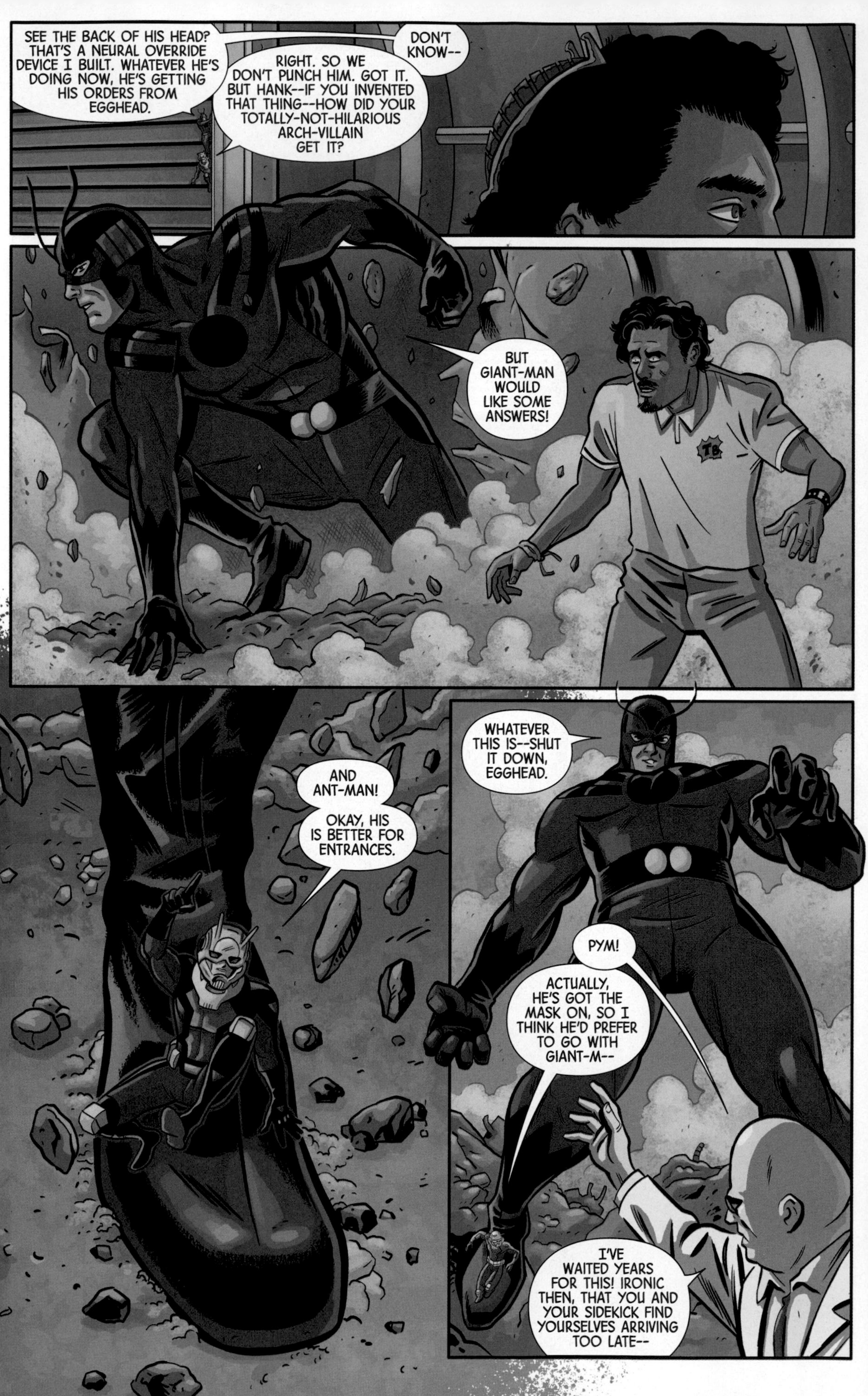
SEE THE BACK OF HIS HEAD? THAT'S A NEURAL OVERRIDE DEVICE I BUILT. WHATEVER HE'S DOING NOW, HE'S GETTING HIS ORDERS FROM EGGHEAD.
RIGHT. SO WE DON'T PUNCH HIM. GOT IT. BUT HANK--IF YOU INVENTED THAT THING--HOW DID YOUR TOTALLY-NOT-HILARIOUS ARCH-VILLAIN GET IT?
DON'T KNOW--
BUT GIANT-MAN WOULD LIKE SOME ANSWERS!
AND ANT-MAN!
OKAY, HIS IS BETTER FOR ENTRANCES.
WHATEVER THIS IS--SHUT IT DOWN, EGGHEAD.
PYM!
ACTUALLY, HE'S GOT THE MASK ON, SO I THINK HE'D PREFER TO GO WITH GIANT-M--
I'VE WAITED YEARS FOR THIS! IRONIC THEN, THAT YOU AND YOUR SIDEKICK FIND YOURSELVES ARRIVING TOO LATE--

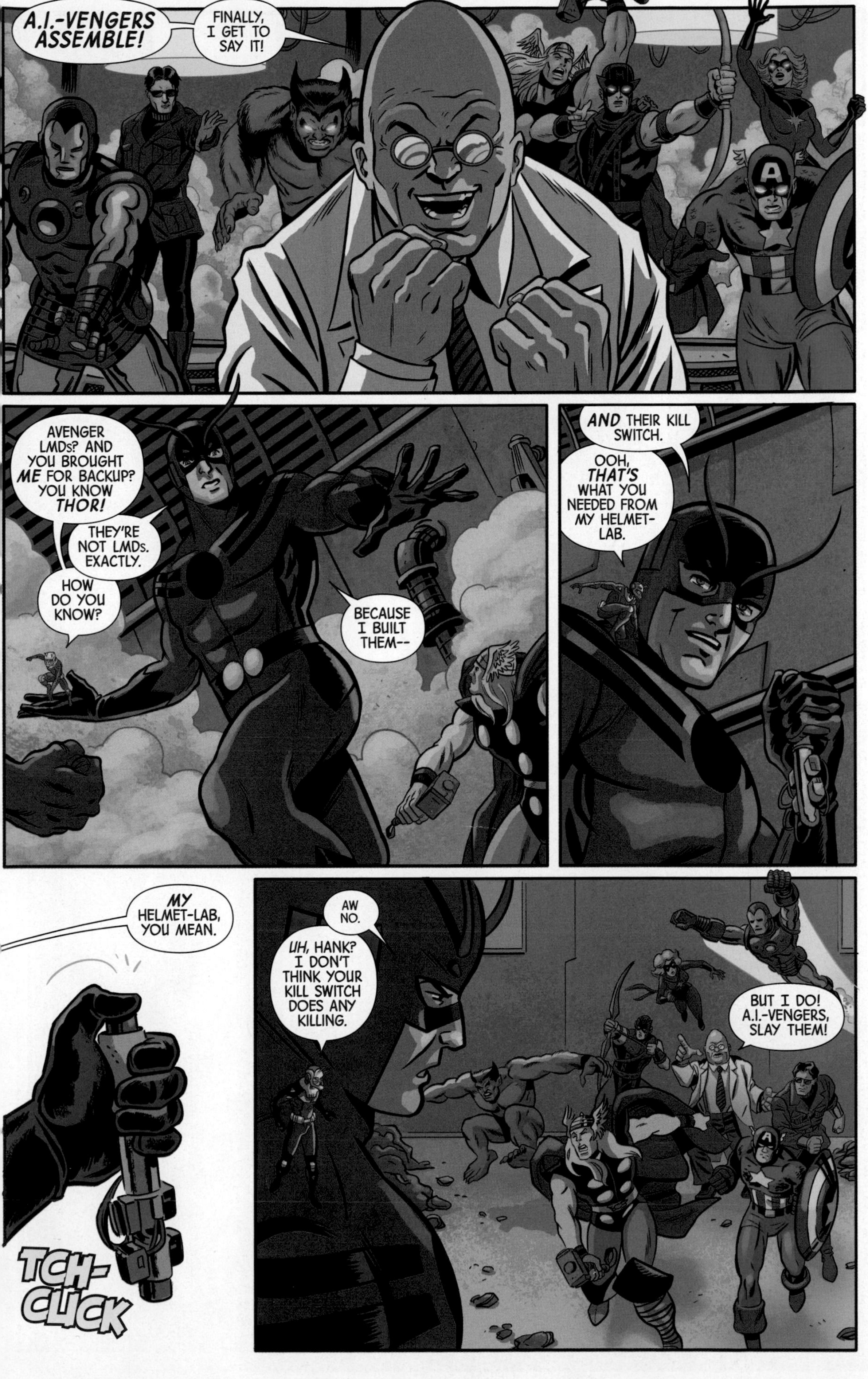
A.I.-VENGERS ASSEMBLE!
FINALLY, I GET TO SAY IT!
AVENGER LMDs? AND YOU BROUGHT ME FOR BACKUP? YOU KNOW THOR!
THEY'RE NOT LMDs. EXACTLY.
HOW DO YOU KNOW?
BECAUSE I BUILT THEM--
AND THEIR KILL SWITCH.
OOH, THAT'S WHAT YOU NEEDED FROM MY HELMET-LAB.
MY HELMET-LAB, YOU MEAN.
TCH-CLICK
AW NO.
UH, HANK? I DON'T THINK YOUR KILL SWITCH DOES ANY KILLING.
BUT I DO! A.I.-VENGERS, SLAY THEM!

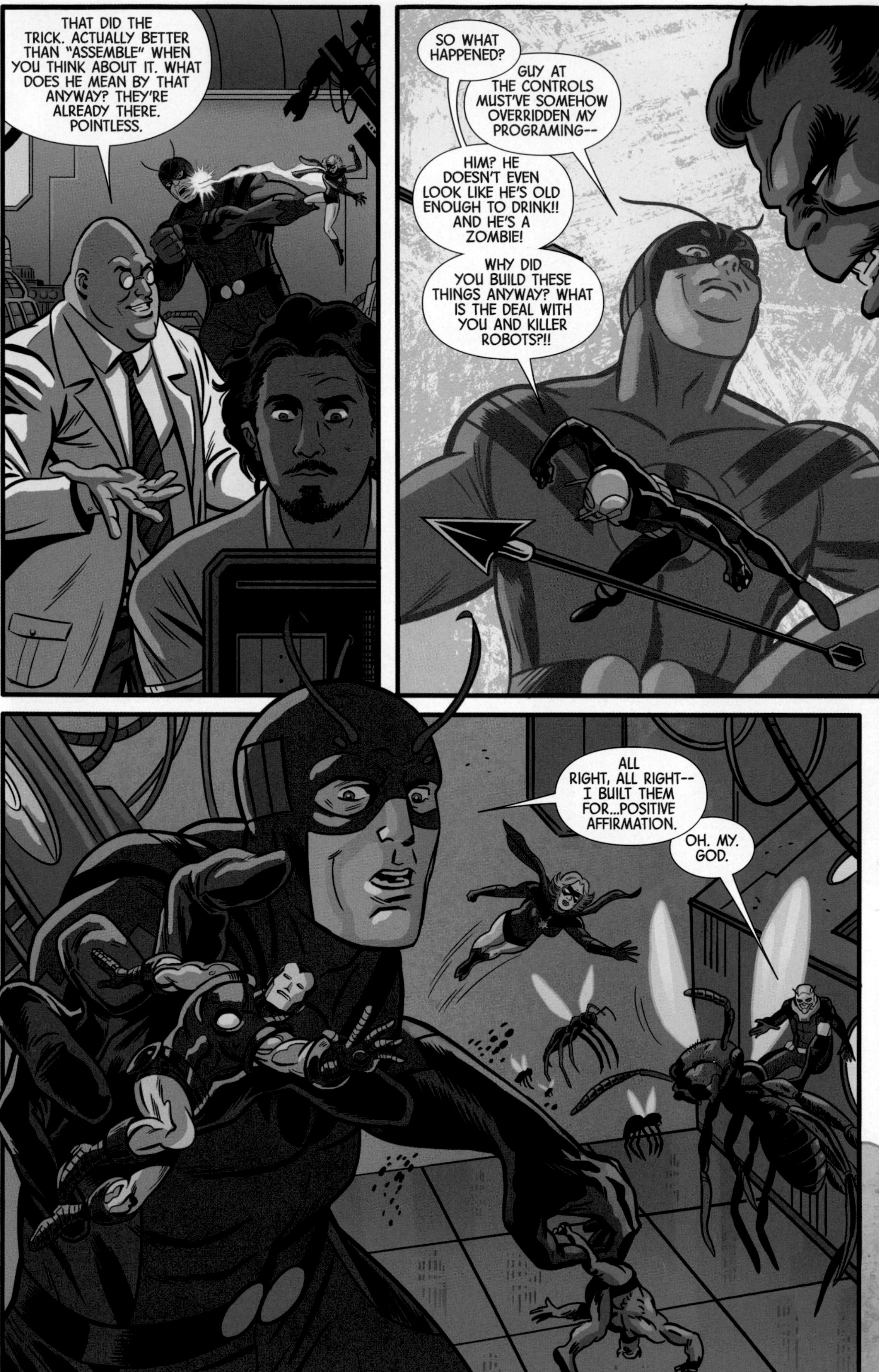
THAT DID THE TRICK. ACTUALLY BETTER THAN "ASSEMBLE" WHEN YOU THINK ABOUT IT. WHAT DOES HE MEAN BY THAT ANYWAY? THEY'RE ALREADY THERE. POINTLESS.
SO WHAT HAPPENED?
GUY AT THE CONTROLS MUST'VE SOMEHOW OVERRIDDEN MY PROGRAMING--
HIM? HE DOESN'T EVEN LOOK LIKE HE'S OLD ENOUGH TO DRINK!! AND HE'S A ZOMBIE!
WHY DID YOU BUILD THESE THINGS ANYWAY? WHAT IS THE DEAL WITH YOU AND KILLER ROBOTS?!!
ALL RIGHT, ALL RIGHT-- I BUILT THEM FOR...POSITIVE AFFIRMATION.
OH. MY. GOD.

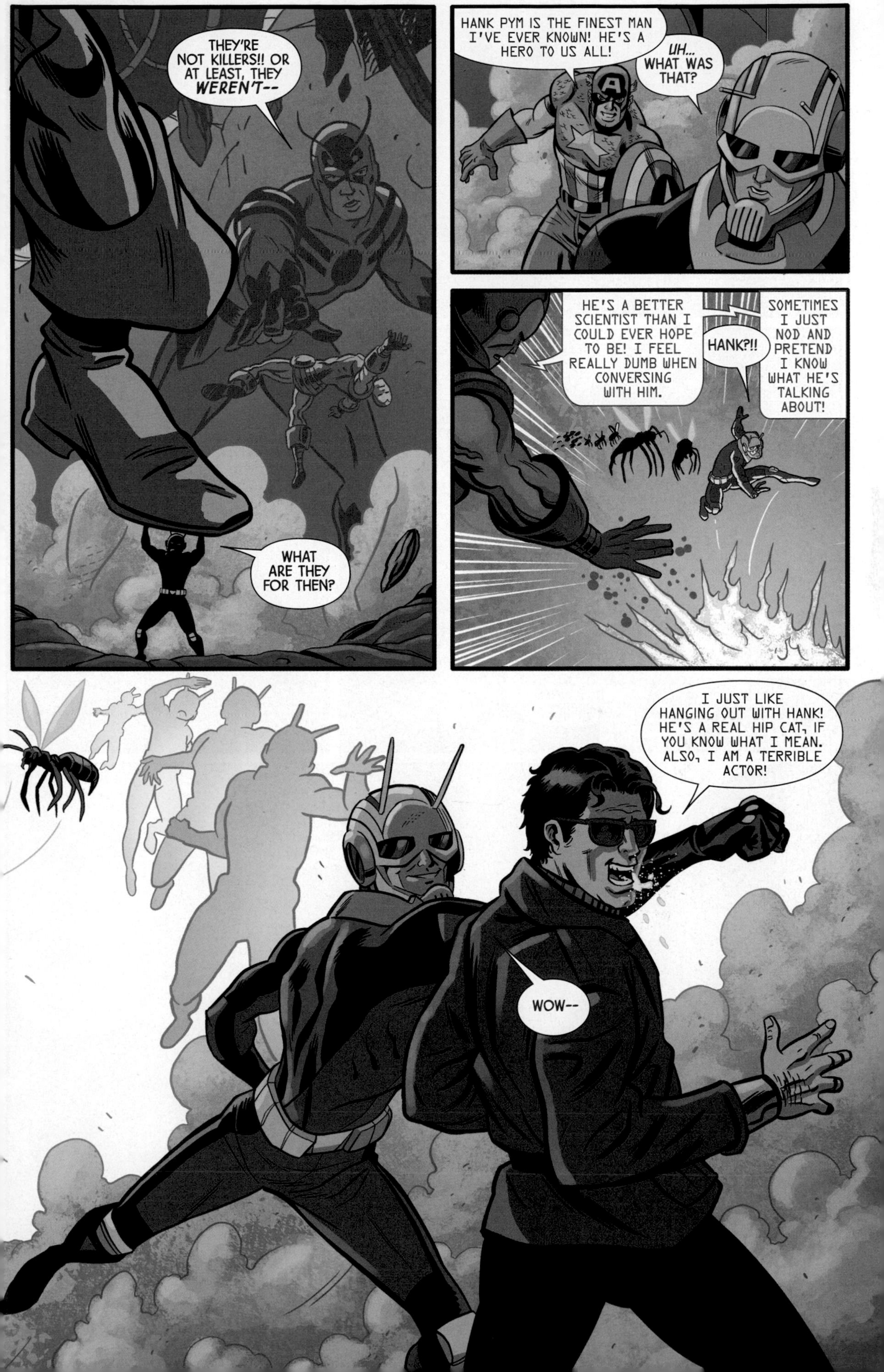
THEY'RE NOT KILLERS!! OR AT LEAST, THEY WEREN'T--
WHAT ARE THEY FOR THEN?
HANK PYM IS THE FINEST MAN I'VE EVER KNOWN! HE'S A HERO TO US ALL!
UH... WHAT WAS THAT?
HE'S A BETTER SCIENTIST THAN I COULD EVER HOPE TO BE! I FEEL REALLY DUMB WHEN CONVERSING WITH HIM.
HANK?!!
SOMETIMES I JUST NOD AND PRETEND I KNOW WHAT HE'S TALKING ABOUT!
I JUST LIKE HANGING OUT WITH HANK! HE'S A REAL HIP CAT, IF YOU KNOW WHAT I MEAN. ALSO, I AM A TERRIBLE ACTOR!
WOW--

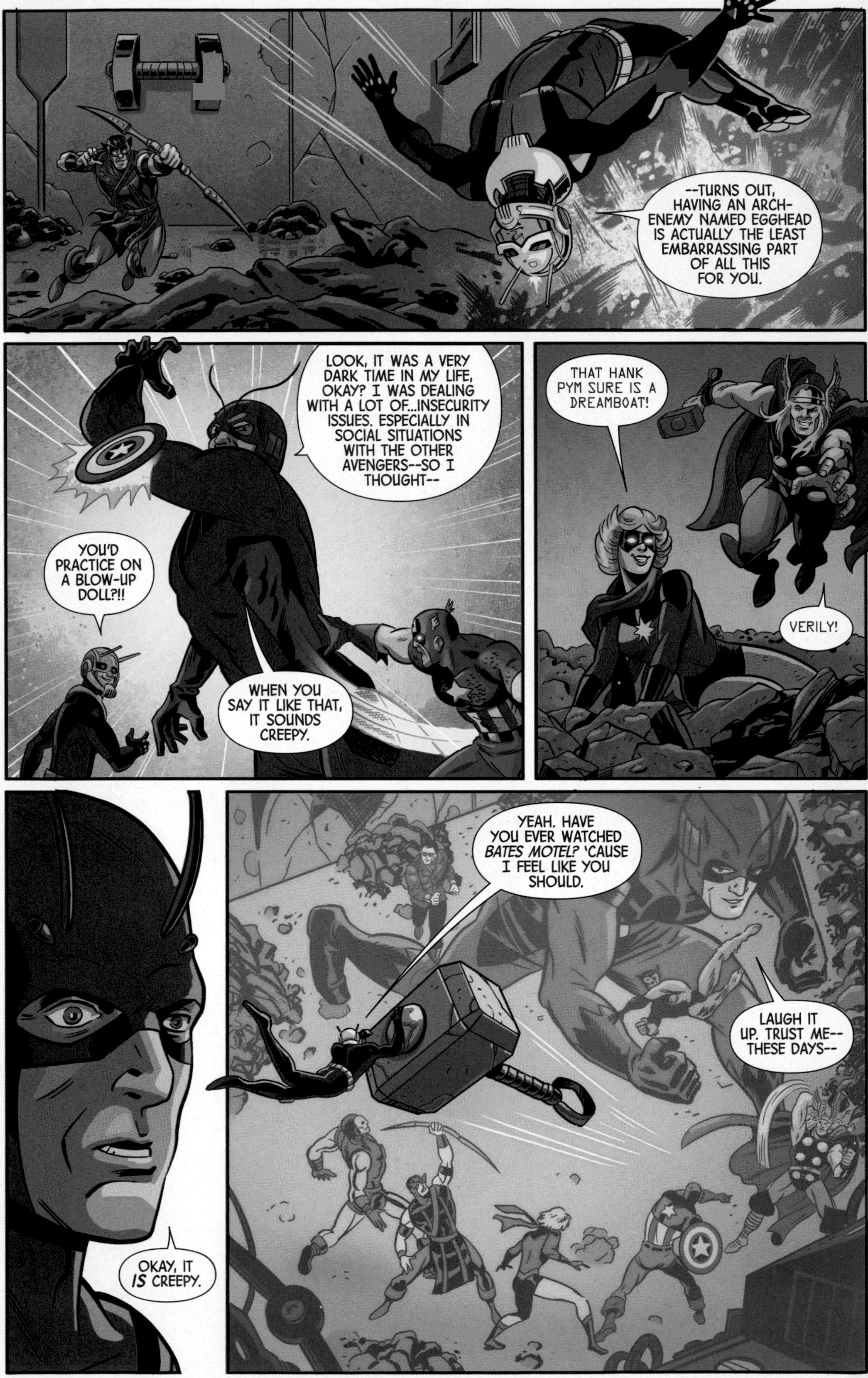
--TURNS OUT, HAVING AN ARCH-ENEMY NAMED EGGHEAD IS ACTUALLY THE LEAST EMBARRASSING PART OF ALL THIS FOR YOU.
LOOK, IT WAS A VERY DARK TIME IN MY LIFE, OKAY? I WAS DEALING WITH A LOT OF...INSECURITY ISSUES. ESPECIALLY IN SOCIAL SITUATIONS WITH THE OTHER AVENGERS--SO I THOUGHT--
YOU'D PRACTICE ON A BLOW-UP DOLL?!!
WHEN YOU SAY IT LIKE THAT, IT SOUNDS CREEPY.
THAT HANK PYM SURE IS A DREAMBOAT!
VERILY!
OKAY, IT *IS* CREEPY.
YEAH. HAVE YOU EVER WATCHED *BATES MOTEL?* 'CAUSE I FEEL LIKE YOU SHOULD.
LAUGH IT UP. TRUST ME--THESE DAYS--

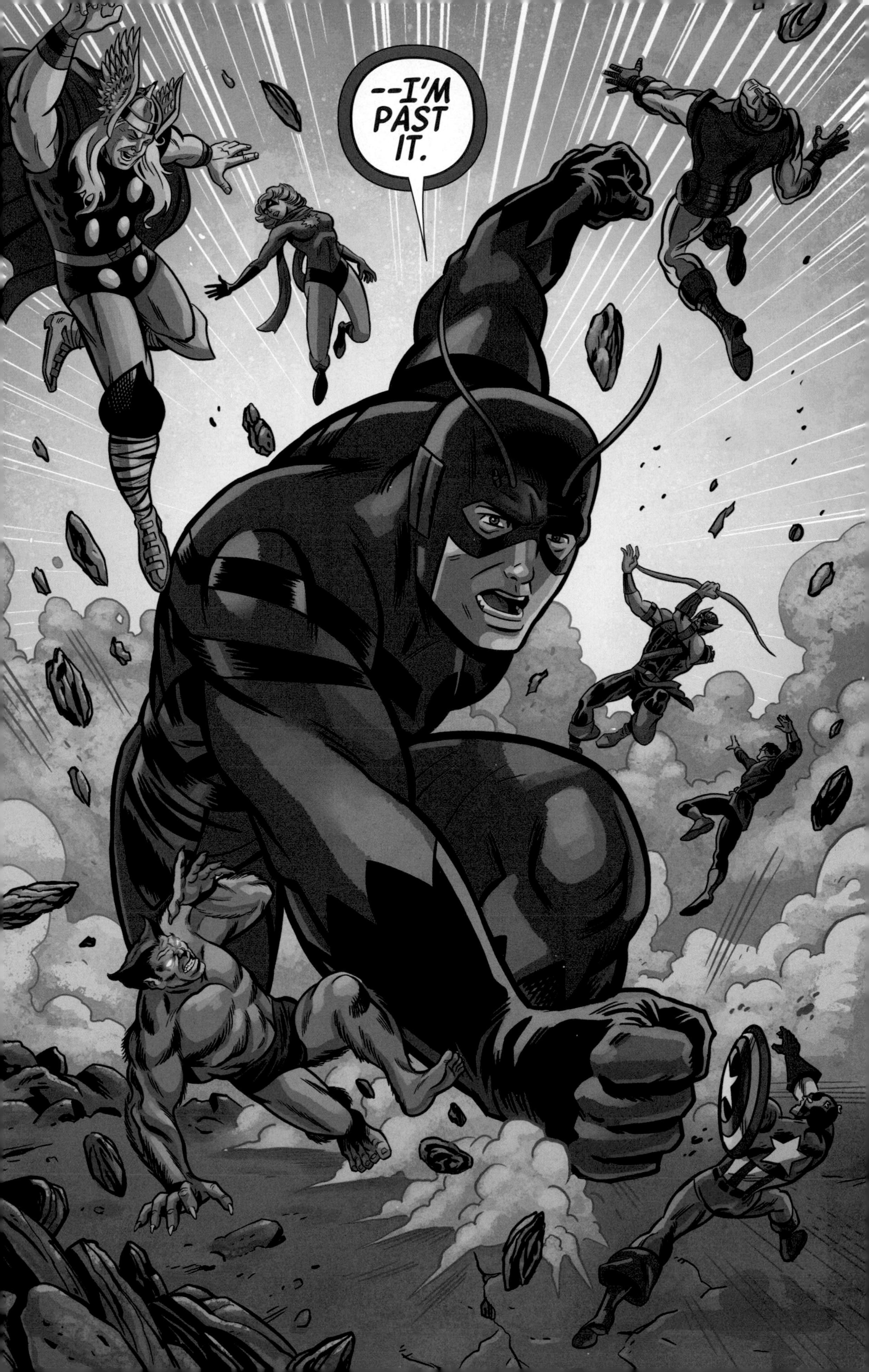
--I'M PAST IT.

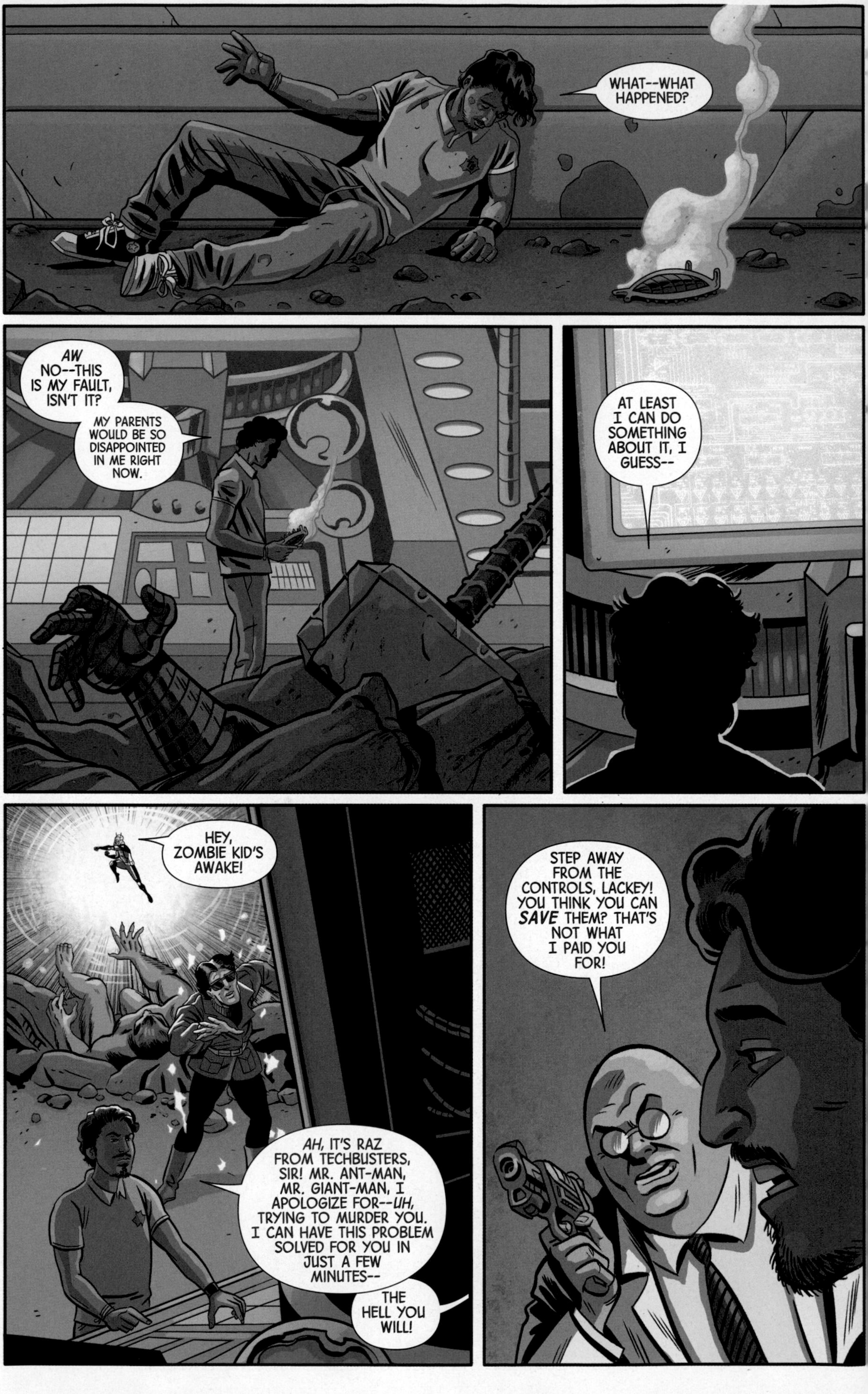
WHAT--WHAT HAPPENED?
AW NO--THIS IS MY FAULT, ISN'T IT?
MY PARENTS WOULD BE SO DISAPPOINTED IN ME RIGHT NOW.
AT LEAST I CAN DO SOMETHING ABOUT IT, I GUESS--
HEY, ZOMBIE KID'S AWAKE!
AH, IT'S RAZ FROM TECHBUSTERS, SIR! MR. ANT-MAN, MR. GIANT-MAN, I APOLOGIZE FOR--UH, TRYING TO MURDER YOU. I CAN HAVE THIS PROBLEM SOLVED FOR YOU IN JUST A FEW MINUTES--
THE HELL YOU WILL!
STEP AWAY FROM THE CONTROLS, LACKEY! YOU THINK YOU CAN SAVE THEM? THAT'S NOT WHAT I PAID YOU FOR!

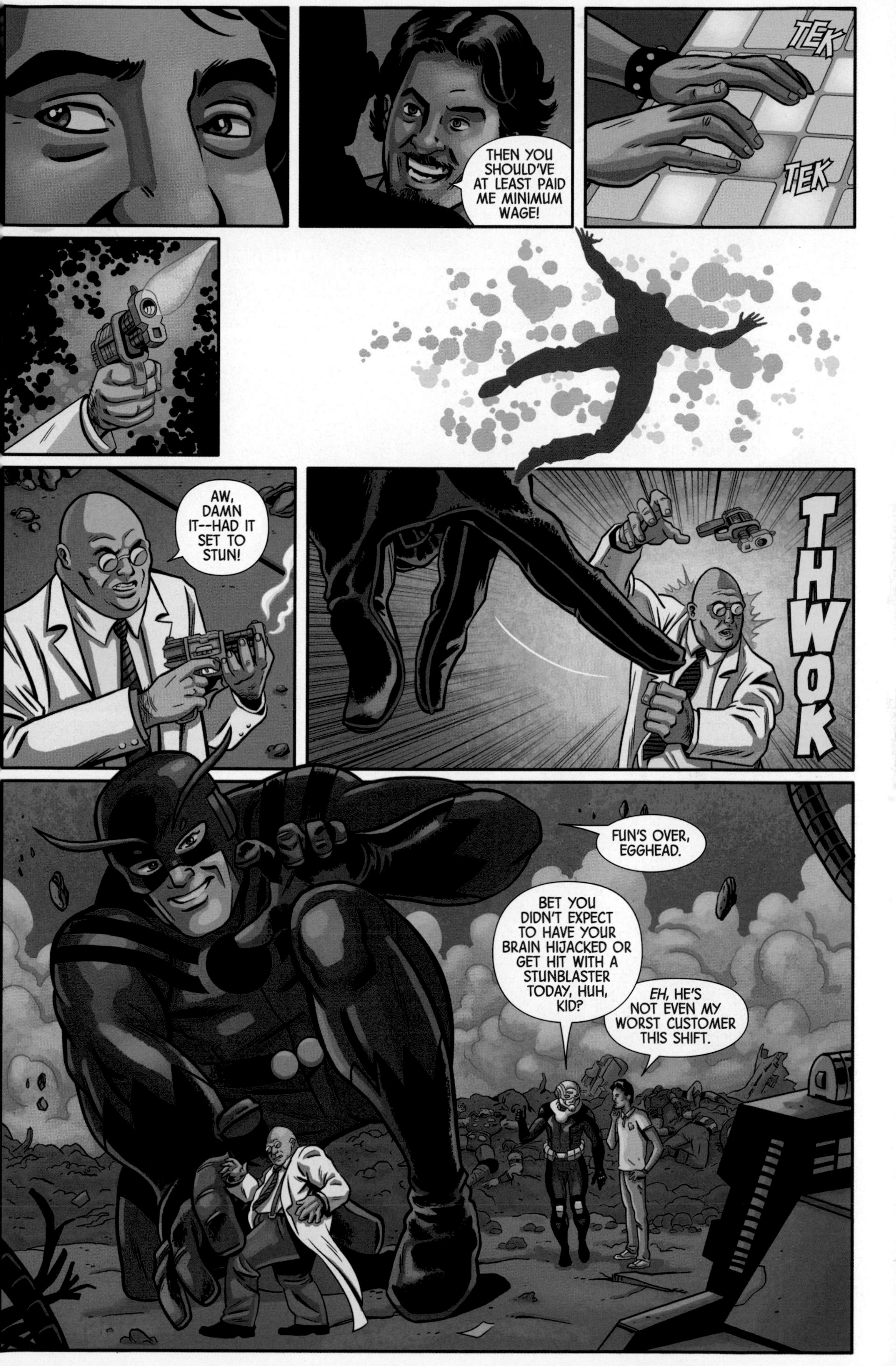
THEN YOU SHOULD'VE AT LEAST PAID ME MINIMUM WAGE!
TEK
TEK
AW, DAMN IT--HAD IT SET TO STUN!
THWOK
FUN'S OVER, EGGHEAD.
BET YOU DIDN'T EXPECT TO HAVE YOUR BRAIN HIJACKED OR GET HIT WITH A STUNBLASTER TODAY, HUH, KID?
EH, HE'S NOT EVEN MY WORST CUSTOMER THIS SHIFT.

SEE, I TOLD YOU TEAMING UP WOULD BE FUN.

PLEASE DON'T RUIN THE VIEW.

ABOUT BACK THERE-- WHEN I FIRST STARTED WITH THE AVENGERS, I WAS SURROUNDED BY THESE GUYS--THOR, IRON MAN, THE HULK--

A BLOND SCANDINAVIAN GUY, A BILLIONAIRE LADIES' MAN WITH A COOL SUIT OF ARMOR, AND THE STRONGEST BEING ON THE PLANET.

AND THERE I WAS, SHRINKING, AND GETTING IN ARGUMENTS WITH ANTS.

I COULDN'T *WAIT* TO BECOME GIANT-MAN. THE MINUTE I WORKED OUT THE SCIENCE, I WAS THERE. AND IT MADE ME FEEL SO BIG, TOWERING OVER ALL OF THEM. I THINK THAT'S REALLY WHEN IT ALL STARTED GOING WRONG.

I WISH I COULD GO BACK-- JUST TO TELL MYSELF--

THAT *THIS* IS PRETTY GREAT.

YEAH, I HEAR YA--I HATE GOING GIANT-SIZE. ALWAYS TRIPPING OVER TACO TRUCKS AND WHATNOT. GETS EXPENSIVE.

YOU SHOULD PROBABLY STAY WHERE YOU ARE, SCOTT. SAFER FOR ALL OF US THAT WAY.

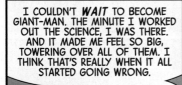

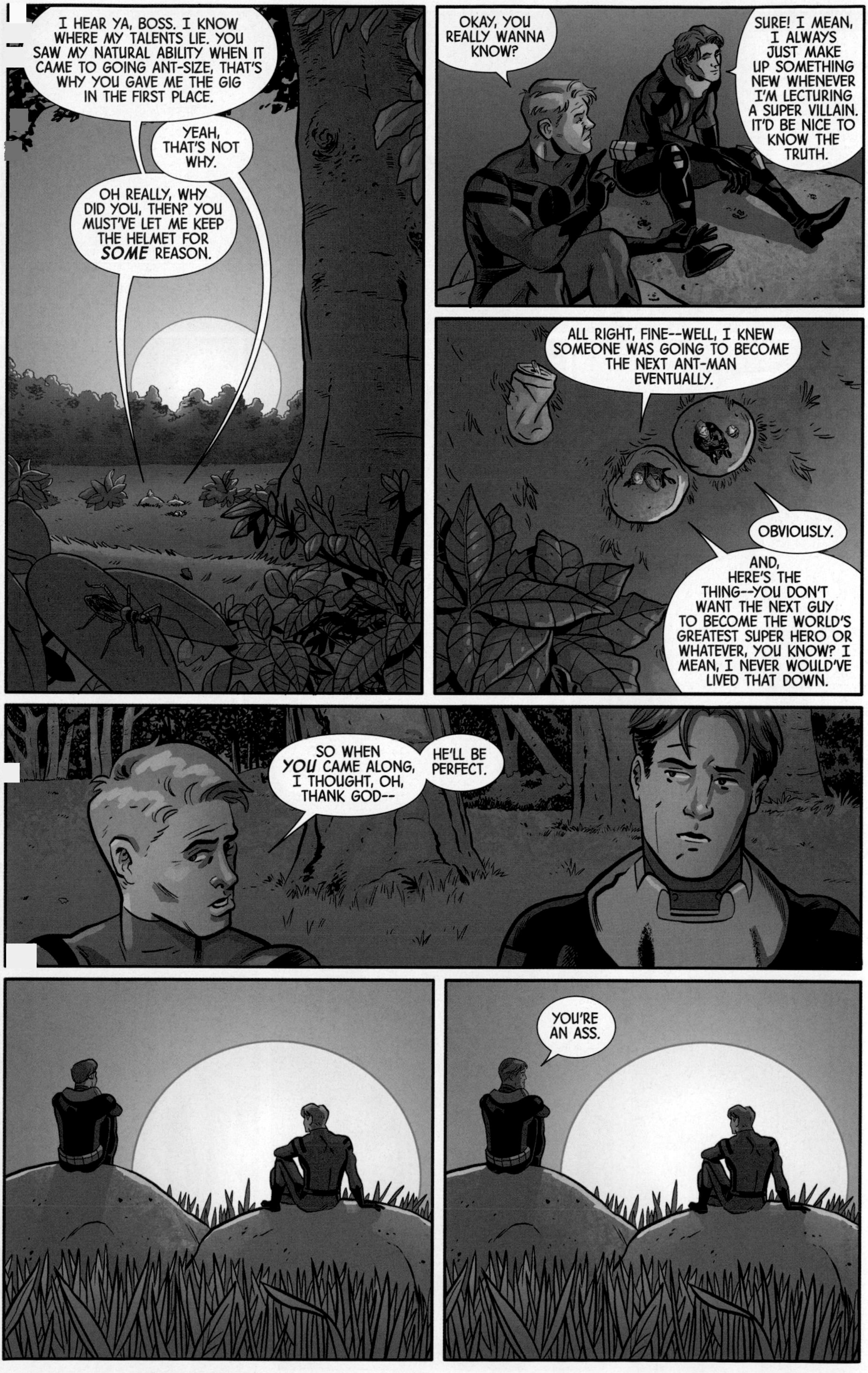
I HEAR YA, BOSS. I KNOW WHERE MY TALENTS LIE. YOU SAW MY NATURAL ABILITY WHEN IT CAME TO GOING ANT-SIZE, THAT'S WHY YOU GAVE ME THE GIG IN THE FIRST PLACE.
YEAH, THAT'S NOT WHY.
OH REALLY, WHY DID YOU, THEN? YOU MUST'VE LET ME KEEP THE HELMET FOR SOME REASON.
OKAY, YOU REALLY WANNA KNOW?
SURE! I MEAN, I ALWAYS JUST MAKE UP SOMETHING NEW WHENEVER I'M LECTURING A SUPER VILLAIN. IT'D BE NICE TO KNOW THE TRUTH.
ALL RIGHT, FINE--WELL, I KNEW SOMEONE WAS GOING TO BECOME THE NEXT ANT-MAN EVENTUALLY.
OBVIOUSLY.
AND, HERE'S THE THING--YOU DON'T WANT THE NEXT GUY TO BECOME THE WORLD'S GREATEST SUPER HERO OR WHATEVER, YOU KNOW? I MEAN, I NEVER WOULD'VE LIVED THAT DOWN.
SO WHEN YOU CAME ALONG, I THOUGHT, OH, THANK GOD--
HE'LL BE PERFECT.
YOU'RE AN ASS.

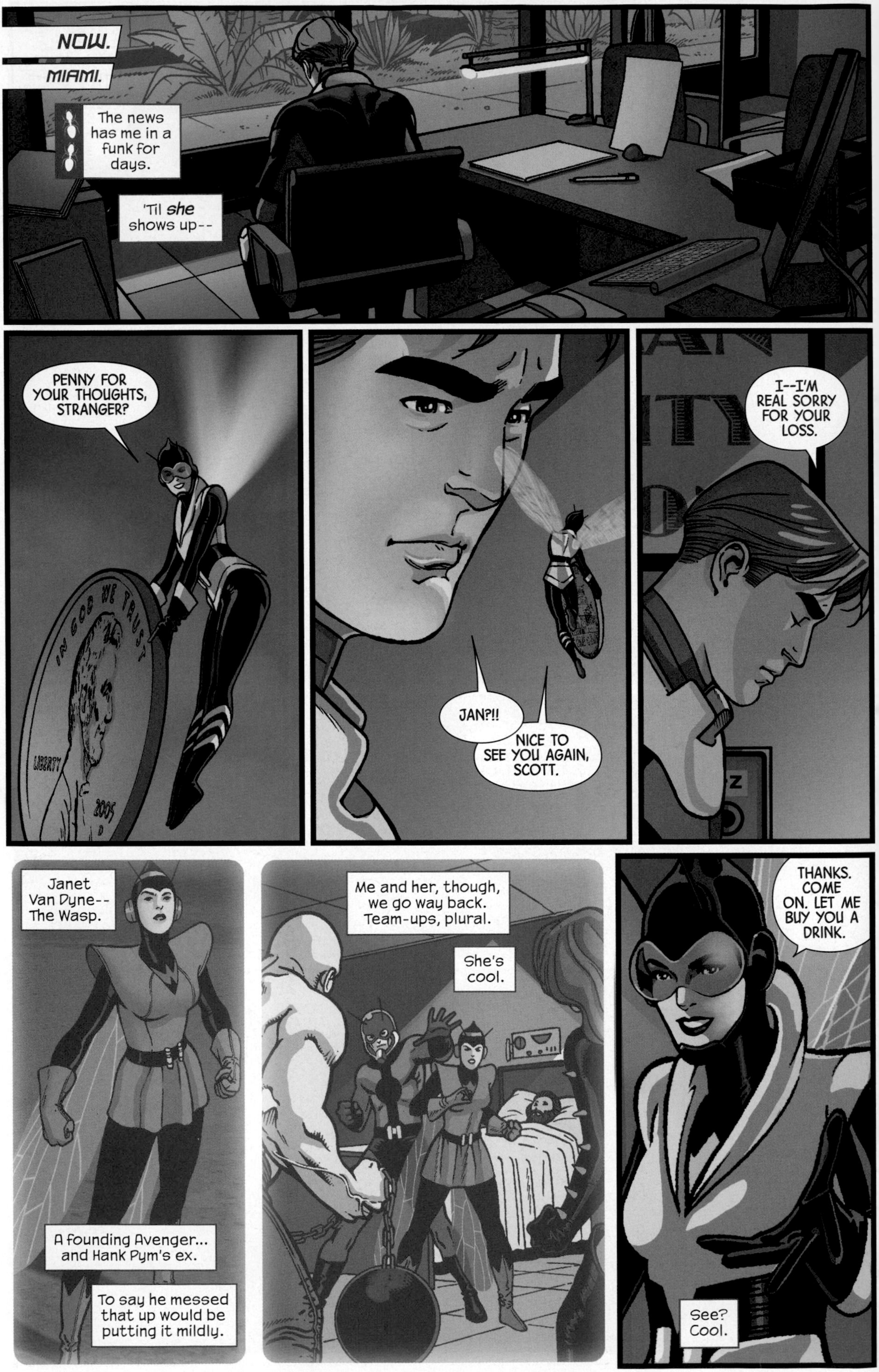
NOW.
MIAMI.
The news has me in a funk for days.
'Til *she* shows up--
PENNY FOR YOUR THOUGHTS, STRANGER?
IN GOD WE TRUST
LIBERTY
2005
D
JAN?!!
NICE TO SEE YOU AGAIN, SCOTT.
I--I'M REAL SORRY FOR YOUR LOSS.
Janet Van Dyne--The Wasp.
A founding Avenger... and Hank Pym's ex.
To say he messed that up would be putting it mildly.
Me and her, though, we go way back. Team-ups, plural.
She's cool.
THANKS. COME ON. LET ME BUY YOU A DRINK.
See? Cool.

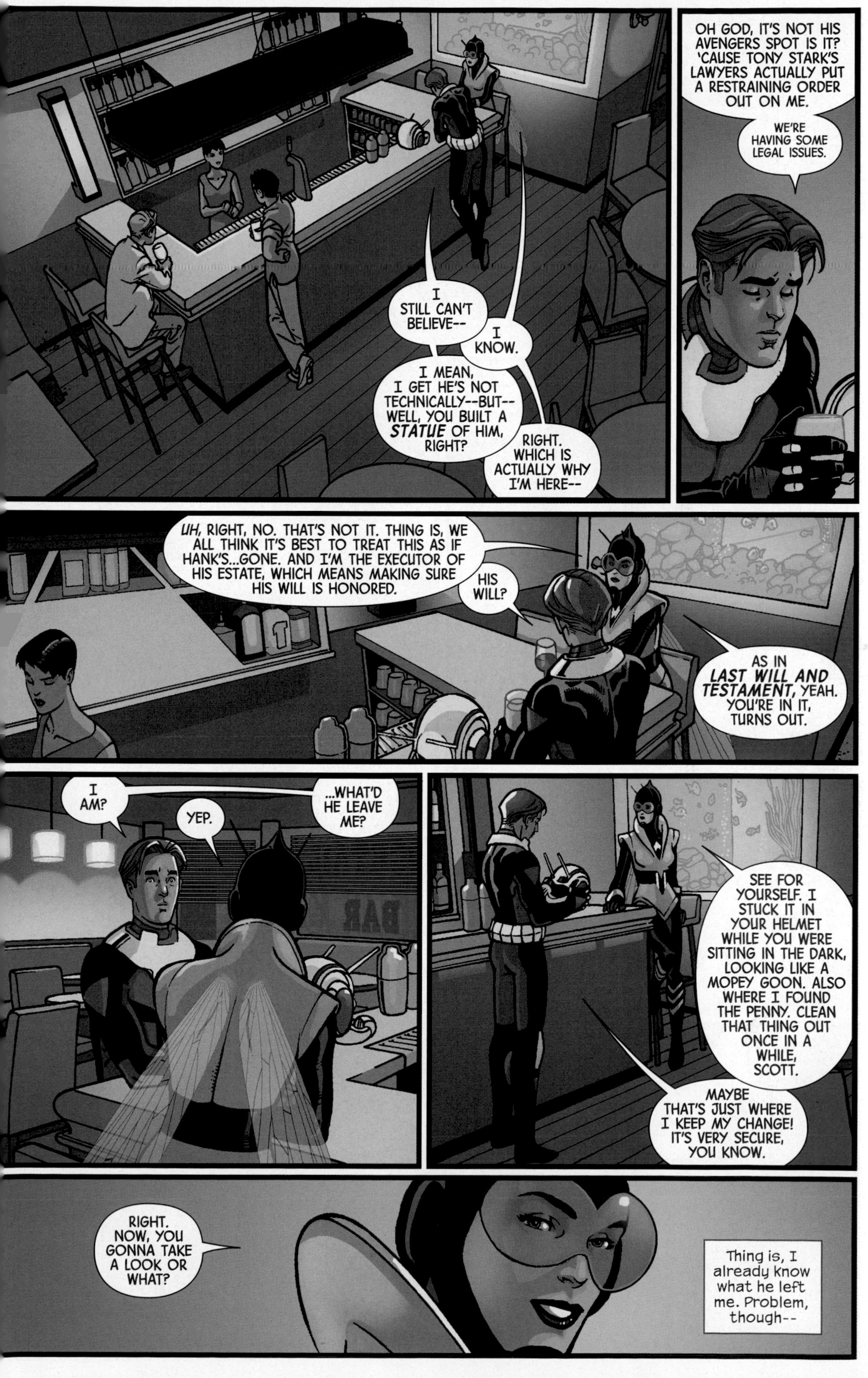
I STILL CAN'T BELIEVE--
I KNOW.
I MEAN, I GET HE'S NOT TECHNICALLY--BUT-- WELL, YOU BUILT A STATUE OF HIM, RIGHT?
RIGHT. WHICH IS ACTUALLY WHY I'M HERE--
OH GOD, IT'S NOT HIS AVENGERS SPOT IS IT? 'CAUSE TONY STARK'S LAWYERS ACTUALLY PUT A RESTRAINING ORDER OUT ON ME.
WE'RE HAVING SOME LEGAL ISSUES.
UH, RIGHT, NO. THAT'S NOT IT. THING IS, WE ALL THINK IT'S BEST TO TREAT THIS AS IF HANK'S...GONE. AND I'M THE EXECUTOR OF HIS ESTATE, WHICH MEANS MAKING SURE HIS WILL IS HONORED.
HIS WILL?
AS IN LAST WILL AND TESTAMENT, YEAH. YOU'RE IN IT, TURNS OUT.
I AM?
YEP.
...WHAT'D HE LEAVE ME?
SEE FOR YOURSELF. I STUCK IT IN YOUR HELMET WHILE YOU WERE SITTING IN THE DARK, LOOKING LIKE A MOPEY GOON. ALSO WHERE I FOUND THE PENNY. CLEAN THAT THING OUT ONCE IN A WHILE, SCOTT.
MAYBE THAT'S JUST WHERE I KEEP MY CHANGE! IT'S VERY SECURE, YOU KNOW.
RIGHT. NOW, YOU GONNA TAKE A LOOK OR WHAT?
Thing is, I already know what he left me. Problem, though--

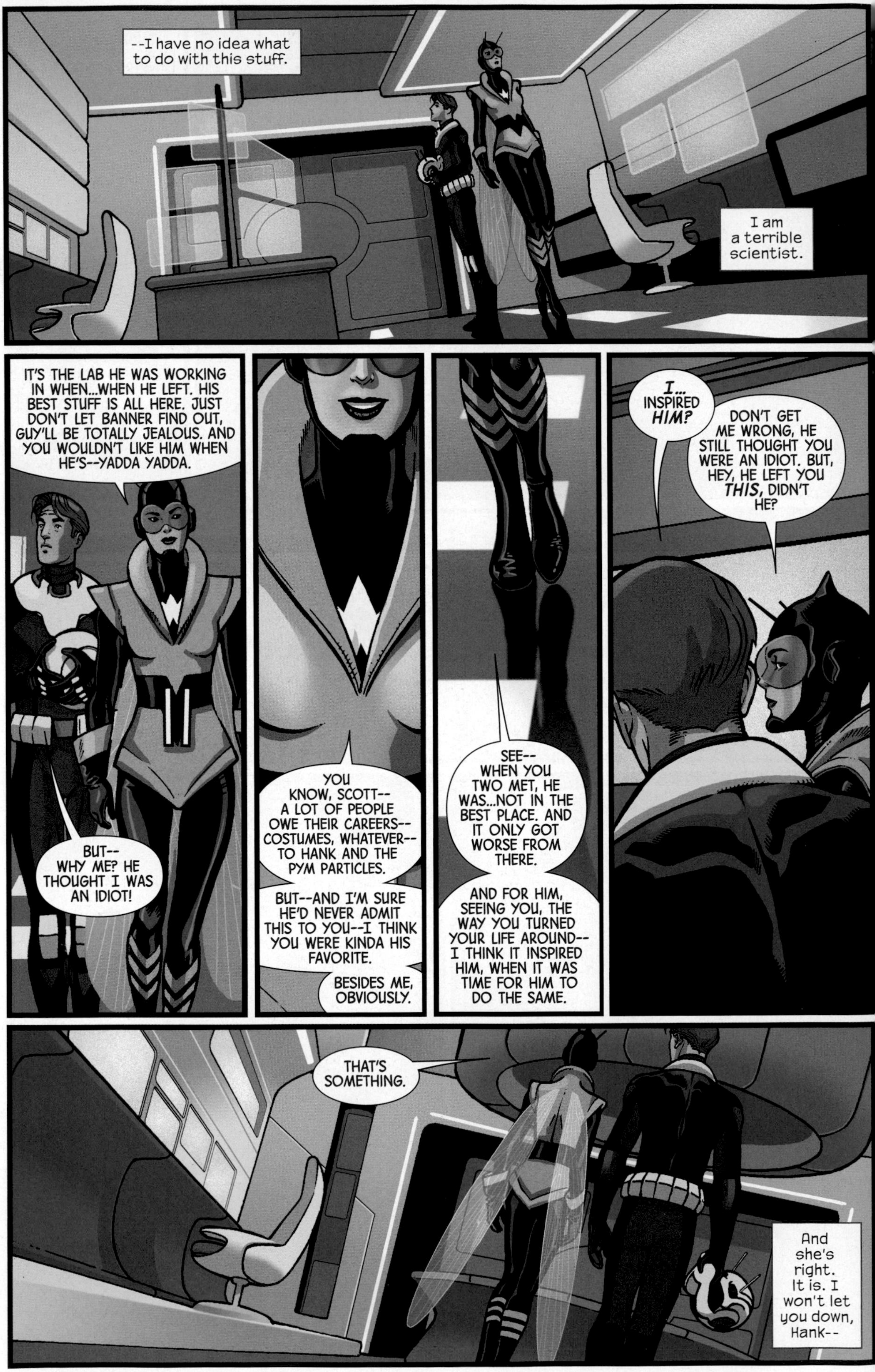
--I have no idea what to do with this stuff.
I am a terrible scientist.
IT'S THE LAB HE WAS WORKING IN WHEN...WHEN HE LEFT. HIS BEST STUFF IS ALL HERE. JUST DON'T LET BANNER FIND OUT, GUY'LL BE TOTALLY JEALOUS. AND YOU WOULDN'T LIKE HIM WHEN HE'S--YADDA YADDA.
BUT-- WHY ME? HE THOUGHT I WAS AN IDIOT!
YOU KNOW, SCOTT-- A LOT OF PEOPLE OWE THEIR CAREERS-- COSTUMES, WHATEVER-- TO HANK AND THE PYM PARTICLES.
BUT--AND I'M SURE HE'D NEVER ADMIT THIS TO YOU--I THINK YOU WERE KINDA HIS FAVORITE.
BESIDES ME, OBVIOUSLY.
SEE-- WHEN YOU TWO MET, HE WAS...NOT IN THE BEST PLACE. AND IT ONLY GOT WORSE FROM THERE.
AND FOR HIM, SEEING YOU, THE WAY YOU TURNED YOUR LIFE AROUND-- I THINK IT INSPIRED HIM, WHEN IT WAS TIME FOR HIM TO DO THE SAME.
I... INSPIRED HIM?
DON'T GET ME WRONG, HE STILL THOUGHT YOU WERE AN IDIOT. BUT, HEY, HE LEFT YOU THIS, DIDN'T HE?
THAT'S SOMETHING.
And she's right. It is. I won't let you down, Hank--

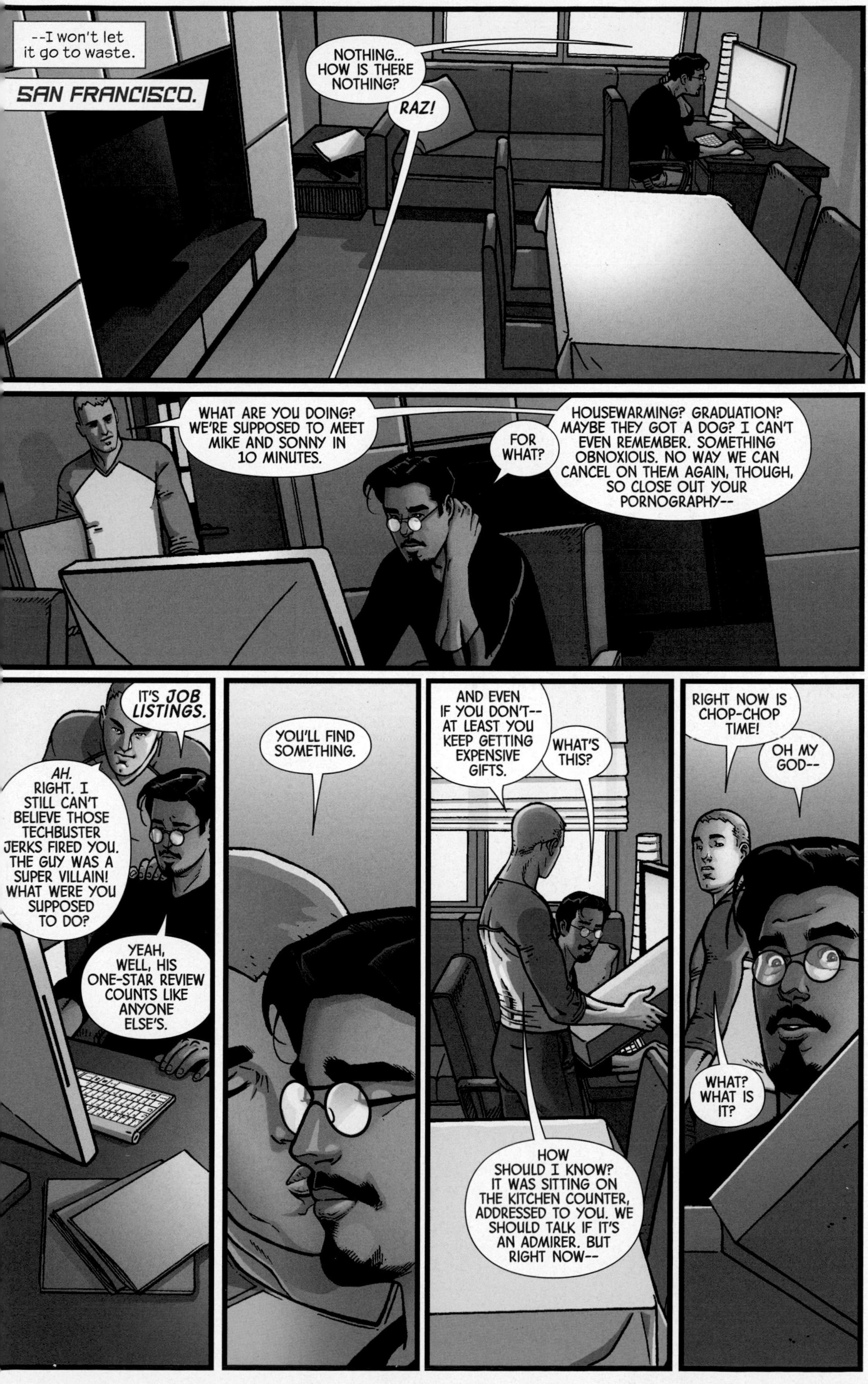
--I won't let it go to waste.
SAN FRANCISCO.
NOTHING... HOW IS THERE NOTHING?
RAZ!
WHAT ARE YOU DOING? WE'RE SUPPOSED TO MEET MIKE AND SONNY IN 10 MINUTES.
FOR WHAT?
HOUSEWARMING? GRADUATION? MAYBE THEY GOT A DOG? I CAN'T EVEN REMEMBER. SOMETHING OBNOXIOUS. NO WAY WE CAN CANCEL ON THEM AGAIN, THOUGH, SO CLOSE OUT YOUR PORNOGRAPHY--
IT'S JOB LISTINGS.
AH. RIGHT. I STILL CAN'T BELIEVE THOSE TECHBUSTER JERKS FIRED YOU. THE GUY WAS A SUPER VILLAIN! WHAT WERE YOU SUPPOSED TO DO?
YEAH, WELL, HIS ONE-STAR REVIEW COUNTS LIKE ANYONE ELSE'S.
YOU'LL FIND SOMETHING.
AND EVEN IF YOU DON'T-- AT LEAST YOU KEEP GETTING EXPENSIVE GIFTS.
WHAT'S THIS?
HOW SHOULD I KNOW? IT WAS SITTING ON THE KITCHEN COUNTER, ADDRESSED TO YOU. WE SHOULD TALK IF IT'S AN ADMIRER. BUT RIGHT NOW--
RIGHT NOW IS CHOP-CHOP TIME!
OH MY GOD--
WHAT? WHAT IS IT?

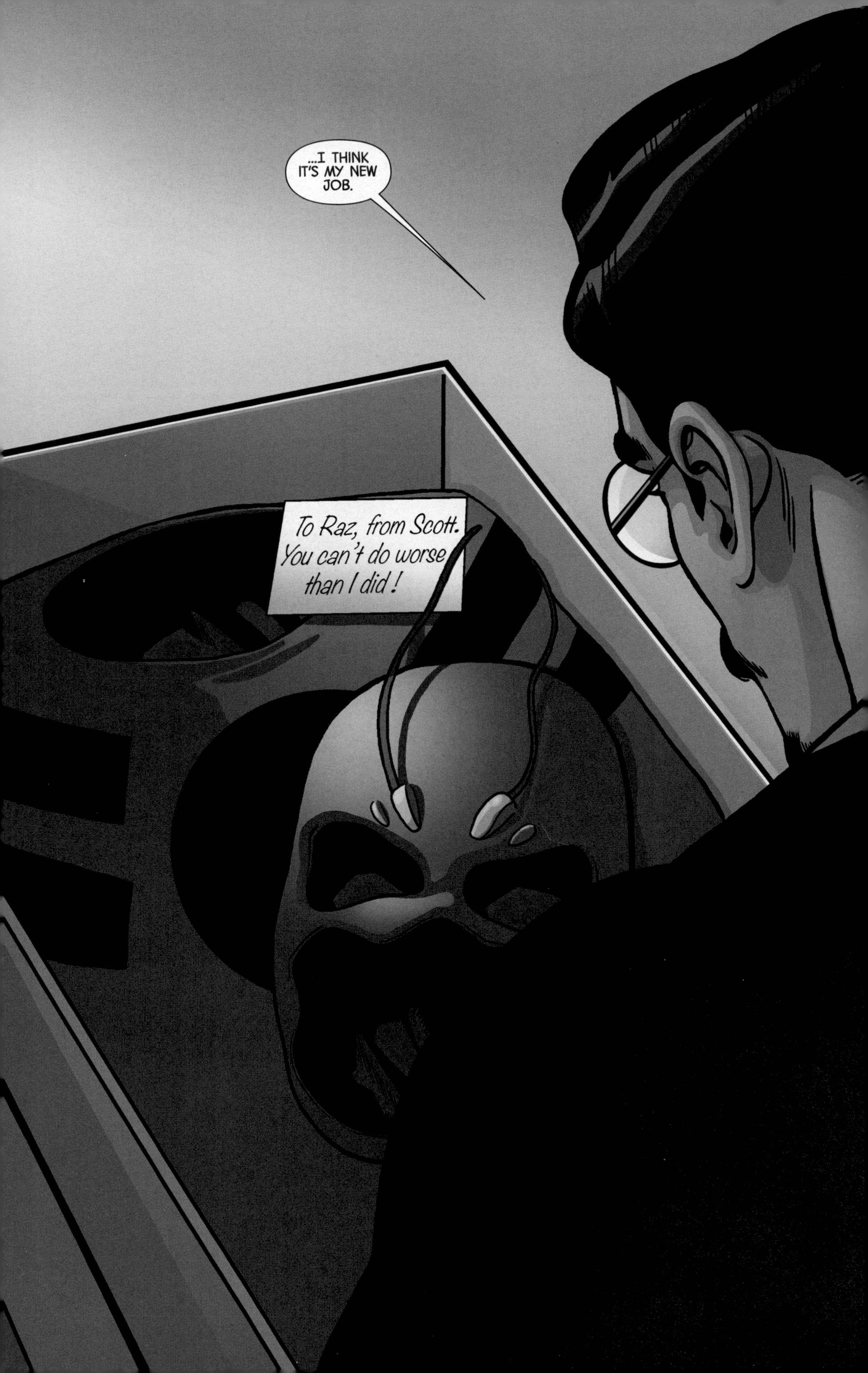
...I THINK IT'S MY NEW JOB.
To Raz, from Scott. You can't do worse than I did!

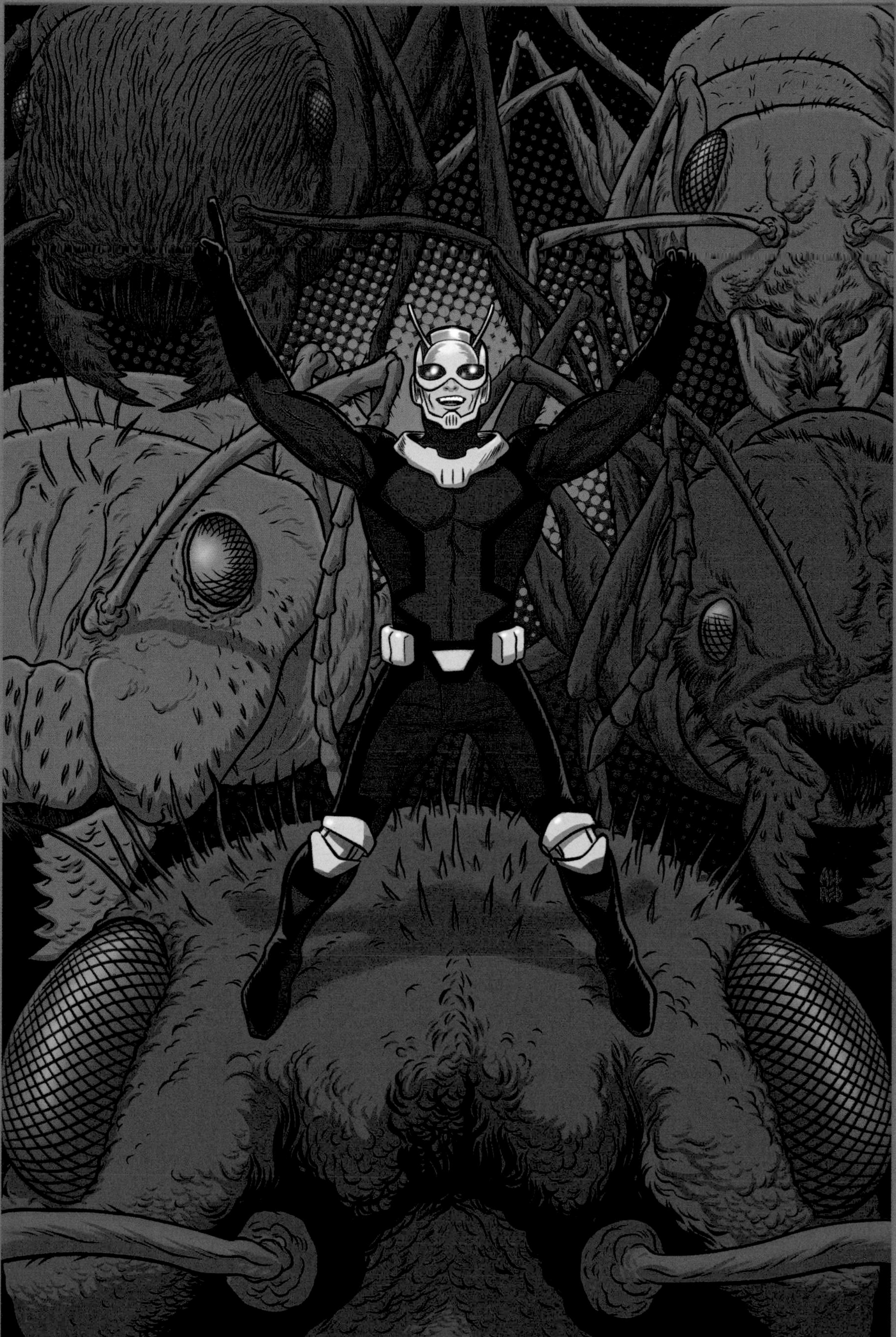

#1 VARIANT
BY **MIKE ALLRED** & **LAURA ALLRED**

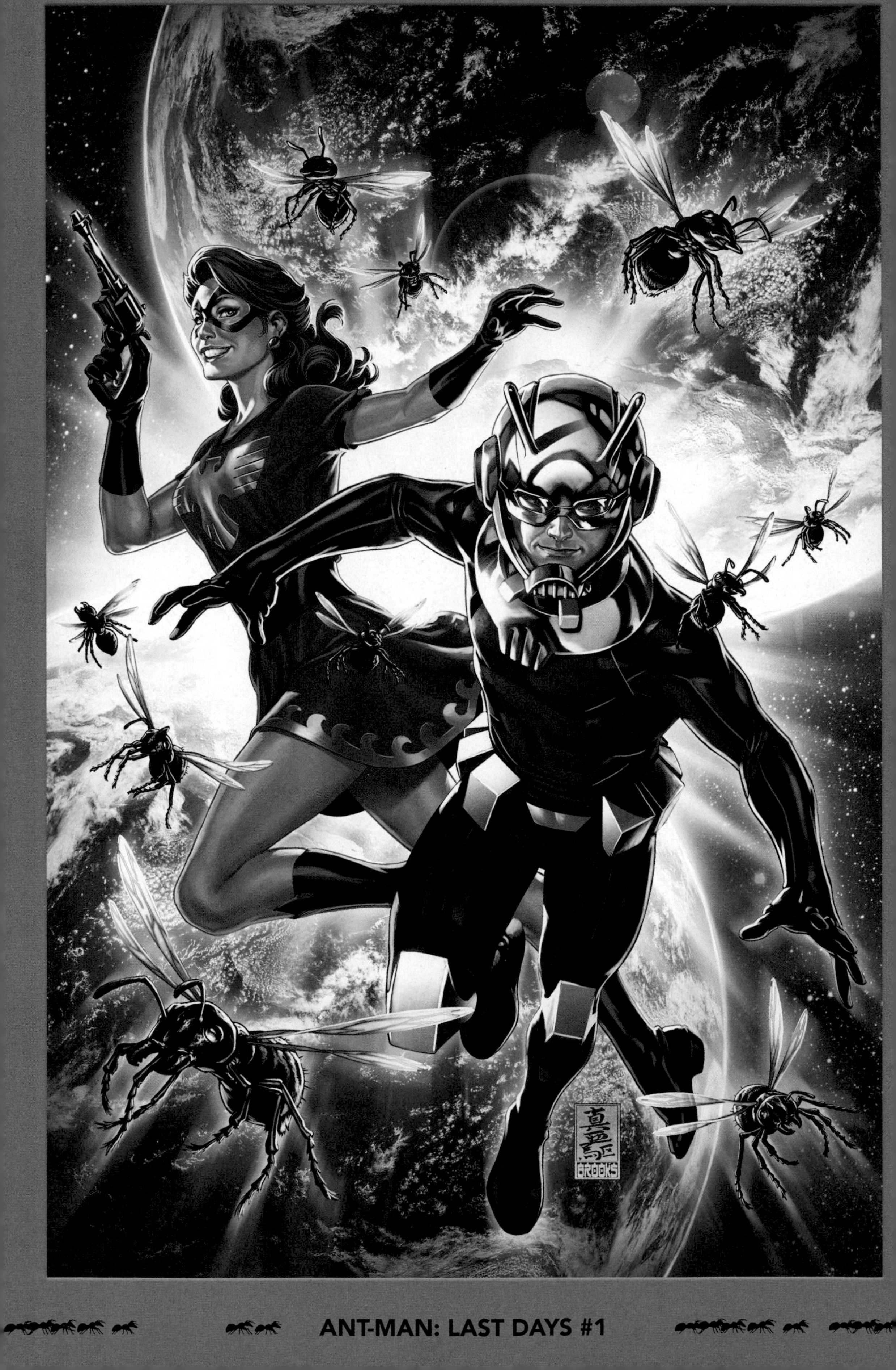
BROOKS

ANT-MAN: LAST DAYS #1

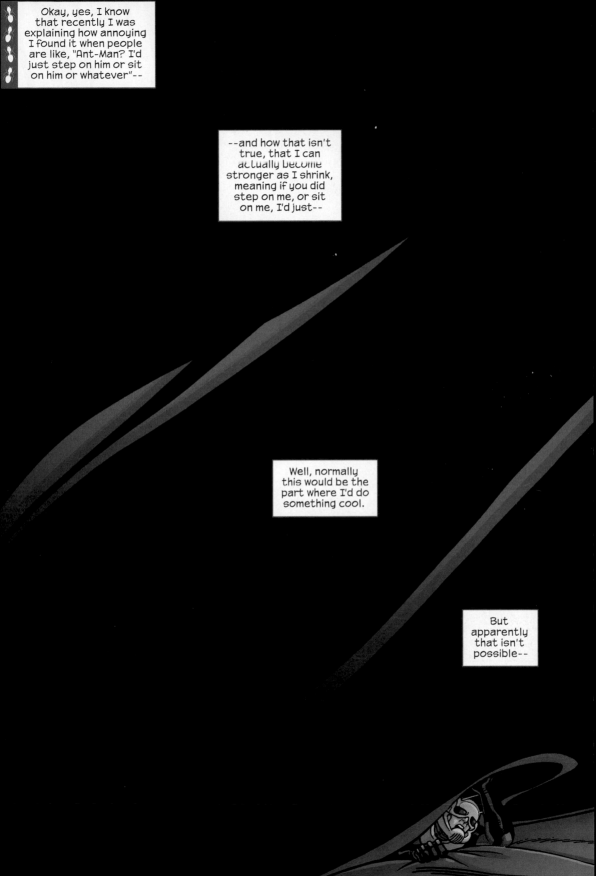

Okay, yes, I know that recently I was explaining how annoying I found it when people are like, "Ant-Man? I'd just step on him or sit on him or whatever"--

--and how that isn't true, that I can actually become stronger as I shrink, meaning if you did step on me, or sit on me, I'd just--

Well, normally this would be the part where I'd do something cool.

But apparently that isn't possible--

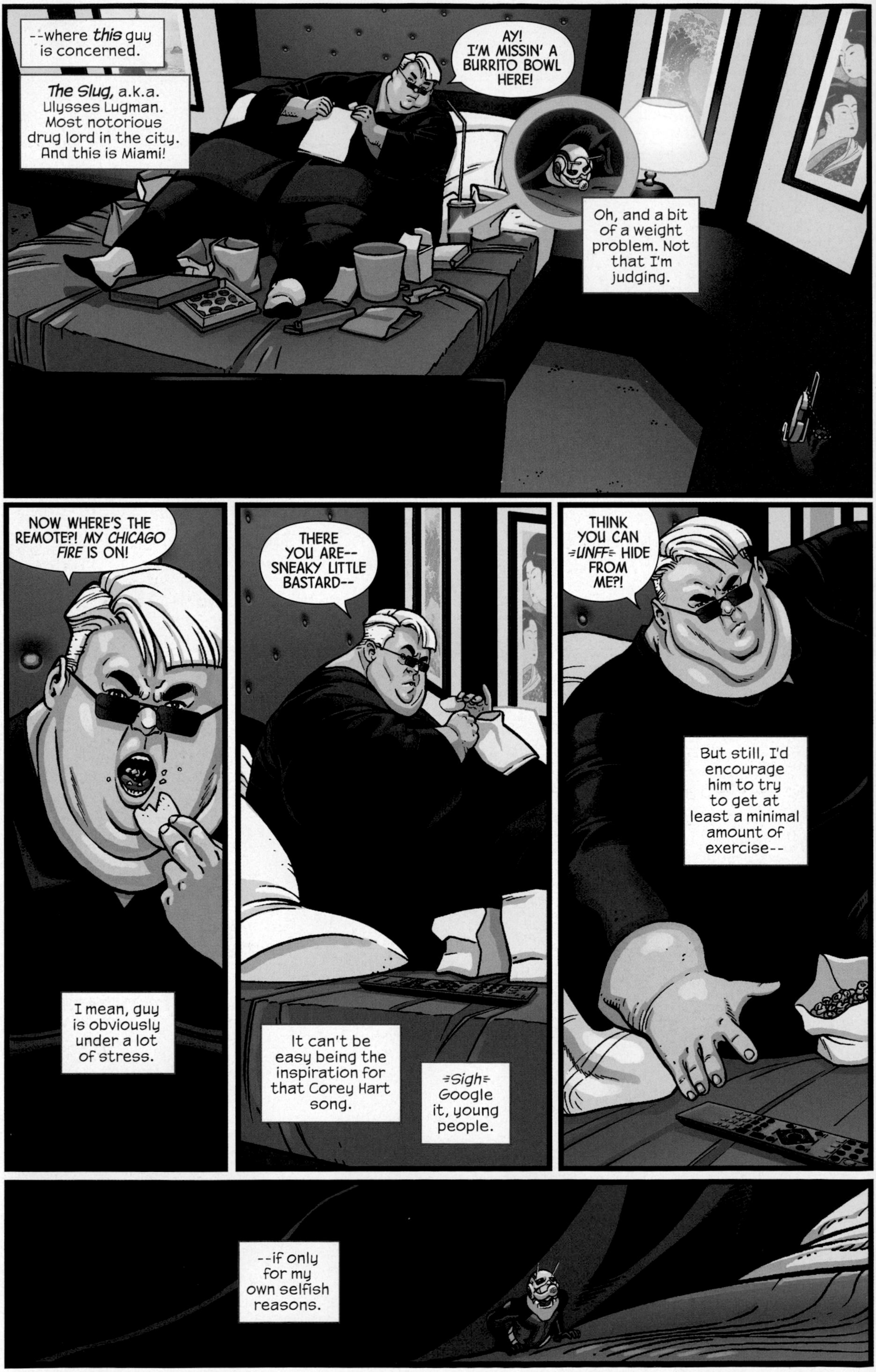
--where *this* guy is concerned.
The Slug, a.k.a. Ulysses Lugman. Most notorious drug lord in the city. And this is Miami!
AY! I'M MISSIN' A BURRITO BOWL HERE!
Oh, and a bit of a weight problem. Not that I'm judging.
NOW WHERE'S THE REMOTE?! MY *CHICAGO FIRE* IS ON!
I mean, guy is obviously under a lot of stress.
THERE YOU ARE-- SNEAKY LITTLE BASTARD--
It can't be easy being the inspiration for that Corey Hart song.
Sigh Google it, young people.
THINK YOU CAN *UNFF* HIDE FROM ME?!
But still, I'd encourage him to try to get at least a minimal amount of exercise--
--if only for my own selfish reasons.

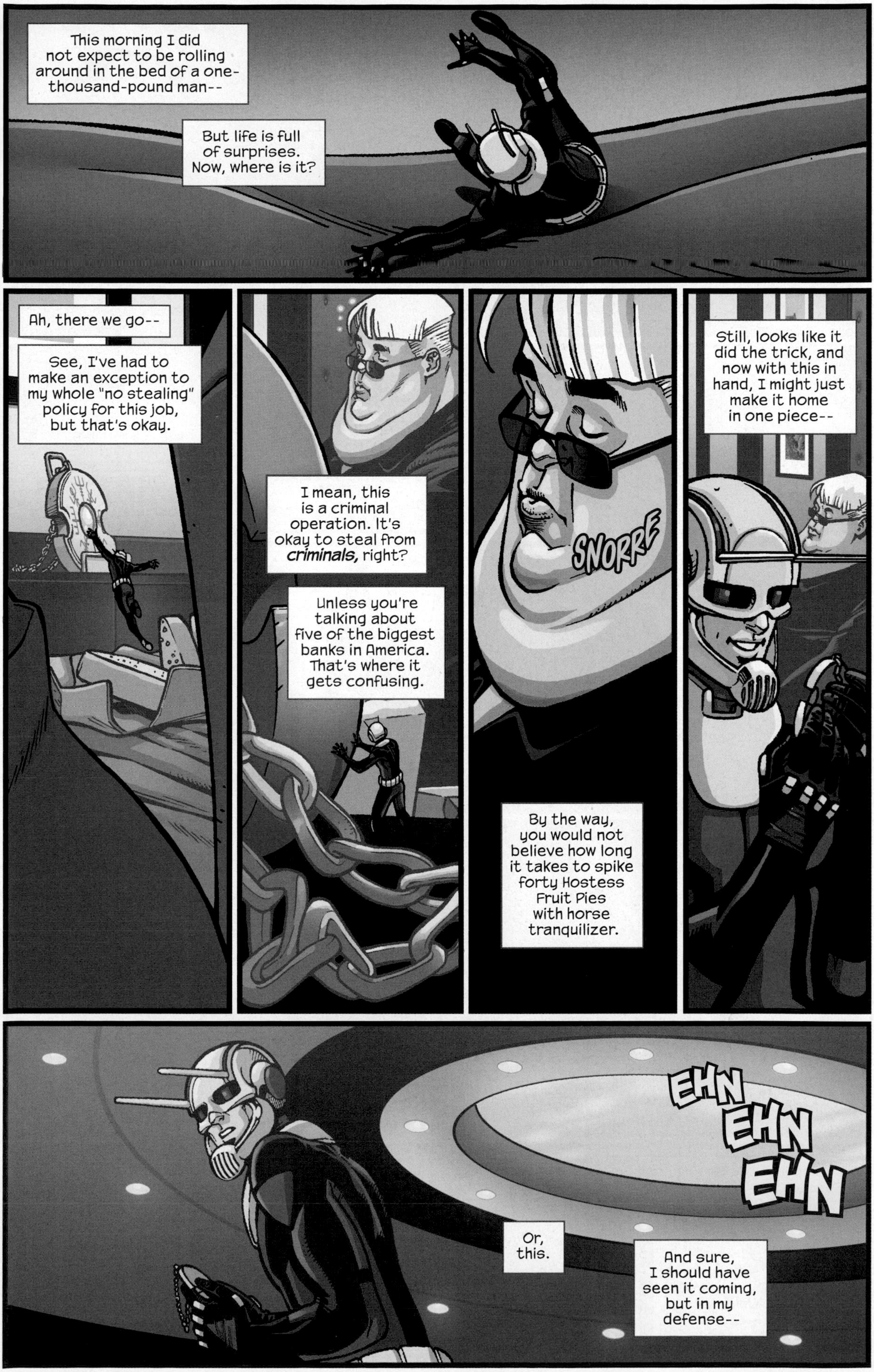
This morning I did not expect to be rolling around in the bed of a one-thousand-pound man--
But life is full of surprises. Now, where is it?
Ah, there we go--
See, I've had to make an exception to my whole "no stealing" policy for this job, but that's okay.
I mean, this is a criminal operation. It's okay to steal from *criminals,* right?
Unless you're talking about five of the biggest banks in America. That's where it gets confusing.
SNORRE
By the way, you would not believe how long it takes to spike forty Hostess Fruit Pies with horse tranquilizer.
Still, looks like it did the trick, and now with this in hand, I might just make it home in one piece--
EHN EHN EHN
Or, this.
And sure, I should have seen it coming, but in my defense--

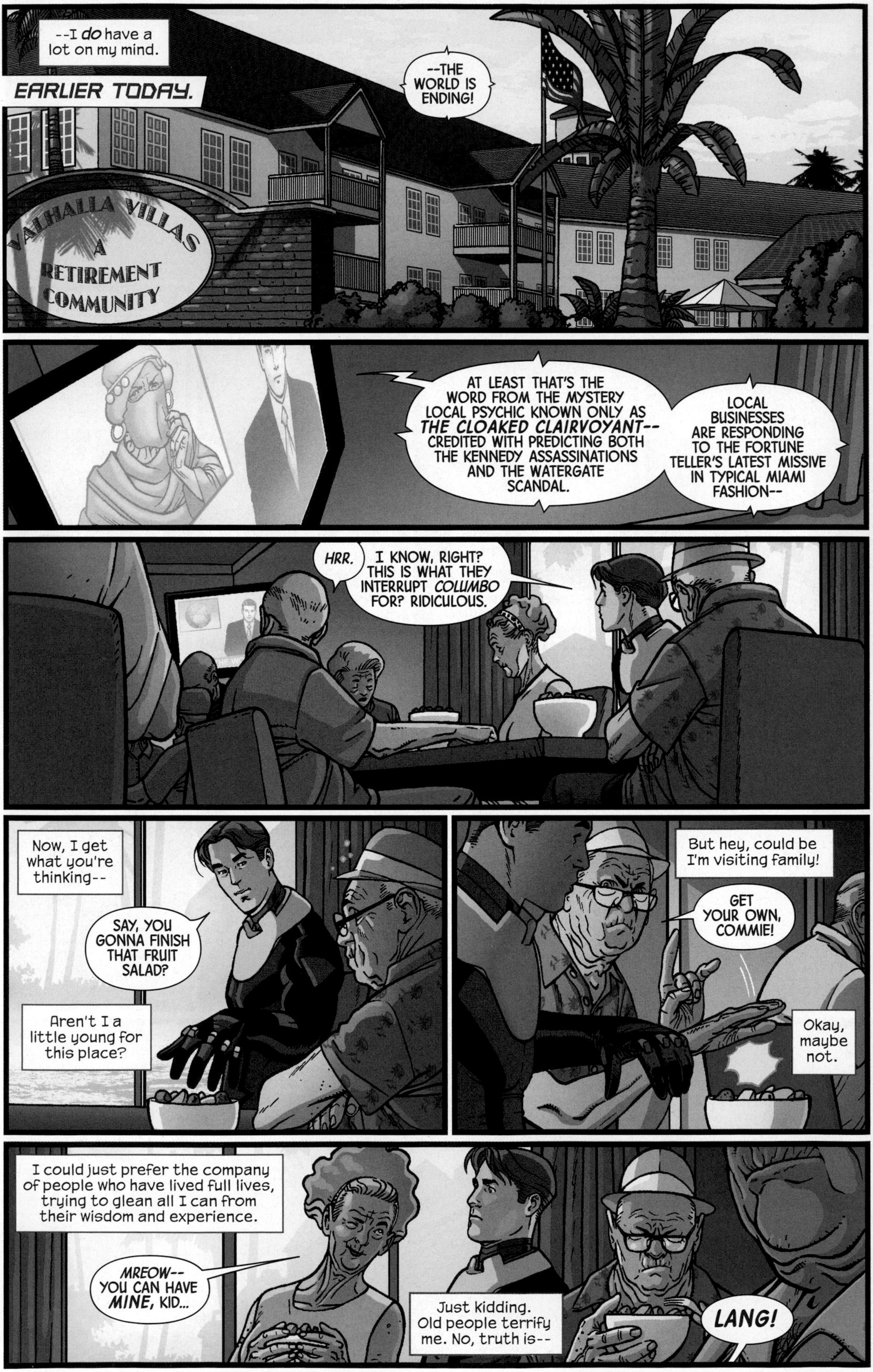

--I *do* have a lot on my mind.
EARLIER TODAY.
--THE WORLD IS ENDING!
VALHALLA VILLAS A RETIREMENT COMMUNITY
AT LEAST THAT'S THE WORD FROM THE MYSTERY LOCAL PSYCHIC KNOWN ONLY AS *THE CLOAKED CLAIRVOYANT*-- CREDITED WITH PREDICTING BOTH THE KENNEDY ASSASSINATIONS AND THE WATERGATE SCANDAL.
LOCAL BUSINESSES ARE RESPONDING TO THE FORTUNE TELLER'S LATEST MISSIVE IN TYPICAL MIAMI FASHION--
HRR.
I KNOW, RIGHT? THIS IS WHAT THEY INTERRUPT *COLUMBO* FOR? RIDICULOUS.
Now, I get what you're thinking--
SAY, YOU GONNA FINISH THAT FRUIT SALAD?
Aren't I a little young for this place?
But hey, could be I'm visiting family!
GET YOUR OWN, COMMIE!
Okay, maybe not.
I could just prefer the company of people who have lived full lives, trying to glean all I can from their wisdom and experience.
MREOW-- YOU CAN HAVE *MINE*, KID...
Just kidding. Old people terrify me. No, truth is--
LANG!

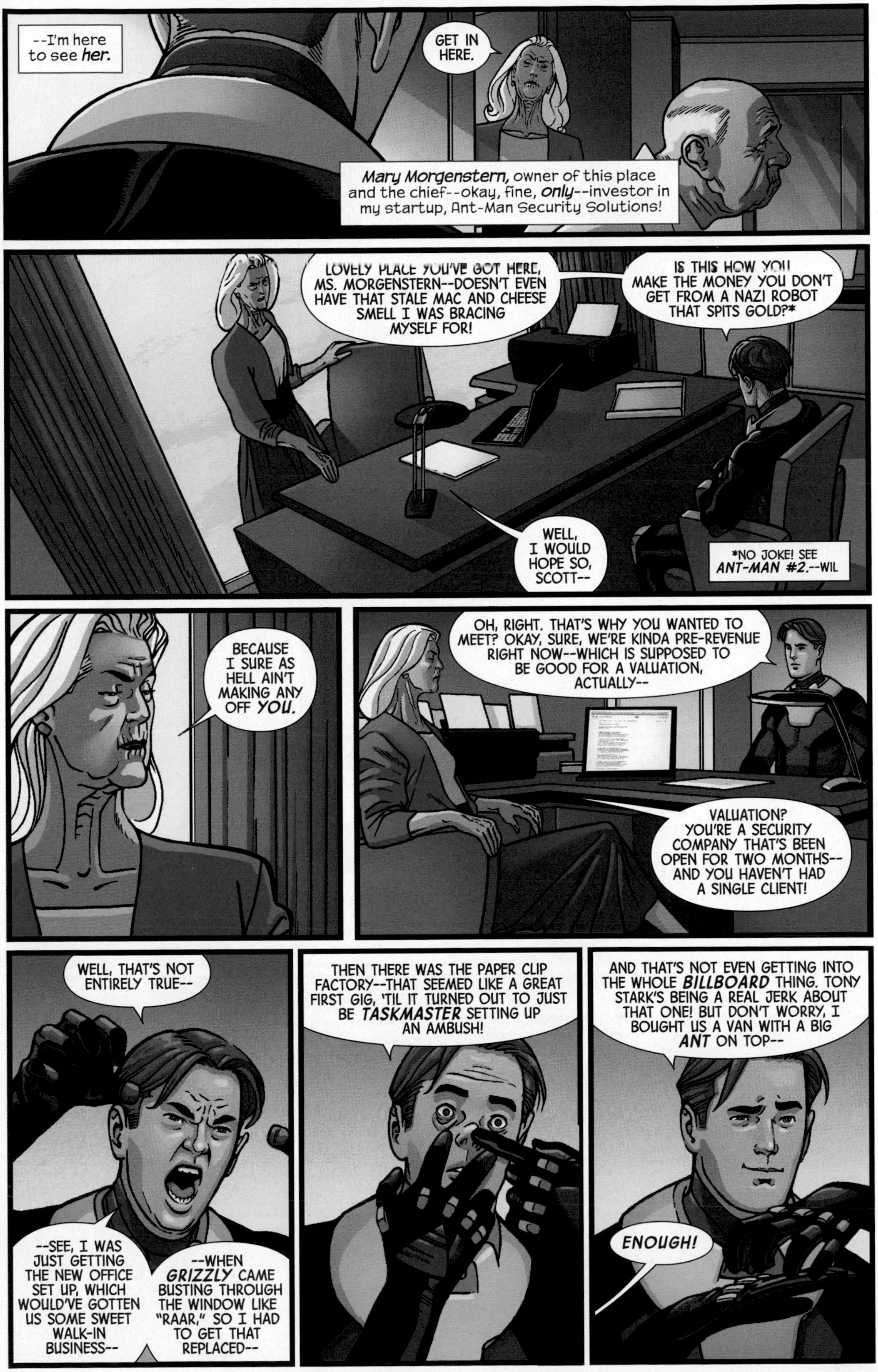
--I'm here to see *her.*
GET IN HERE.
Mary Morgenstern, owner of this place and the chief--okay, fine, *only*--investor in my startup, Ant-Man Security Solutions!
LOVELY PLACE YOU'VE GOT HERE, MS. MORGENSTERN--DOESN'T EVEN HAVE THAT STALE MAC AND CHEESE SMELL I WAS BRACING MYSELF FOR!
IS THIS HOW YOU MAKE THE MONEY YOU DON'T GET FROM A NAZI ROBOT THAT SPITS GOLD?*
WELL, I WOULD HOPE SO, SCOTT--
*NO JOKE! SEE *ANT-MAN #2.*--WIL
BECAUSE I SURE AS HELL AIN'T MAKING ANY OFF *YOU.*
OH, RIGHT. THAT'S WHY YOU WANTED TO MEET? OKAY, SURE, WE'RE KINDA PRE-REVENUE RIGHT NOW--WHICH IS SUPPOSED TO BE GOOD FOR A VALUATION, ACTUALLY--
VALUATION? YOU'RE A SECURITY COMPANY THAT'S BEEN OPEN FOR TWO MONTHS--AND YOU HAVEN'T HAD A SINGLE CLIENT!
WELL, THAT'S NOT ENTIRELY TRUE--
--SEE, I WAS JUST GETTING THE NEW OFFICE SET UP, WHICH WOULD'VE GOTTEN US SOME SWEET WALK-IN BUSINESS--
--WHEN *GRIZZLY* CAME BUSTING THROUGH THE WINDOW LIKE "RAAR," SO I HAD TO GET THAT REPLACED--
THEN THERE WAS THE PAPER CLIP FACTORY--THAT SEEMED LIKE A GREAT FIRST GIG, 'TIL IT TURNED OUT TO JUST BE *TASKMASTER* SETTING UP AN AMBUSH!
AND THAT'S NOT EVEN GETTING INTO THE WHOLE *BILLBOARD* THING. TONY STARK'S BEING A REAL JERK ABOUT THAT ONE! BUT DON'T WORRY, I BOUGHT US A VAN WITH A BIG *ANT* ON TOP--
ENOUGH!

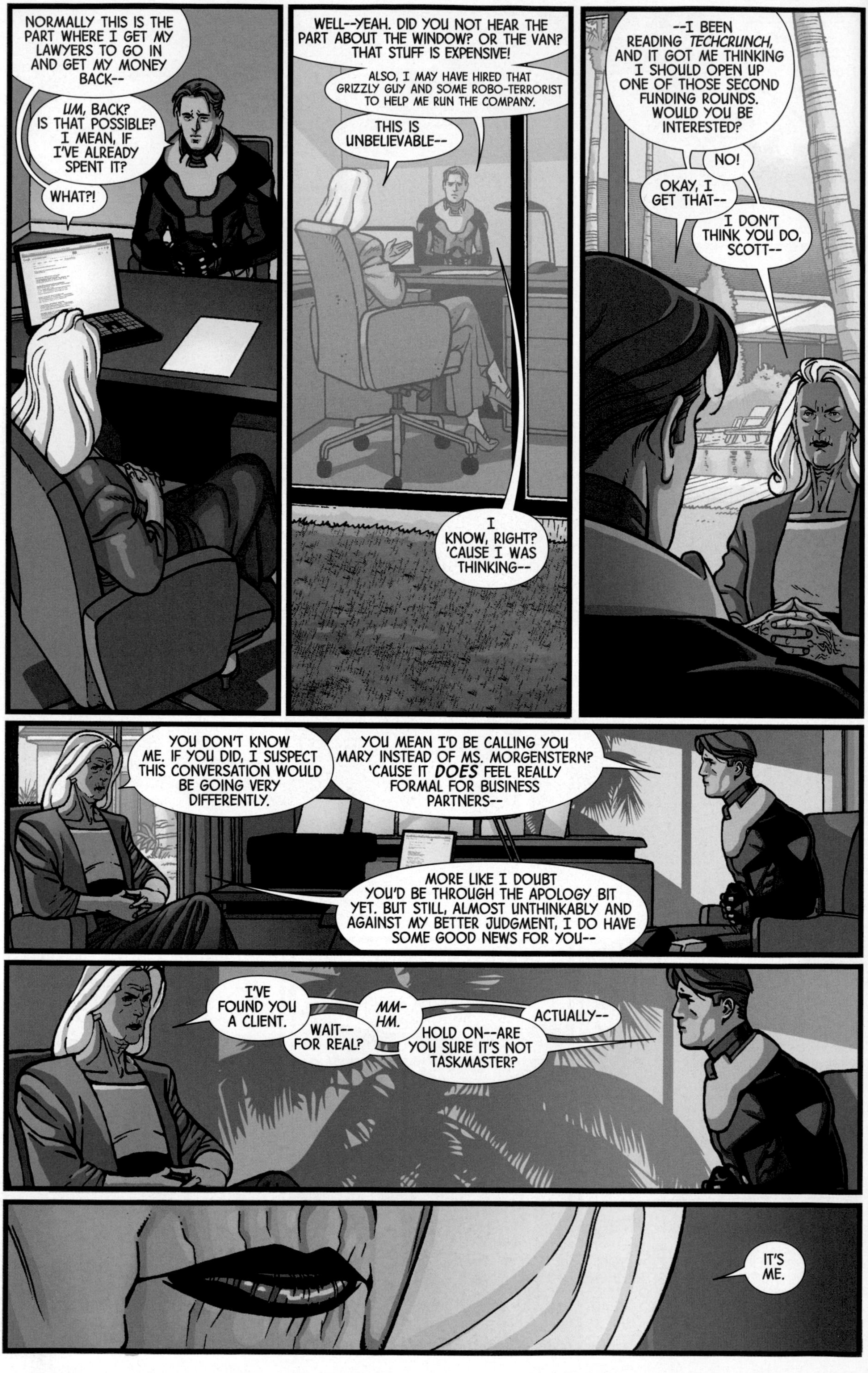
NORMALLY THIS IS THE PART WHERE I GET MY LAWYERS TO GO IN AND GET MY MONEY BACK--
UM, BACK? IS THAT POSSIBLE? I MEAN, IF I'VE ALREADY SPENT IT?
WHAT?!
WELL--YEAH. DID YOU NOT HEAR THE PART ABOUT THE WINDOW? OR THE VAN? THAT STUFF IS EXPENSIVE!
ALSO, I MAY HAVE HIRED THAT GRIZZLY GUY AND SOME ROBO-TERRORIST TO HELP ME RUN THE COMPANY.
THIS IS UNBELIEVABLE--
I KNOW, RIGHT? 'CAUSE I WAS THINKING--
--I BEEN READING TECHCRUNCH, AND IT GOT ME THINKING I SHOULD OPEN UP ONE OF THOSE SECOND FUNDING ROUNDS. WOULD YOU BE INTERESTED?
NO!
OKAY, I GET THAT--
I DON'T THINK YOU DO, SCOTT--
YOU DON'T KNOW ME. IF YOU DID, I SUSPECT THIS CONVERSATION WOULD BE GOING VERY DIFFERENTLY.
YOU MEAN I'D BE CALLING YOU MARY INSTEAD OF MS. MORGENSTERN? 'CAUSE IT DOES FEEL REALLY FORMAL FOR BUSINESS PARTNERS--
MORE LIKE I DOUBT YOU'D BE THROUGH THE APOLOGY BIT YET. BUT STILL, ALMOST UNTHINKABLY AND AGAINST MY BETTER JUDGMENT, I DO HAVE SOME GOOD NEWS FOR YOU--
I'VE FOUND YOU A CLIENT.
WAIT-- FOR REAL?
MM-HM.
HOLD ON--ARE YOU SURE IT'S NOT TASKMASTER?
ACTUALLY--
IT'S ME.

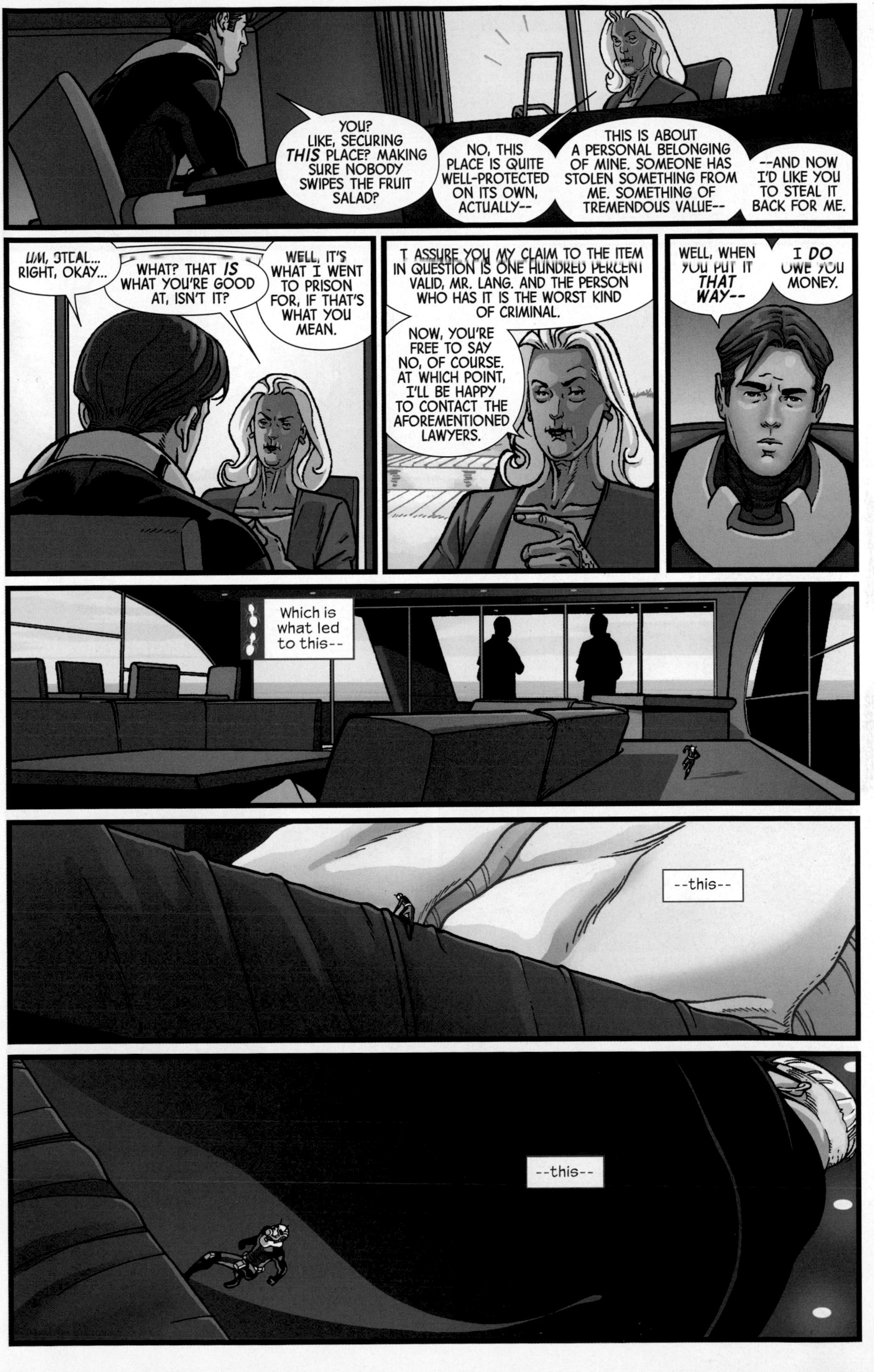

YOU? LIKE, SECURING THIS PLACE? MAKING SURE NOBODY SWIPES THE FRUIT SALAD?
NO, THIS PLACE IS QUITE WELL-PROTECTED ON ITS OWN, ACTUALLY--
THIS IS ABOUT A PERSONAL BELONGING OF MINE. SOMEONE HAS STOLEN SOMETHING FROM ME. SOMETHING OF TREMENDOUS VALUE--
--AND NOW I'D LIKE YOU TO STEAL IT BACK FOR ME.
UM, STEAL... RIGHT, OKAY...
WHAT? THAT IS WHAT YOU'RE GOOD AT, ISN'T IT?
WELL, IT'S WHAT I WENT TO PRISON FOR, IF THAT'S WHAT YOU MEAN.
I ASSURE YOU MY CLAIM TO THE ITEM IN QUESTION IS ONE HUNDRED PERCENT VALID, MR. LANG. AND THE PERSON WHO HAS IT IS THE WORST KIND OF CRIMINAL.
NOW, YOU'RE FREE TO SAY NO, OF COURSE. AT WHICH POINT, I'LL BE HAPPY TO CONTACT THE AFOREMENTIONED LAWYERS.
WELL, WHEN YOU PUT IT THAT WAY--
I DO OWE YOU MONEY.
Which is what led to this--
--this--
--this--

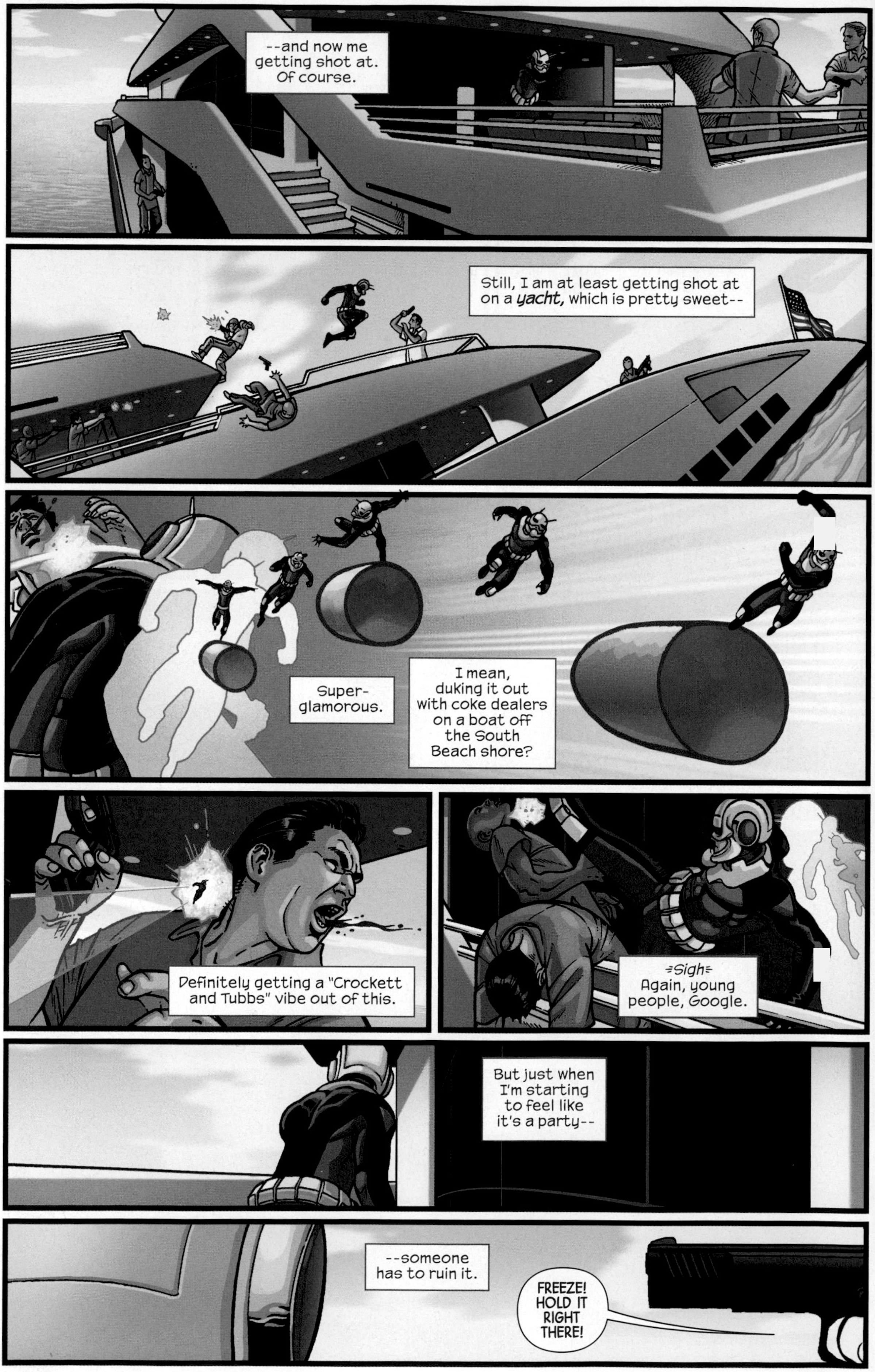
--and now me getting shot at. Of course.
Still, I am at least getting shot at on a *yacht,* which is pretty sweet--
Super-glamorous.
I mean, duking it out with coke dealers on a boat off the South Beach shore?
Definitely getting a "Crockett and Tubbs" vibe out of this.
Sigh
Again, young people, Google.
But just when I'm starting to feel like it's a party--
--someone has to ruin it.
FREEZE! HOLD IT RIGHT THERE!

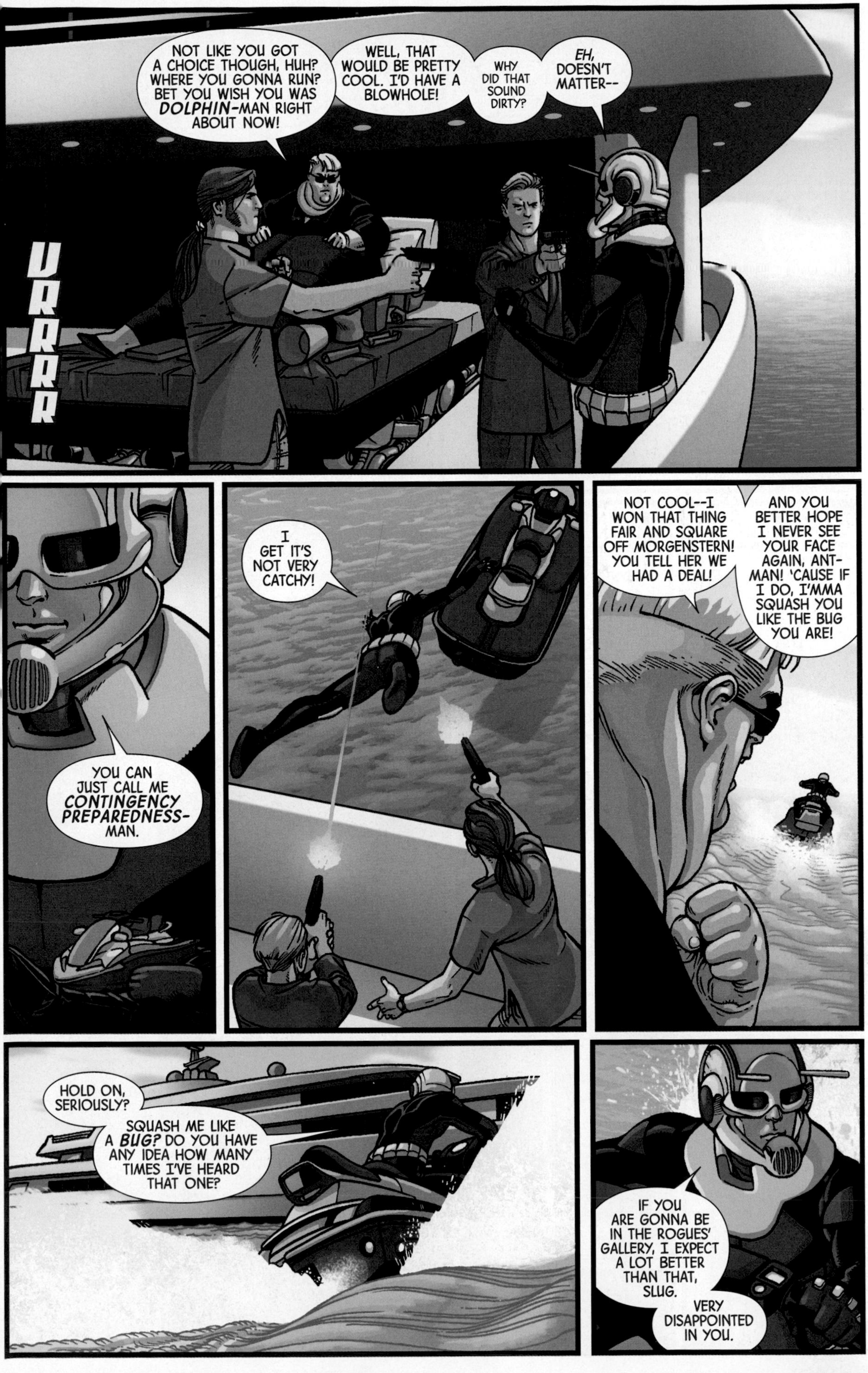
NOT LIKE YOU GOT A CHOICE THOUGH, HUH? WHERE YOU GONNA RUN? BET YOU WISH YOU WAS DOLPHIN-MAN RIGHT ABOUT NOW!
WELL, THAT WOULD BE PRETTY COOL. I'D HAVE A BLOWHOLE!
WHY DID THAT SOUND DIRTY?
EH, DOESN'T MATTER--
VRRRR
YOU CAN JUST CALL ME CONTINGENCY PREPAREDNESS-MAN.
I GET IT'S NOT VERY CATCHY!
NOT COOL--I WON THAT THING FAIR AND SQUARE OFF MORGENSTERN! YOU TELL HER WE HAD A DEAL!
AND YOU BETTER HOPE I NEVER SEE YOUR FACE AGAIN, ANT-MAN! 'CAUSE IF I DO, I'MMA SQUASH YOU LIKE THE BUG YOU ARE!
HOLD ON, SERIOUSLY?
SQUASH ME LIKE A BUG? DO YOU HAVE ANY IDEA HOW MANY TIMES I'VE HEARD THAT ONE?
IF YOU ARE GONNA BE IN THE ROGUES' GALLERY, I EXPECT A LOT BETTER THAN THAT, SLUG.
VERY DISAPPOINTED IN YOU.

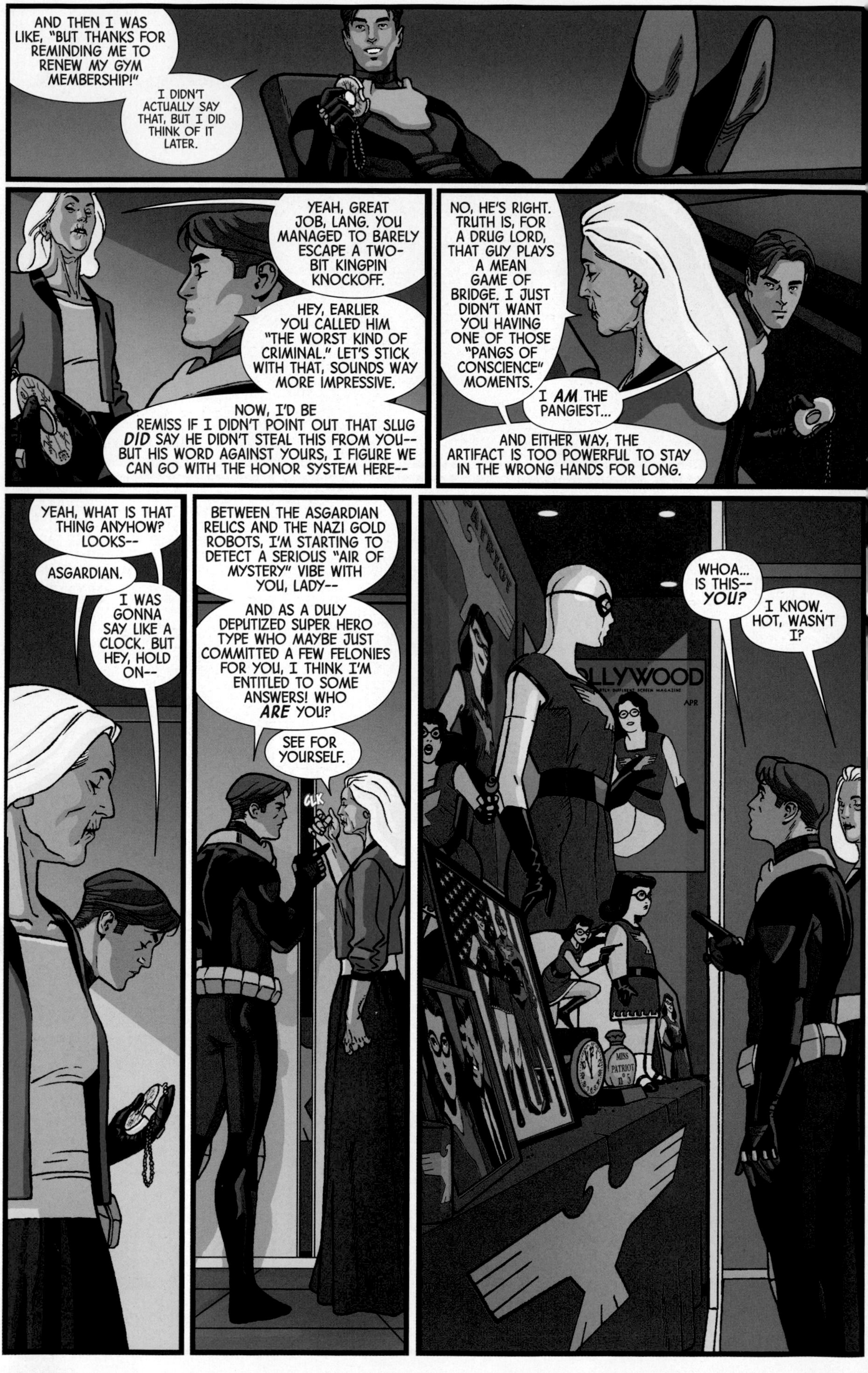
AND THEN I WAS LIKE, "BUT THANKS FOR REMINDING ME TO RENEW MY GYM MEMBERSHIP!"
I DIDN'T ACTUALLY SAY THAT, BUT I DID THINK OF IT LATER.
YEAH, GREAT JOB, LANG. YOU MANAGED TO BARELY ESCAPE A TWO-BIT KINGPIN KNOCKOFF.
HEY, EARLIER YOU CALLED HIM "THE WORST KIND OF CRIMINAL." LET'S STICK WITH THAT, SOUNDS WAY MORE IMPRESSIVE.
NOW, I'D BE REMISS IF I DIDN'T POINT OUT THAT SLUG *DID* SAY HE DIDN'T STEAL THIS FROM YOU-- BUT HIS WORD AGAINST YOURS, I FIGURE WE CAN GO WITH THE HONOR SYSTEM HERE--
NO, HE'S RIGHT. TRUTH IS, FOR A DRUG LORD, THAT GUY PLAYS A MEAN GAME OF BRIDGE. I JUST DIDN'T WANT YOU HAVING ONE OF THOSE "PANGS OF CONSCIENCE" MOMENTS.
I *AM* THE PANGIEST...
AND EITHER WAY, THE ARTIFACT IS TOO POWERFUL TO STAY IN THE WRONG HANDS FOR LONG.
YEAH, WHAT IS THAT THING ANYHOW? LOOKS--
ASGARDIAN.
I WAS GONNA SAY LIKE A CLOCK. BUT HEY, HOLD ON--
BETWEEN THE ASGARDIAN RELICS AND THE NAZI GOLD ROBOTS, I'M STARTING TO DETECT A SERIOUS "AIR OF MYSTERY" VIBE WITH YOU, LADY--
AND AS A DULY DEPUTIZED SUPER HERO TYPE WHO MAYBE JUST COMMITTED A FEW FELONIES FOR YOU, I THINK I'M ENTITLED TO SOME ANSWERS! WHO *ARE* YOU?
SEE FOR YOURSELF.
CLK
WHOA... IS THIS-- *YOU?*
I KNOW. HOT, WASN'T I?
LLYWOOD
APR
MISS PATRIOT

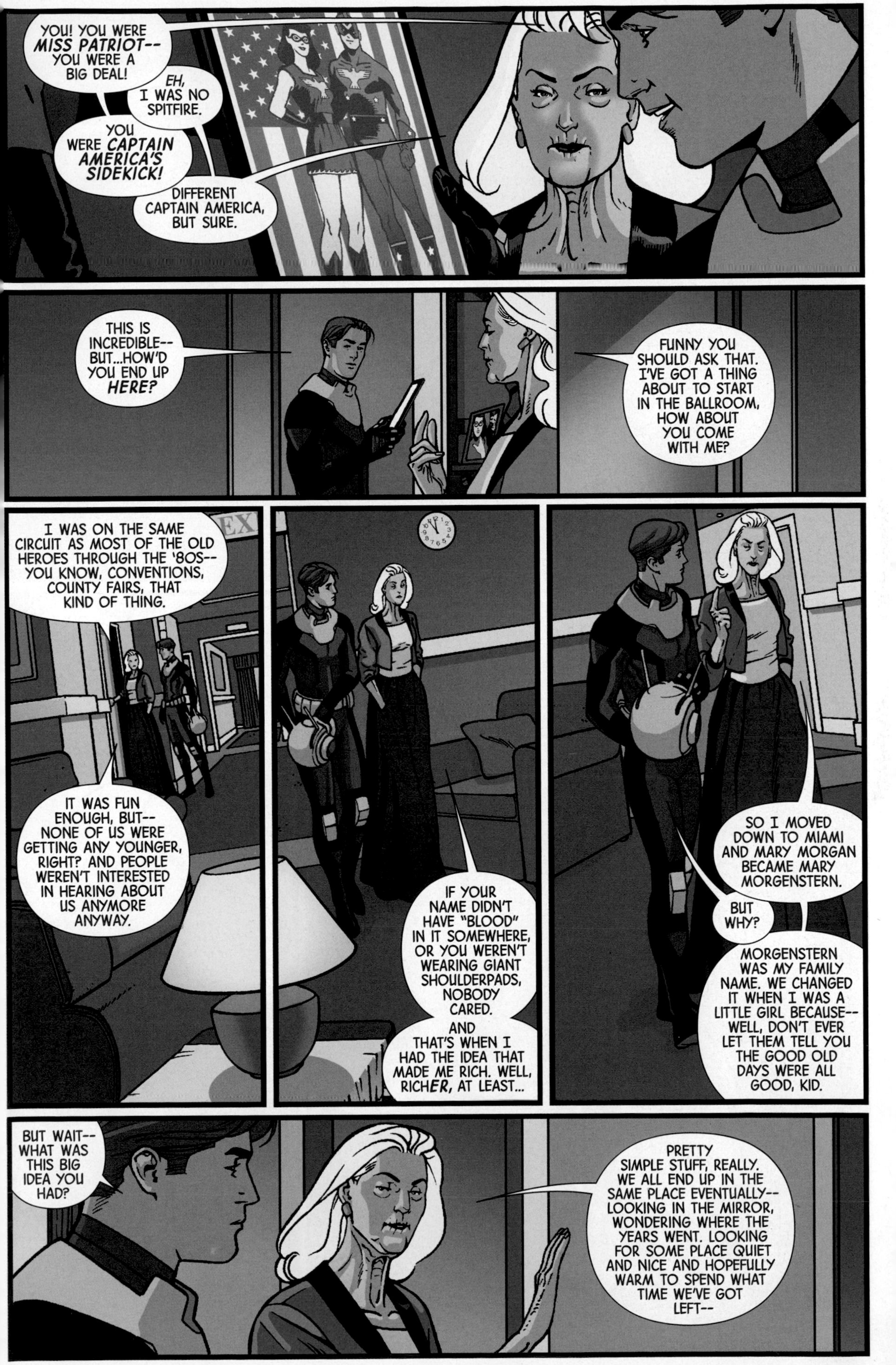
YOU! YOU WERE MISS PATRIOT-- YOU WERE A BIG DEAL!
EH, I WAS NO SPITFIRE.
YOU WERE CAPTAIN AMERICA'S SIDEKICK!
DIFFERENT CAPTAIN AMERICA, BUT SURE.
THIS IS INCREDIBLE-- BUT...HOW'D YOU END UP HERE?
FUNNY YOU SHOULD ASK THAT. I'VE GOT A THING ABOUT TO START IN THE BALLROOM, HOW ABOUT YOU COME WITH ME?
I WAS ON THE SAME CIRCUIT AS MOST OF THE OLD HEROES THROUGH THE '80S-- YOU KNOW, CONVENTIONS, COUNTY FAIRS, THAT KIND OF THING.
IT WAS FUN ENOUGH, BUT-- NONE OF US WERE GETTING ANY YOUNGER, RIGHT? AND PEOPLE WEREN'T INTERESTED IN HEARING ABOUT US ANYMORE ANYWAY.
IF YOUR NAME DIDN'T HAVE "BLOOD" IN IT SOMEWHERE, OR YOU WEREN'T WEARING GIANT SHOULDERPADS, NOBODY CARED.
AND THAT'S WHEN I HAD THE IDEA THAT MADE ME RICH. WELL, RICHER, AT LEAST...
SO I MOVED DOWN TO MIAMI AND MARY MORGAN BECAME MARY MORGENSTERN.
BUT WHY?
MORGENSTERN WAS MY FAMILY NAME. WE CHANGED IT WHEN I WAS A LITTLE GIRL BECAUSE-- WELL, DON'T EVER LET THEM TELL YOU THE GOOD OLD DAYS WERE ALL GOOD, KID.
BUT WAIT-- WHAT WAS THIS BIG IDEA YOU HAD?
PRETTY SIMPLE STUFF, REALLY. WE ALL END UP IN THE SAME PLACE EVENTUALLY-- LOOKING IN THE MIRROR, WONDERING WHERE THE YEARS WENT. LOOKING FOR SOME PLACE QUIET AND NICE AND HOPEFULLY WARM TO SPEND WHAT TIME WE'VE GOT LEFT--

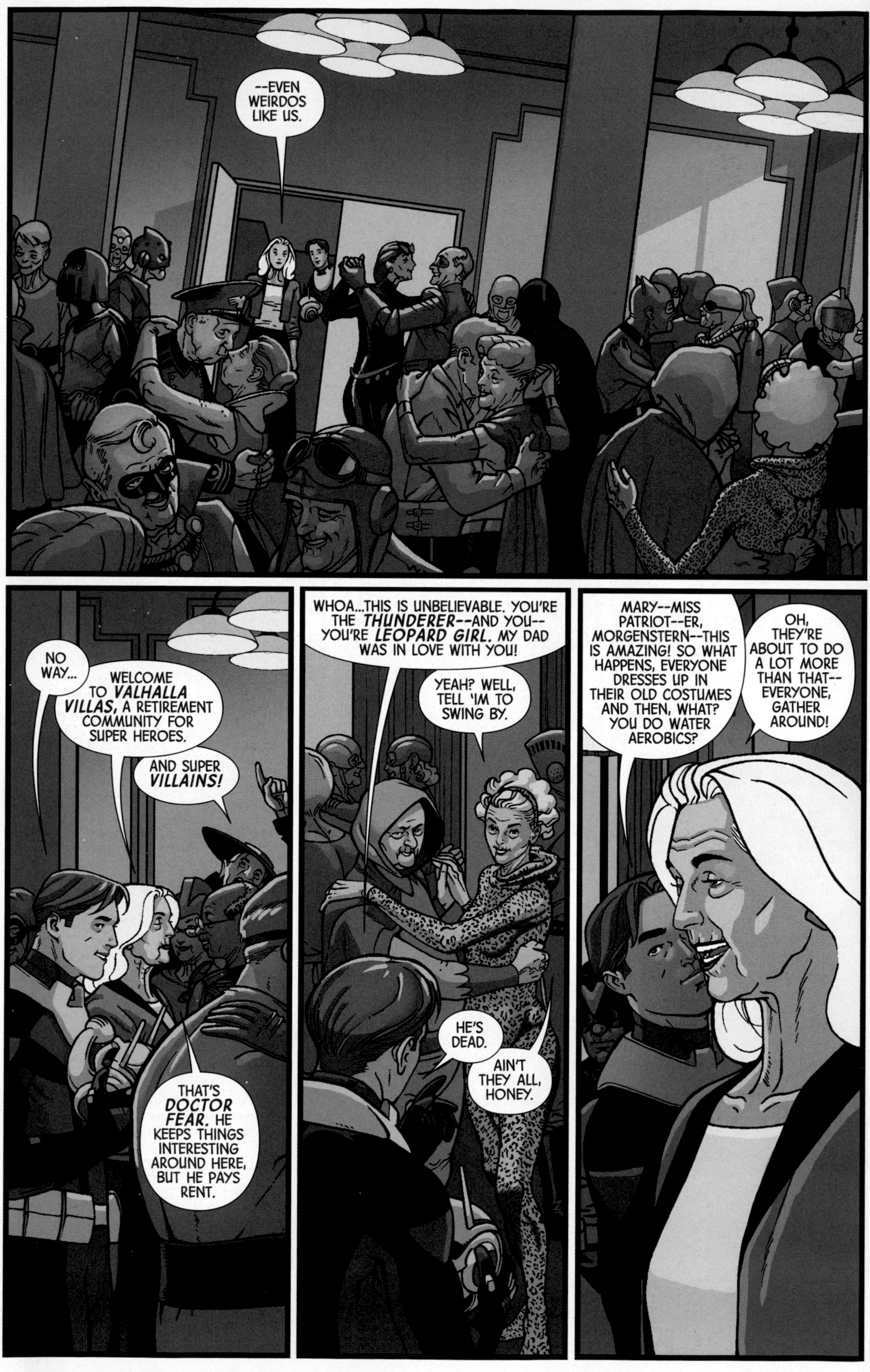
--EVEN WEIRDOS LIKE US.
NO WAY...
WELCOME TO VALHALLA VILLAS, A RETIREMENT COMMUNITY FOR SUPER HEROES.
AND SUPER VILLAINS!
THAT'S DOCTOR FEAR. HE KEEPS THINGS INTERESTING AROUND HERE, BUT HE PAYS RENT.
WHOA...THIS IS UNBELIEVABLE. YOU'RE THE THUNDERER--AND YOU--YOU'RE LEOPARD GIRL. MY DAD WAS IN LOVE WITH YOU!
YEAH? WELL, TELL 'IM TO SWING BY.
HE'S DEAD.
AIN'T THEY ALL, HONEY.
MARY--MISS PATRIOT--ER, MORGENSTERN--THIS IS AMAZING! SO WHAT HAPPENS, EVERYONE DRESSES UP IN THEIR OLD COSTUMES AND THEN, WHAT? YOU DO WATER AEROBICS?
OH, THEY'RE ABOUT TO DO A LOT MORE THAN THAT--EVERYONE, GATHER AROUND!

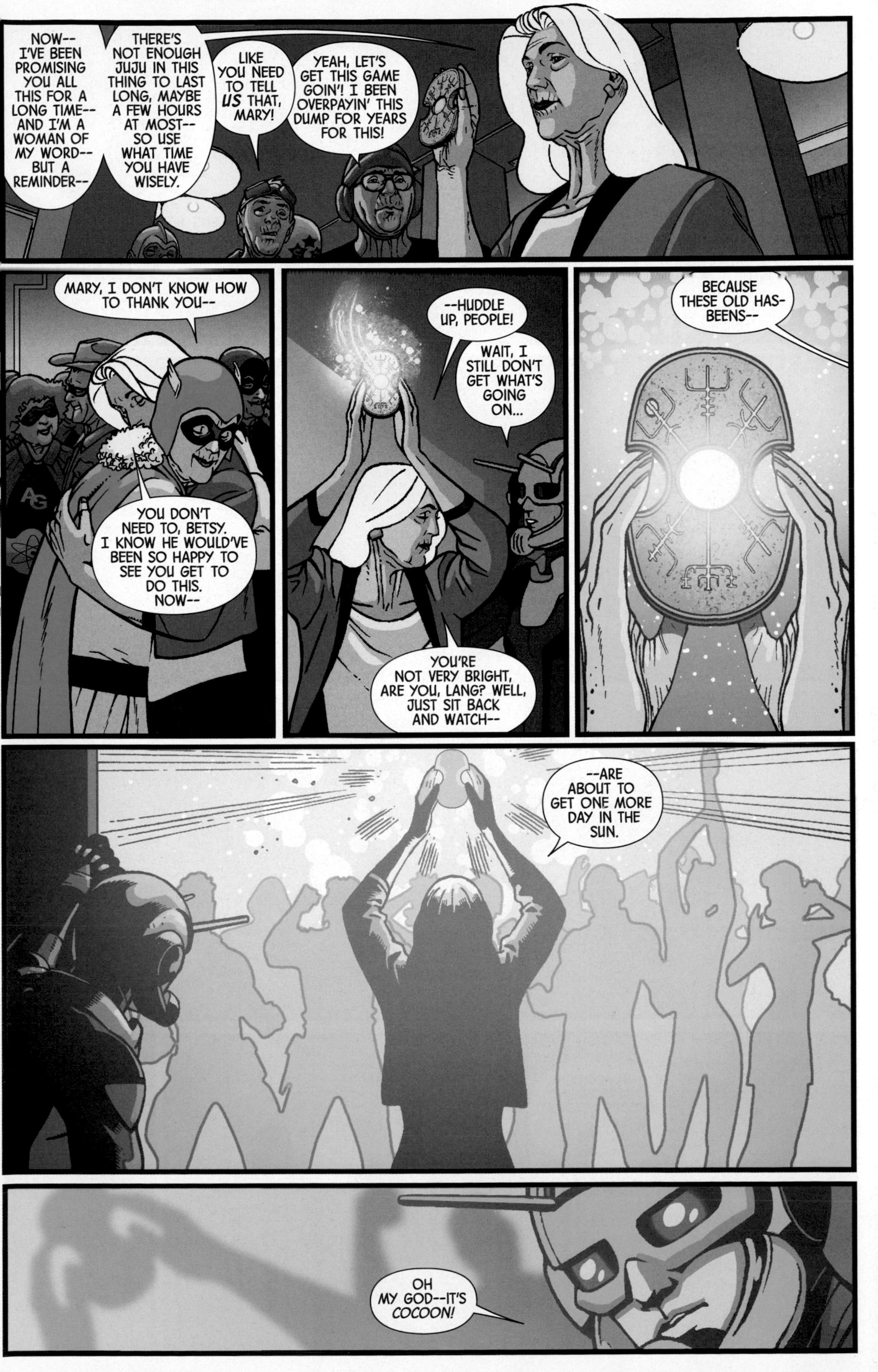
NOW-- I'VE BEEN PROMISING YOU ALL THIS FOR A LONG TIME-- AND I'M A WOMAN OF MY WORD-- BUT A REMINDER--
THERE'S NOT ENOUGH JUJU IN THIS THING TO LAST LONG, MAYBE A FEW HOURS AT MOST-- SO USE WHAT TIME YOU HAVE WISELY.
LIKE YOU NEED TO TELL US THAT, MARY!
YEAH, LET'S GET THIS GAME GOIN'! I BEEN OVERPAYIN' THIS DUMP FOR YEARS FOR THIS!
MARY, I DON'T KNOW HOW TO THANK YOU--
YOU DON'T NEED TO, BETSY. I KNOW HE WOULD'VE BEEN SO HAPPY TO SEE YOU GET TO DO THIS. NOW--
--HUDDLE UP, PEOPLE!
WAIT, I STILL DON'T GET WHAT'S GOING ON...
YOU'RE NOT VERY BRIGHT, ARE YOU, LANG? WELL, JUST SIT BACK AND WATCH--
BECAUSE THESE OLD HAS-BEENS--
--ARE ABOUT TO GET ONE MORE DAY IN THE SUN.
OH MY GOD--IT'S COCOON!

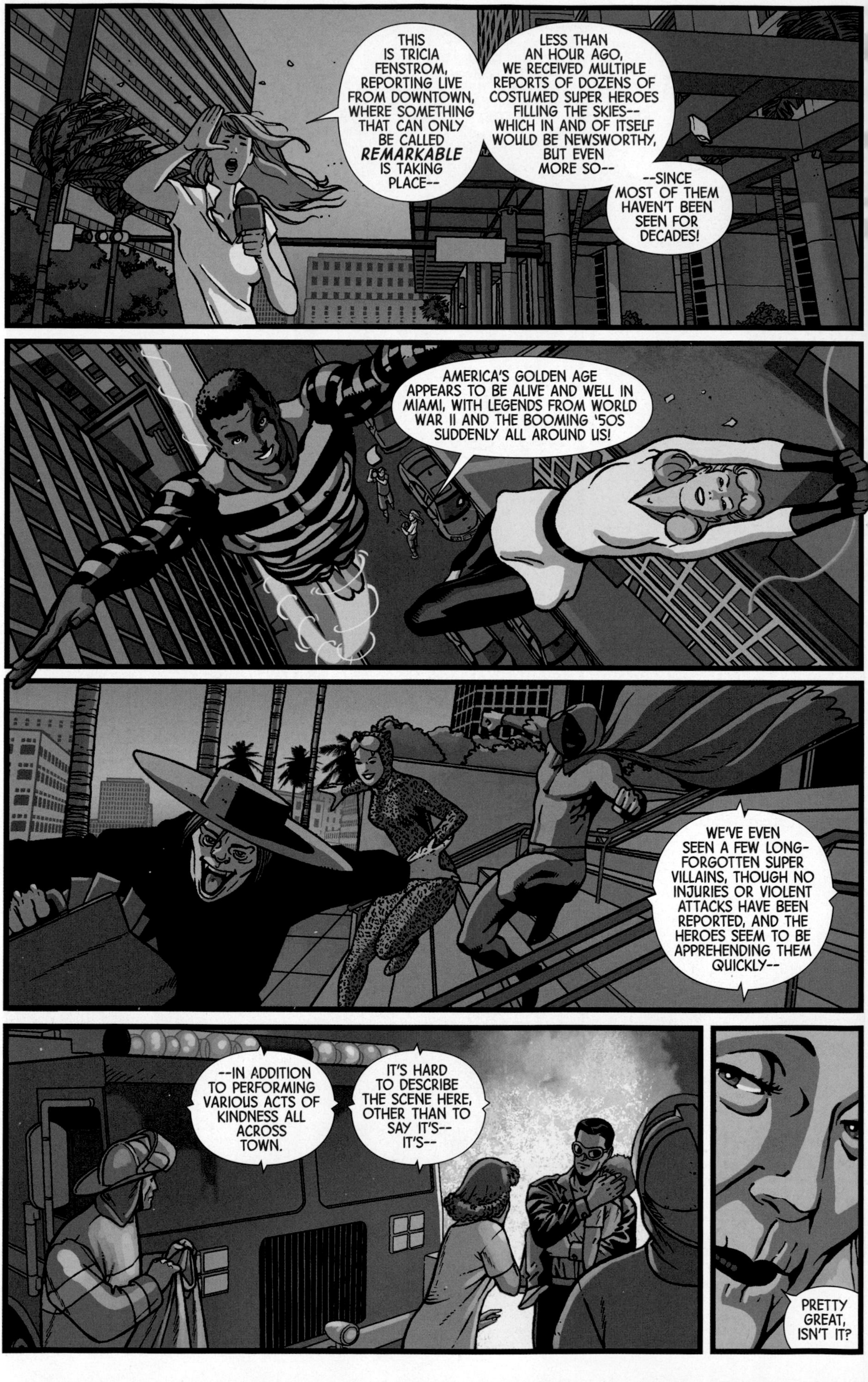
THIS IS TRICIA FENSTROM, REPORTING LIVE FROM DOWNTOWN, WHERE SOMETHING THAT CAN ONLY BE CALLED *REMARKABLE* IS TAKING PLACE--
LESS THAN AN HOUR AGO, WE RECEIVED MULTIPLE REPORTS OF DOZENS OF COSTUMED SUPER HEROES FILLING THE SKIES-- WHICH IN AND OF ITSELF WOULD BE NEWSWORTHY, BUT EVEN MORE SO--
--SINCE MOST OF THEM HAVEN'T BEEN SEEN FOR DECADES!
AMERICA'S GOLDEN AGE APPEARS TO BE ALIVE AND WELL IN MIAMI, WITH LEGENDS FROM WORLD WAR II AND THE BOOMING '50S SUDDENLY ALL AROUND US!
WE'VE EVEN SEEN A FEW LONG-FORGOTTEN SUPER VILLAINS, THOUGH NO INJURIES OR VIOLENT ATTACKS HAVE BEEN REPORTED, AND THE HEROES SEEM TO BE APPREHENDING THEM QUICKLY--
--IN ADDITION TO PERFORMING VARIOUS ACTS OF KINDNESS ALL ACROSS TOWN.
IT'S HARD TO DESCRIBE THE SCENE HERE, OTHER THAN TO SAY IT'S-- IT'S--
PRETTY GREAT, ISN'T IT?

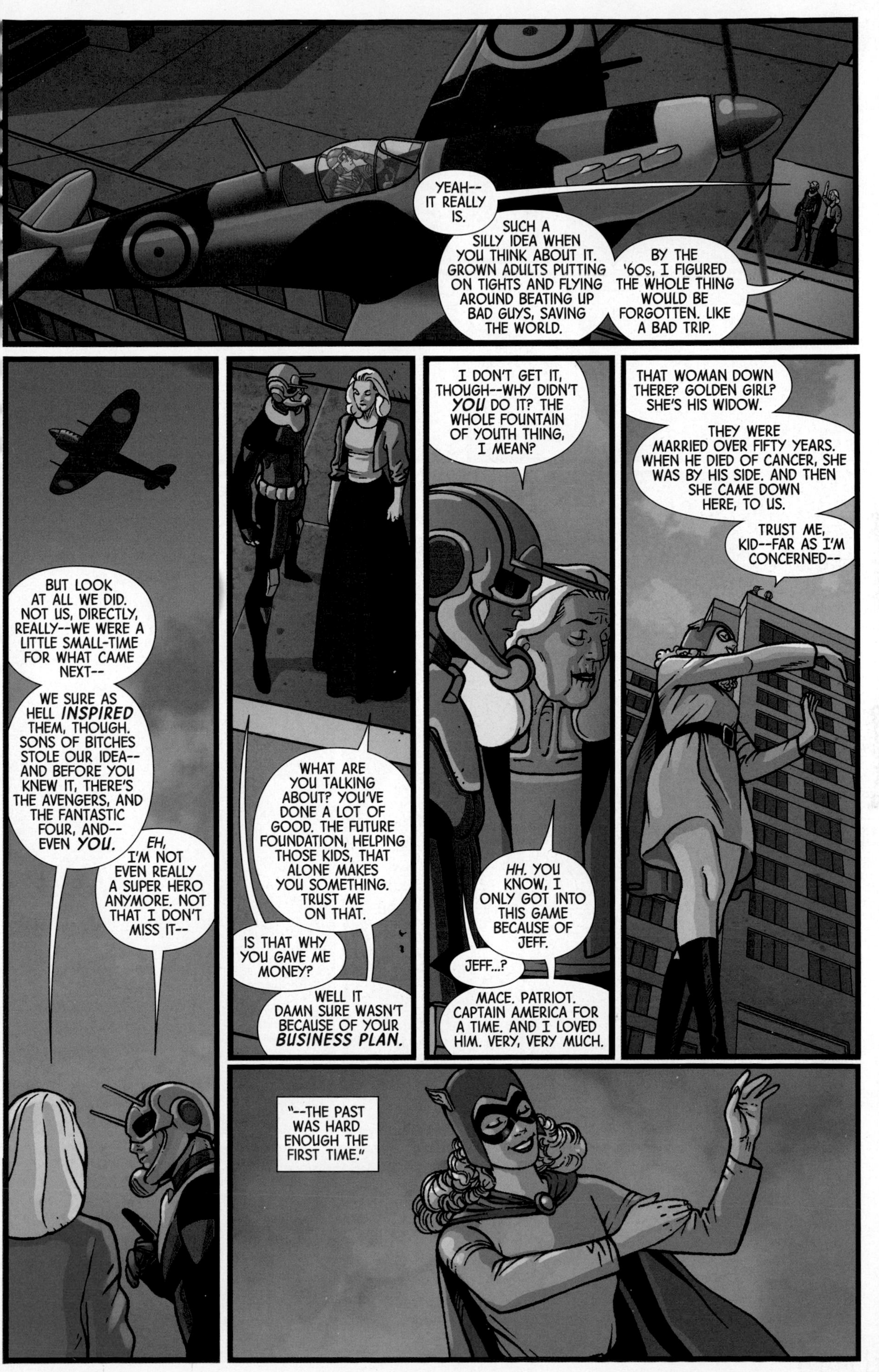
YEAH--IT REALLY IS.
SUCH A SILLY IDEA WHEN YOU THINK ABOUT IT. GROWN ADULTS PUTTING ON TIGHTS AND FLYING AROUND BEATING UP BAD GUYS, SAVING THE WORLD.
BY THE '60s, I FIGURED THE WHOLE THING WOULD BE FORGOTTEN. LIKE A BAD TRIP.
BUT LOOK AT ALL WE DID. NOT US, DIRECTLY, REALLY--WE WERE A LITTLE SMALL-TIME FOR WHAT CAME NEXT--
WE SURE AS HELL INSPIRED THEM, THOUGH. SONS OF BITCHES STOLE OUR IDEA--AND BEFORE YOU KNEW IT, THERE'S THE AVENGERS, AND THE FANTASTIC FOUR, AND--EVEN YOU.
EH, I'M NOT EVEN REALLY A SUPER HERO ANYMORE. NOT THAT I DON'T MISS IT--
WHAT ARE YOU TALKING ABOUT? YOU'VE DONE A LOT OF GOOD. THE FUTURE FOUNDATION, HELPING THOSE KIDS, THAT ALONE MAKES YOU SOMETHING. TRUST ME ON THAT.
IS THAT WHY YOU GAVE ME MONEY?
WELL IT DAMN SURE WASN'T BECAUSE OF YOUR BUSINESS PLAN.
I DON'T GET IT, THOUGH--WHY DIDN'T YOU DO IT? THE WHOLE FOUNTAIN OF YOUTH THING, I MEAN?
HH. YOU KNOW, I ONLY GOT INTO THIS GAME BECAUSE OF JEFF.
JEFF...?
MACE. PATRIOT. CAPTAIN AMERICA FOR A TIME. AND I LOVED HIM. VERY, VERY MUCH.
THAT WOMAN DOWN THERE? GOLDEN GIRL? SHE'S HIS WIDOW.
THEY WERE MARRIED OVER FIFTY YEARS. WHEN HE DIED OF CANCER, SHE WAS BY HIS SIDE. AND THEN SHE CAME DOWN HERE, TO US.
TRUST ME, KID--FAR AS I'M CONCERNED--
"--THE PAST WAS HARD ENOUGH THE FIRST TIME."

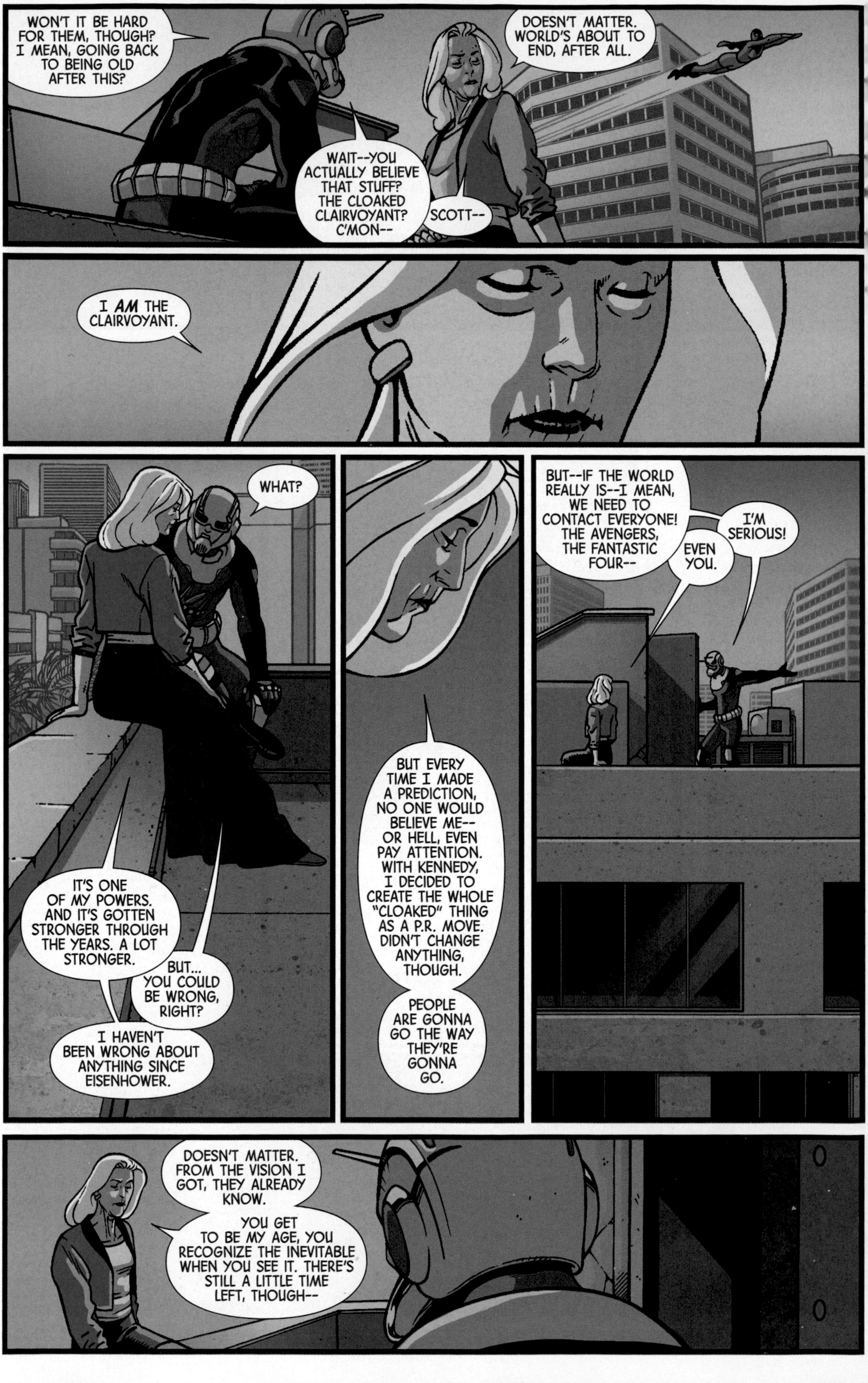
WON'T IT BE HARD FOR THEM, THOUGH? I MEAN, GOING BACK TO BEING OLD AFTER THIS?
DOESN'T MATTER. WORLD'S ABOUT TO END, AFTER ALL.
WAIT--YOU ACTUALLY BELIEVE THAT STUFF? THE CLOAKED CLAIRVOYANT? C'MON--
SCOTT--
I AM THE CLAIRVOYANT.
WHAT?
IT'S ONE OF MY POWERS. AND IT'S GOTTEN STRONGER THROUGH THE YEARS. A LOT STRONGER.
BUT... YOU COULD BE WRONG, RIGHT?
I HAVEN'T BEEN WRONG ABOUT ANYTHING SINCE EISENHOWER.
BUT EVERY TIME I MADE A PREDICTION, NO ONE WOULD BELIEVE ME-- OR HELL, EVEN PAY ATTENTION. WITH KENNEDY, I DECIDED TO CREATE THE WHOLE "CLOAKED" THING AS A P.R. MOVE. DIDN'T CHANGE ANYTHING, THOUGH.
PEOPLE ARE GONNA GO THE WAY THEY'RE GONNA GO.
BUT--IF THE WORLD REALLY IS--I MEAN, WE NEED TO CONTACT EVERYONE! THE AVENGERS, THE FANTASTIC FOUR--
EVEN YOU.
I'M SERIOUS!
DOESN'T MATTER. FROM THE VISION I GOT, THEY ALREADY KNOW.
YOU GET TO BE MY AGE, YOU RECOGNIZE THE INEVITABLE WHEN YOU SEE IT. THERE'S STILL A LITTLE TIME LEFT, THOUGH--

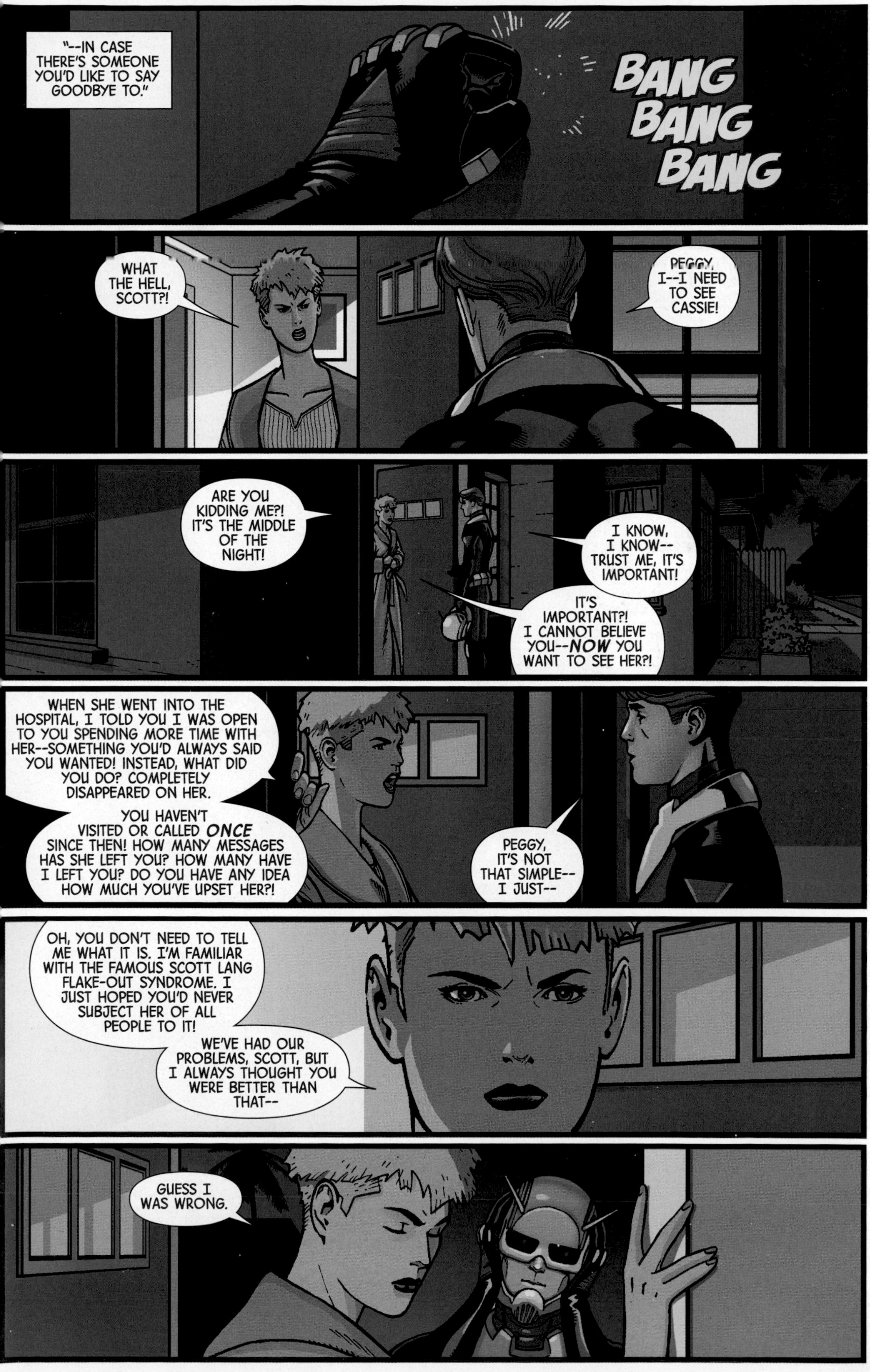
"--IN CASE THERE'S SOMEONE YOU'D LIKE TO SAY GOODBYE TO."
BANG BANG BANG
WHAT THE HELL, SCOTT?!
PEGGY, I--I NEED TO SEE CASSIE!
ARE YOU KIDDING ME?! IT'S THE MIDDLE OF THE NIGHT!
I KNOW, I KNOW-- TRUST ME, IT'S IMPORTANT!
IT'S IMPORTANT?! I CANNOT BELIEVE YOU--*NOW* YOU WANT TO SEE HER?!
WHEN SHE WENT INTO THE HOSPITAL, I TOLD YOU I WAS OPEN TO YOU SPENDING MORE TIME WITH HER--SOMETHING YOU'D ALWAYS SAID YOU WANTED! INSTEAD, WHAT DID YOU DO? COMPLETELY DISAPPEARED ON HER.
YOU HAVEN'T VISITED OR CALLED *ONCE* SINCE THEN! HOW MANY MESSAGES HAS SHE LEFT YOU? HOW MANY HAVE I LEFT YOU? DO YOU HAVE ANY IDEA HOW MUCH YOU'VE UPSET HER?!
PEGGY, IT'S NOT THAT SIMPLE-- I JUST--
OH, YOU DON'T NEED TO TELL ME WHAT IT IS. I'M FAMILIAR WITH THE FAMOUS SCOTT LANG FLAKE-OUT SYNDROME. I JUST HOPED YOU'D NEVER SUBJECT HER OF ALL PEOPLE TO IT!
WE'VE HAD OUR PROBLEMS, SCOTT, BUT I ALWAYS THOUGHT YOU WERE BETTER THAN THAT--
GUESS I WAS WRONG.

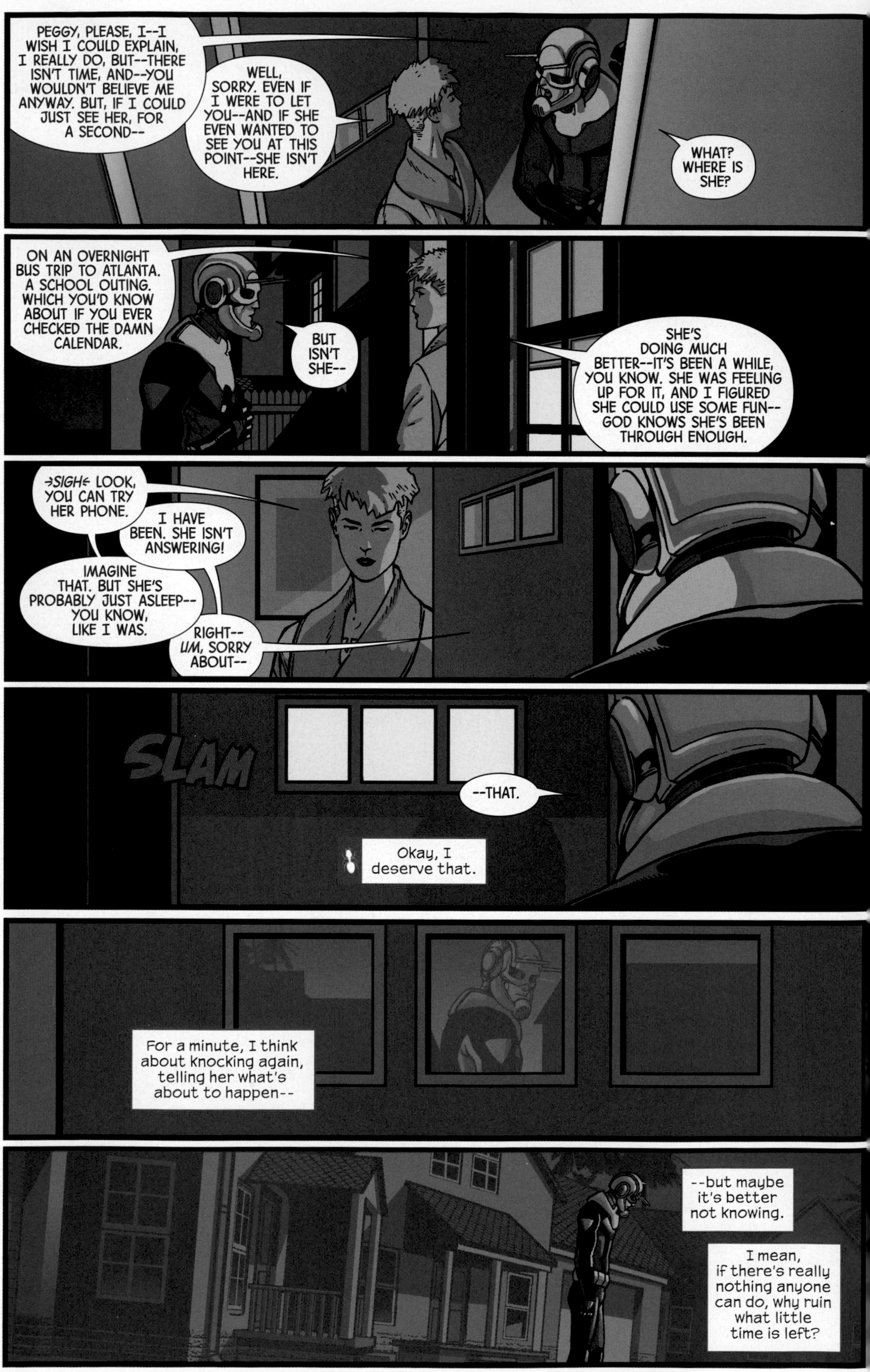
PEGGY, PLEASE, I--I WISH I COULD EXPLAIN, I REALLY DO, BUT--THERE ISN'T TIME, AND--YOU WOULDN'T BELIEVE ME ANYWAY. BUT, IF I COULD JUST SEE HER, FOR A SECOND--
WELL, SORRY. EVEN IF I WERE TO LET YOU--AND IF SHE EVEN WANTED TO SEE YOU AT THIS POINT--SHE ISN'T HERE.
WHAT? WHERE IS SHE?
ON AN OVERNIGHT BUS TRIP TO ATLANTA. A SCHOOL OUTING. WHICH YOU'D KNOW ABOUT IF YOU EVER CHECKED THE DAMN CALENDAR.
BUT ISN'T SHE--
SHE'S DOING MUCH BETTER--IT'S BEEN A WHILE, YOU KNOW. SHE WAS FEELING UP FOR IT, AND I FIGURED SHE COULD USE SOME FUN--GOD KNOWS SHE'S BEEN THROUGH ENOUGH.
→SIGH← LOOK, YOU CAN TRY HER PHONE.
I HAVE BEEN. SHE ISN'T ANSWERING!
IMAGINE THAT. BUT SHE'S PROBABLY JUST ASLEEP--YOU KNOW, LIKE I WAS.
RIGHT--UM, SORRY ABOUT--
SLAM
--THAT.
Okay, I deserve that.
For a minute, I think about knocking again, telling her what's about to happen--
--but maybe it's better not knowing.
I mean, if there's really nothing anyone can do, why ruin what little time is left?

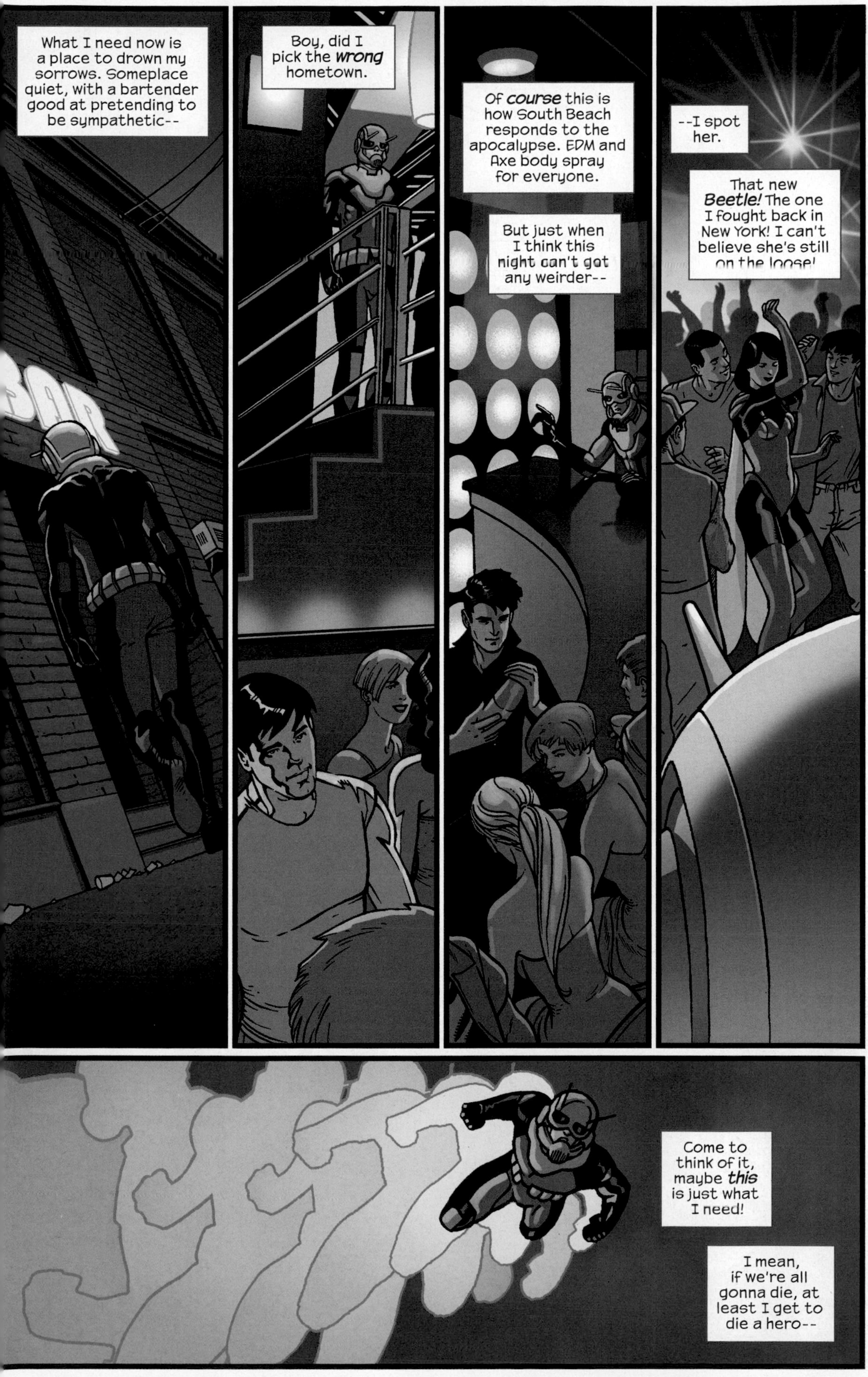
What I need now is a place to drown my sorrows. Someplace quiet, with a bartender good at pretending to be sympathetic--
Boy, did I pick the *wrong* hometown.
Of *course* this is how South Beach responds to the apocalypse. EDM and Axe body spray for everyone.
But just when I think this night can't get any weirder--
--I spot her.
That new *Beetle!* The one I fought back in New York! I can't believe she's still on the loose!
Come to think of it, maybe *this* is just what I need!
I mean, if we're all gonna die, at least I get to die a hero--

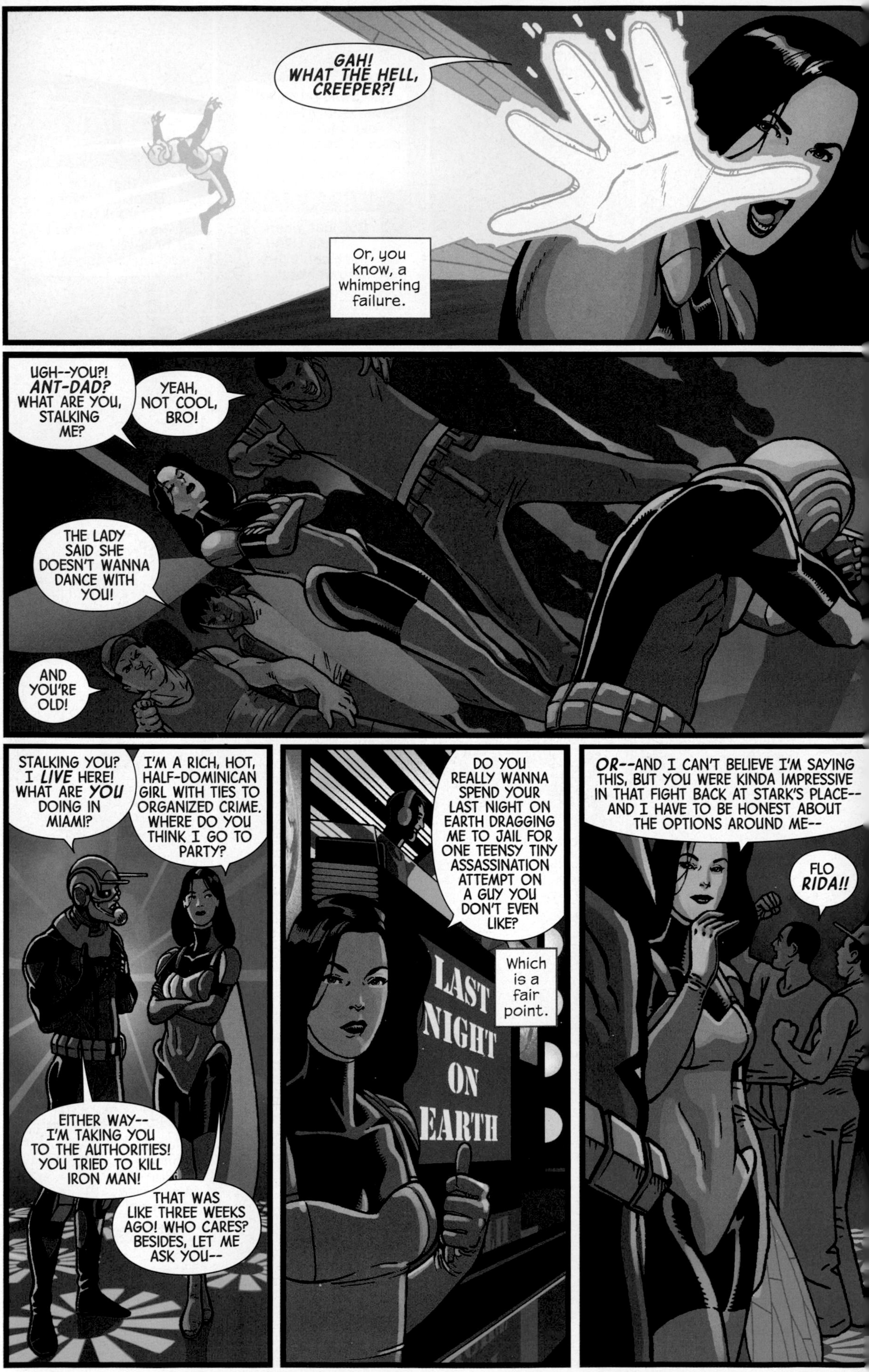
GAH! WHAT THE HELL, CREEPER?!
Or, you know, a whimpering failure.
UGH--YOU?! ANT-DAD? WHAT ARE YOU, STALKING ME?
YEAH, NOT COOL, BRO!
THE LADY SAID SHE DOESN'T WANNA DANCE WITH YOU!
AND YOU'RE OLD!
STALKING YOU? I LIVE HERE! WHAT ARE YOU DOING IN MIAMI?
I'M A RICH, HOT, HALF-DOMINICAN GIRL WITH TIES TO ORGANIZED CRIME. WHERE DO YOU THINK I GO TO PARTY?
EITHER WAY-- I'M TAKING YOU TO THE AUTHORITIES! YOU TRIED TO KILL IRON MAN!
THAT WAS LIKE THREE WEEKS AGO! WHO CARES? BESIDES, LET ME ASK YOU--
DO YOU REALLY WANNA SPEND YOUR LAST NIGHT ON EARTH DRAGGING ME TO JAIL FOR ONE TEENSY TINY ASSASSINATION ATTEMPT ON A GUY YOU DON'T EVEN LIKE?
LAST NIGHT ON EARTH
Which is a fair point.
OR--AND I CAN'T BELIEVE I'M SAYING THIS, BUT YOU WERE KINDA IMPRESSIVE IN THAT FIGHT BACK AT STARK'S PLACE-- AND I HAVE TO BE HONEST ABOUT THE OPTIONS AROUND ME--
FLO RIDA!!

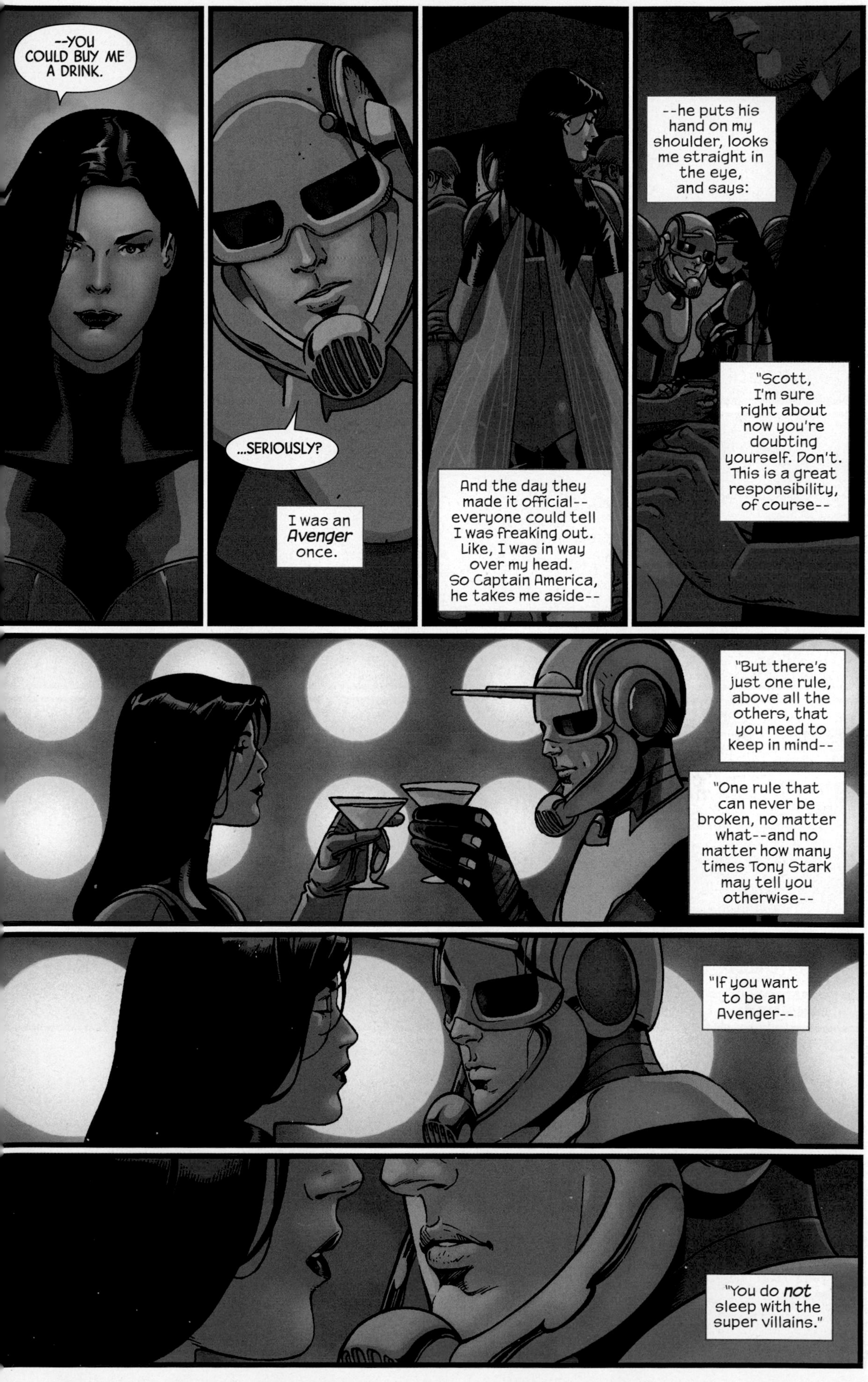
--YOU COULD BUY ME A DRINK.
...SERIOUSLY?
I was an *Avenger* once.
And the day they made it official--everyone could tell I was freaking out. Like, I was in way over my head. So Captain America, he takes me aside--
--he puts his hand on my shoulder, looks me straight in the eye, and says:
"Scott, I'm sure right about now you're doubting yourself. Don't. This is a great responsibility, of course--
"But there's just one rule, above all the others, that you need to keep in mind--
"One rule that can never be broken, no matter what--and no matter how many times Tony Stark may tell you otherwise--
"If you want to be an Avenger--
"You do ***not*** sleep with the super villains."

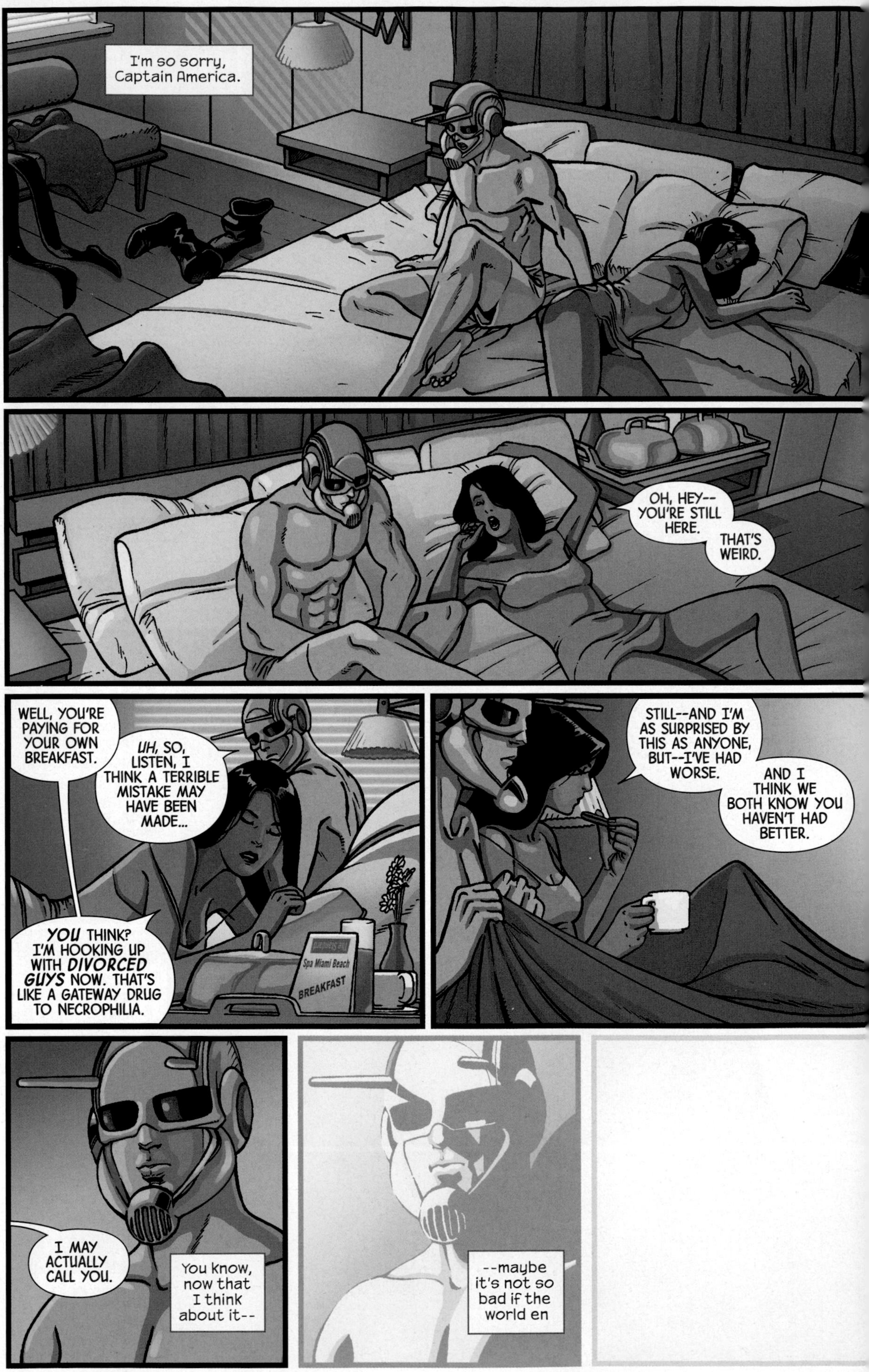
I'm so sorry, Captain America.
OH, HEY-- YOU'RE STILL HERE.
THAT'S WEIRD.
WELL, YOU'RE PAYING FOR YOUR OWN BREAKFAST.
UH, SO, LISTEN, I THINK A TERRIBLE MISTAKE MAY HAVE BEEN MADE...
YOU THINK? I'M HOOKING UP WITH DIVORCED GUYS NOW. THAT'S LIKE A GATEWAY DRUG TO NECROPHILIA.
Spa Miami Beach
BREAKFAST
STILL--AND I'M AS SURPRISED BY THIS AS ANYONE, BUT--I'VE HAD WORSE.
AND I THINK WE BOTH KNOW YOU HAVEN'T HAD BETTER.
I MAY ACTUALLY CALL YOU.
You know, now that I think about it--
--maybe it's not so bad if the world en

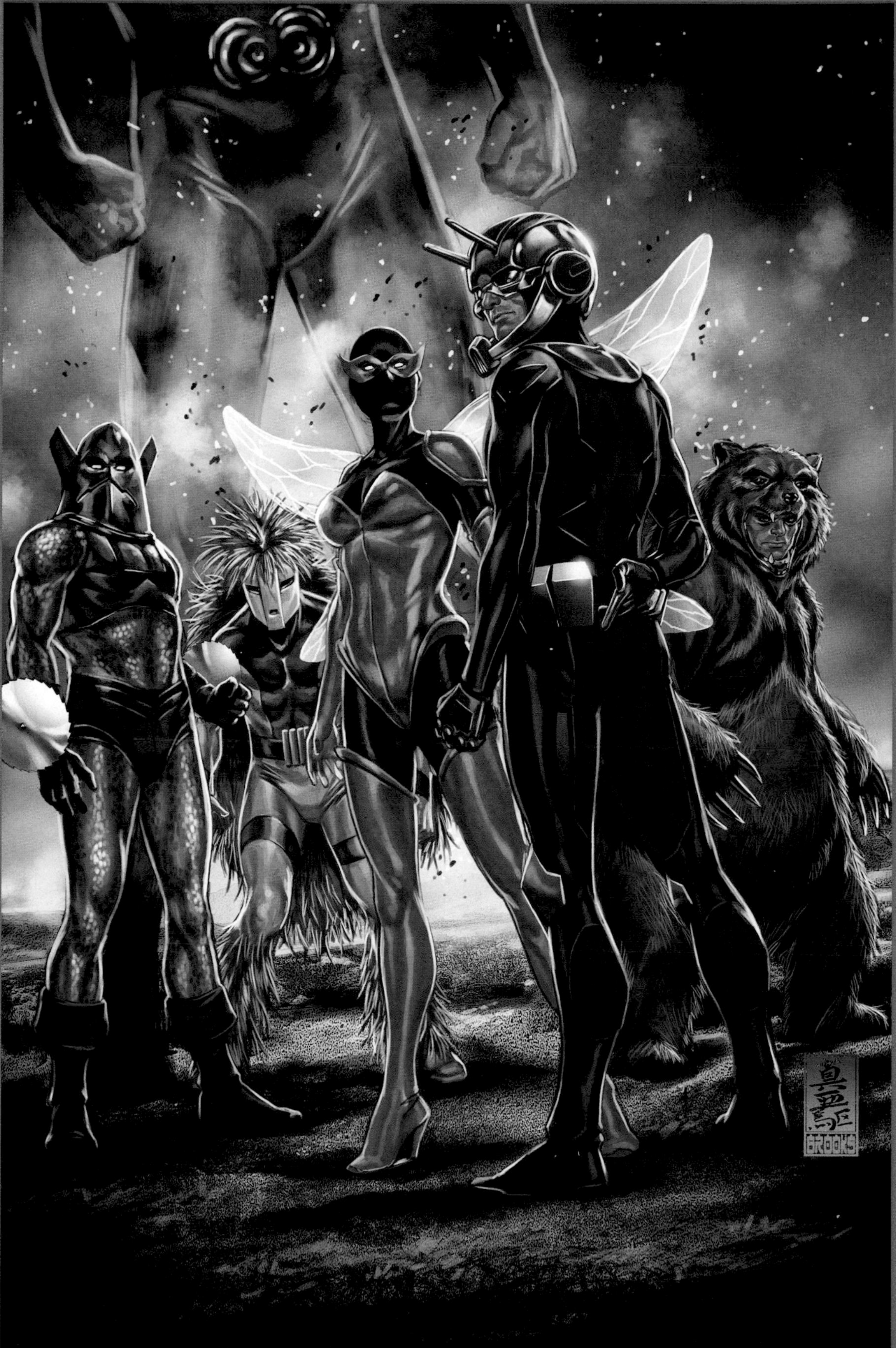

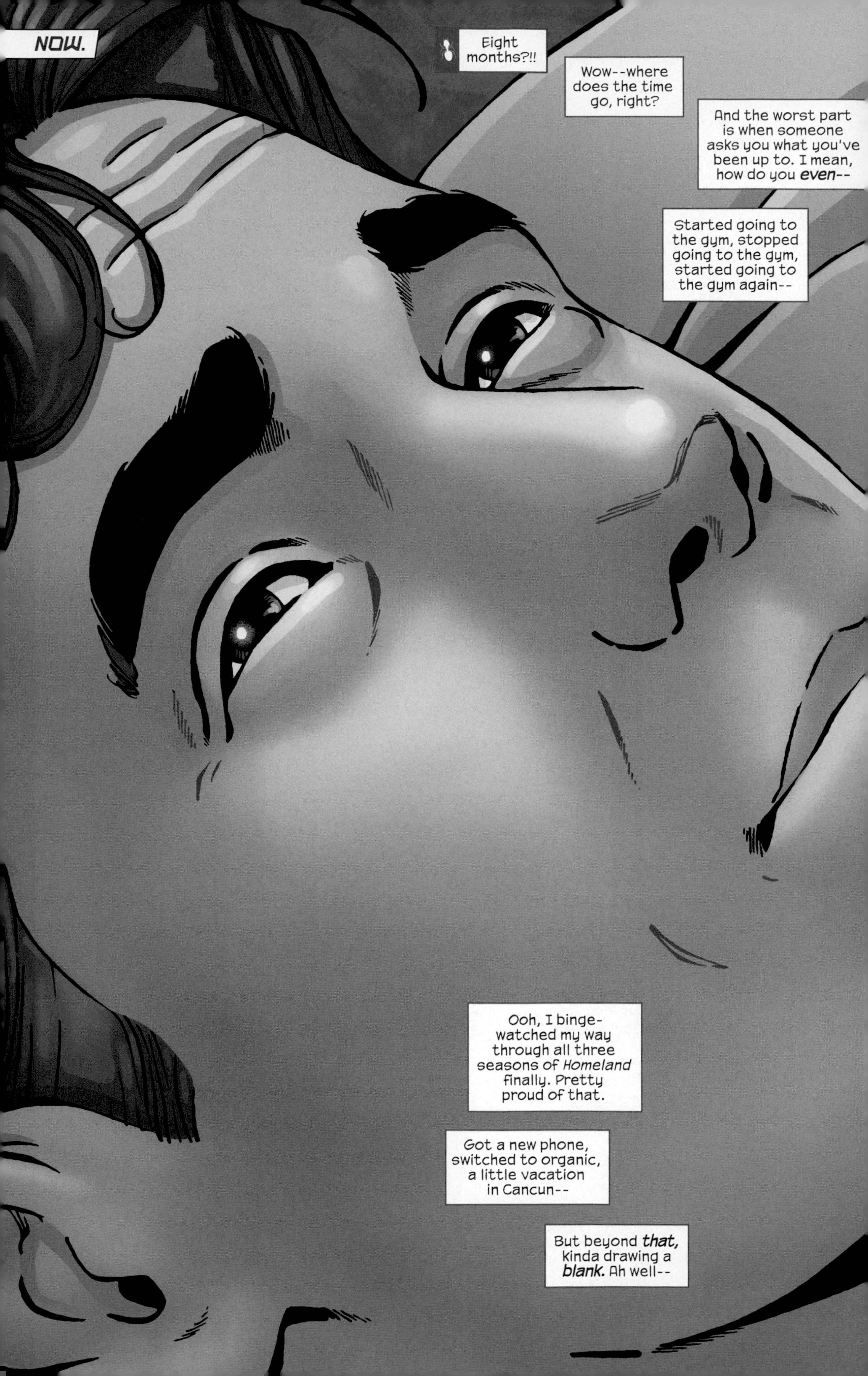
NOW.
Eight months?!!
Wow--where does the time go, right?
And the worst part is when someone asks you what you've been up to. I mean, how do you *even*--
Started going to the gym, stopped going to the gym, started going to the gym again--
Ooh, I binge-watched my way through all three seasons of *Homeland* finally. Pretty proud of that.
Got a new phone, switched to organic, a little vacation in Cancun--
But beyond *that,* kinda drawing a *blank.* Ah well--

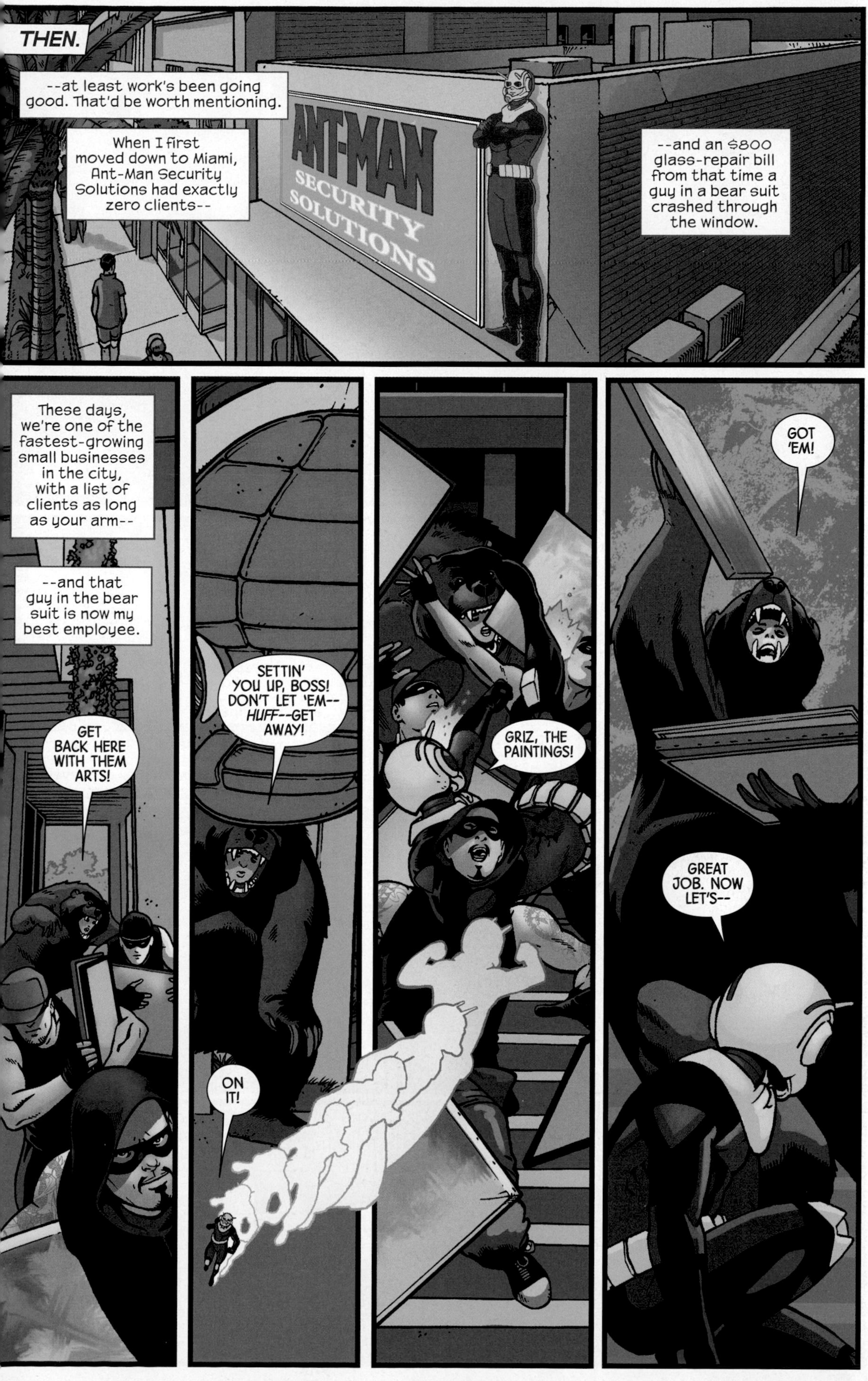
THEN.
--at least work's been going good. That'd be worth mentioning.
When I first moved down to Miami, Ant-Man Security Solutions had exactly zero clients--
ANT-MAN SECURITY SOLUTIONS
--and an $800 glass-repair bill from that time a guy in a bear suit crashed through the window.
These days, we're one of the fastest-growing small businesses in the city, with a list of clients as long as your arm--
--and that guy in the bear suit is now my best employee.
GET BACK HERE WITH THEM ARTS!
SETTIN' YOU UP, BOSS! DON'T LET 'EM--HUFF--GET AWAY!
ON IT!
GRIZ, THE PAINTINGS!
GOT 'EM!
GREAT JOB. NOW LET'S--

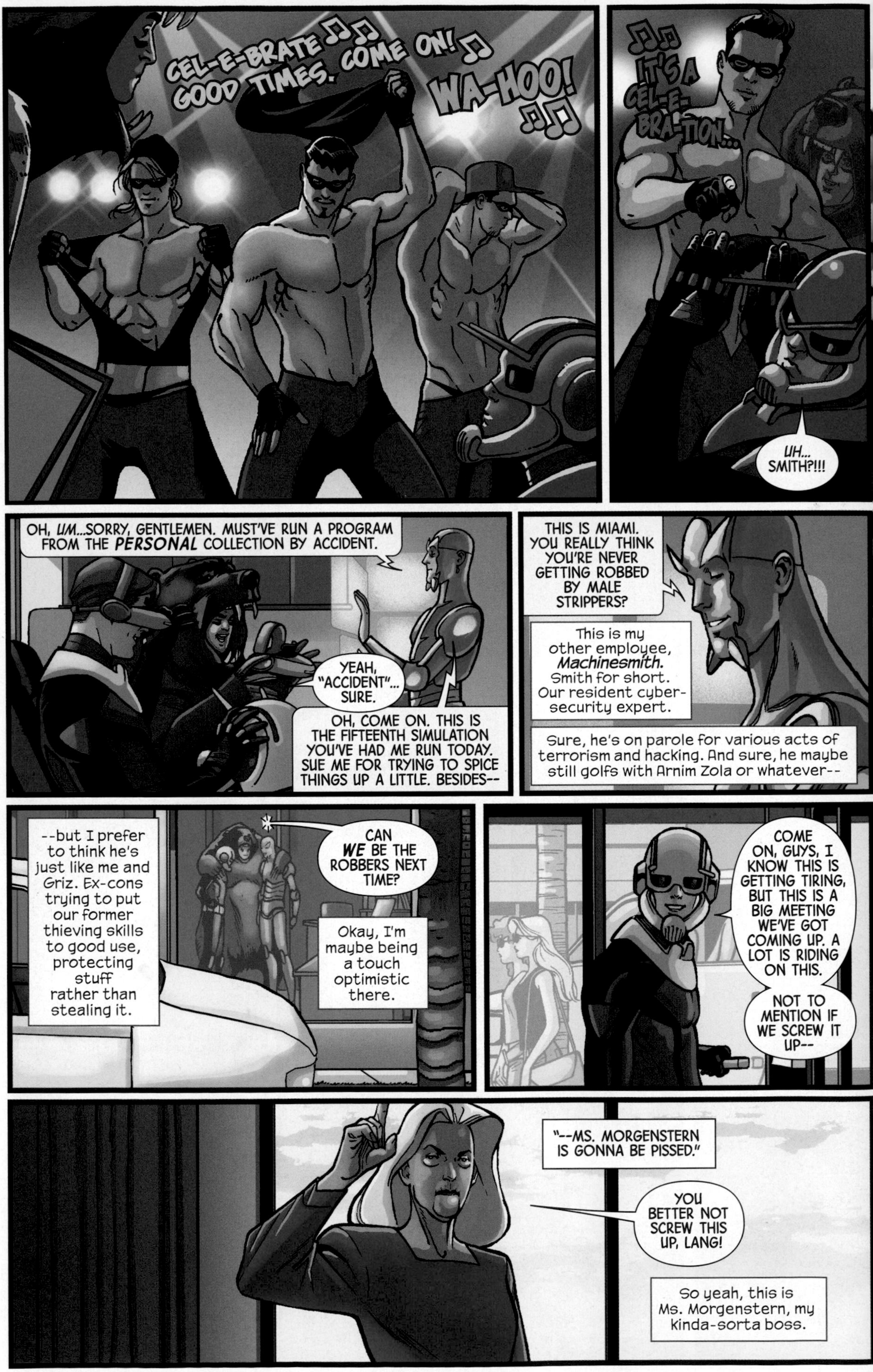
CEL-E-BRATE ♫♫ GOOD TIMES. COME ON! ♫
WA-HOO! ♫♫
♫♫ IT'S A CEL-E-BRA-TION...
UH... SMITH?!!!
OH, UM...SORRY, GENTLEMEN. MUST'VE RUN A PROGRAM FROM THE PERSONAL COLLECTION BY ACCIDENT.
YEAH, "ACCIDENT"... SURE.
OH, COME ON. THIS IS THE FIFTEENTH SIMULATION YOU'VE HAD ME RUN TODAY. SUE ME FOR TRYING TO SPICE THINGS UP A LITTLE. BESIDES--
THIS IS MIAMI. YOU REALLY THINK YOU'RE NEVER GETTING ROBBED BY MALE STRIPPERS?
This is my other employee, Machinesmith. Smith for short. Our resident cyber-security expert.
Sure, he's on parole for various acts of terrorism and hacking. And sure, he maybe still golfs with Arnim Zola or whatever--
--but I prefer to think he's just like me and Griz. Ex-cons trying to put our former thieving skills to good use, protecting stuff rather than stealing it.
CAN WE BE THE ROBBERS NEXT TIME?
Okay, I'm maybe being a touch optimistic there.
COME ON, GUYS, I KNOW THIS IS GETTING TIRING, BUT THIS IS A BIG MEETING WE'VE GOT COMING UP. A LOT IS RIDING ON THIS.
NOT TO MENTION IF WE SCREW IT UP--
"--MS. MORGENSTERN IS GONNA BE PISSED."
YOU BETTER NOT SCREW THIS UP, LANG!
So yeah, this is Ms. Morgenstern, my kinda-sorta boss.

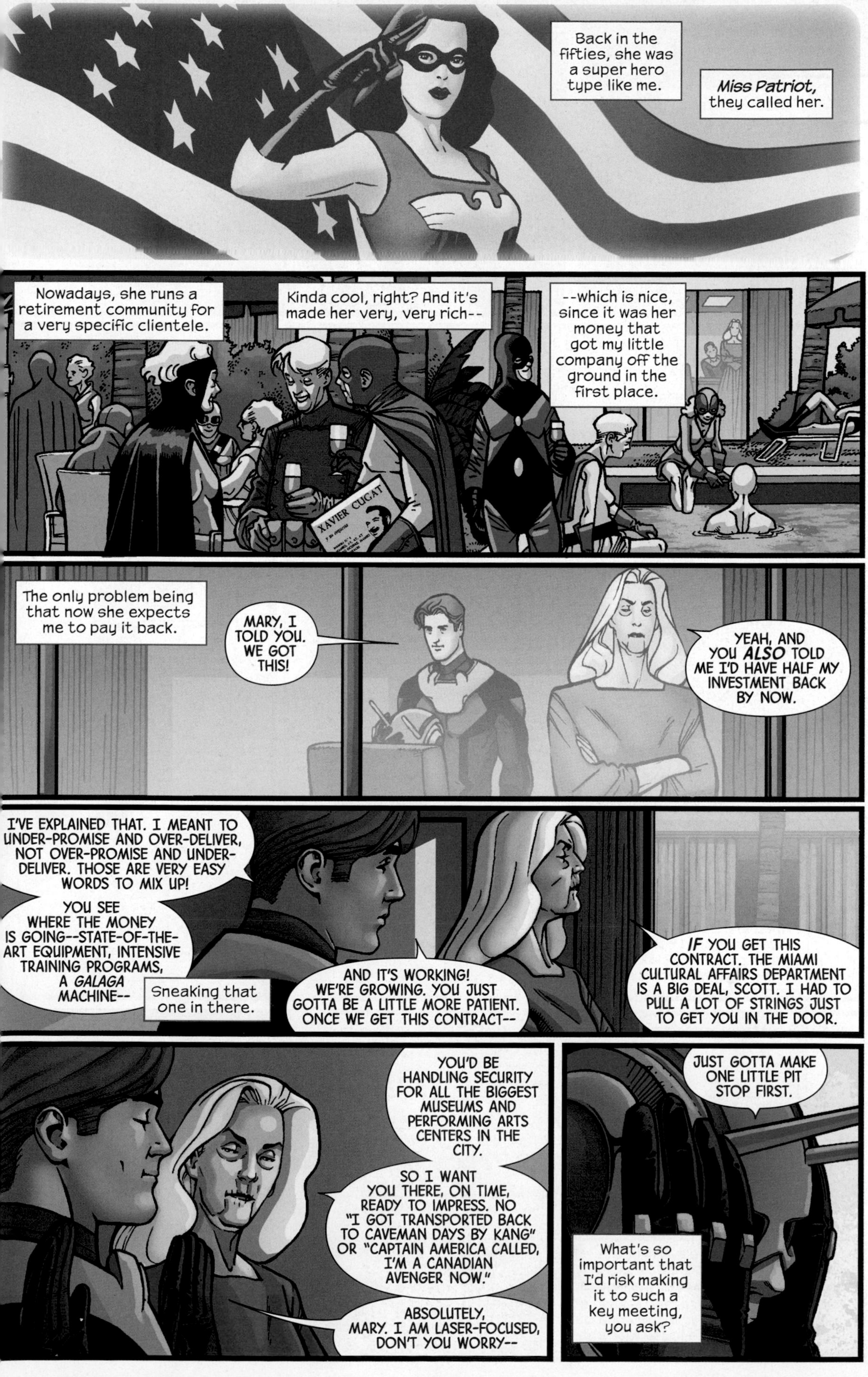

Back in the fifties, she was a super hero type like me.
Miss Patriot, they called her.
Nowadays, she runs a retirement community for a very specific clientele.
Kinda cool, right? And it's made her very, very rich--
--which is nice, since it was her money that got my little company off the ground in the first place.
XAVIER CUGAT
The only problem being that now she expects me to pay it back.
MARY, I TOLD YOU. WE GOT THIS!
YEAH, AND YOU *ALSO* TOLD ME I'D HAVE HALF MY INVESTMENT BACK BY NOW.
I'VE EXPLAINED THAT. I MEANT TO UNDER-PROMISE AND OVER-DELIVER, NOT OVER-PROMISE AND UNDER-DELIVER. THOSE ARE VERY EASY WORDS TO MIX UP!
YOU SEE WHERE THE MONEY IS GOING--STATE-OF-THE-ART EQUIPMENT, INTENSIVE TRAINING PROGRAMS, A *GALAGA* MACHINE--
Sneaking that one in there.
AND IT'S WORKING! WE'RE GROWING. YOU JUST GOTTA BE A LITTLE MORE PATIENT. ONCE WE GET THIS CONTRACT--
IF YOU GET THIS CONTRACT. THE MIAMI CULTURAL AFFAIRS DEPARTMENT IS A BIG DEAL, SCOTT. I HAD TO PULL A LOT OF STRINGS JUST TO GET YOU IN THE DOOR.
YOU'D BE HANDLING SECURITY FOR ALL THE BIGGEST MUSEUMS AND PERFORMING ARTS CENTERS IN THE CITY.
SO I WANT YOU THERE, ON TIME, READY TO IMPRESS. NO "I GOT TRANSPORTED BACK TO CAVEMAN DAYS BY KANG" OR "CAPTAIN AMERICA CALLED, I'M A CANADIAN AVENGER NOW."
ABSOLUTELY, MARY. I AM LASER-FOCUSED, DON'T YOU WORRY--
JUST GOTTA MAKE ONE LITTLE PIT STOP FIRST.
What's so important that I'd risk making it to such a key meeting, you ask?

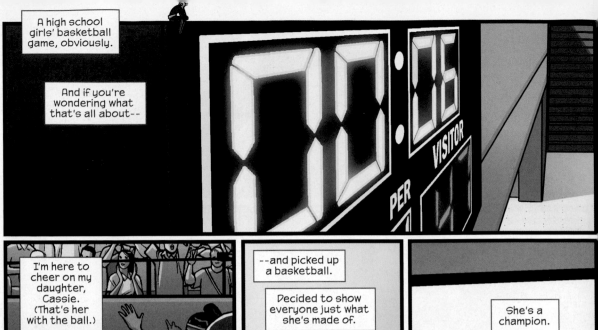

A high school girls' basketball game, obviously.

And if you're wondering what that's all about--

I'm here to cheer on my daughter, Cassie. (That's her with the ball.)

You wouldn't know it to look at her, but my little girl is just a few months removed from major heart surgery.

When she came back to school, everyone told her to go slow, take it easy. So what did she do? She put down her drumsticks--

--and picked up a basketball.

Decided to show everyone just what she's made of.

But then, that's my girl--

She's a champion.

NICE TRY, LANG!

BLZZZ

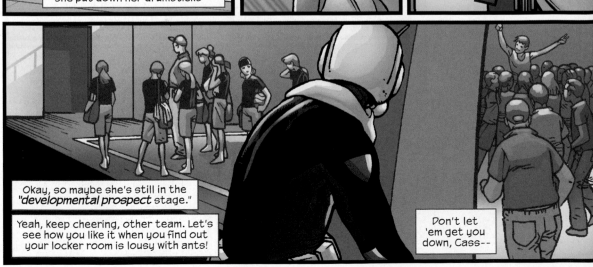

Okay, so maybe she's still in the *developmental prospect* stage.

Yeah, keep cheering, other team. Let's see how you like it when you find out your locker room is lousy with ants!

Don't let 'em get you down, Cass--

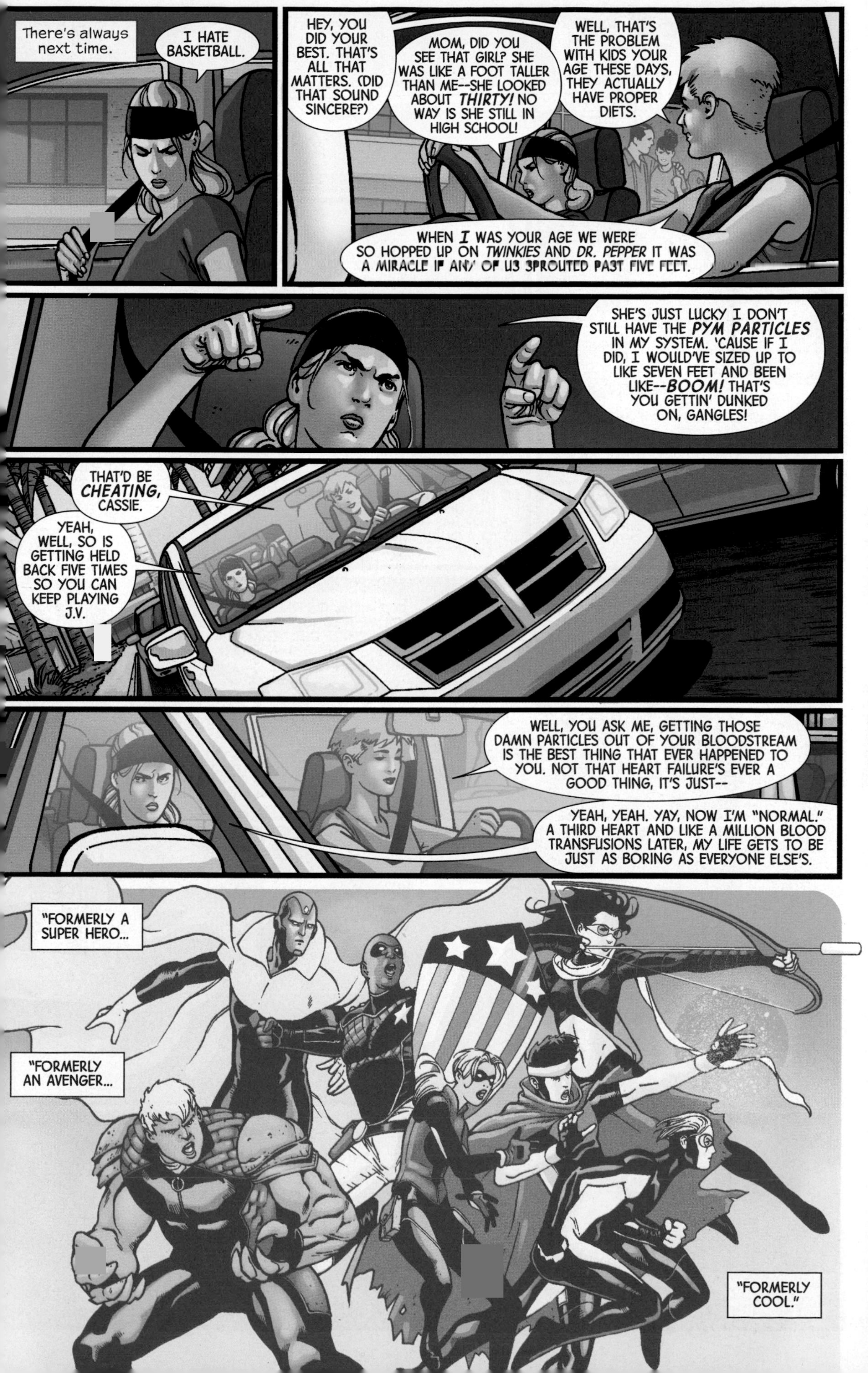
There's always next time.
I HATE BASKETBALL.
HEY, YOU DID YOUR BEST. THAT'S ALL THAT MATTERS. (DID THAT SOUND SINCERE?)
MOM, DID YOU SEE THAT GIRL? SHE WAS LIKE A FOOT TALLER THAN ME--SHE LOOKED ABOUT THIRTY! NO WAY IS SHE STILL IN HIGH SCHOOL!
WELL, THAT'S THE PROBLEM WITH KIDS YOUR AGE THESE DAYS, THEY ACTUALLY HAVE PROPER DIETS.
WHEN I WAS YOUR AGE WE WERE SO HOPPED UP ON TWINKIES AND DR. PEPPER IT WAS A MIRACLE IF ANY OF US SPROUTED PAST FIVE FEET.
SHE'S JUST LUCKY I DON'T STILL HAVE THE PYM PARTICLES IN MY SYSTEM. 'CAUSE IF I DID, I WOULD'VE SIZED UP TO LIKE SEVEN FEET AND BEEN LIKE--BOOM! THAT'S YOU GETTIN' DUNKED ON, GANGLES!
THAT'D BE CHEATING, CASSIE.
YEAH, WELL, SO IS GETTING HELD BACK FIVE TIMES SO YOU CAN KEEP PLAYING J.V.
WELL, YOU ASK ME, GETTING THOSE DAMN PARTICLES OUT OF YOUR BLOODSTREAM IS THE BEST THING THAT EVER HAPPENED TO YOU. NOT THAT HEART FAILURE'S EVER A GOOD THING, IT'S JUST--
YEAH, YEAH. YAY, NOW I'M "NORMAL." A THIRD HEART AND LIKE A MILLION BLOOD TRANSFUSIONS LATER, MY LIFE GETS TO BE JUST AS BORING AS EVERYONE ELSE'S.
"FORMERLY A SUPER HERO...
"FORMERLY AN AVENGER...
"FORMERLY COOL."

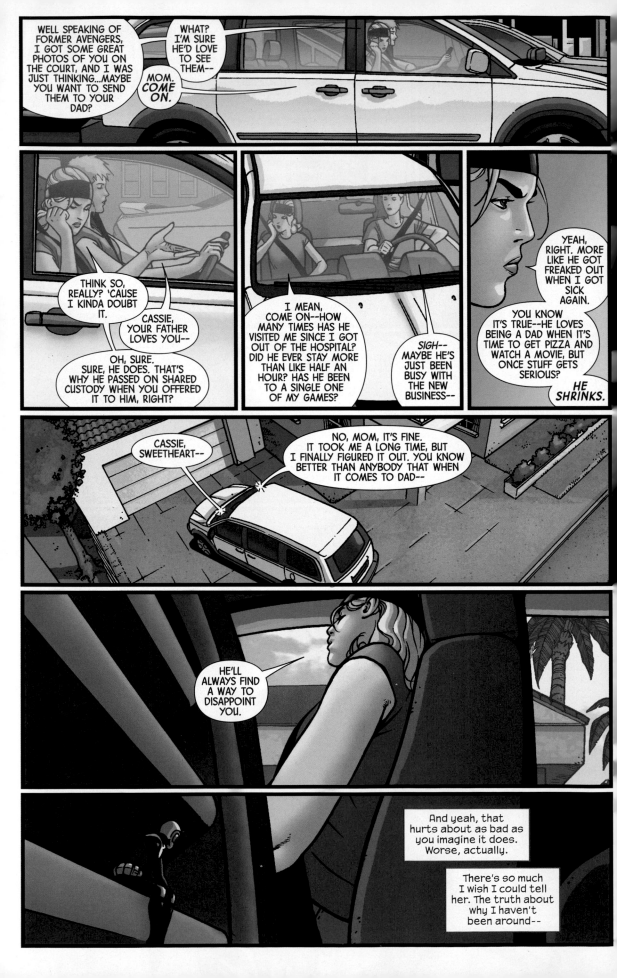

WELL SPEAKING OF FORMER AVENGERS, I GOT SOME GREAT PHOTOS OF YOU ON THE COURT, AND I WAS JUST THINKING...MAYBE YOU WANT TO SEND THEM TO YOUR DAD?

WHAT? I'M SURE HE'D LOVE TO SEE THEM--

MOM. COME ON.

THINK SO, REALLY? 'CAUSE I KINDA DOUBT IT.

CASSIE, YOUR FATHER LOVES YOU--

OH, SURE. SURE, HE DOES. THAT'S WHY HE PASSED ON SHARED CUSTODY WHEN YOU OFFERED IT TO HIM, RIGHT?

I MEAN, COME ON--HOW MANY TIMES HAS HE VISITED ME SINCE I GOT OUT OF THE HOSPITAL? DID HE EVER STAY MORE THAN LIKE HALF AN HOUR? HAS HE BEEN TO A SINGLE ONE OF MY GAMES?

SIGH-- MAYBE HE'S JUST BEEN BUSY WITH THE NEW BUSINESS--

YEAH, RIGHT. MORE LIKE HE GOT FREAKED OUT WHEN I GOT SICK AGAIN.

YOU KNOW IT'S TRUE--HE LOVES BEING A DAD WHEN IT'S TIME TO GET PIZZA AND WATCH A MOVIE, BUT ONCE STUFF GETS SERIOUS?

HE SHRINKS.

CASSIE, SWEETHEART--

NO, MOM, IT'S FINE. IT TOOK ME A LONG TIME, BUT I FINALLY FIGURED IT OUT. YOU KNOW BETTER THAN ANYBODY THAT WHEN IT COMES TO DAD--

HE'LL ALWAYS FIND A WAY TO DISAPPOINT YOU.

And yeah, that hurts about as bad as you imagine it does. Worse, actually.

There's so much I wish I could tell her. The truth about why I haven't been around--

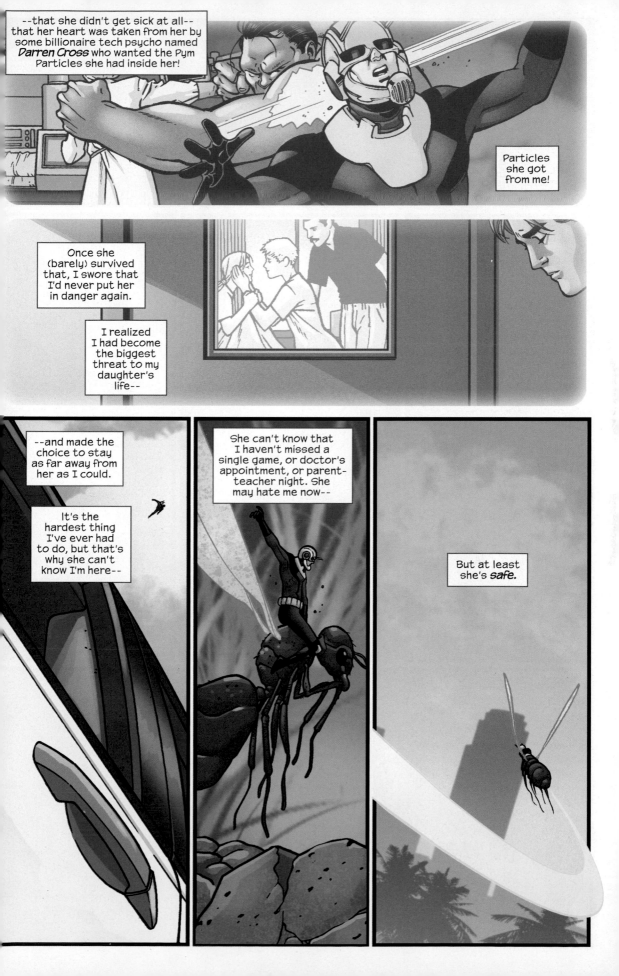

--that she didn't get sick at all-- that her heart was taken from her by some billionaire tech psycho named *Darren Cross* who wanted the Pym Particles she had inside her!

Particles she got from me!

Once she (barely) survived that, I swore that I'd never put her in danger again.

I realized I had become the biggest threat to my daughter's life--

--and made the choice to stay as far away from her as I could.

It's the hardest thing I've ever had to do, but that's why she can't know I'm here--

She can't know that I haven't missed a single game, or doctor's appointment, or parent-teacher night. She may hate me now--

But at least she's *safe.*

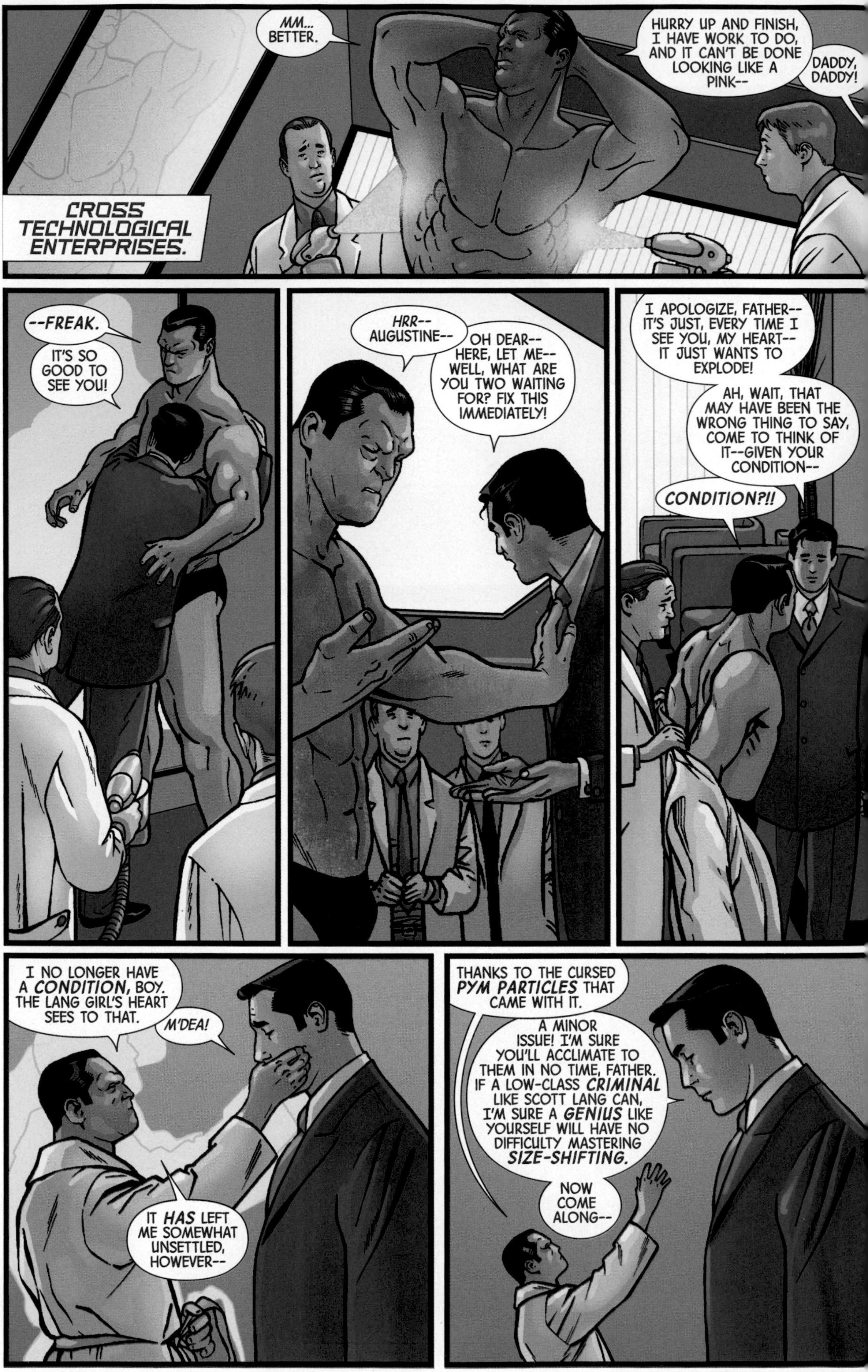

CROSS TECHNOLOGICAL ENTERPRISES.
MM... BETTER.
HURRY UP AND FINISH, I HAVE WORK TO DO, AND IT CAN'T BE DONE LOOKING LIKE A PINK--
DADDY, DADDY!
--FREAK.
IT'S SO GOOD TO SEE YOU!
HRR-- AUGUSTINE--
OH DEAR-- HERE, LET ME-- WELL, WHAT ARE YOU TWO WAITING FOR? FIX THIS IMMEDIATELY!
I APOLOGIZE, FATHER-- IT'S JUST, EVERY TIME I SEE YOU, MY HEART-- IT JUST WANTS TO EXPLODE!
AH, WAIT, THAT MAY HAVE BEEN THE WRONG THING TO SAY, COME TO THINK OF IT--GIVEN YOUR CONDITION--
CONDITION?!!
I NO LONGER HAVE A CONDITION, BOY. THE LANG GIRL'S HEART SEES TO THAT.
M'DEA!
IT HAS LEFT ME SOMEWHAT UNSETTLED, HOWEVER--
THANKS TO THE CURSED PYM PARTICLES THAT CAME WITH IT.
A MINOR ISSUE! I'M SURE YOU'LL ACCLIMATE TO THEM IN NO TIME, FATHER. IF A LOW-CLASS CRIMINAL LIKE SCOTT LANG CAN, I'M SURE A GENIUS LIKE YOURSELF WILL HAVE NO DIFFICULTY MASTERING SIZE-SHIFTING.
NOW COME ALONG--

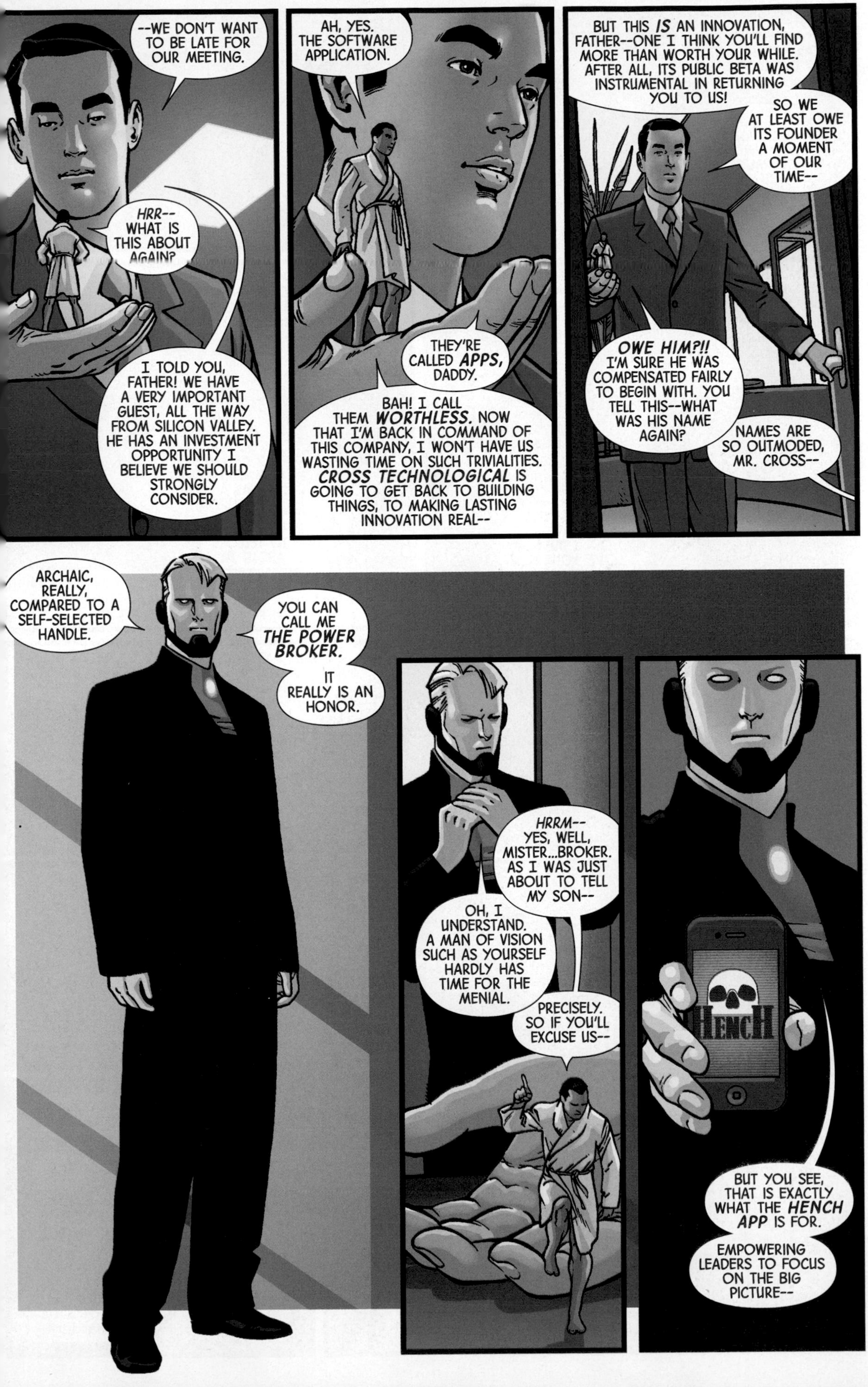
--WE DON'T WANT TO BE LATE FOR OUR MEETING.
HRR-- WHAT IS THIS ABOUT AGAIN?
I TOLD YOU, FATHER! WE HAVE A VERY IMPORTANT GUEST, ALL THE WAY FROM SILICON VALLEY. HE HAS AN INVESTMENT OPPORTUNITY I BELIEVE WE SHOULD STRONGLY CONSIDER.
AH, YES. THE SOFTWARE APPLICATION.
THEY'RE CALLED APPS, DADDY.
BAH! I CALL THEM WORTHLESS. NOW THAT I'M BACK IN COMMAND OF THIS COMPANY, I WON'T HAVE US WASTING TIME ON SUCH TRIVIALITIES. CROSS TECHNOLOGICAL IS GOING TO GET BACK TO BUILDING THINGS, TO MAKING LASTING INNOVATION REAL--
BUT THIS IS AN INNOVATION, FATHER--ONE I THINK YOU'LL FIND MORE THAN WORTH YOUR WHILE. AFTER ALL, ITS PUBLIC BETA WAS INSTRUMENTAL IN RETURNING YOU TO US!
SO WE AT LEAST OWE ITS FOUNDER A MOMENT OF OUR TIME--
OWE HIM?!! I'M SURE HE WAS COMPENSATED FAIRLY TO BEGIN WITH. YOU TELL THIS--WHAT WAS HIS NAME AGAIN?
NAMES ARE SO OUTMODED, MR. CROSS--
ARCHAIC, REALLY, COMPARED TO A SELF-SELECTED HANDLE.
YOU CAN CALL ME THE POWER BROKER.
IT REALLY IS AN HONOR.
HRRM-- YES, WELL, MISTER...BROKER. AS I WAS JUST ABOUT TO TELL MY SON--
OH, I UNDERSTAND. A MAN OF VISION SUCH AS YOURSELF HARDLY HAS TIME FOR THE MENIAL.
PRECISELY. SO IF YOU'LL EXCUSE US--
HENCH
BUT YOU SEE, THAT IS EXACTLY WHAT THE HENCH APP IS FOR.
EMPOWERING LEADERS TO FOCUS ON THE BIG PICTURE--

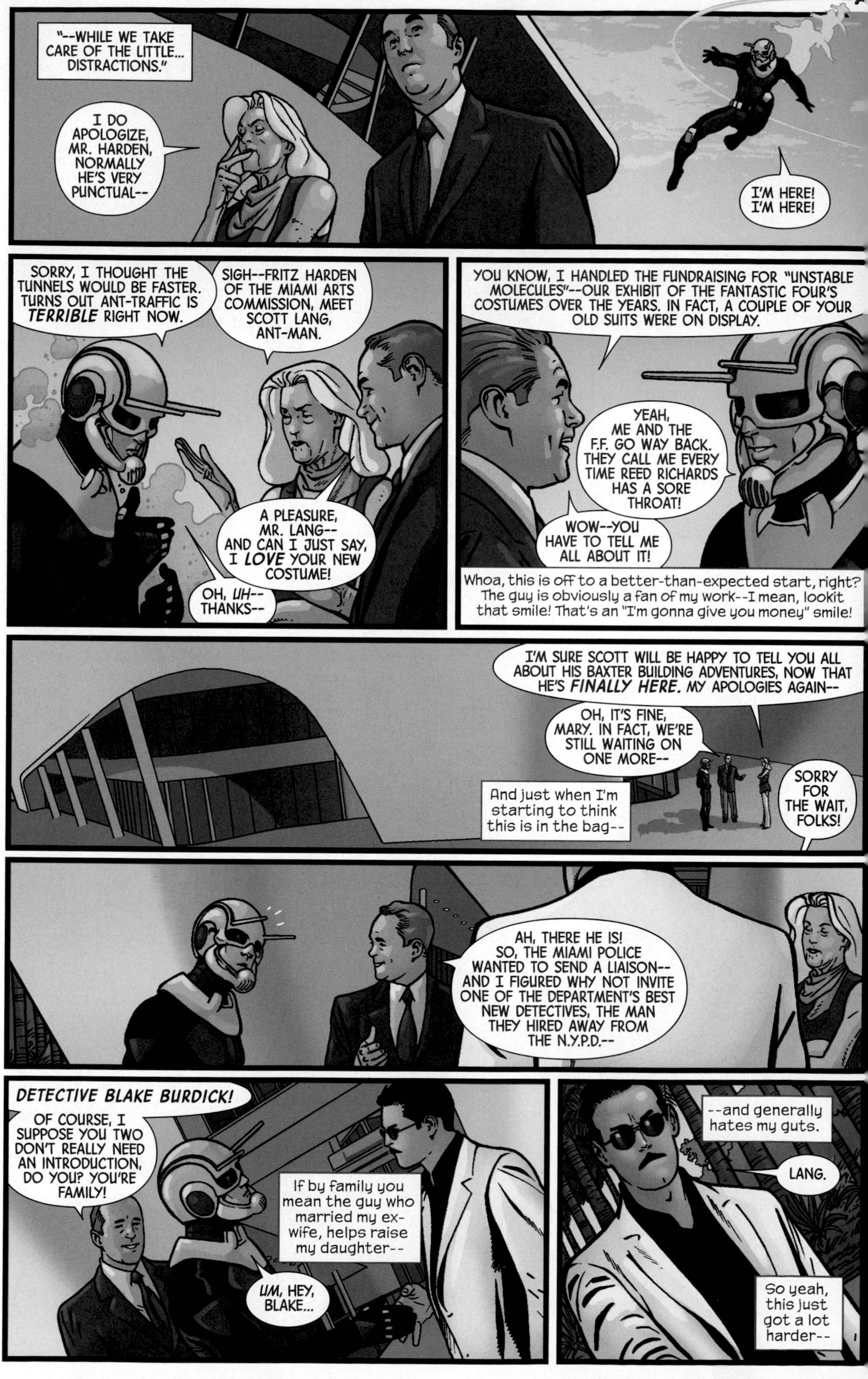
"--WHILE WE TAKE CARE OF THE LITTLE... DISTRACTIONS."
I DO APOLOGIZE, MR. HARDEN, NORMALLY HE'S VERY PUNCTUAL--
I'M HERE! I'M HERE!
SORRY, I THOUGHT THE TUNNELS WOULD BE FASTER. TURNS OUT ANT-TRAFFIC IS TERRIBLE RIGHT NOW.
SIGH--FRITZ HARDEN OF THE MIAMI ARTS COMMISSION, MEET SCOTT LANG, ANT-MAN.
A PLEASURE, MR. LANG-- AND CAN I JUST SAY, I LOVE YOUR NEW COSTUME!
OH, UH-- THANKS--
YOU KNOW, I HANDLED THE FUNDRAISING FOR "UNSTABLE MOLECULES"--OUR EXHIBIT OF THE FANTASTIC FOUR'S COSTUMES OVER THE YEARS. IN FACT, A COUPLE OF YOUR OLD SUITS WERE ON DISPLAY.
YEAH, ME AND THE F.F. GO WAY BACK. THEY CALL ME EVERY TIME REED RICHARDS HAS A SORE THROAT!
WOW--YOU HAVE TO TELL ME ALL ABOUT IT!
Whoa, this is off to a better-than-expected start, right? The guy is obviously a fan of my work--I mean, lookit that smile! That's an "I'm gonna give you money" smile!
I'M SURE SCOTT WILL BE HAPPY TO TELL YOU ALL ABOUT HIS BAXTER BUILDING ADVENTURES, NOW THAT HE'S FINALLY HERE. MY APOLOGIES AGAIN--
OH, IT'S FINE, MARY. IN FACT, WE'RE STILL WAITING ON ONE MORE--
And just when I'm starting to think this is in the bag--
SORRY FOR THE WAIT, FOLKS!
AH, THERE HE IS! SO, THE MIAMI POLICE WANTED TO SEND A LIAISON-- AND I FIGURED WHY NOT INVITE ONE OF THE DEPARTMENT'S BEST NEW DETECTIVES, THE MAN THEY HIRED AWAY FROM THE N.Y.P.D.--
DETECTIVE BLAKE BURDICK!
OF COURSE, I SUPPOSE YOU TWO DON'T REALLY NEED AN INTRODUCTION, DO YOU? YOU'RE FAMILY!
If by family you mean the guy who married my ex-wife, helps raise my daughter--
UM, HEY, BLAKE...
--and generally hates my guts.
LANG.
So yeah, this just got a lot harder--

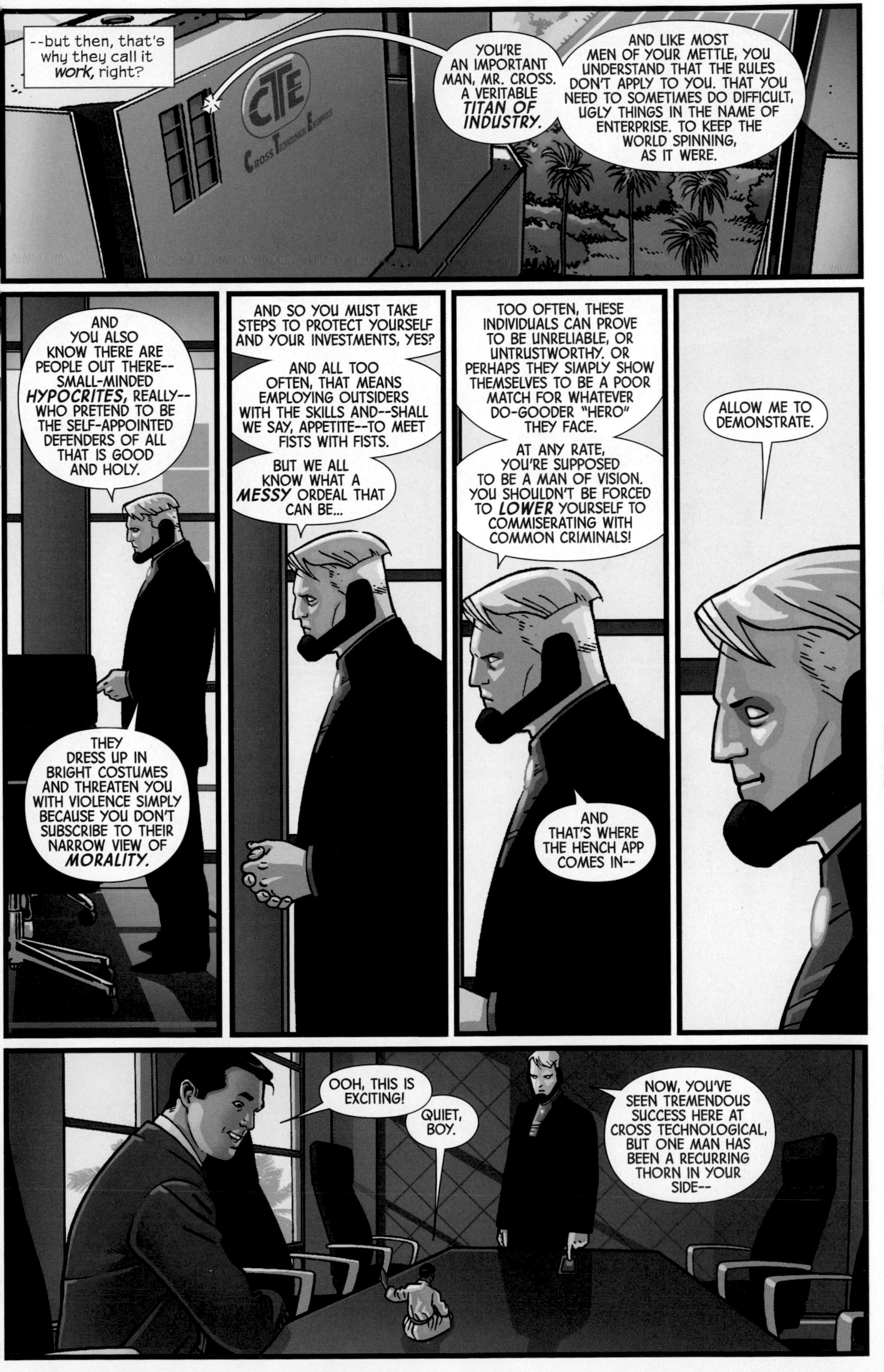
--but then, that's why they call it *work,* right?
CTE
CROSS TECHNOLOGICAL ENTERPRISES
YOU'RE AN IMPORTANT MAN, MR. CROSS. A VERITABLE *TITAN OF INDUSTRY.*
AND LIKE MOST MEN OF YOUR METTLE, YOU UNDERSTAND THAT THE RULES DON'T APPLY TO YOU. THAT YOU NEED TO SOMETIMES DO DIFFICULT, UGLY THINGS IN THE NAME OF ENTERPRISE. TO KEEP THE WORLD SPINNING, AS IT WERE.
AND YOU ALSO KNOW THERE ARE PEOPLE OUT THERE--SMALL-MINDED *HYPOCRITES,* REALLY--WHO PRETEND TO BE THE SELF-APPOINTED DEFENDERS OF ALL THAT IS GOOD AND HOLY.
THEY DRESS UP IN BRIGHT COSTUMES AND THREATEN YOU WITH VIOLENCE SIMPLY BECAUSE YOU DON'T SUBSCRIBE TO THEIR NARROW VIEW OF *MORALITY.*
AND SO YOU MUST TAKE STEPS TO PROTECT YOURSELF AND YOUR INVESTMENTS, YES?
AND ALL TOO OFTEN, THAT MEANS EMPLOYING OUTSIDERS WITH THE SKILLS AND--SHALL WE SAY, APPETITE--TO MEET FISTS WITH FISTS.
BUT WE ALL KNOW WHAT A *MESSY* ORDEAL THAT CAN BE...
TOO OFTEN, THESE INDIVIDUALS CAN PROVE TO BE UNRELIABLE, OR UNTRUSTWORTHY. OR PERHAPS THEY SIMPLY SHOW THEMSELVES TO BE A POOR MATCH FOR WHATEVER DO-GOODER "HERO" THEY FACE.
AT ANY RATE, YOU'RE SUPPOSED TO BE A MAN OF VISION. YOU SHOULDN'T BE FORCED TO *LOWER* YOURSELF TO COMMISERATING WITH COMMON CRIMINALS!
AND THAT'S WHERE THE HENCH APP COMES IN--
ALLOW ME TO DEMONSTRATE.
OOH, THIS IS EXCITING!
QUIET, BOY.
NOW, YOU'VE SEEN TREMENDOUS SUCCESS HERE AT CROSS TECHNOLOGICAL, BUT ONE MAN HAS BEEN A RECURRING THORN IN YOUR SIDE--

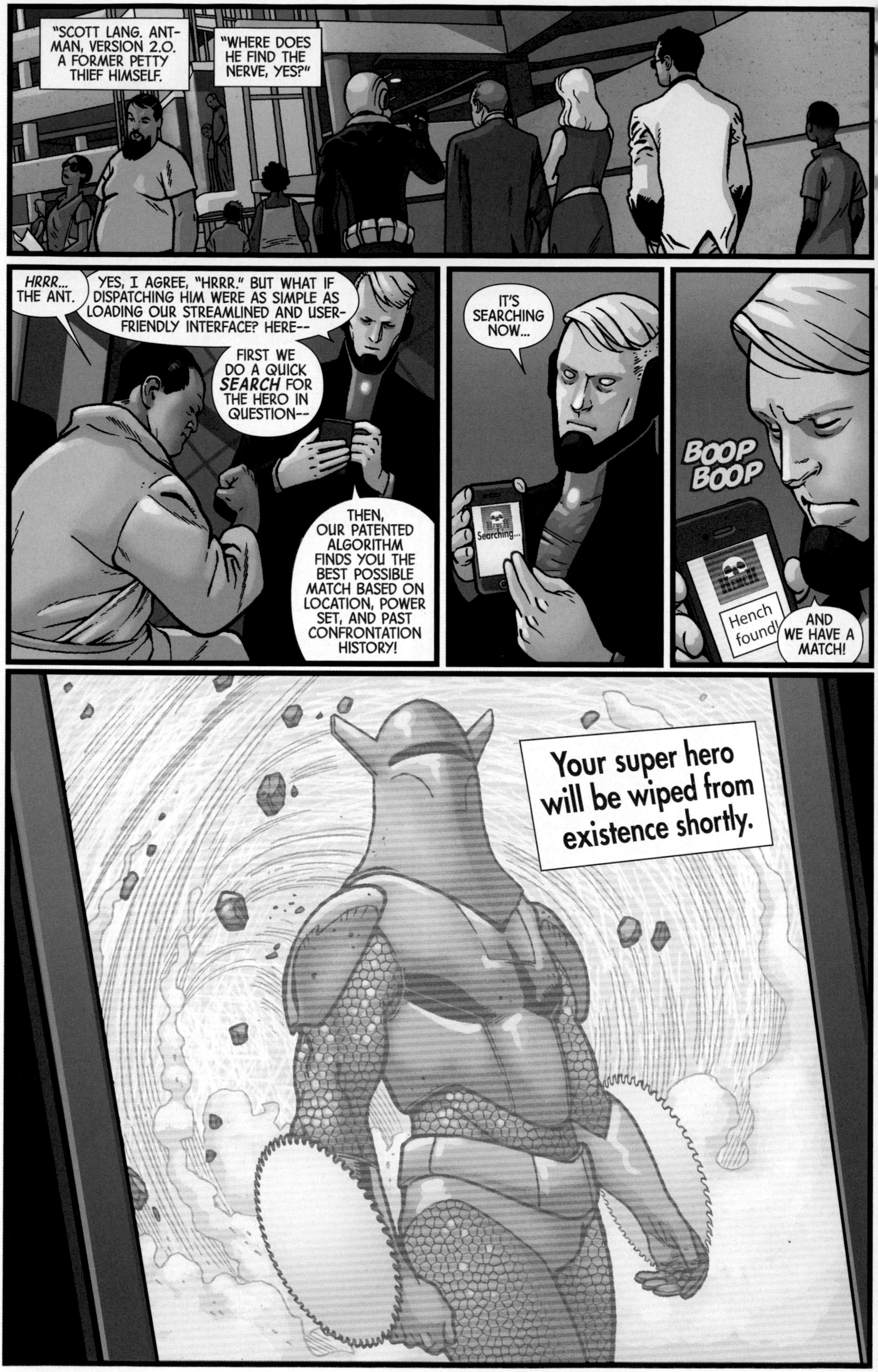
"SCOTT LANG. ANT-MAN, VERSION 2.O. A FORMER PETTY THIEF HIMSELF.
"WHERE DOES HE FIND THE NERVE, YES?"
HRRR... THE ANT.
YES, I AGREE, "HRRR." BUT WHAT IF DISPATCHING HIM WERE AS SIMPLE AS LOADING OUR STREAMLINED AND USER-FRIENDLY INTERFACE? HERE--
FIRST WE DO A QUICK SEARCH FOR THE HERO IN QUESTION--
THEN, OUR PATENTED ALGORITHM FINDS YOU THE BEST POSSIBLE MATCH BASED ON LOCATION, POWER SET, AND PAST CONFRONTATION HISTORY!
IT'S SEARCHING NOW...
Searching...
BOOP BOOP
Hench found!
AND WE HAVE A MATCH!
Your super hero will be wiped from existence shortly.

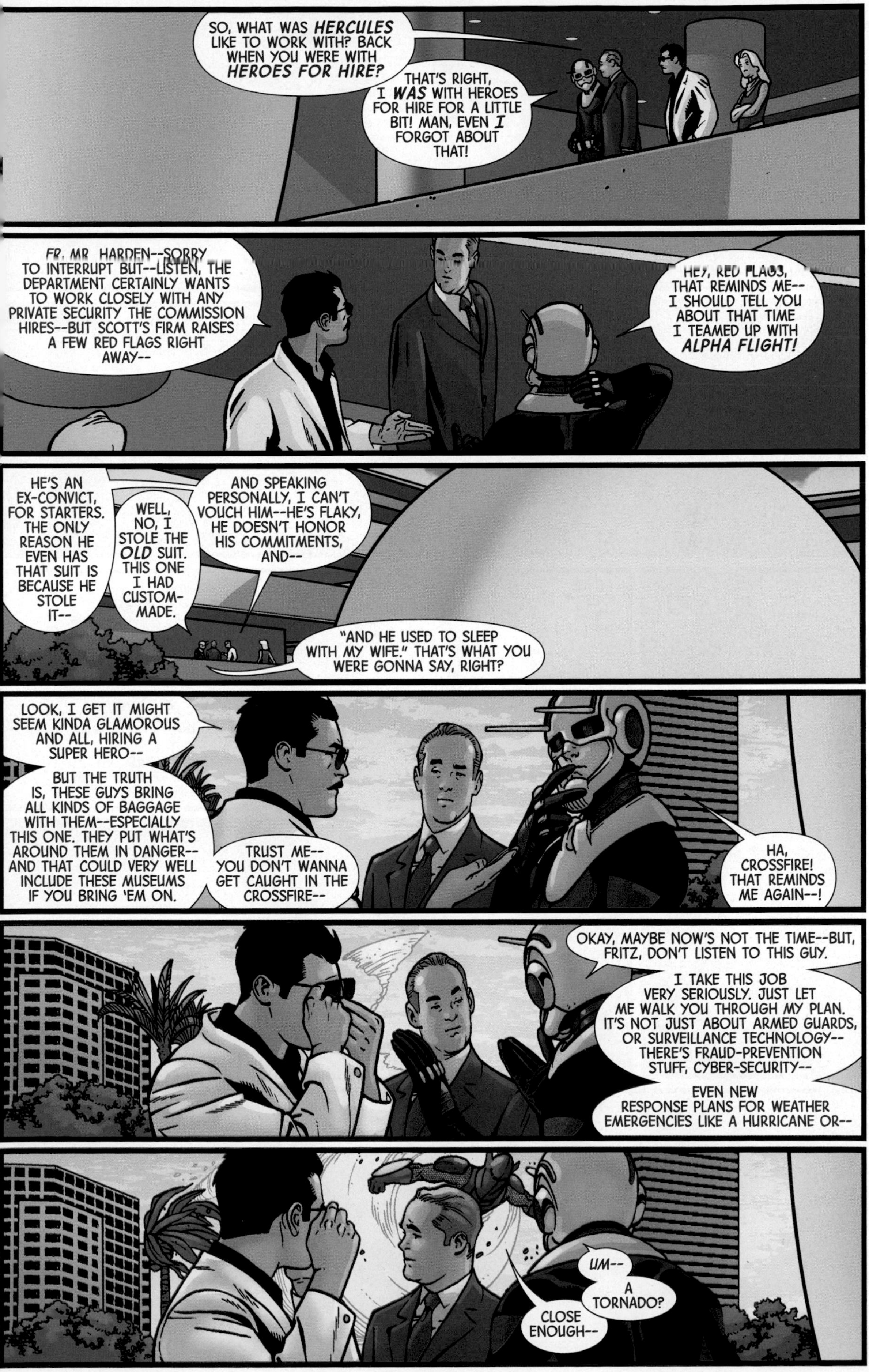

SO, WHAT WAS HERCULES LIKE TO WORK WITH? BACK WHEN YOU WERE WITH HEROES FOR HIRE?
THAT'S RIGHT, I WAS WITH HEROES FOR HIRE FOR A LITTLE BIT! MAN, EVEN I FORGOT ABOUT THAT!
ER, MR. HARDEN--SORRY TO INTERRUPT BUT--LISTEN, THE DEPARTMENT CERTAINLY WANTS TO WORK CLOSELY WITH ANY PRIVATE SECURITY THE COMMISSION HIRES--BUT SCOTT'S FIRM RAISES A FEW RED FLAGS RIGHT AWAY--
HEY, RED FLAGS, THAT REMINDS ME--I SHOULD TELL YOU ABOUT THAT TIME I TEAMED UP WITH ALPHA FLIGHT!
HE'S AN EX-CONVICT, FOR STARTERS. THE ONLY REASON HE EVEN HAS THAT SUIT IS BECAUSE HE STOLE IT--
WELL, NO, I STOLE THE OLD SUIT. THIS ONE I HAD CUSTOM-MADE.
AND SPEAKING PERSONALLY, I CAN'T VOUCH HIM--HE'S FLAKY, HE DOESN'T HONOR HIS COMMITMENTS, AND--
"AND HE USED TO SLEEP WITH MY WIFE." THAT'S WHAT YOU WERE GONNA SAY, RIGHT?
LOOK, I GET IT MIGHT SEEM KINDA GLAMOROUS AND ALL, HIRING A SUPER HERO--
BUT THE TRUTH IS, THESE GUYS BRING ALL KINDS OF BAGGAGE WITH THEM--ESPECIALLY THIS ONE. THEY PUT WHAT'S AROUND THEM IN DANGER--AND THAT COULD VERY WELL INCLUDE THESE MUSEUMS IF YOU BRING 'EM ON.
TRUST ME--YOU DON'T WANNA GET CAUGHT IN THE CROSSFIRE--
HA, CROSSFIRE! THAT REMINDS ME AGAIN--!
OKAY, MAYBE NOW'S NOT THE TIME--BUT, FRITZ, DON'T LISTEN TO THIS GUY.
I TAKE THIS JOB VERY SERIOUSLY. JUST LET ME WALK YOU THROUGH MY PLAN. IT'S NOT JUST ABOUT ARMED GUARDS, OR SURVEILLANCE TECHNOLOGY--THERE'S FRAUD-PREVENTION STUFF, CYBER-SECURITY--
EVEN NEW RESPONSE PLANS FOR WEATHER EMERGENCIES LIKE A HURRICANE OR--
UM--
A TORNADO?
CLOSE ENOUGH--

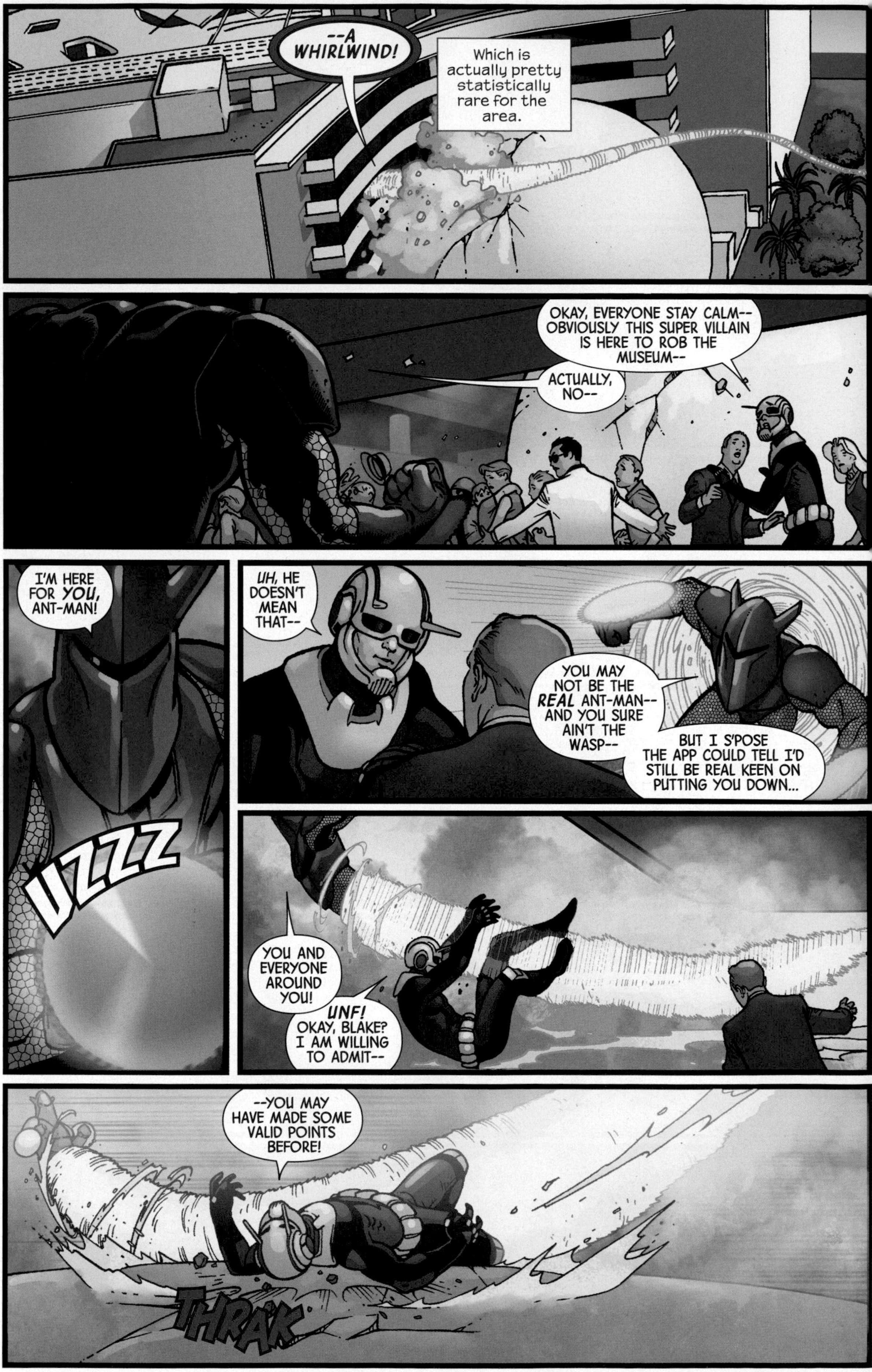
--A WHIRLWIND!
Which is actually pretty statistically rare for the area.
OKAY, EVERYONE STAY CALM-- OBVIOUSLY THIS SUPER VILLAIN IS HERE TO ROB THE MUSEUM--
ACTUALLY, NO--
I'M HERE FOR YOU, ANT-MAN!
UZZZ
UH, HE DOESN'T MEAN THAT--
YOU MAY NOT BE THE REAL ANT-MAN-- AND YOU SURE AIN'T THE WASP--
BUT I S'POSE THE APP COULD TELL I'D STILL BE REAL KEEN ON PUTTING YOU DOWN...
YOU AND EVERYONE AROUND YOU!
UNF! OKAY, BLAKE? I AM WILLING TO ADMIT--
--YOU MAY HAVE MADE SOME VALID POINTS BEFORE!
THRAK

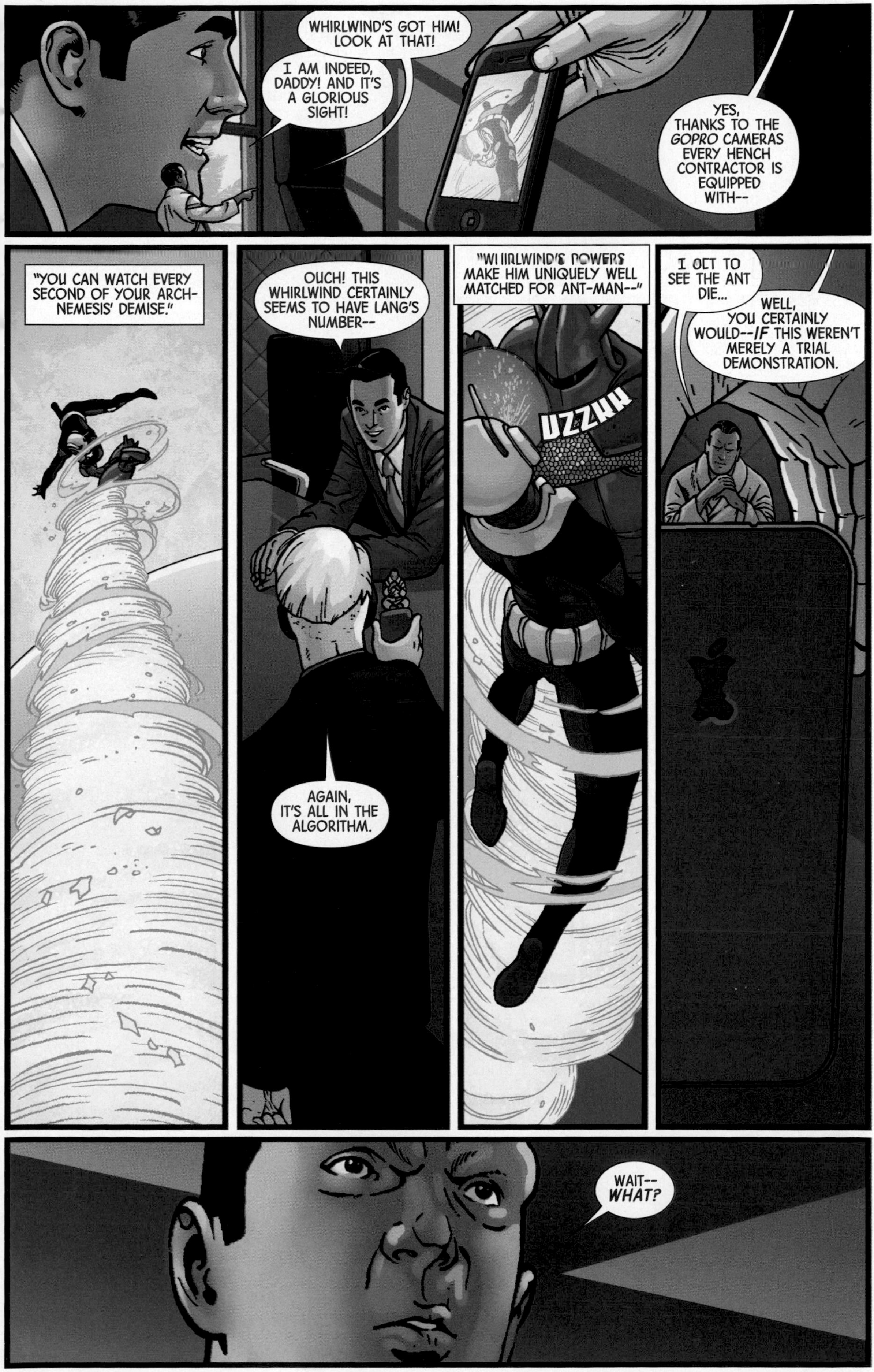
WHIRLWIND'S GOT HIM! LOOK AT THAT!
I AM INDEED, DADDY! AND IT'S A GLORIOUS SIGHT!
YES, THANKS TO THE GOPRO CAMERAS EVERY HENCH CONTRACTOR IS EQUIPPED WITH--
"YOU CAN WATCH EVERY SECOND OF YOUR ARCH-NEMESIS' DEMISE."
OUCH! THIS WHIRLWIND CERTAINLY SEEMS TO HAVE LANG'S NUMBER--
AGAIN, IT'S ALL IN THE ALGORITHM.
"WHIRLWIND'S POWERS MAKE HIM UNIQUELY WELL MATCHED FOR ANT-MAN--"
UZZHH
I OCT TO SEE THE ANT DIE...
WELL, YOU CERTAINLY WOULD--IF THIS WEREN'T MERELY A TRIAL DEMONSTRATION.
WAIT-- WHAT?

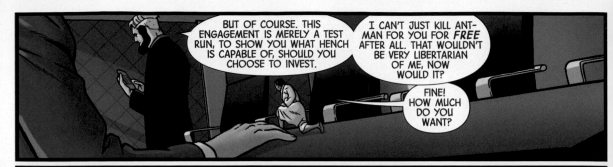

BUT OF COURSE. THIS ENGAGEMENT IS MERELY A TEST RUN, TO SHOW YOU WHAT HENCH IS CAPABLE OF, SHOULD YOU CHOOSE TO INVEST.

I CAN'T JUST KILL ANT-MAN FOR YOU FOR *FREE* AFTER ALL. THAT WOULDN'T BE VERY LIBERTARIAN OF ME, NOW WOULD IT?

FINE! HOW MUCH DO YOU WANT?

ZZZKKKK

"ANYTHING TO SEE LANG'S HEAD COME OFF!"

WELL, I'M GLAD TO HEAR YOU SAY THAT, MR. CROSS. YOU SEE, OUR FIRST FUNDING ROUND WAS QUITE SUCCESSFUL, WITH A NUMBER OF V.C.'s AND ANGELS INVESTING.

NOW WE'RE HOPING TO MATCH THAT HERE IN OUR SECOND, BUT WITHOUT BRINGING IN TOO MANY NEW BOARD SEATS. IF WE WERE TO FIND ONE *DEEP-POCKETED* INVESTOR WITH THE WILL--

STOP BLATHERING AND NAME YOUR PRICE, BROKER! FIFTY THOUSAND?!! ONE HUNDRED THOUSAND?!!

MR. CROSS--

OUR LAST ROUND RAISED *1.2 BILLION.*

...B-BILLION?

YOU--YOU EXPECT ME TO GIVE YOU 1.2 BILLION DOLLARS JUST TO EXTERMINATE ONE MEASLY INSECT?!! THAT'S--THAT'S INSANE! THAT'S *CRIMINAL!*

NO SIR, THAT'S SILICON VALLEY.

THIS IS EXTORTION! WE WON'T PAY IT.

OH? WELL, THAT IS QUITE A SHAME--

ARE YOU SURE YOU WANT TO CANCEL THE ASSASSINATION?

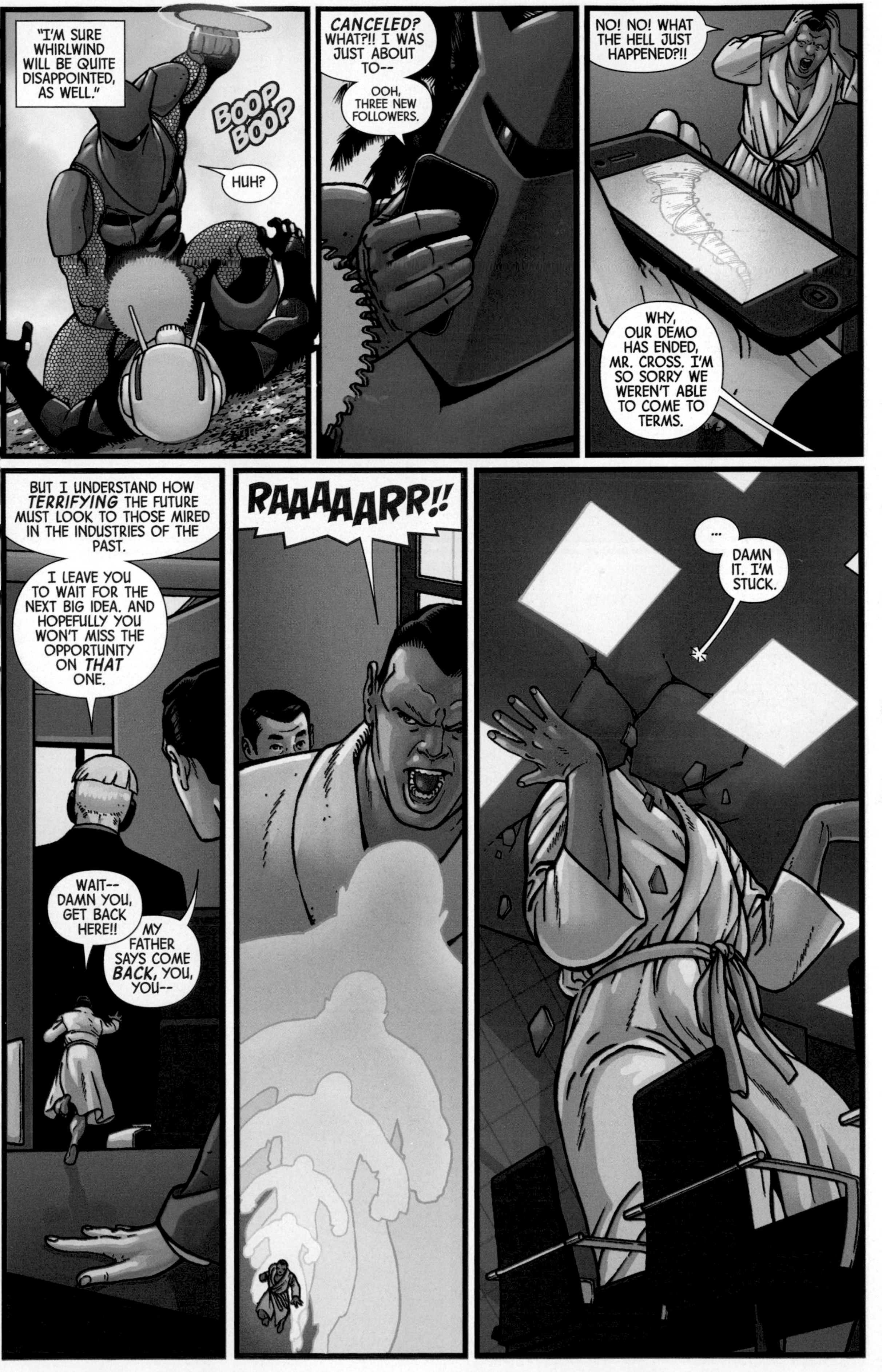
"I'M SURE WHIRLWIND WILL BE QUITE DISAPPOINTED, AS WELL."
BOOP BOOP
HUH?
CANCELED? WHAT?!! I WAS JUST ABOUT TO--
OOH, THREE NEW FOLLOWERS.
NO! NO! WHAT THE HELL JUST HAPPENED?!!
WHY, OUR DEMO HAS ENDED, MR. CROSS. I'M SO SORRY WE WEREN'T ABLE TO COME TO TERMS.
BUT I UNDERSTAND HOW TERRIFYING THE FUTURE MUST LOOK TO THOSE MIRED IN THE INDUSTRIES OF THE PAST.
I LEAVE YOU TO WAIT FOR THE NEXT BIG IDEA. AND HOPEFULLY YOU WON'T MISS THE OPPORTUNITY ON THAT ONE.
WAIT-- DAMN YOU, GET BACK HERE!!
MY FATHER SAYS COME BACK, YOU, YOU--
RAAAAARR!!
...
DAMN IT. I'M STUCK.

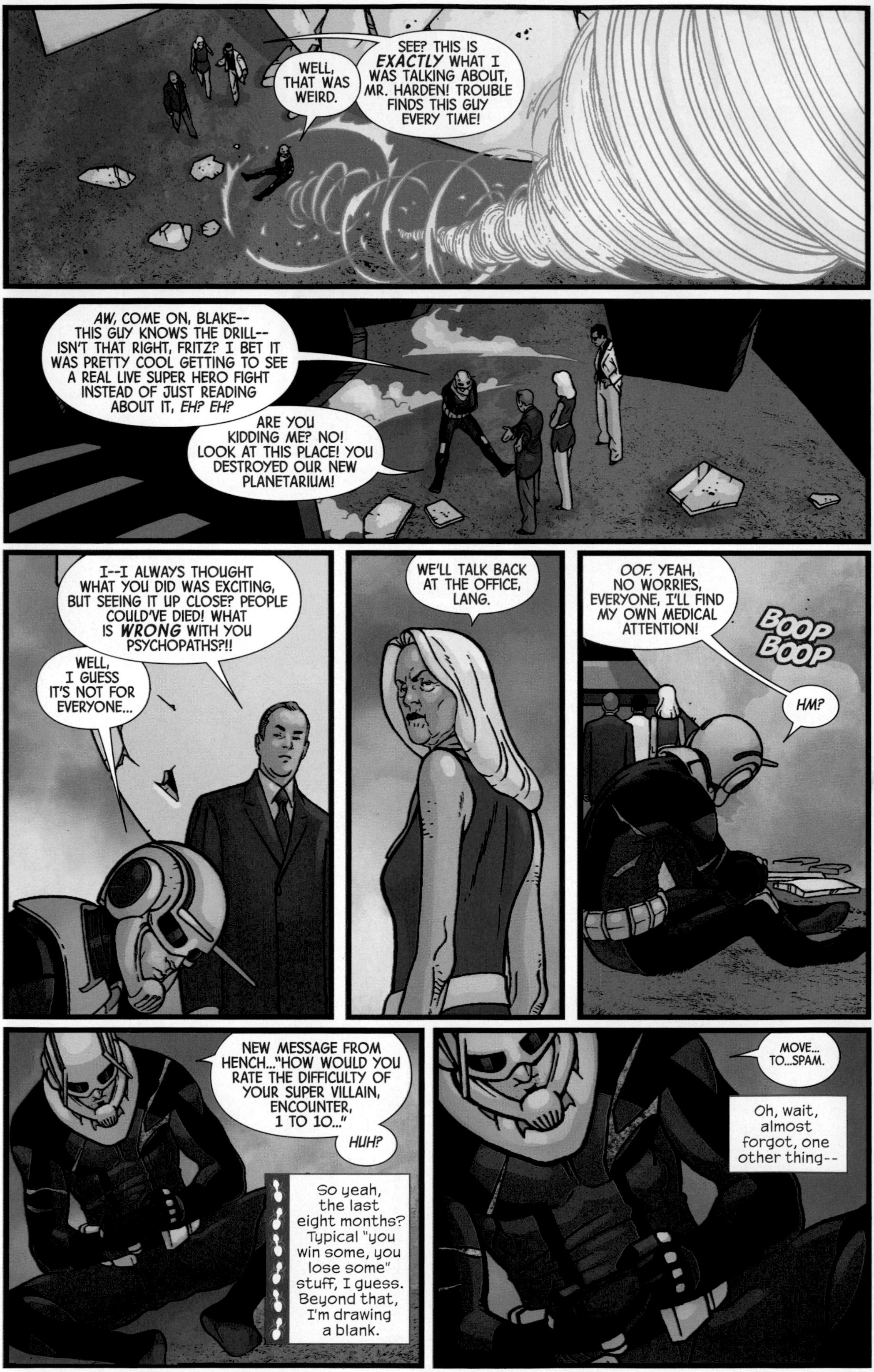
WELL, THAT WAS WEIRD.
SEE? THIS IS EXACTLY WHAT I WAS TALKING ABOUT, MR. HARDEN! TROUBLE FINDS THIS GUY EVERY TIME!
AW, COME ON, BLAKE-- THIS GUY KNOWS THE DRILL-- ISN'T THAT RIGHT, FRITZ? I BET IT WAS PRETTY COOL GETTING TO SEE A REAL LIVE SUPER HERO FIGHT INSTEAD OF JUST READING ABOUT IT, EH? EH?
ARE YOU KIDDING ME? NO! LOOK AT THIS PLACE! YOU DESTROYED OUR NEW PLANETARIUM!
I--I ALWAYS THOUGHT WHAT YOU DID WAS EXCITING, BUT SEEING IT UP CLOSE? PEOPLE COULD'VE DIED! WHAT IS WRONG WITH YOU PSYCHOPATHS?!!
WELL, I GUESS IT'S NOT FOR EVERYONE...
WE'LL TALK BACK AT THE OFFICE, LANG.
OOF. YEAH, NO WORRIES, EVERYONE, I'LL FIND MY OWN MEDICAL ATTENTION!
BOOP BOOP
HM?
NEW MESSAGE FROM HENCH..."HOW WOULD YOU RATE THE DIFFICULTY OF YOUR SUPER VILLAIN, ENCOUNTER, 1 TO 10..."
HUH?
So yeah, the last eight months? Typical "you win some, you lose some" stuff, I guess. Beyond that, I'm drawing a blank.
MOVE... TO...SPAM.
Oh, wait, almost forgot, one other thing--

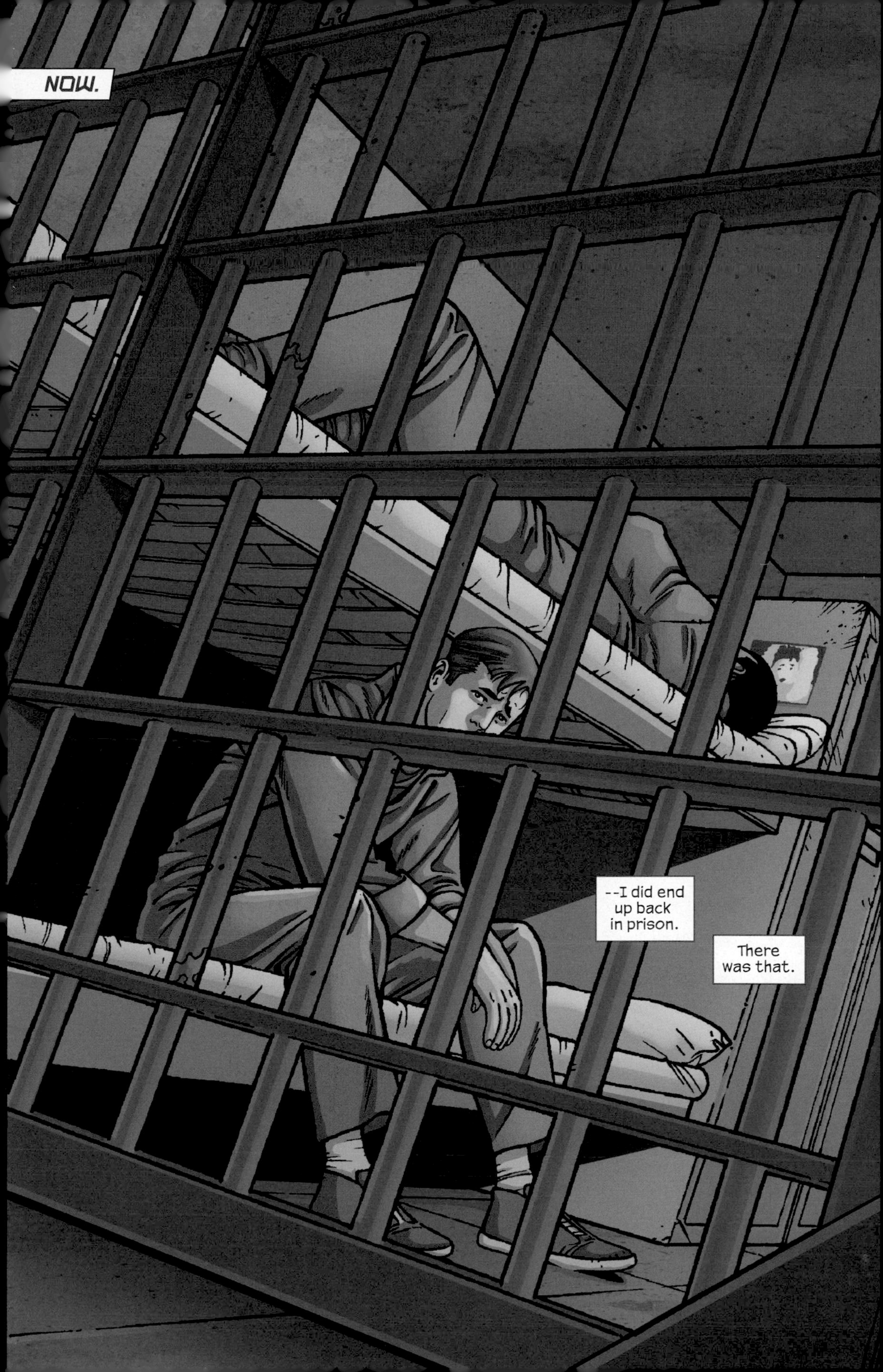
NOW.
--I did end up back in prison.
There was that.

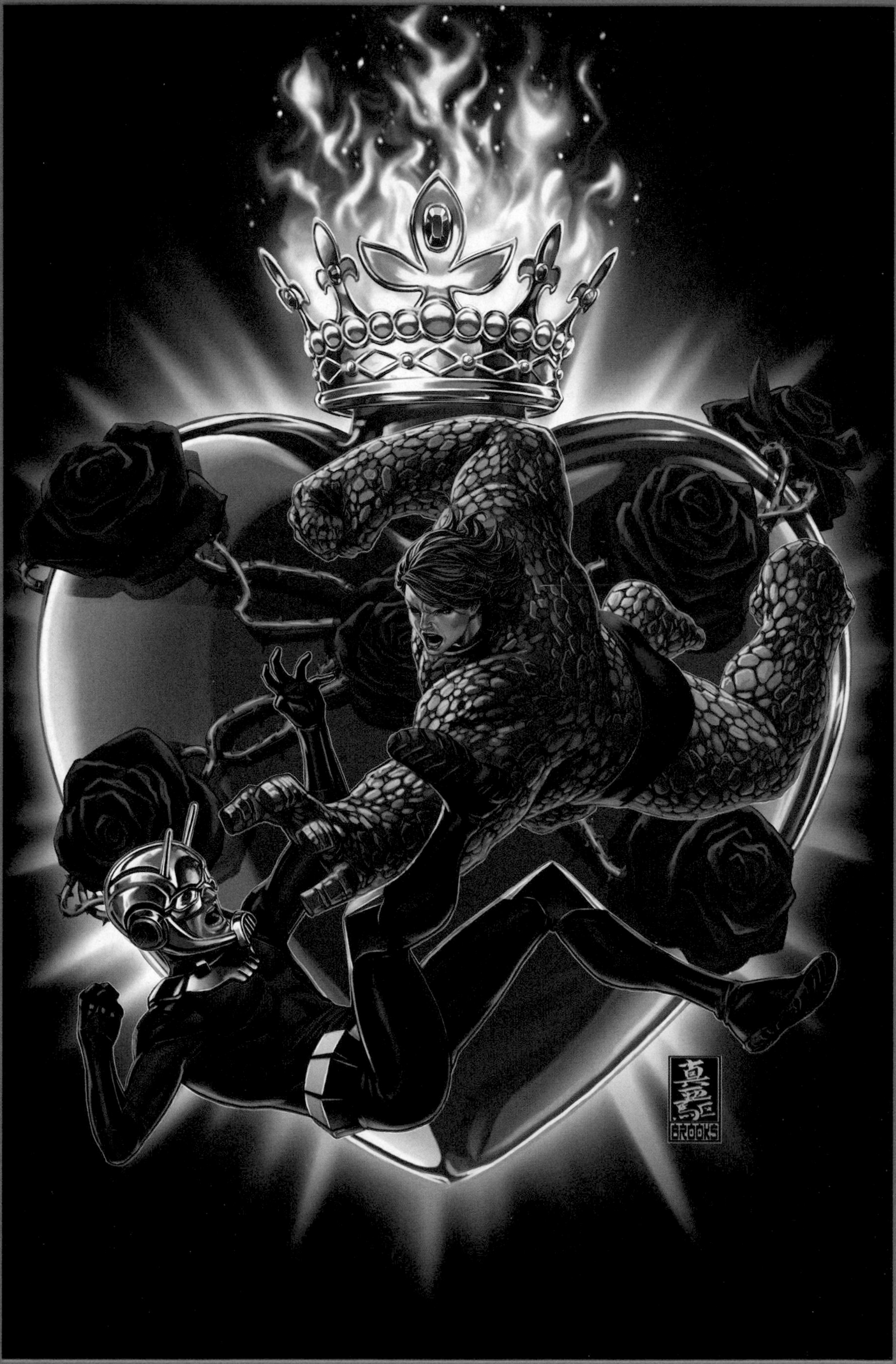
BROOKS

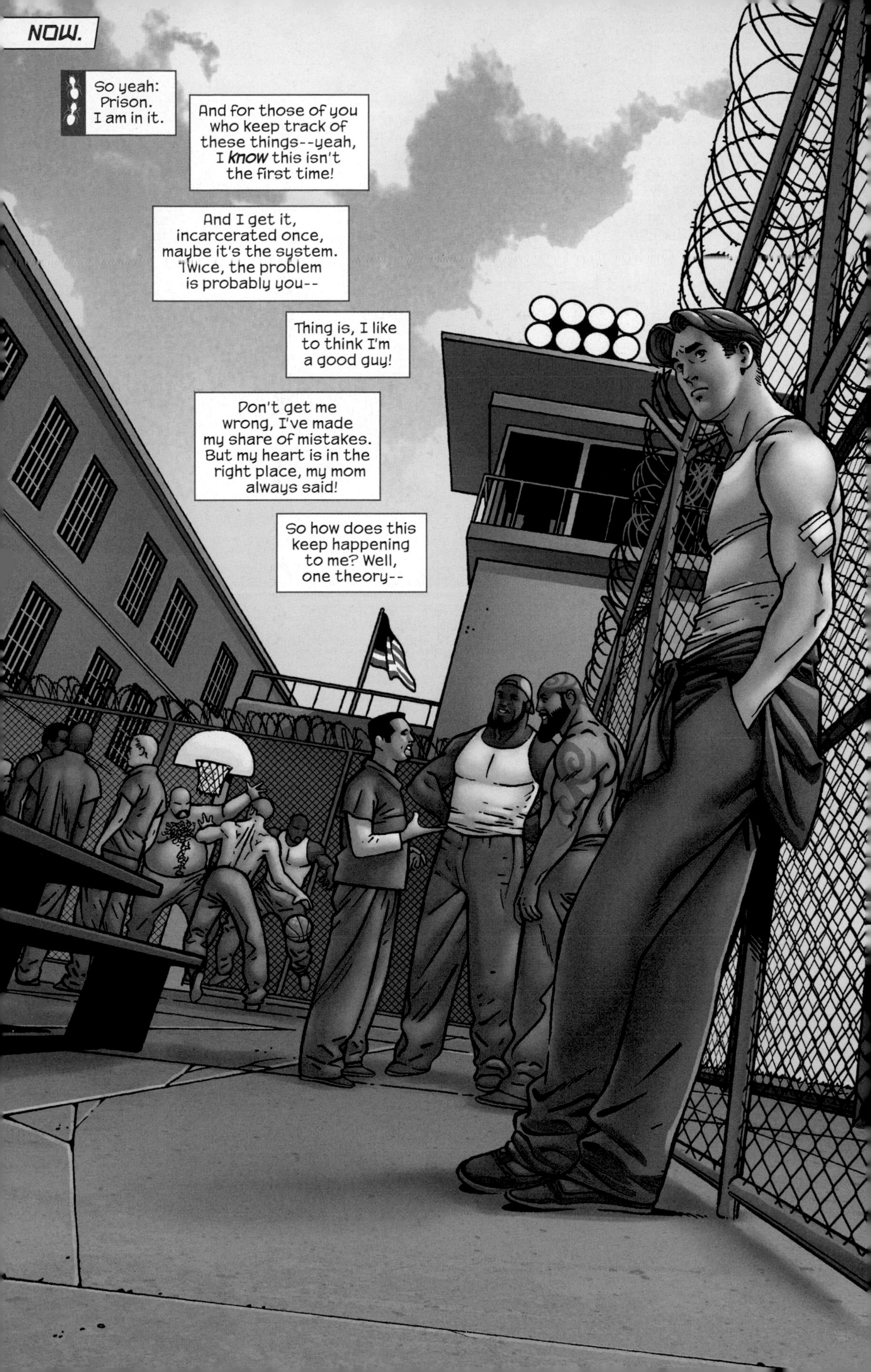
NOW.
So yeah: Prison. I am in it.
And for those of you who keep track of these things--yeah, I *KNOW* this isn't the first time!
And I get it, incarcerated once, maybe it's the system. Twice, the problem is probably you--
Thing is, I like to think I'm a good guy!
Don't get me wrong, I've made my share of mistakes. But my heart is in the right place, my mom always said!
So how does this keep happening to me? Well, one theory--

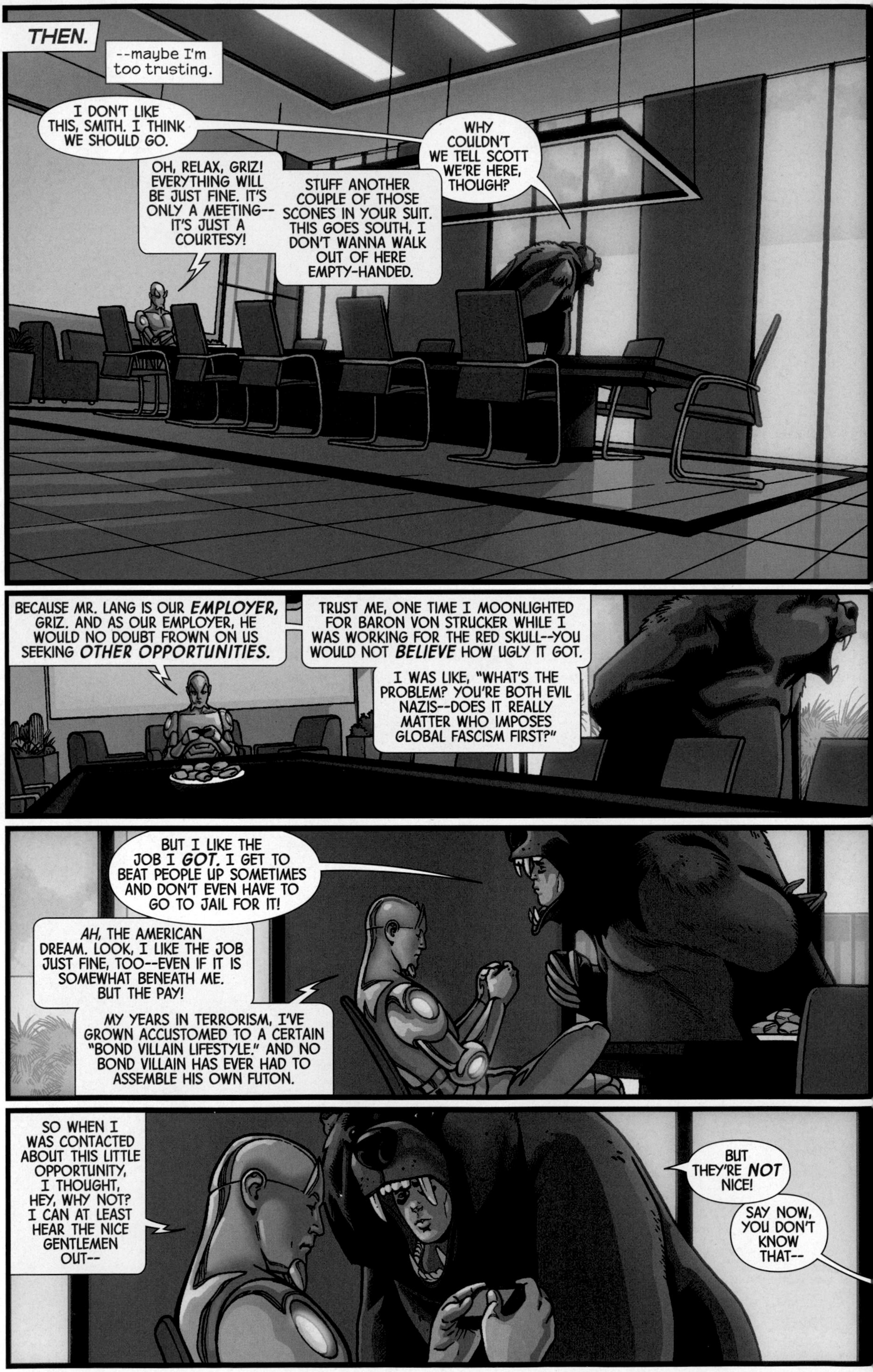

THEN.
--maybe I'm too trusting.
I DON'T LIKE THIS, SMITH. I THINK WE SHOULD GO.
WHY COULDN'T WE TELL SCOTT WE'RE HERE, THOUGH?
OH, RELAX, GRIZ! EVERYTHING WILL BE JUST FINE. IT'S ONLY A MEETING-- IT'S JUST A COURTESY!
STUFF ANOTHER COUPLE OF THOSE SCONES IN YOUR SUIT. THIS GOES SOUTH, I DON'T WANNA WALK OUT OF HERE EMPTY-HANDED.
BECAUSE MR. LANG IS OUR *EMPLOYER,* GRIZ. AND AS OUR EMPLOYER, HE WOULD NO DOUBT FROWN ON US SEEKING *OTHER OPPORTUNITIES.*
TRUST ME, ONE TIME I MOONLIGHTED FOR BARON VON STRUCKER WHILE I WAS WORKING FOR THE RED SKULL--YOU WOULD NOT *BELIEVE* HOW UGLY IT GOT.
I WAS LIKE, "WHAT'S THE PROBLEM? YOU'RE BOTH EVIL NAZIS--DOES IT REALLY MATTER WHO IMPOSES GLOBAL FASCISM FIRST?"
BUT I LIKE THE JOB I *GOT.* I GET TO BEAT PEOPLE UP SOMETIMES AND DON'T EVEN HAVE TO GO TO JAIL FOR IT!
AH, THE AMERICAN DREAM. LOOK, I LIKE THE JOB JUST FINE, TOO--EVEN IF IT IS SOMEWHAT BENEATH ME. BUT THE PAY!
MY YEARS IN TERRORISM, I'VE GROWN ACCUSTOMED TO A CERTAIN "BOND VILLAIN LIFESTYLE." AND NO BOND VILLAIN HAS EVER HAD TO ASSEMBLE HIS OWN FUTON.
SO WHEN I WAS CONTACTED ABOUT THIS LITTLE OPPORTUNITY, I THOUGHT, HEY, WHY NOT? I CAN AT LEAST HEAR THE NICE GENTLEMEN OUT--
BUT THEY'RE *NOT* NICE!
SAY NOW, YOU DON'T KNOW THAT--

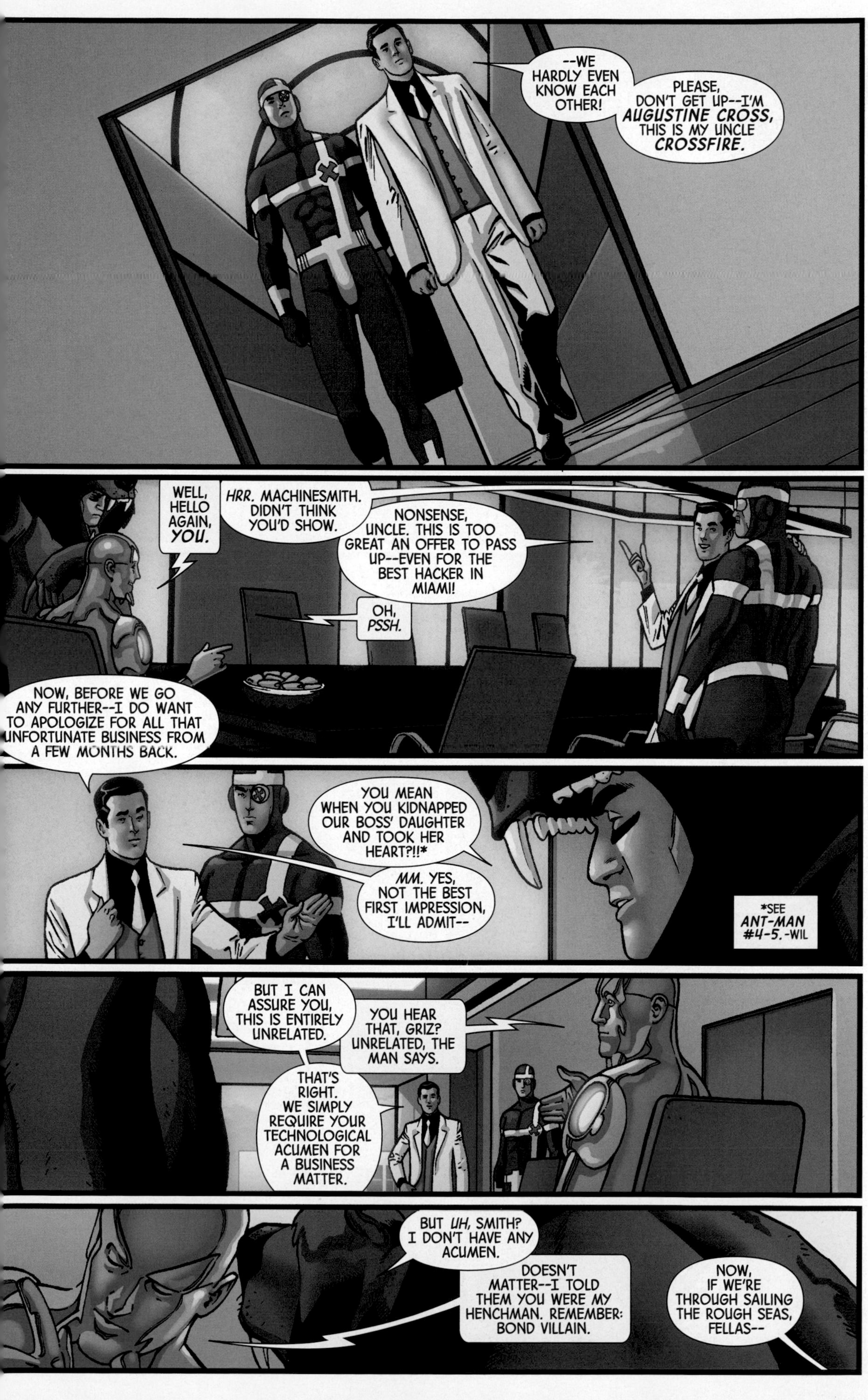
--WE HARDLY EVEN KNOW EACH OTHER!
PLEASE, DON'T GET UP--I'M AUGUSTINE CROSS, THIS IS MY UNCLE CROSSFIRE.
WELL, HELLO AGAIN, YOU.
HRR. MACHINESMITH. DIDN'T THINK YOU'D SHOW.
NONSENSE, UNCLE. THIS IS TOO GREAT AN OFFER TO PASS UP--EVEN FOR THE BEST HACKER IN MIAMI!
OH, PSSH.
NOW, BEFORE WE GO ANY FURTHER--I DO WANT TO APOLOGIZE FOR ALL THAT UNFORTUNATE BUSINESS FROM A FEW MONTHS BACK.
YOU MEAN WHEN YOU KIDNAPPED OUR BOSS' DAUGHTER AND TOOK HER HEART?!!*
MM. YES, NOT THE BEST FIRST IMPRESSION, I'LL ADMIT--
*SEE ANT-MAN #4-5. -WIL
BUT I CAN ASSURE YOU, THIS IS ENTIRELY UNRELATED.
YOU HEAR THAT, GRIZ? UNRELATED, THE MAN SAYS.
THAT'S RIGHT. WE SIMPLY REQUIRE YOUR TECHNOLOGICAL ACUMEN FOR A BUSINESS MATTER.
BUT UH, SMITH? I DON'T HAVE ANY ACUMEN.
DOESN'T MATTER--I TOLD THEM YOU WERE MY HENCHMAN. REMEMBER: BOND VILLAIN.
NOW, IF WE'RE THROUGH SAILING THE ROUGH SEAS, FELLAS--

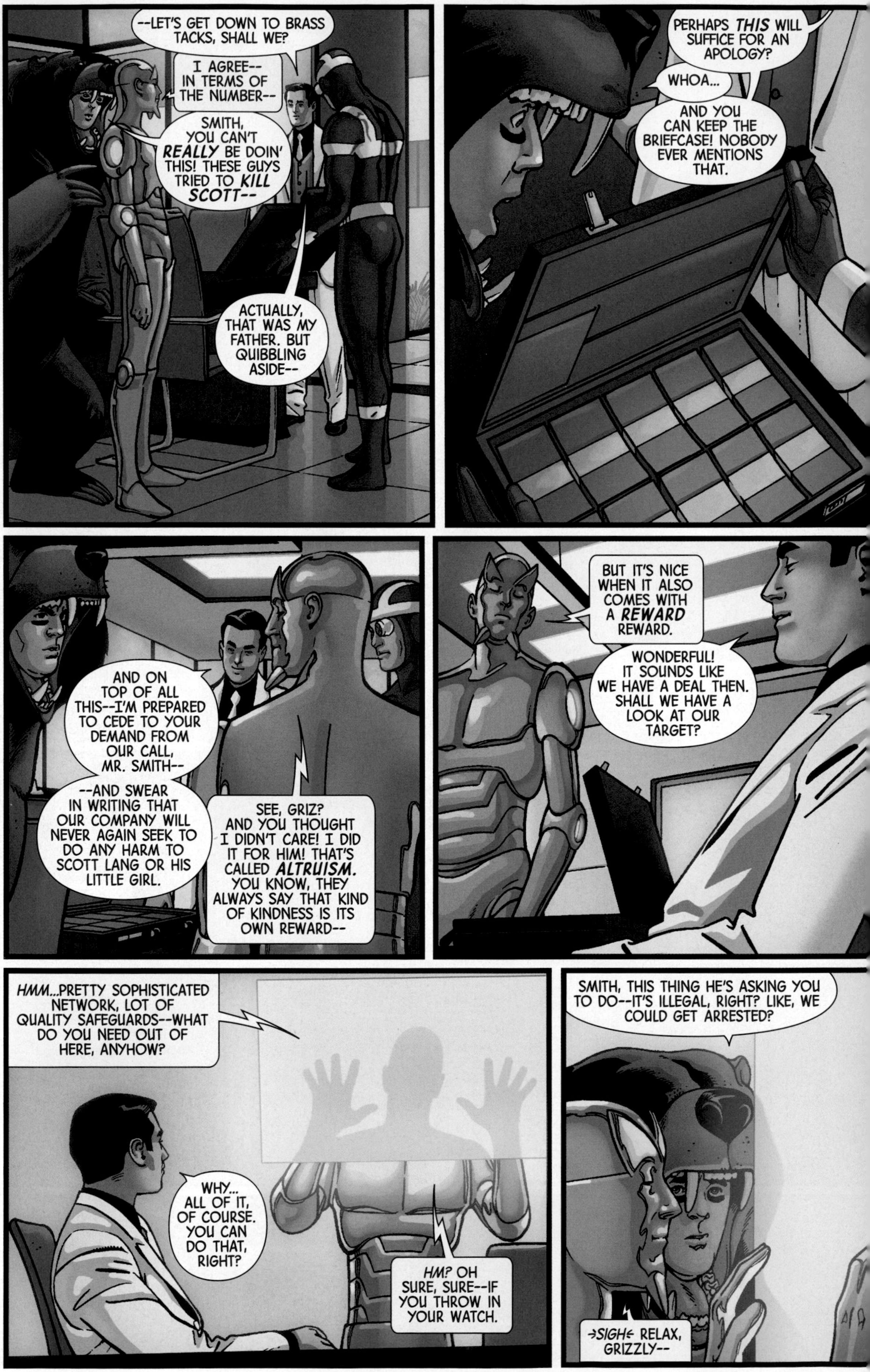
--LET'S GET DOWN TO BRASS TACKS, SHALL WE?
I AGREE-- IN TERMS OF THE NUMBER--
SMITH, YOU CAN'T REALLY BE DOIN' THIS! THESE GUYS TRIED TO KILL SCOTT--
ACTUALLY, THAT WAS MY FATHER. BUT QUIBBLING ASIDE--
PERHAPS THIS WILL SUFFICE FOR AN APOLOGY?
WHOA...
AND YOU CAN KEEP THE BRIEFCASE! NOBODY EVER MENTIONS THAT.
AND ON TOP OF ALL THIS--I'M PREPARED TO CEDE TO YOUR DEMAND FROM OUR CALL, MR. SMITH--
--AND SWEAR IN WRITING THAT OUR COMPANY WILL NEVER AGAIN SEEK TO DO ANY HARM TO SCOTT LANG OR HIS LITTLE GIRL.
SEE, GRIZ? AND YOU THOUGHT I DIDN'T CARE! I DID IT FOR HIM! THAT'S CALLED ALTRUISM. YOU KNOW, THEY ALWAYS SAY THAT KIND OF KINDNESS IS ITS OWN REWARD--
BUT IT'S NICE WHEN IT ALSO COMES WITH A REWARD REWARD.
WONDERFUL! IT SOUNDS LIKE WE HAVE A DEAL THEN. SHALL WE HAVE A LOOK AT OUR TARGET?
HMM...PRETTY SOPHISTICATED NETWORK, LOT OF QUALITY SAFEGUARDS--WHAT DO YOU NEED OUT OF HERE, ANYHOW?
WHY... ALL OF IT, OF COURSE. YOU CAN DO THAT, RIGHT?
HM? OH SURE, SURE--IF YOU THROW IN YOUR WATCH.
SMITH, THIS THING HE'S ASKING YOU TO DO--IT'S ILLEGAL, RIGHT? LIKE, WE COULD GET ARRESTED?
>SIGH< RELAX, GRIZZLY--

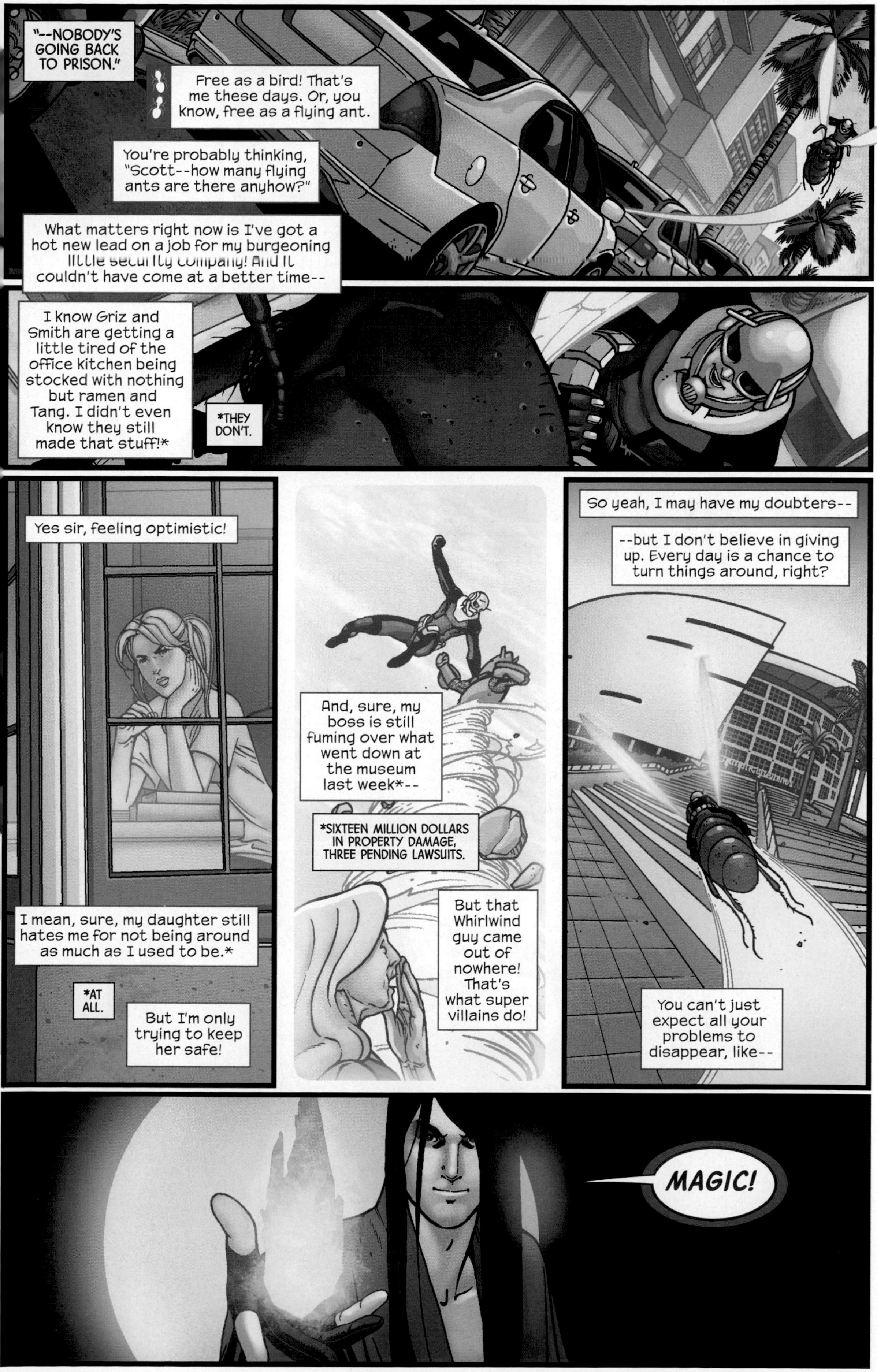
"--NOBODY'S GOING BACK TO PRISON."
Free as a bird! That's me these days. Or, you know, free as a flying ant.
You're probably thinking, "Scott--how many flying ants are there anyhow?"
What matters right now is I've got a hot new lead on a job for my burgeoning little security company! And it couldn't have come at a better time--
I know Griz and Smith are getting a little tired of the office kitchen being stocked with nothing but ramen and Tang. I didn't even know they still made that stuff!*
*THEY DON'T.
Yes sir, feeling optimistic!
I mean, sure, my daughter still hates me for not being around as much as I used to be.*
*AT ALL.
But I'm only trying to keep her safe!
And, sure, my boss is still fuming over what went down at the museum last week*--
*SIXTEEN MILLION DOLLARS IN PROPERTY DAMAGE, THREE PENDING LAWSUITS.
But that Whirlwind guy came out of nowhere! That's what super villains do!
So yeah, I may have my doubters--
--but I don't believe in giving up. Every day is a chance to turn things around, right?
You can't just expect all your problems to disappear, like--
MAGIC!

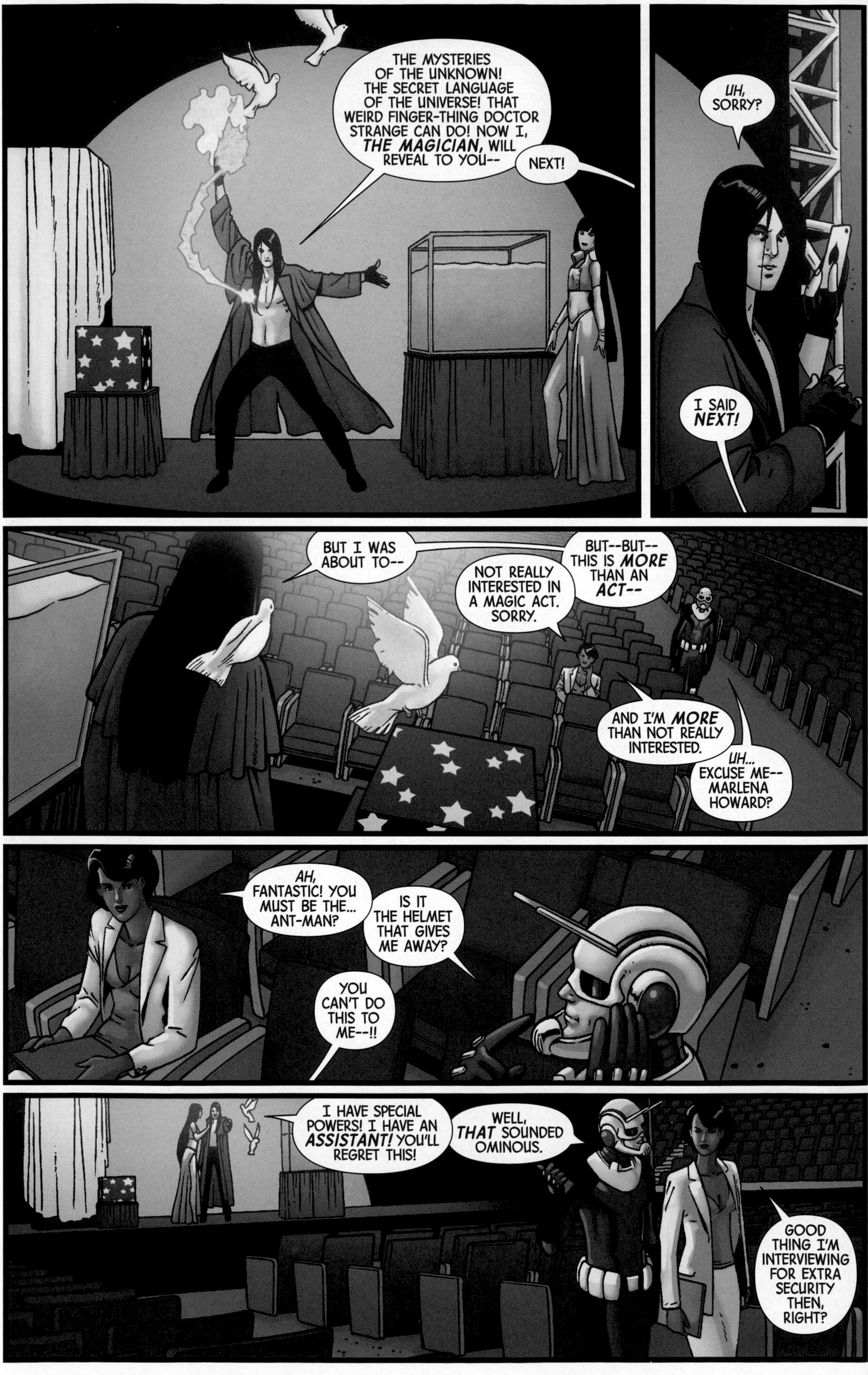
THE MYSTERIES OF THE UNKNOWN! THE SECRET LANGUAGE OF THE UNIVERSE! THAT WEIRD FINGER-THING DOCTOR STRANGE CAN DO! NOW I, *THE MAGICIAN,* WILL REVEAL TO YOU--
NEXT!
UH, SORRY?
I SAID *NEXT!*
BUT I WAS ABOUT TO--
NOT REALLY INTERESTED IN A MAGIC ACT. SORRY.
BUT--BUT-- THIS IS *MORE* THAN AN *ACT*--
AND I'M *MORE* THAN NOT REALLY INTERESTED.
UH... EXCUSE ME-- MARLENA HOWARD?
AH, FANTASTIC! YOU MUST BE THE... ANT-MAN?
IS IT THE HELMET THAT GIVES ME AWAY?
YOU CAN'T DO THIS TO ME--!!
I HAVE SPECIAL POWERS! I HAVE AN *ASSISTANT!* YOU'LL REGRET THIS!
WELL, *THAT* SOUNDED OMINOUS.
GOOD THING I'M INTERVIEWING FOR EXTRA SECURITY THEN, RIGHT?

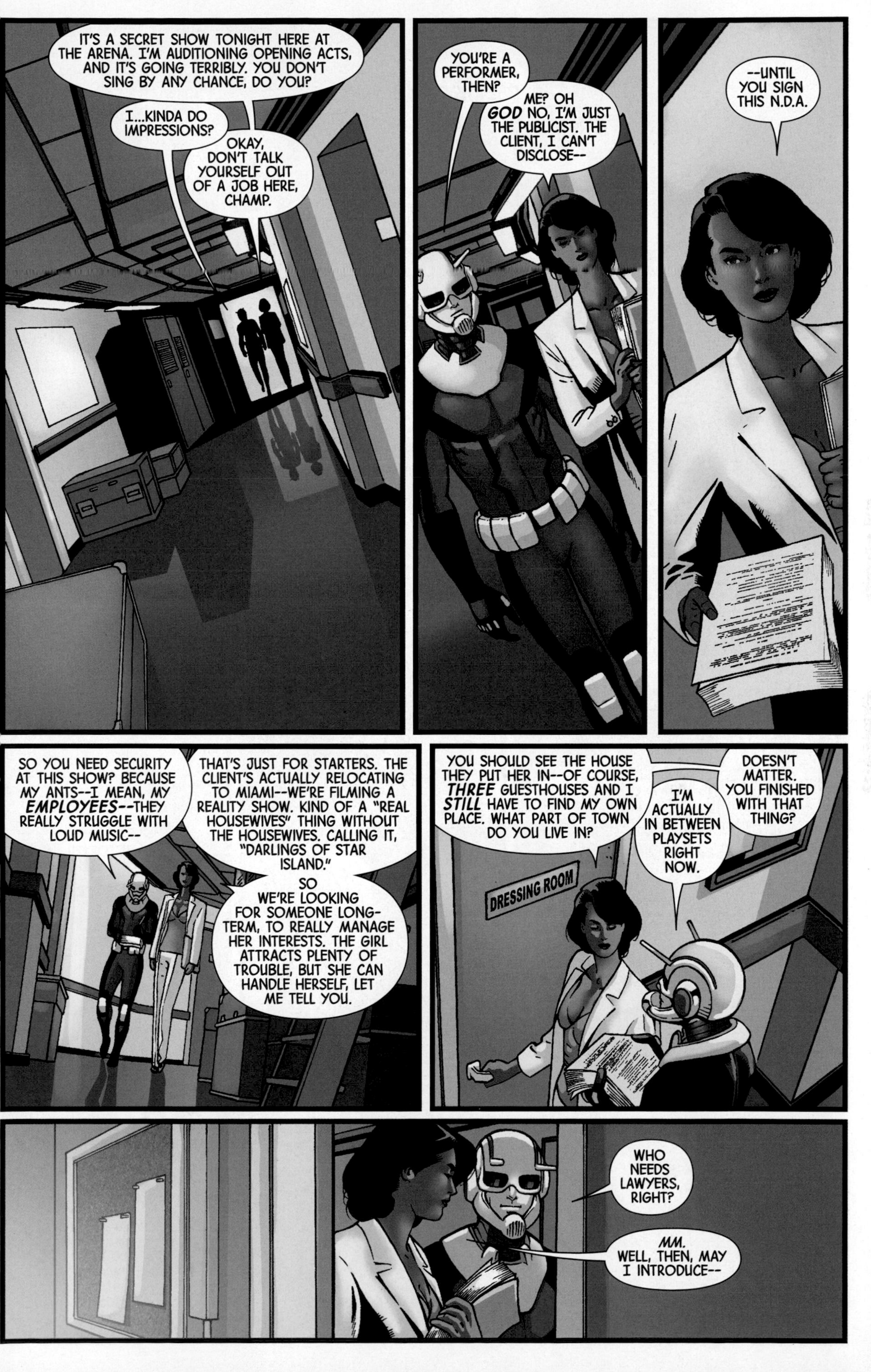
IT'S A SECRET SHOW TONIGHT HERE AT THE ARENA. I'M AUDITIONING OPENING ACTS, AND IT'S GOING TERRIBLY. YOU DON'T SING BY ANY CHANCE, DO YOU?
I...KINDA DO IMPRESSIONS?
OKAY, DON'T TALK YOURSELF OUT OF A JOB HERE, CHAMP.
YOU'RE A PERFORMER, THEN?
ME? OH *GOD* NO, I'M JUST THE PUBLICIST. THE CLIENT, I CAN'T DISCLOSE--
--UNTIL YOU SIGN THIS N.D.A.
SO YOU NEED SECURITY AT THIS SHOW? BECAUSE MY ANTS--I MEAN, MY *EMPLOYEES*--THEY REALLY STRUGGLE WITH LOUD MUSIC--
THAT'S JUST FOR STARTERS. THE CLIENT'S ACTUALLY RELOCATING TO MIAMI--WE'RE FILMING A REALITY SHOW. KIND OF A "REAL HOUSEWIVES" THING WITHOUT THE HOUSEWIVES. CALLING IT, "DARLINGS OF STAR ISLAND."
SO WE'RE LOOKING FOR SOMEONE LONG-TERM, TO REALLY MANAGE HER INTERESTS. THE GIRL ATTRACTS PLENTY OF TROUBLE, BUT SHE CAN HANDLE HERSELF, LET ME TELL YOU.
YOU SHOULD SEE THE HOUSE THEY PUT HER IN--OF COURSE, *THREE* GUESTHOUSES AND I *STILL* HAVE TO FIND MY OWN PLACE. WHAT PART OF TOWN DO YOU LIVE IN?
I'M ACTUALLY IN BETWEEN PLAYSETS RIGHT NOW.
DOESN'T MATTER. YOU FINISHED WITH THAT THING?
DRESSING ROOM
WHO NEEDS LAWYERS, RIGHT?
MM. WELL, THEN, MAY I INTRODUCE--

--DARLA DEERING!

Uh-oh.

SCOTT?!!

OH, UM-- HEY, DARLA...

WAIT-- YOU TWO KNOW EACH OTHER?

WE, UM-- WE KINDA DATED--

KINDA?!! DATED?!!

OH, WOW--THIS IS EMBARRASSING...

AND YOU--HOW COULD YOU NOT KNOW THIS?!!

I DON'T KNOW--I KINDA TUNE OUT SUPER HERO STUFF! IT'S LIKE POLITICS, RIGHT? IT'S ALL FAKE ANYWAY. BUT IF I'D KNOWN YOU TWO HAD HISTORY--

HISTORY?!! OH YEAH--

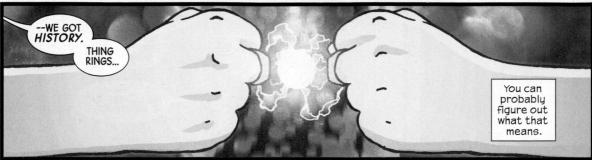

--WE GOT HISTORY.

THING RINGS...

You can probably figure out what that means.

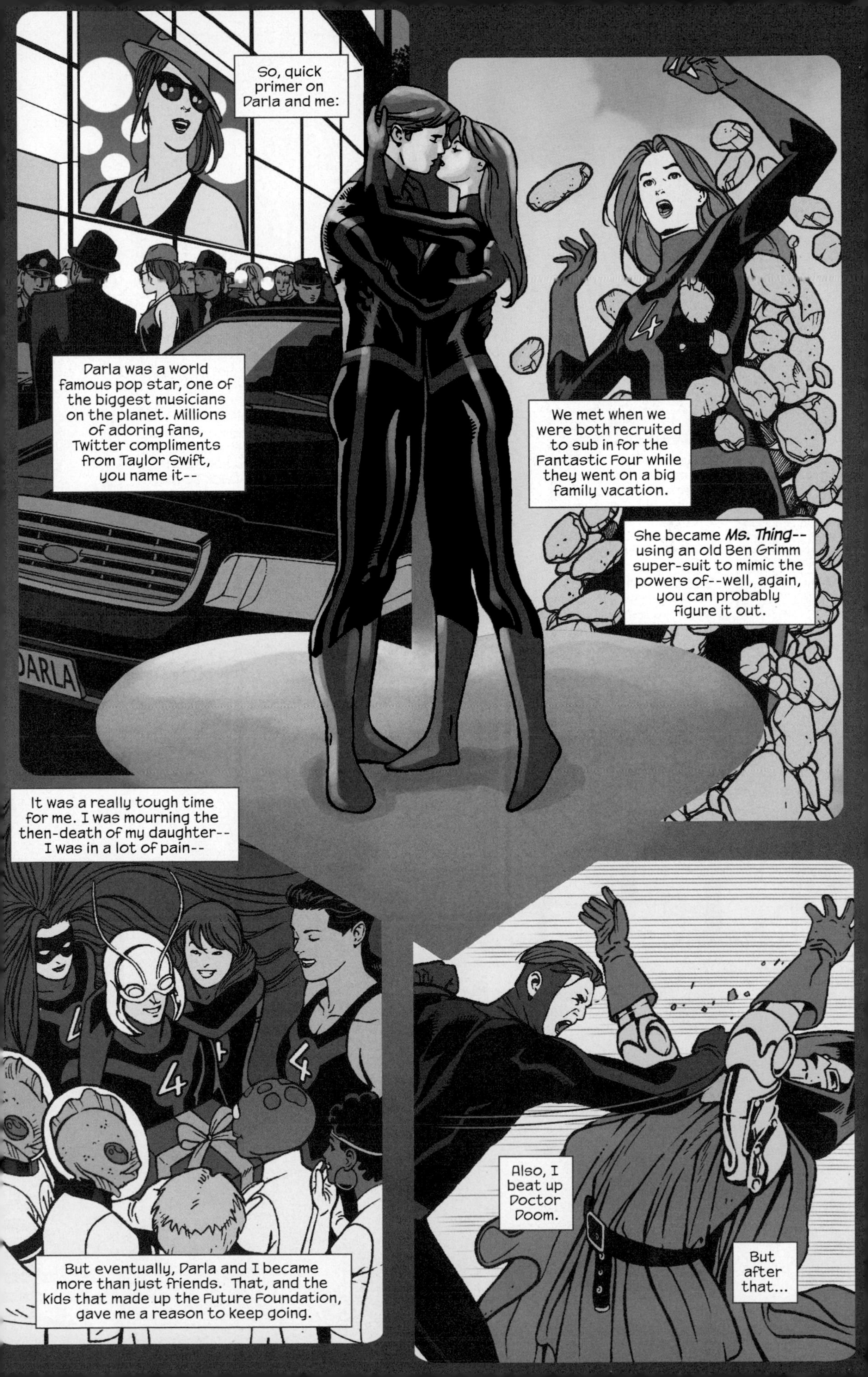
So, quick primer on Darla and me:
Darla was a world famous pop star, one of the biggest musicians on the planet. Millions of adoring fans, Twitter compliments from Taylor Swift, you name it--
DARLA
We met when we were both recruited to sub in for the Fantastic Four while they went on a big family vacation.
She became *Ms. Thing*-- using an old Ben Grimm super-suit to mimic the powers of--well, again, you can probably figure it out.
It was a really tough time for me. I was mourning the then-death of my daughter-- I was in a lot of pain--
But eventually, Darla and I became more than just friends. That, and the kids that made up the Future Foundation, gave me a reason to keep going.
Also, I beat up Doctor Doom.
But after that...

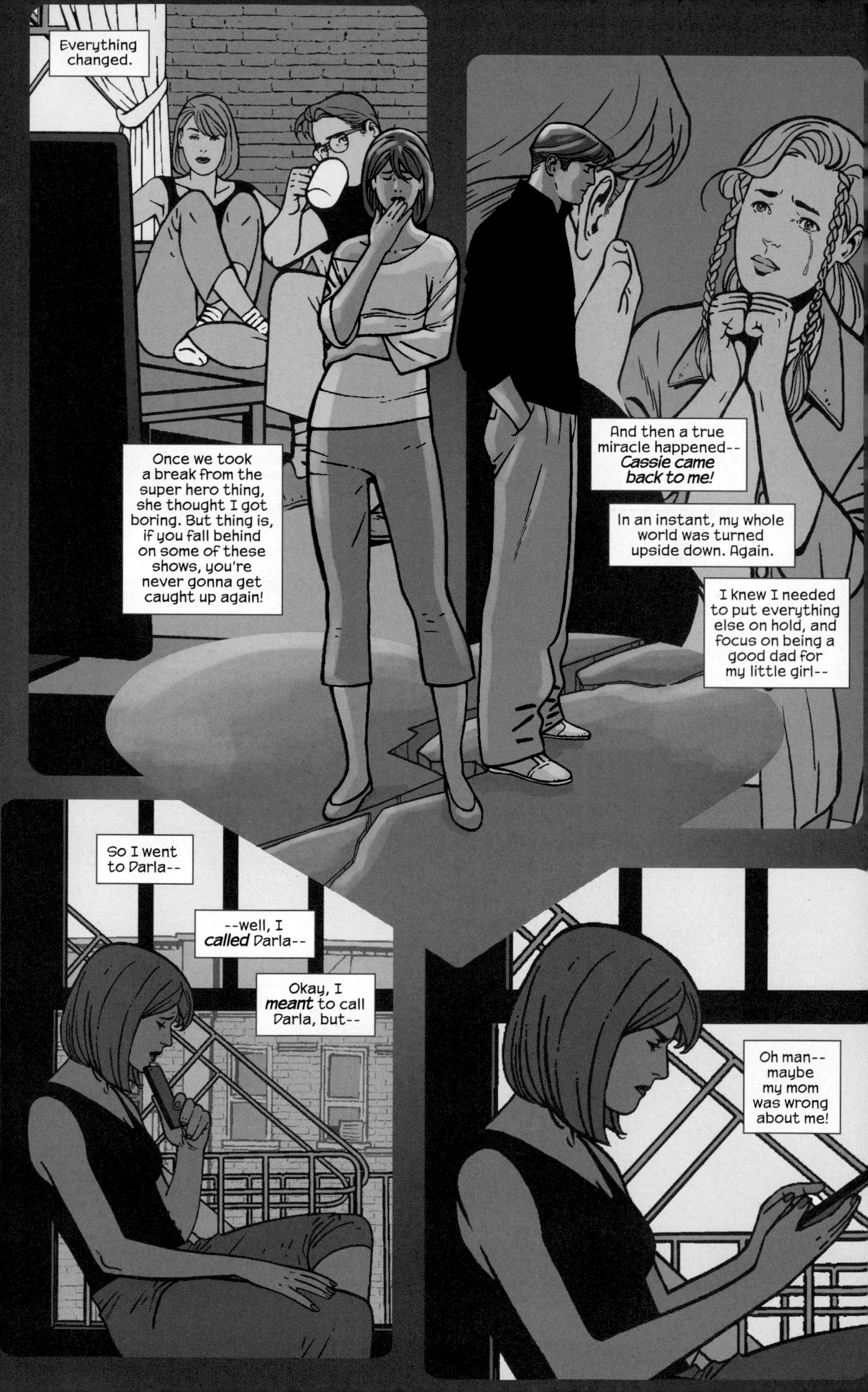
Everything changed.
Once we took a break from the super hero thing, she thought I got boring. But thing is, if you fall behind on some of these shows, you're never gonna get caught up again!
And then a true miracle happened-- *Cassie came back to me!*
In an instant, my whole world was turned upside down. Again.
I knew I needed to put everything else on hold, and focus on being a good dad for my little girl--
So I went to Darla--
--well, I *called* Darla--
Okay, I *meant* to call Darla, but--
Oh man-- maybe my mom was wrong about me!

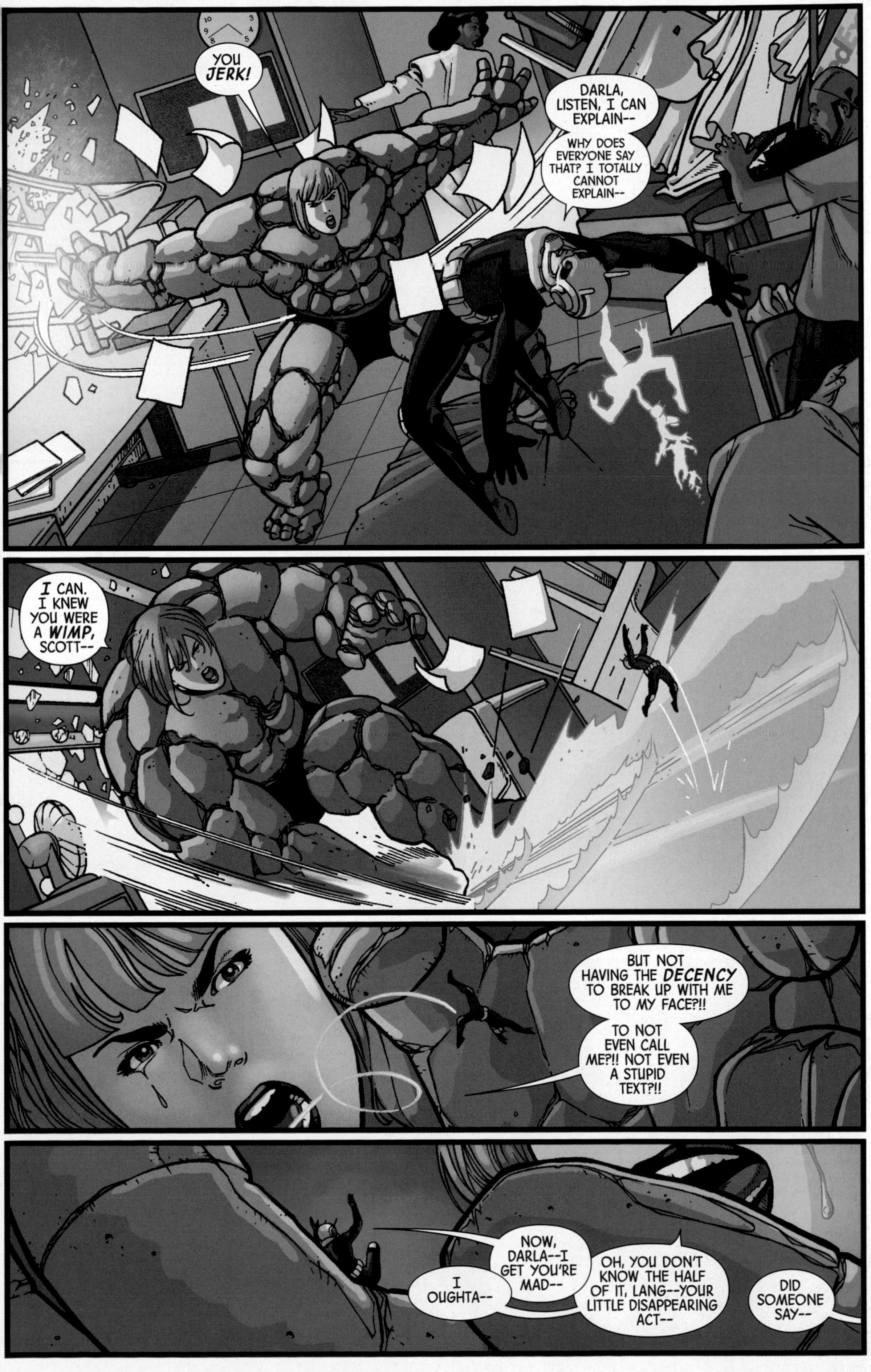
YOU JERK!
DARLA, LISTEN, I CAN EXPLAIN--
WHY DOES EVERYONE SAY THAT? I TOTALLY CANNOT EXPLAIN--
I CAN. I KNEW YOU WERE A WIMP, SCOTT--
BUT NOT HAVING THE DECENCY TO BREAK UP WITH ME TO MY FACE?!!
TO NOT EVEN CALL ME?!! NOT EVEN A STUPID TEXT?!!
I OUGHTA--
NOW, DARLA--I GET YOU'RE MAD--
OH, YOU DON'T KNOW THE HALF OF IT, LANG--YOUR LITTLE DISAPPEARING ACT--
DID SOMEONE SAY--

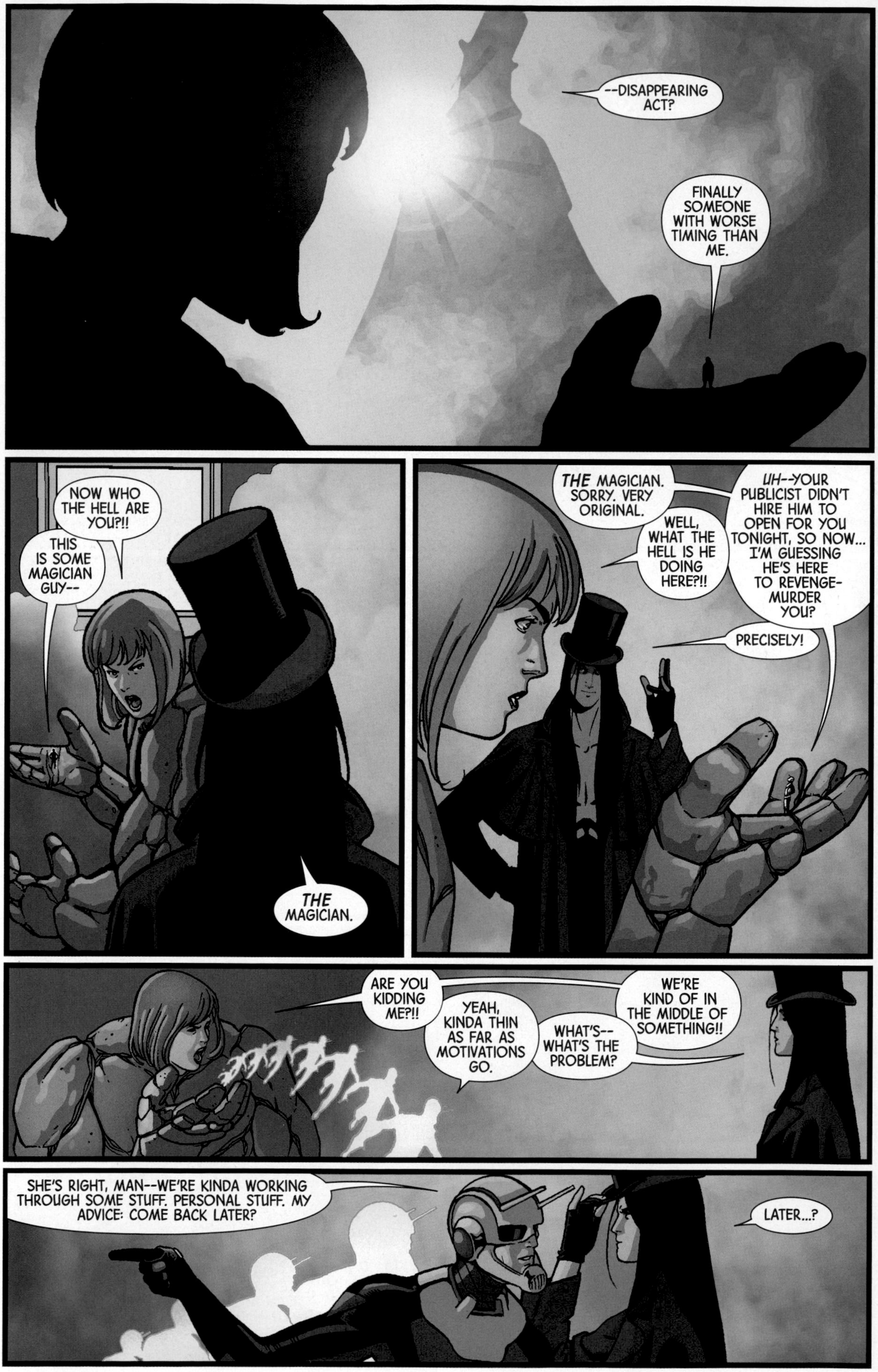
--DISAPPEARING ACT?
FINALLY SOMEONE WITH WORSE TIMING THAN ME.
NOW WHO THE HELL ARE YOU?!!
THIS IS SOME MAGICIAN GUY--
THE MAGICIAN.
THE MAGICIAN. SORRY. VERY ORIGINAL.
WELL, WHAT THE HELL IS HE DOING HERE?!!
UH--YOUR PUBLICIST DIDN'T HIRE HIM TO OPEN FOR YOU TONIGHT, SO NOW... I'M GUESSING HE'S HERE TO REVENGE-MURDER YOU?
PRECISELY!
ARE YOU KIDDING ME?!!
YEAH, KINDA THIN AS FAR AS MOTIVATIONS GO.
WE'RE KIND OF IN THE MIDDLE OF SOMETHING!!
WHAT'S-- WHAT'S THE PROBLEM?
SHE'S RIGHT, MAN--WE'RE KINDA WORKING THROUGH SOME STUFF. PERSONAL STUFF. MY ADVICE: COME BACK LATER?
LATER...?

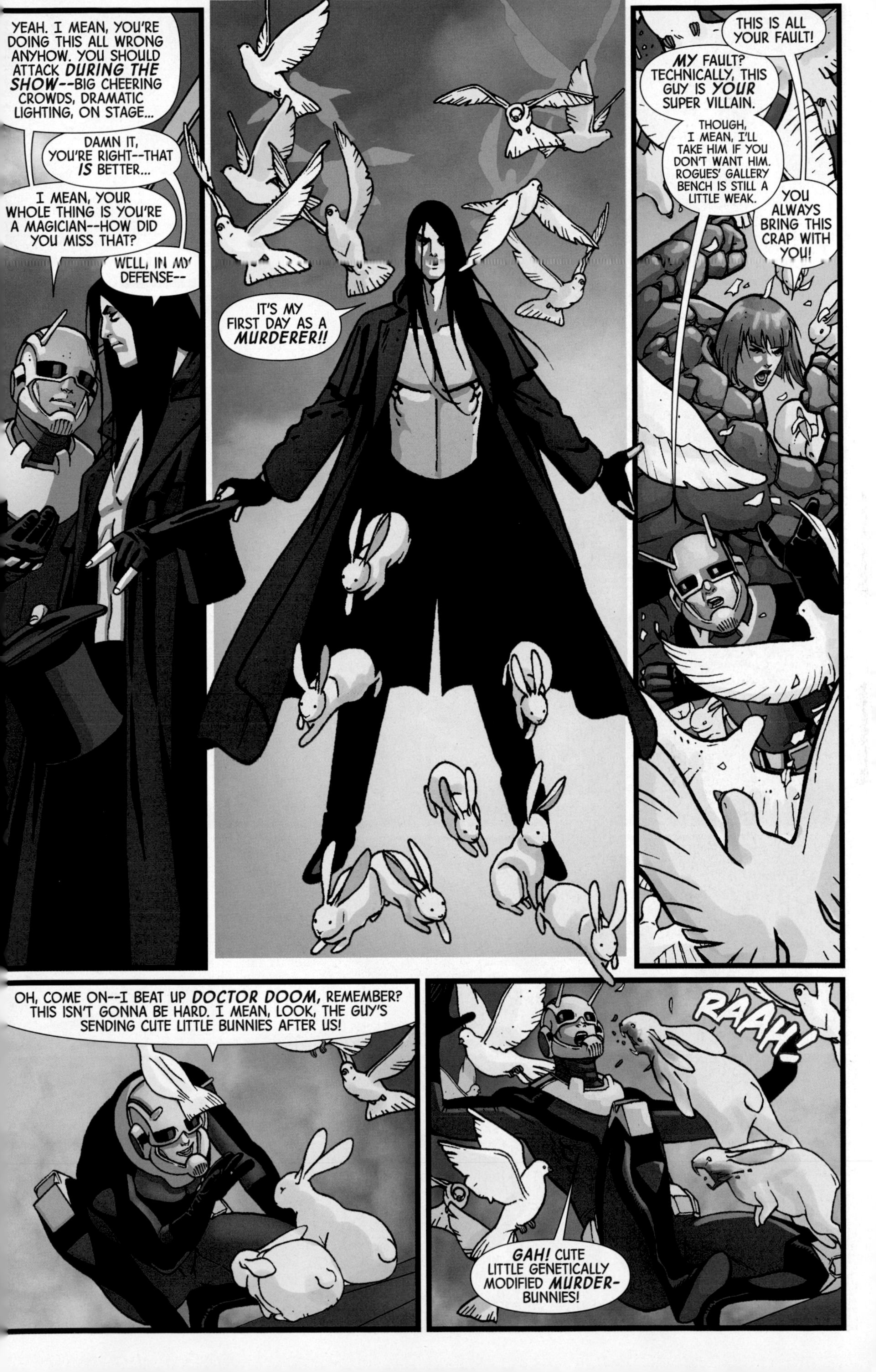

YEAH. I MEAN, YOU'RE DOING THIS ALL WRONG ANYHOW. YOU SHOULD ATTACK DURING THE SHOW--BIG CHEERING CROWDS, DRAMATIC LIGHTING, ON STAGE...
DAMN IT, YOU'RE RIGHT--THAT IS BETTER...
I MEAN, YOUR WHOLE THING IS YOU'RE A MAGICIAN--HOW DID YOU MISS THAT?
WELL, IN MY DEFENSE--
IT'S MY FIRST DAY AS A MURDERER!!
THIS IS ALL YOUR FAULT!
MY FAULT? TECHNICALLY, THIS GUY IS YOUR SUPER VILLAIN.
THOUGH, I MEAN, I'LL TAKE HIM IF YOU DON'T WANT HIM. ROGUES' GALLERY BENCH IS STILL A LITTLE WEAK.
YOU ALWAYS BRING THIS CRAP WITH YOU!
OH, COME ON--I BEAT UP DOCTOR DOOM, REMEMBER? THIS ISN'T GONNA BE HARD. I MEAN, LOOK, THE GUY'S SENDING CUTE LITTLE BUNNIES AFTER US!
RAAH!
GAH! CUTE LITTLE GENETICALLY MODIFIED MURDER-BUNNIES!

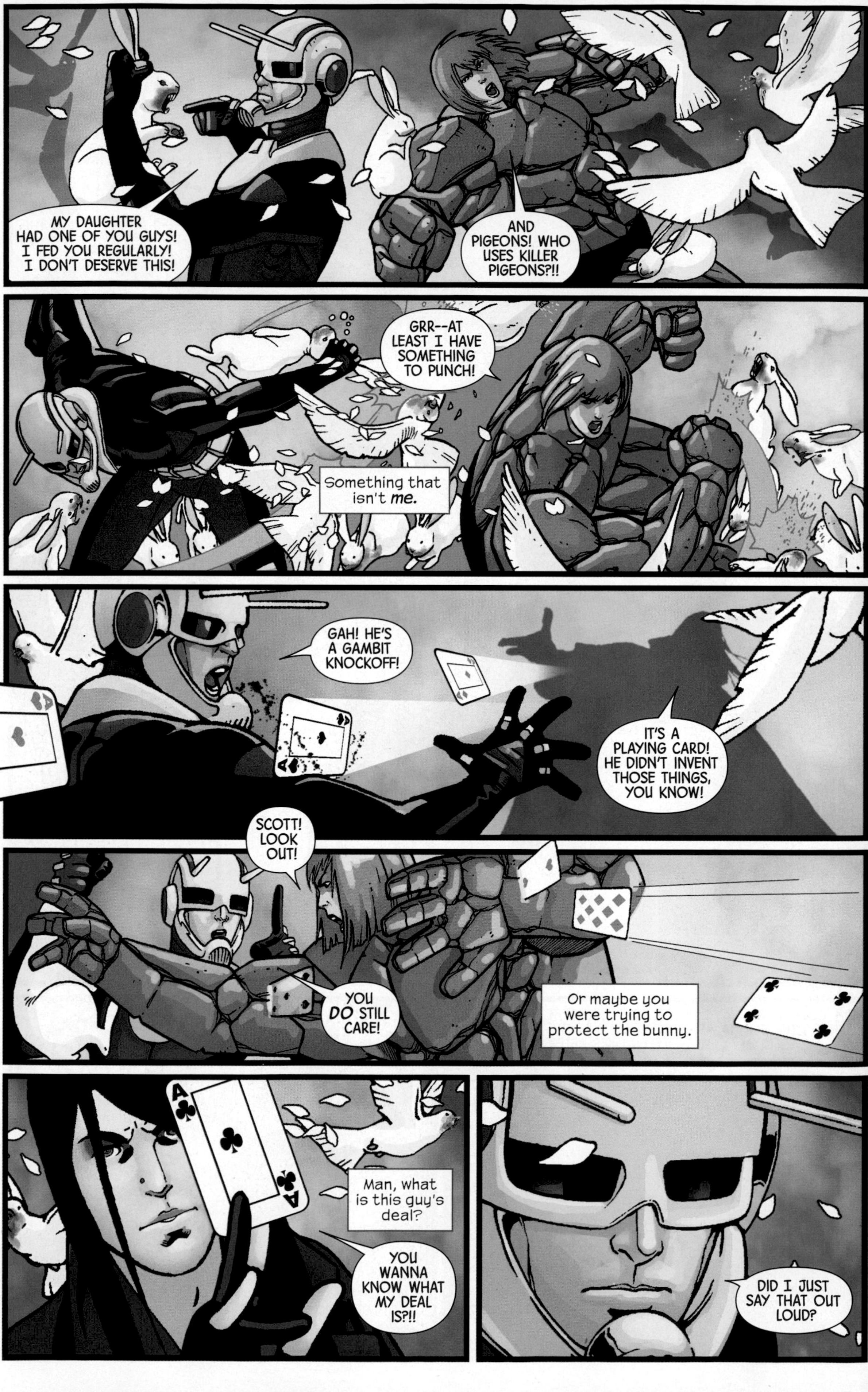
MY DAUGHTER HAD ONE OF YOU GUYS! I FED YOU REGULARLY! I DON'T DESERVE THIS!
AND PIGEONS! WHO USES KILLER PIGEONS?!!
GRR--AT LEAST I HAVE SOMETHING TO PUNCH!
Something that isn't *me.*
GAH! HE'S A GAMBIT KNOCKOFF!
IT'S A PLAYING CARD! HE DIDN'T INVENT THOSE THINGS, YOU KNOW!
SCOTT! LOOK OUT!
YOU **DO** STILL CARE!
Or maybe you were trying to protect the bunny.
Man, what is this guy's deal?
YOU WANNA KNOW WHAT MY DEAL IS?!!
DID I JUST SAY THAT OUT LOUD?

"MY FATHER WAS THE ORIGINAL MAGICIAN--WELL, THERE WERE MAGICIANS BEFORE HIM, HE DIDN'T INVENT--"

R HURRY, MY ED FRIEND ?? LIKE

GIANT-MAN.!! WHERE DID YOU COME FROM? WELL NO MATTER KNOW WHO I'LL KNO FIG

"IT DOESN'T MATTER! THE POINT IS, HE USED HIS SKILLS FOR CRIME, ROBBING THE WEALTHY DURING HIS SHOWS-- UNTIL HE WAS STOPPED BY YOUR PREDECESSOR, GIANT-MAN."

"NOT TECHNICALLY MY PREDECESSOR IF HE WAS GIANT-MAN AT THE TIME--"

"THAT DOESN'T MATTER EITHER!"

"HE ONLY STOLE TO MAKE ENDS MEET (AND TO IMPRESS WOMEN)-- BECAUSE HE ENCOUNTERED THE SAME ANTI-MAGICIAN PREJUDICE WE STILL FIGHT AGAINST TODAY!"

"IS THAT A THING?"

"OF COURSE IT'S A THING!"

"BUT GIANT-MAN DIDN'T CARE-- HE STILL PUT MY FATHER BEHIND BARS.

"BEFORE HE WENT AWAY, THOUGH, HE MADE ME PROMISE THAT I WOULD REDEEM THE FAMILY NAME-- AND CONTINUE THE MORTGAGE PAYMENTS-- THROUGH MAGIC!"

"AND SO I DEDICATED MY LIFE TO BECOMING THE MAGICIAN HE WOULD'VE BEEN PROUD OF!"

"AW NO, DID HE DIE IN PRISON?"

NO. MOVED TO TAMPA WITH SOME DANCER GIRL, YOUNGER THAN ME. NEW FAMILY NOW.

AND THIS SHOW WAS MY LAST SHOT AT REAL FAME! NOW DO YOU SEE WHY I'M SO ANGRY?!!

EH, A LITTLE BETTER ON THE MOTIVATION--STILL A BIT WEAK, BUT THE DADDY ISSUES DO HELP.

ONE THING, THOUGH-- SUPER VILLAINS DON'T REALLY DO THE WHOLE "STOP AND TELL YOUR SECRET ORIGIN" THING SO MUCH ANYMORE--

WHY NOT?

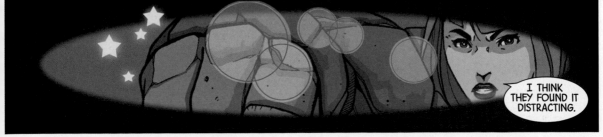

I THINK THEY FOUND IT DISTRACTING.

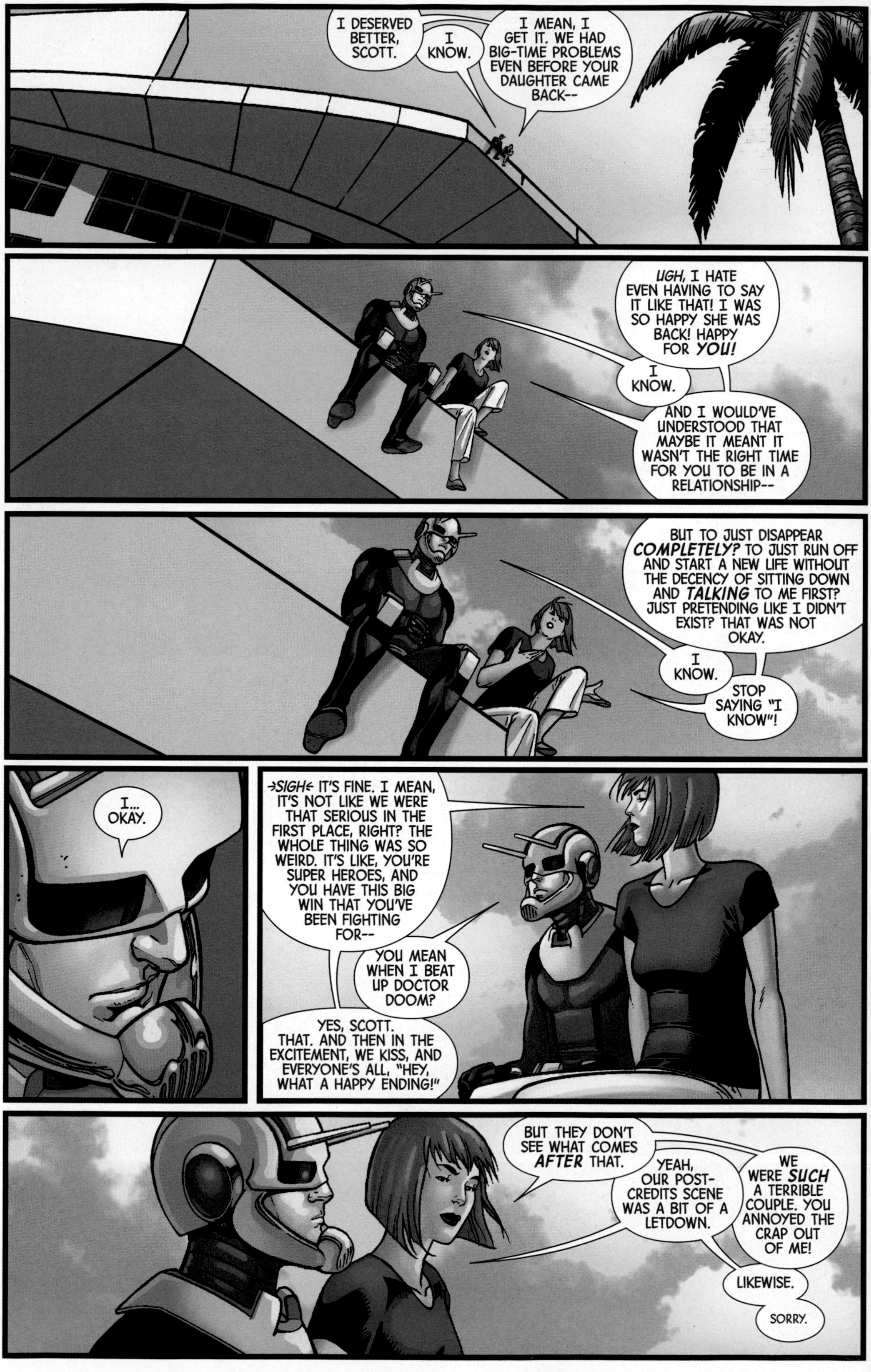
I DESERVED BETTER, SCOTT.
I KNOW.
I MEAN, I GET IT. WE HAD BIG-TIME PROBLEMS EVEN BEFORE YOUR DAUGHTER CAME BACK--
UGH, I HATE EVEN HAVING TO SAY IT LIKE THAT! I WAS SO HAPPY SHE WAS BACK! HAPPY FOR YOU!
I KNOW.
AND I WOULD'VE UNDERSTOOD THAT MAYBE IT MEANT IT WASN'T THE RIGHT TIME FOR YOU TO BE IN A RELATIONSHIP--
BUT TO JUST DISAPPEAR COMPLETELY? TO JUST RUN OFF AND START A NEW LIFE WITHOUT THE DECENCY OF SITTING DOWN AND TALKING TO ME FIRST? JUST PRETENDING LIKE I DIDN'T EXIST? THAT WAS NOT OKAY.
I KNOW.
STOP SAYING "I KNOW"!
I... OKAY.
›SIGH‹ IT'S FINE. I MEAN, IT'S NOT LIKE WE WERE THAT SERIOUS IN THE FIRST PLACE, RIGHT? THE WHOLE THING WAS SO WEIRD. IT'S LIKE, YOU'RE SUPER HEROES, AND YOU HAVE THIS BIG WIN THAT YOU'VE BEEN FIGHTING FOR--
YOU MEAN WHEN I BEAT UP DOCTOR DOOM?
YES, SCOTT. THAT. AND THEN IN THE EXCITEMENT, WE KISS, AND EVERYONE'S ALL, "HEY, WHAT A HAPPY ENDING!"
BUT THEY DON'T SEE WHAT COMES AFTER THAT.
YEAH, OUR POST-CREDITS SCENE WAS A BIT OF A LETDOWN.
WE WERE SUCH A TERRIBLE COUPLE. YOU ANNOYED THE CRAP OUT OF ME!
LIKEWISE.
SORRY.

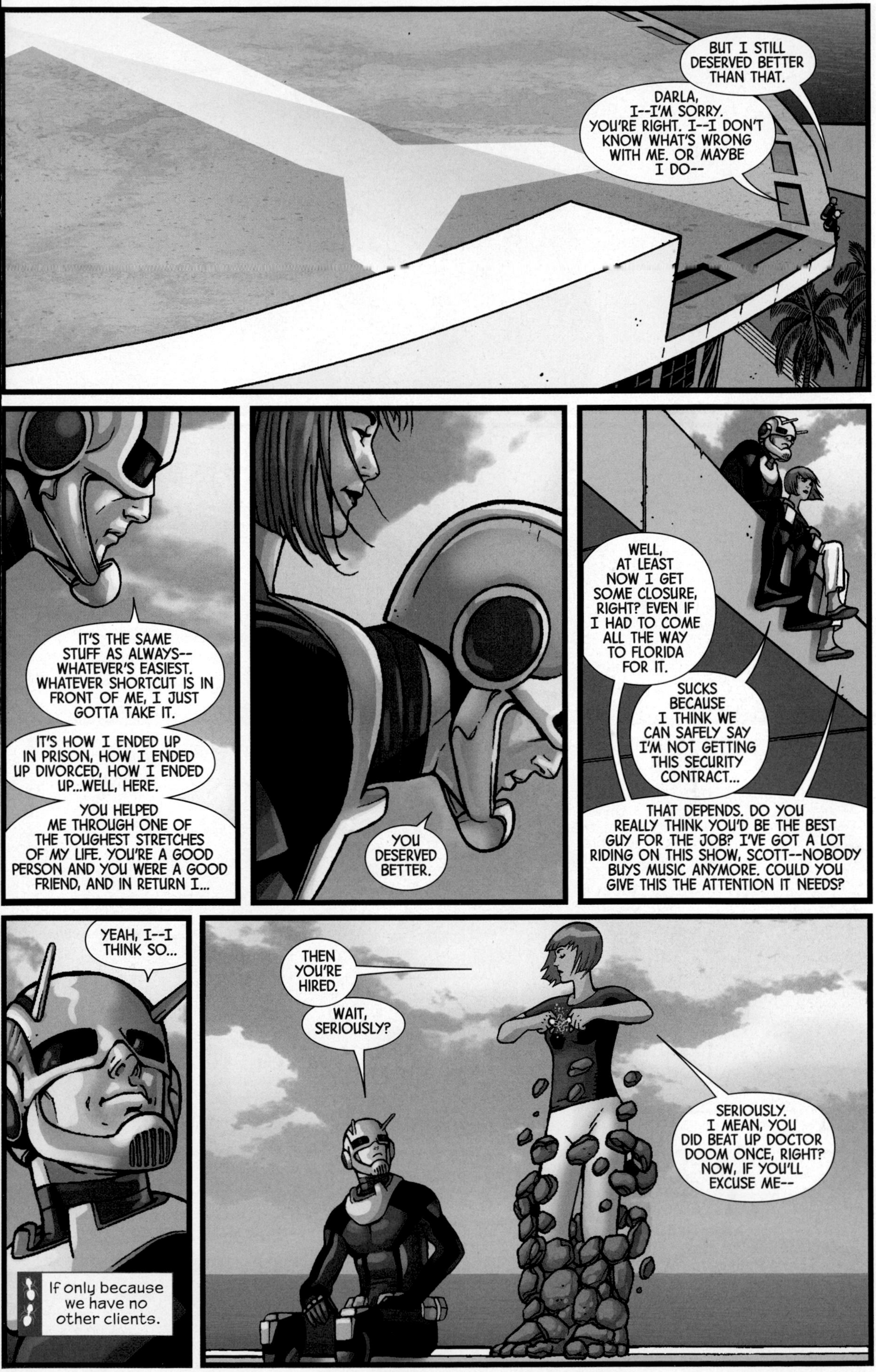
BUT I STILL DESERVED BETTER THAN THAT.
DARLA, I--I'M SORRY. YOU'RE RIGHT. I--I DON'T KNOW WHAT'S WRONG WITH ME. OR MAYBE I DO--
IT'S THE SAME STUFF AS ALWAYS-- WHATEVER'S EASIEST. WHATEVER SHORTCUT IS IN FRONT OF ME, I JUST GOTTA TAKE IT.
IT'S HOW I ENDED UP IN PRISON, HOW I ENDED UP DIVORCED, HOW I ENDED UP...WELL, HERE.
YOU HELPED ME THROUGH ONE OF THE TOUGHEST STRETCHES OF MY LIFE. YOU'RE A GOOD PERSON AND YOU WERE A GOOD FRIEND, AND IN RETURN I...
YOU DESERVED BETTER.
WELL, AT LEAST NOW I GET SOME CLOSURE, RIGHT? EVEN IF I HAD TO COME ALL THE WAY TO FLORIDA FOR IT.
SUCKS BECAUSE I THINK WE CAN SAFELY SAY I'M NOT GETTING THIS SECURITY CONTRACT...
THAT DEPENDS. DO YOU REALLY THINK YOU'D BE THE BEST GUY FOR THE JOB? I'VE GOT A LOT RIDING ON THIS SHOW, SCOTT--NOBODY BUYS MUSIC ANYMORE. COULD YOU GIVE THIS THE ATTENTION IT NEEDS?
YEAH, I--I THINK SO...
If only because we have no other clients.
THEN YOU'RE HIRED.
WAIT, SERIOUSLY?
SERIOUSLY. I MEAN, YOU DID BEAT UP DOCTOR DOOM ONCE, RIGHT? NOW, IF YOU'LL EXCUSE ME--

--I'M GONNA GO FIRE MY PUBLICIST.

PROBABLY A GOOD IDEA.

BE SEEING YOU, SCOTT--

TRY NOT TO SCREW IT UP THIS TIME.

Wow, that was nice of her. And it means things actually worked out for me in the end!

So why do I feel so terrible? Oh, right--

It's because when I think about the people I've really cared about in my life--

--no matter what I do--

--I just end up being a huge disappointment.

Maybe the reason I end up in such bad spots isn't because I'm too trusting.

Maybe the real problem is other people being dumb enough to trust me.

Then again--

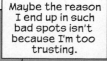

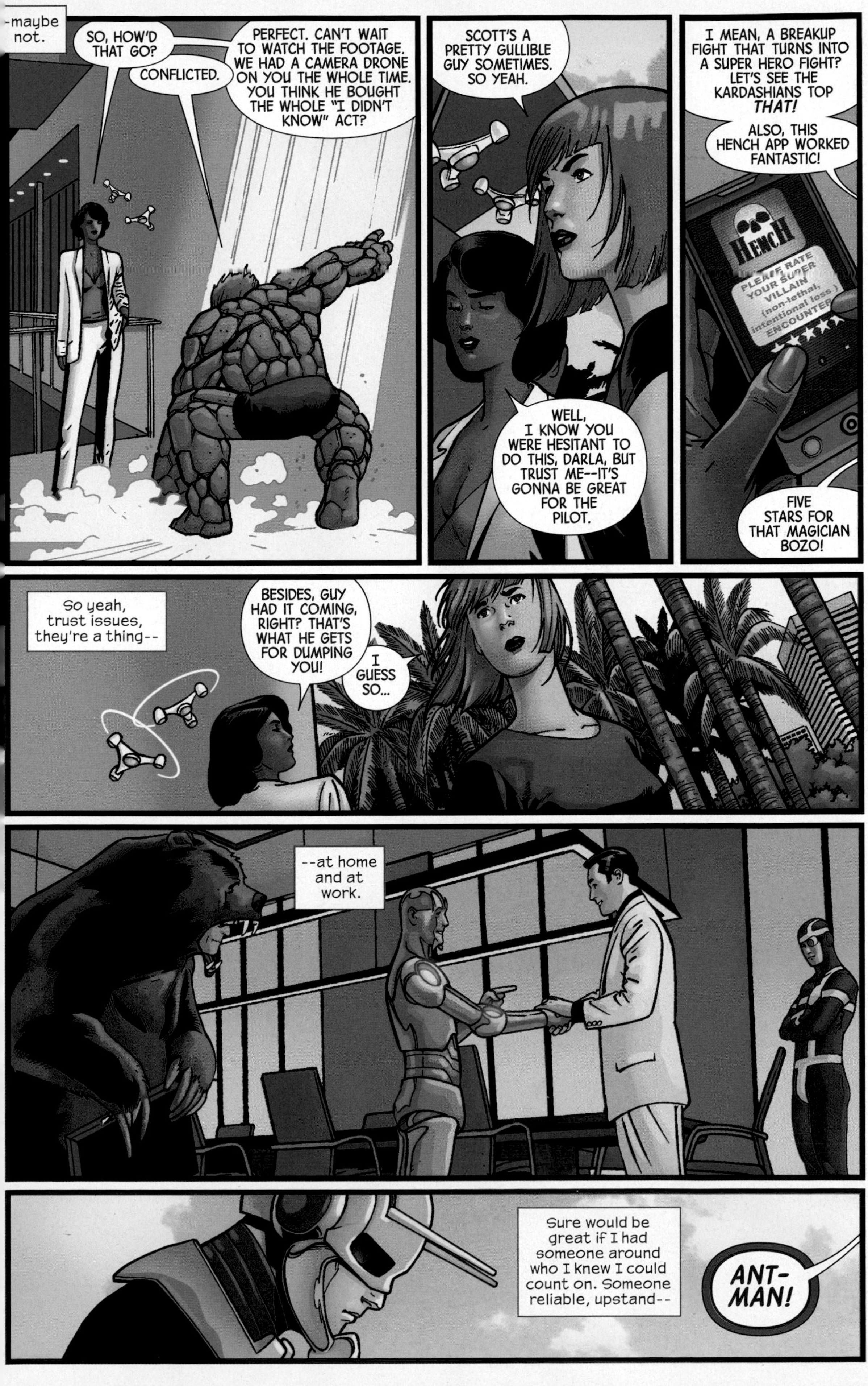
-maybe not.
SO, HOW'D THAT GO?
CONFLICTED.
PERFECT. CAN'T WAIT TO WATCH THE FOOTAGE. WE HAD A CAMERA DRONE ON YOU THE WHOLE TIME. YOU THINK HE BOUGHT THE WHOLE "I DIDN'T KNOW" ACT?
SCOTT'S A PRETTY GULLIBLE GUY SOMETIMES. SO YEAH.
WELL, I KNOW YOU WERE HESITANT TO DO THIS, DARLA, BUT TRUST ME--IT'S GONNA BE GREAT FOR THE PILOT.
I MEAN, A BREAKUP FIGHT THAT TURNS INTO A SUPER HERO FIGHT? LET'S SEE THE KARDASHIANS TOP *THAT!*
ALSO, THIS HENCH APP WORKED FANTASTIC!
HENCH
PLEASE RATE YOUR SUPER VILLAIN (non-lethal, intentional loss) ENCOUNTER
FIVE STARS FOR THAT MAGICIAN BOZO!
So yeah, trust issues, they're a thing--
BESIDES, GUY HAD IT COMING, RIGHT? THAT'S WHAT HE GETS FOR DUMPING YOU!
I GUESS SO...
--at home and at work.
Sure would be great if I had someone around who I knew I could count on. Someone reliable, upstand--
ANT-MAN!

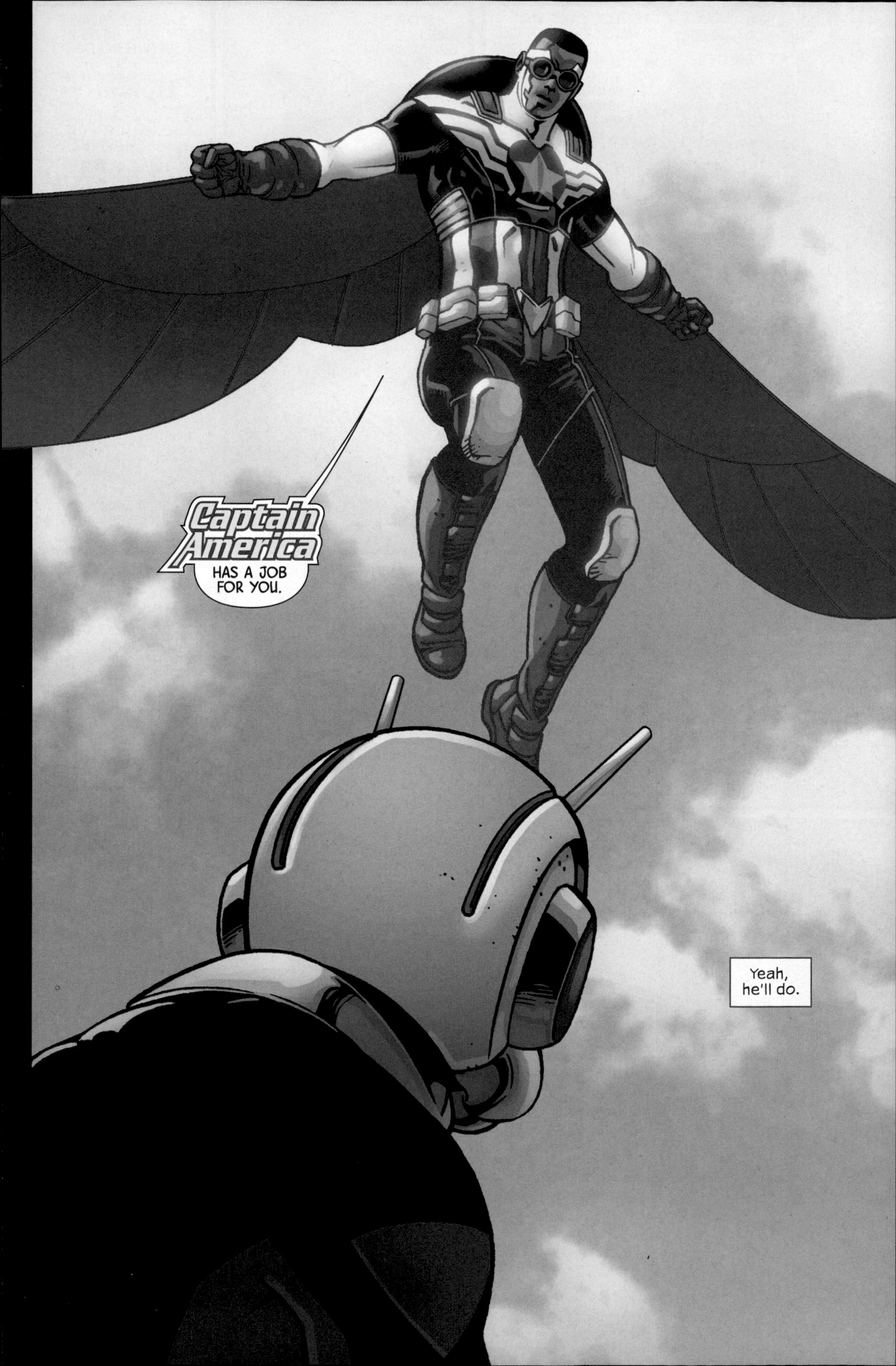
Captain America
HAS A JOB FOR YOU.
Yeah, he'll do.

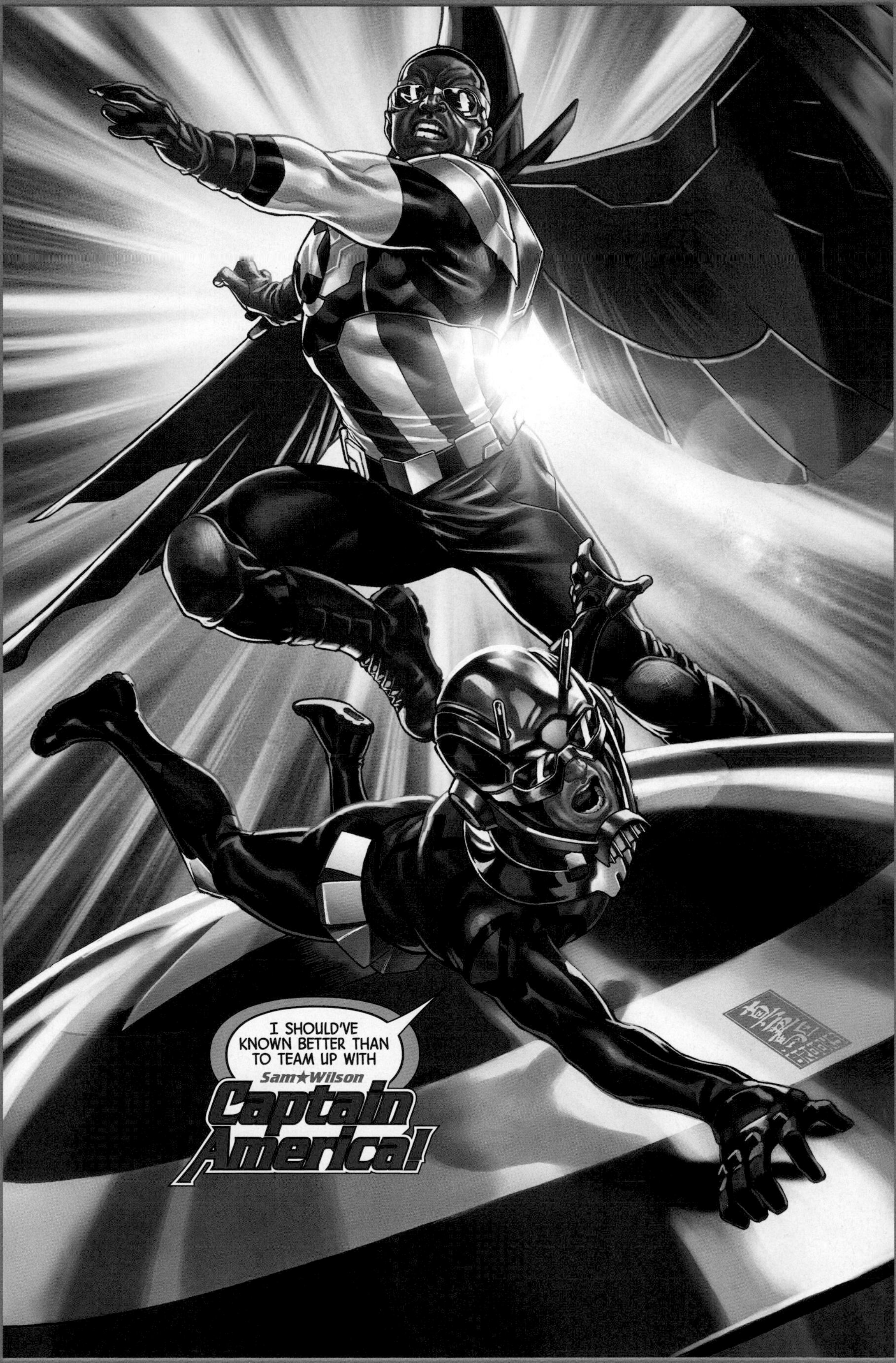
I SHOULD'VE KNOWN BETTER THAN TO TEAM UP WITH
Sam★Wilson
Captain America!

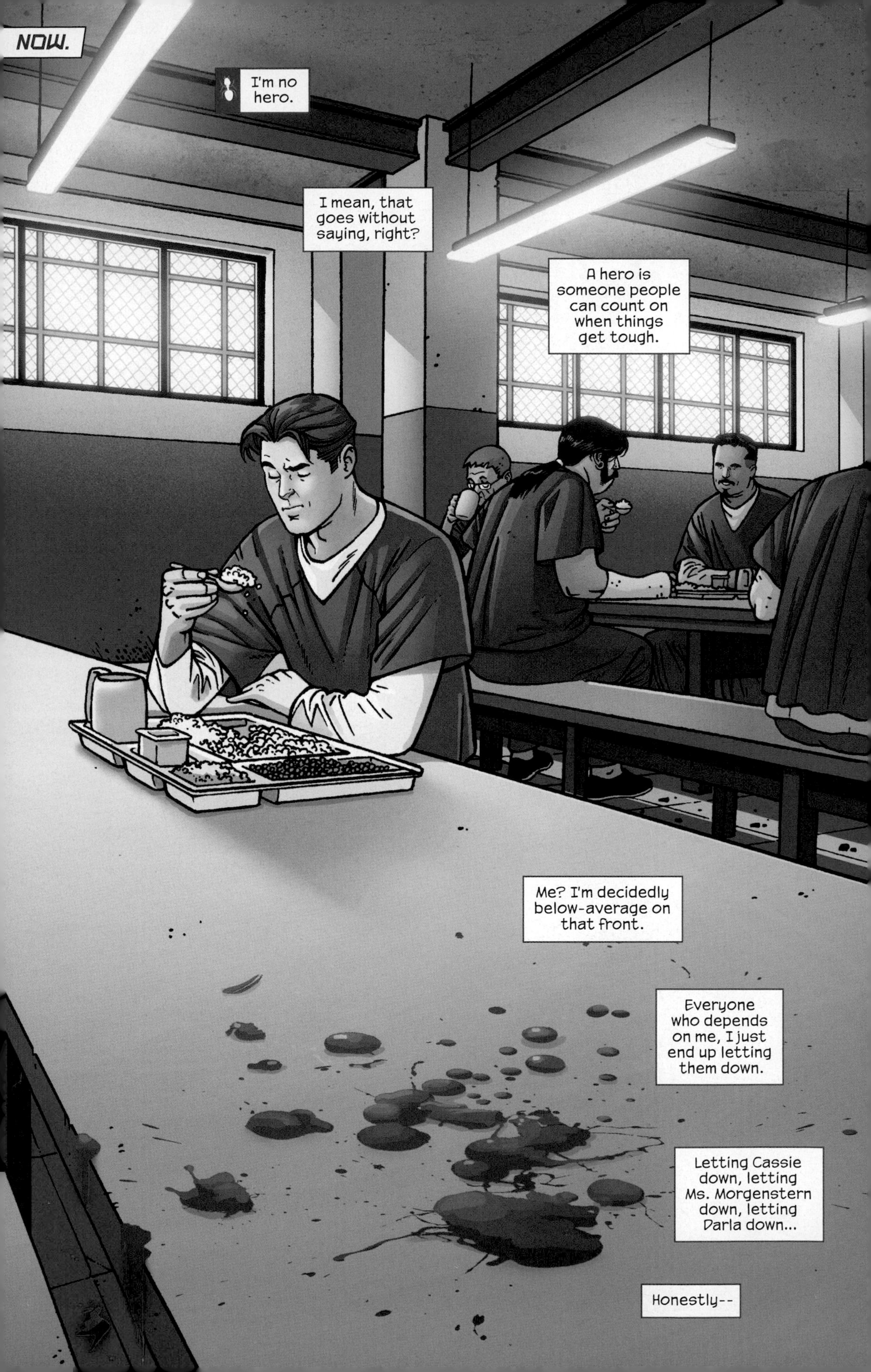
NOW.
I'm no hero.
I mean, that goes without saying, right?
A hero is someone people can count on when things get tough.
Me? I'm decidedly below-average on that front.
Everyone who depends on me, I just end up letting them down.
Letting Cassie down, letting Ms. Morgenstern down, letting Darla down...
Honestly--

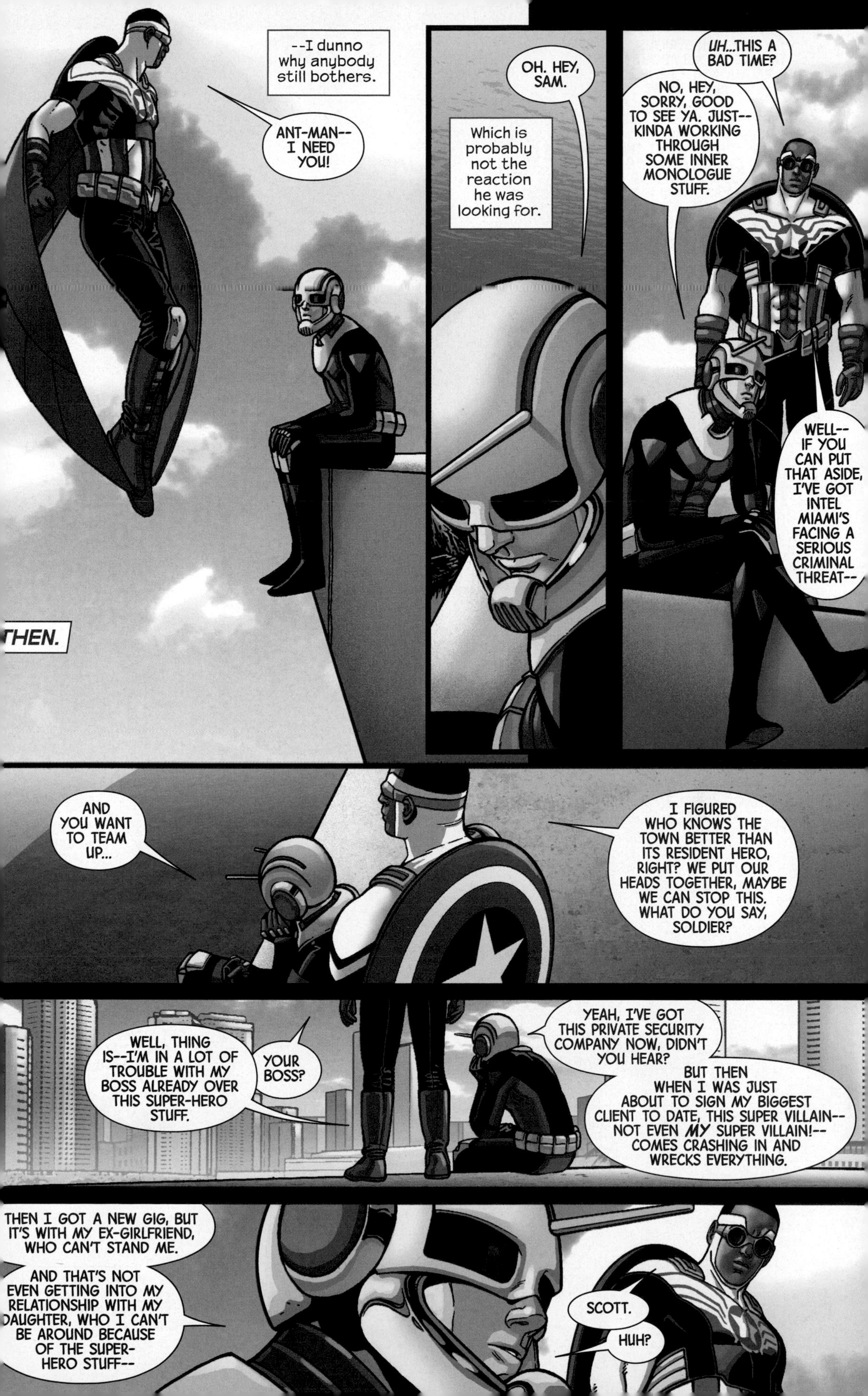

--I dunno why anybody still bothers.
ANT-MAN-- I NEED YOU!
THEN.
OH. HEY, SAM.
Which is probably not the reaction he was looking for.
UH...THIS A BAD TIME?
NO, HEY, SORRY, GOOD TO SEE YA. JUST-- KINDA WORKING THROUGH SOME INNER MONOLOGUE STUFF.
WELL-- IF YOU CAN PUT THAT ASIDE, I'VE GOT INTEL MIAMI'S FACING A SERIOUS CRIMINAL THREAT--
AND YOU WANT TO TEAM UP...
I FIGURED WHO KNOWS THE TOWN BETTER THAN ITS RESIDENT HERO, RIGHT? WE PUT OUR HEADS TOGETHER, MAYBE WE CAN STOP THIS. WHAT DO YOU SAY, SOLDIER?
WELL, THING IS--I'M IN A LOT OF TROUBLE WITH MY BOSS ALREADY OVER THIS SUPER-HERO STUFF.
YOUR BOSS?
YEAH, I'VE GOT THIS PRIVATE SECURITY COMPANY NOW, DIDN'T YOU HEAR?
BUT THEN WHEN I WAS JUST ABOUT TO SIGN MY BIGGEST CLIENT TO DATE, THIS SUPER VILLAIN-- NOT EVEN MY SUPER VILLAIN!-- COMES CRASHING IN AND WRECKS EVERYTHING.
THEN I GOT A NEW GIG, BUT IT'S WITH MY EX-GIRLFRIEND, WHO CAN'T STAND ME.
AND THAT'S NOT EVEN GETTING INTO MY RELATIONSHIP WITH MY DAUGHTER, WHO I CAN'T BE AROUND BECAUSE OF THE SUPER-HERO STUFF--
SCOTT.
HUH?

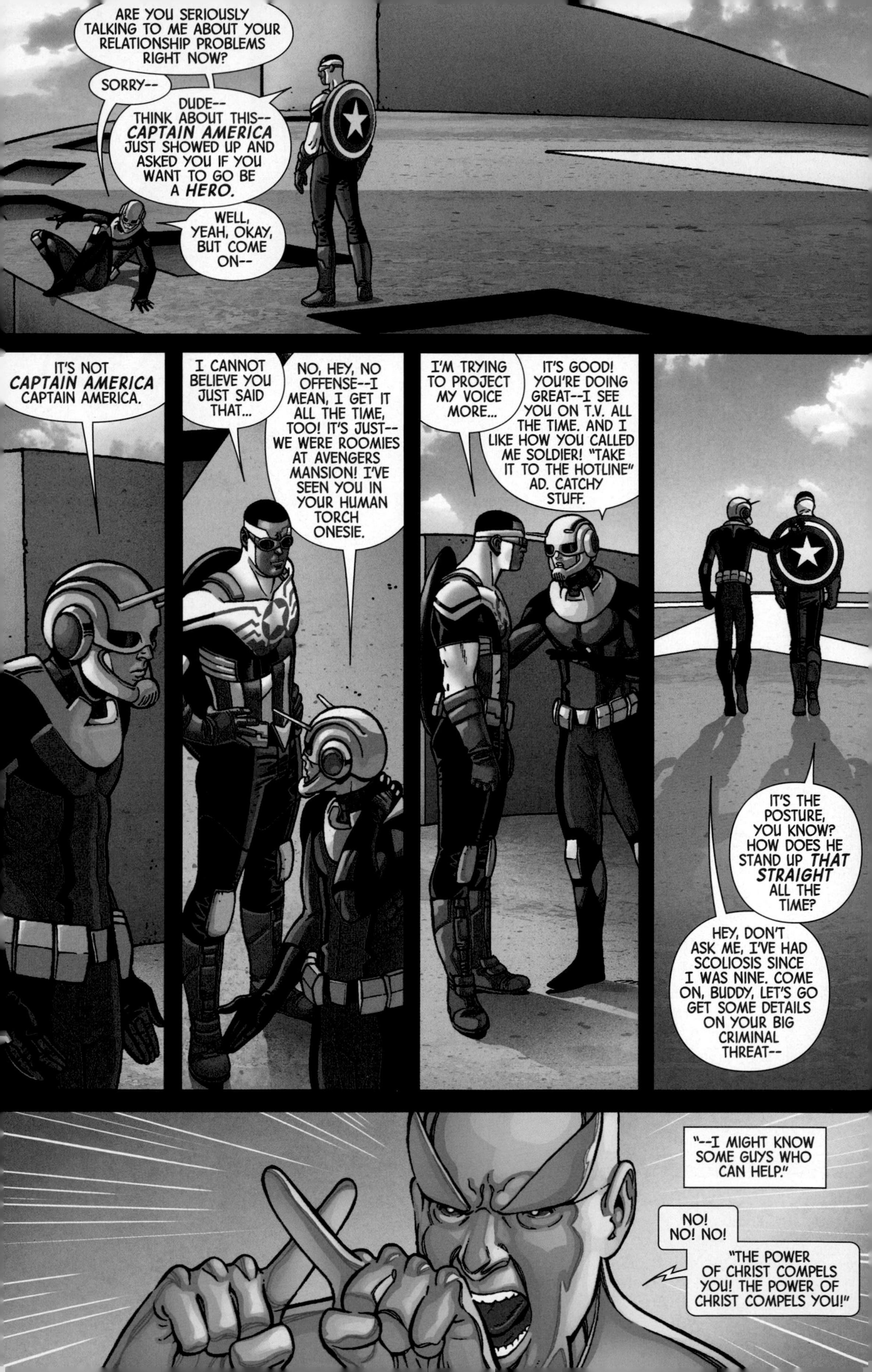
ARE YOU SERIOUSLY TALKING TO ME ABOUT YOUR RELATIONSHIP PROBLEMS RIGHT NOW?
SORRY--
DUDE-- THINK ABOUT THIS-- CAPTAIN AMERICA JUST SHOWED UP AND ASKED YOU IF YOU WANT TO GO BE A HERO.
WELL, YEAH, OKAY, BUT COME ON--
IT'S NOT CAPTAIN AMERICA CAPTAIN AMERICA.
I CANNOT BELIEVE YOU JUST SAID THAT...
NO, HEY, NO OFFENSE--I MEAN, I GET IT ALL THE TIME, TOO! IT'S JUST-- WE WERE ROOMIES AT AVENGERS MANSION! I'VE SEEN YOU IN YOUR HUMAN TORCH ONESIE.
I'M TRYING TO PROJECT MY VOICE MORE...
IT'S GOOD! YOU'RE DOING GREAT--I SEE YOU ON T.V. ALL THE TIME. AND I LIKE HOW YOU CALLED ME SOLDIER! "TAKE IT TO THE HOTLINE" AD. CATCHY STUFF.
IT'S THE POSTURE, YOU KNOW? HOW DOES HE STAND UP THAT STRAIGHT ALL THE TIME?
HEY, DON'T ASK ME, I'VE HAD SCOLIOSIS SINCE I WAS NINE. COME ON, BUDDY, LET'S GO GET SOME DETAILS ON YOUR BIG CRIMINAL THREAT--
"--I MIGHT KNOW SOME GUYS WHO CAN HELP."
NO! NO! NO!
"THE POWER OF CHRIST COMPELS YOU! THE POWER OF CHRIST COMPELS YOU!"

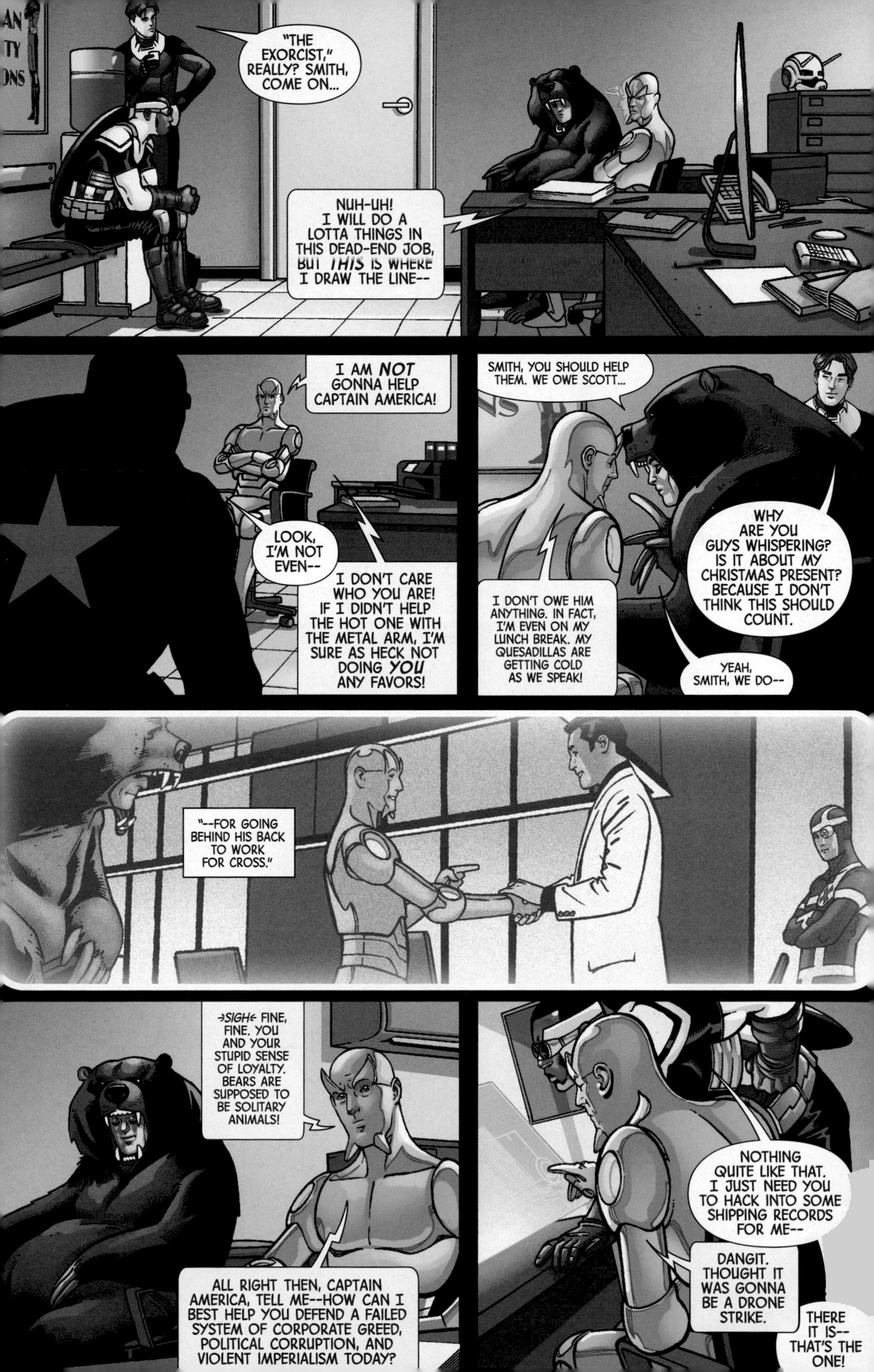

"THE EXORCIST," REALLY? SMITH, COME ON...
NUH-UH! I WILL DO A LOTTA THINGS IN THIS DEAD-END JOB, BUT THIS IS WHERE I DRAW THE LINE--
I AM NOT GONNA HELP CAPTAIN AMERICA!
LOOK, I'M NOT EVEN--
I DON'T CARE WHO YOU ARE! IF I DIDN'T HELP THE HOT ONE WITH THE METAL ARM, I'M SURE AS HECK NOT DOING YOU ANY FAVORS!
SMITH, YOU SHOULD HELP THEM. WE OWE SCOTT...
I DON'T OWE HIM ANYTHING. IN FACT, I'M EVEN ON MY LUNCH BREAK. MY QUESADILLAS ARE GETTING COLD AS WE SPEAK!
WHY ARE YOU GUYS WHISPERING? IS IT ABOUT MY CHRISTMAS PRESENT? BECAUSE I DON'T THINK THIS SHOULD COUNT.
YEAH, SMITH, WE DO--
"--FOR GOING BEHIND HIS BACK TO WORK FOR CROSS."
›SIGH‹ FINE, FINE. YOU AND YOUR STUPID SENSE OF LOYALTY. BEARS ARE SUPPOSED TO BE SOLITARY ANIMALS!
ALL RIGHT THEN, CAPTAIN AMERICA, TELL ME--HOW CAN I BEST HELP YOU DEFEND A FAILED SYSTEM OF CORPORATE GREED, POLITICAL CORRUPTION, AND VIOLENT IMPERIALISM TODAY?
NOTHING QUITE LIKE THAT. I JUST NEED YOU TO HACK INTO SOME SHIPPING RECORDS FOR ME--
DANGIT. THOUGHT IT WAS GONNA BE A DRONE STRIKE.
THERE IT IS-- THAT'S THE ONE!

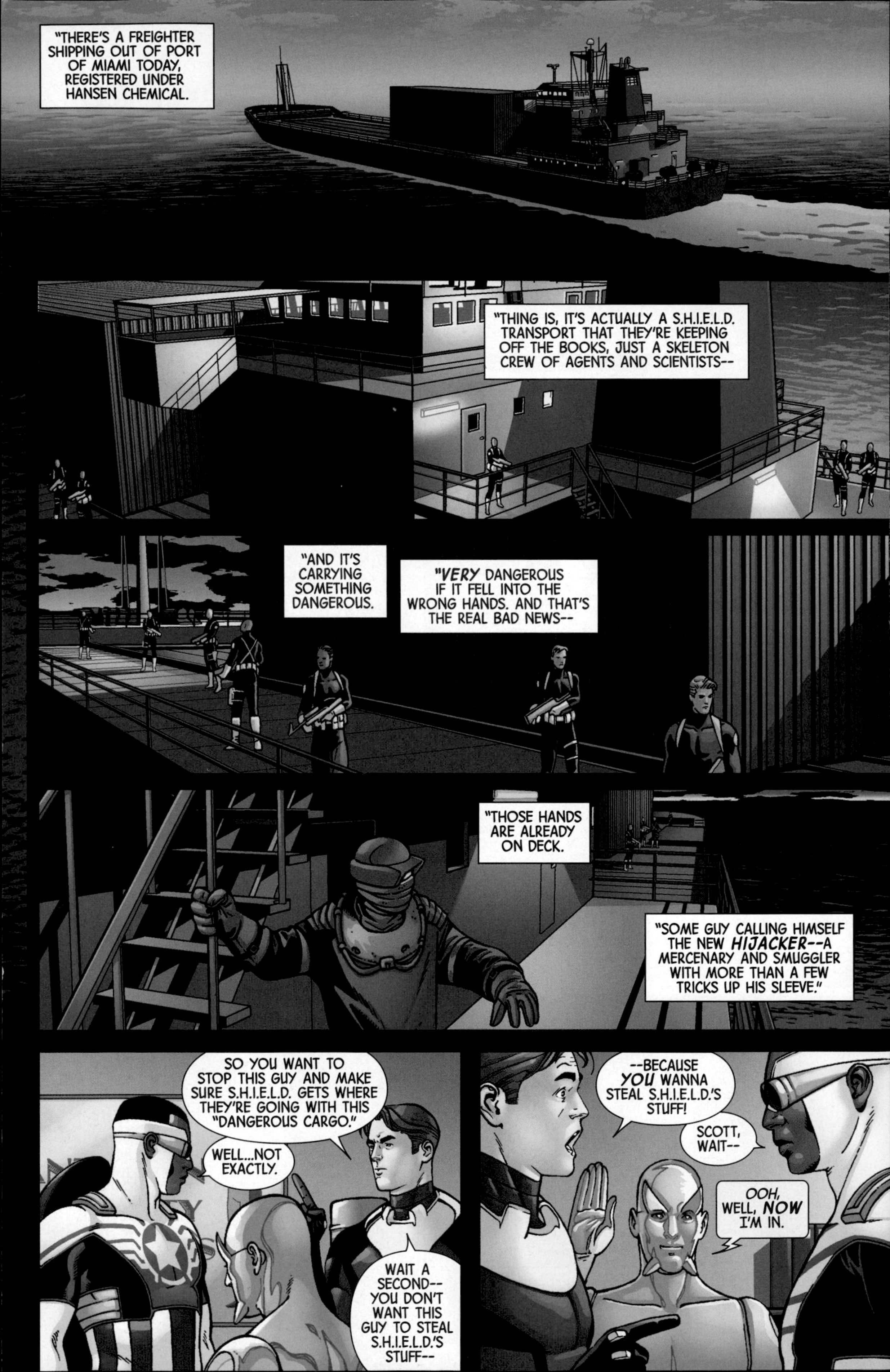
"THERE'S A FREIGHTER SHIPPING OUT OF PORT OF MIAMI TODAY, REGISTERED UNDER HANSEN CHEMICAL.
"THING IS, IT'S ACTUALLY A S.H.I.E.L.D. TRANSPORT THAT THEY'RE KEEPING OFF THE BOOKS, JUST A SKELETON CREW OF AGENTS AND SCIENTISTS--
"AND IT'S CARRYING SOMETHING DANGEROUS.
"VERY DANGEROUS IF IT FELL INTO THE WRONG HANDS. AND THAT'S THE REAL BAD NEWS--
"THOSE HANDS ARE ALREADY ON DECK.
"SOME GUY CALLING HIMSELF THE NEW HIJACKER--A MERCENARY AND SMUGGLER WITH MORE THAN A FEW TRICKS UP HIS SLEEVE."
SO YOU WANT TO STOP THIS GUY AND MAKE SURE S.H.I.E.L.D. GETS WHERE THEY'RE GOING WITH THIS "DANGEROUS CARGO."
WELL...NOT EXACTLY.
WAIT A SECOND-- YOU DON'T WANT THIS GUY TO STEAL S.H.I.E.L.D.'S STUFF--
--BECAUSE YOU WANNA STEAL S.H.I.E.L.D.'S STUFF!
SCOTT, WAIT--
OOH, WELL, NOW I'M IN.

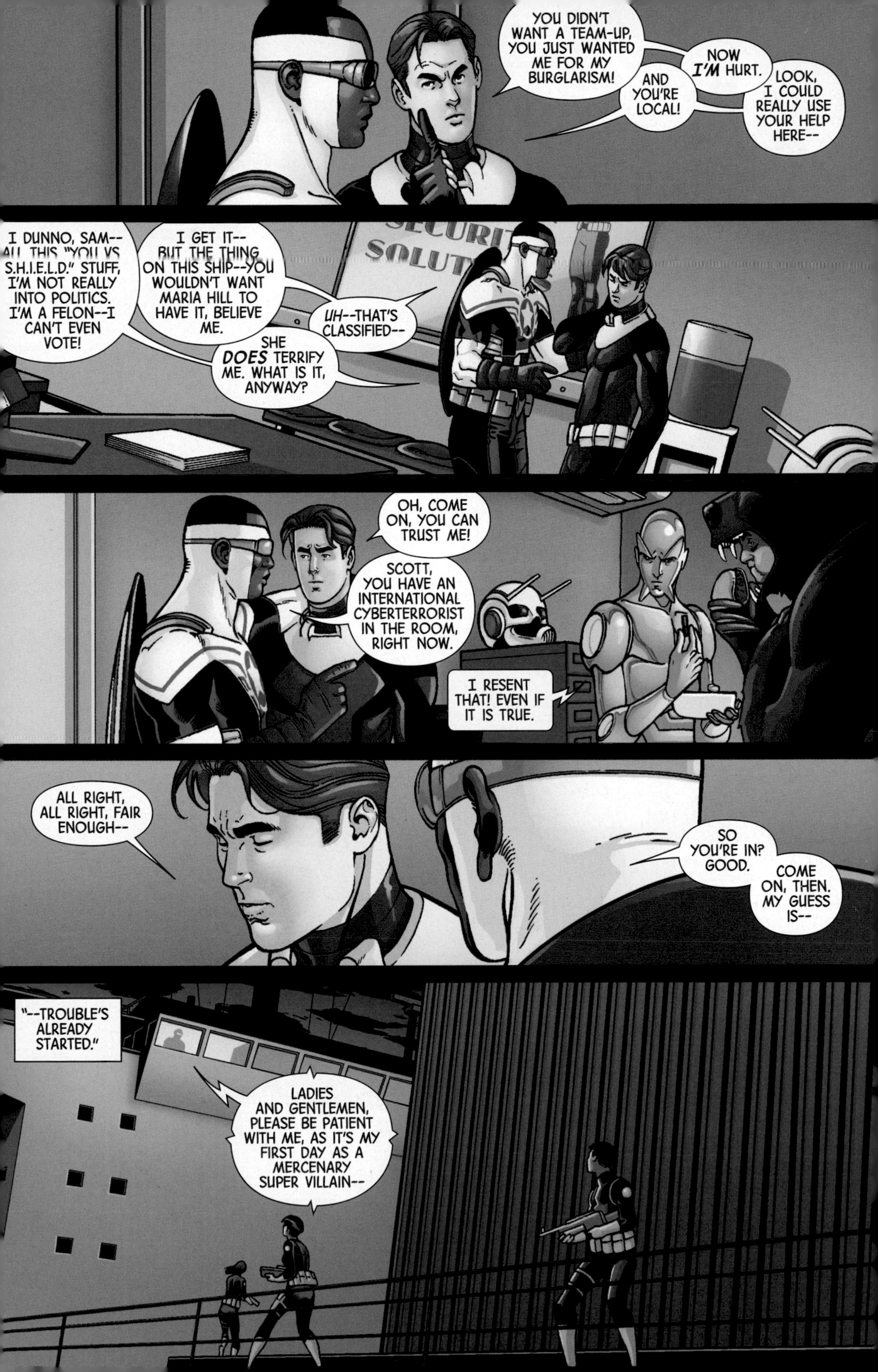
YOU DIDN'T WANT A TEAM-UP, YOU JUST WANTED ME FOR MY BURGLARISM!
NOW I'M HURT.
AND YOU'RE LOCAL!
LOOK, I COULD REALLY USE YOUR HELP HERE--
I DUNNO, SAM-- ALL THIS "YOU VS S.H.I.E.L.D." STUFF, I'M NOT REALLY INTO POLITICS. I'M A FELON--I CAN'T EVEN VOTE!
I GET IT-- BUT THE THING ON THIS SHIP--YOU WOULDN'T WANT MARIA HILL TO HAVE IT, BELIEVE ME.
SHE DOES TERRIFY ME. WHAT IS IT, ANYWAY?
UH--THAT'S CLASSIFIED--
OH, COME ON, YOU CAN TRUST ME!
SCOTT, YOU HAVE AN INTERNATIONAL CYBERTERRORIST IN THE ROOM, RIGHT NOW.
I RESENT THAT! EVEN IF IT IS TRUE.
ALL RIGHT, ALL RIGHT, FAIR ENOUGH--
SO YOU'RE IN? GOOD.
COME ON, THEN. MY GUESS IS--
"--TROUBLE'S ALREADY STARTED."
LADIES AND GENTLEMEN, PLEASE BE PATIENT WITH ME, AS IT'S MY FIRST DAY AS A MERCENARY SUPER VILLAIN--

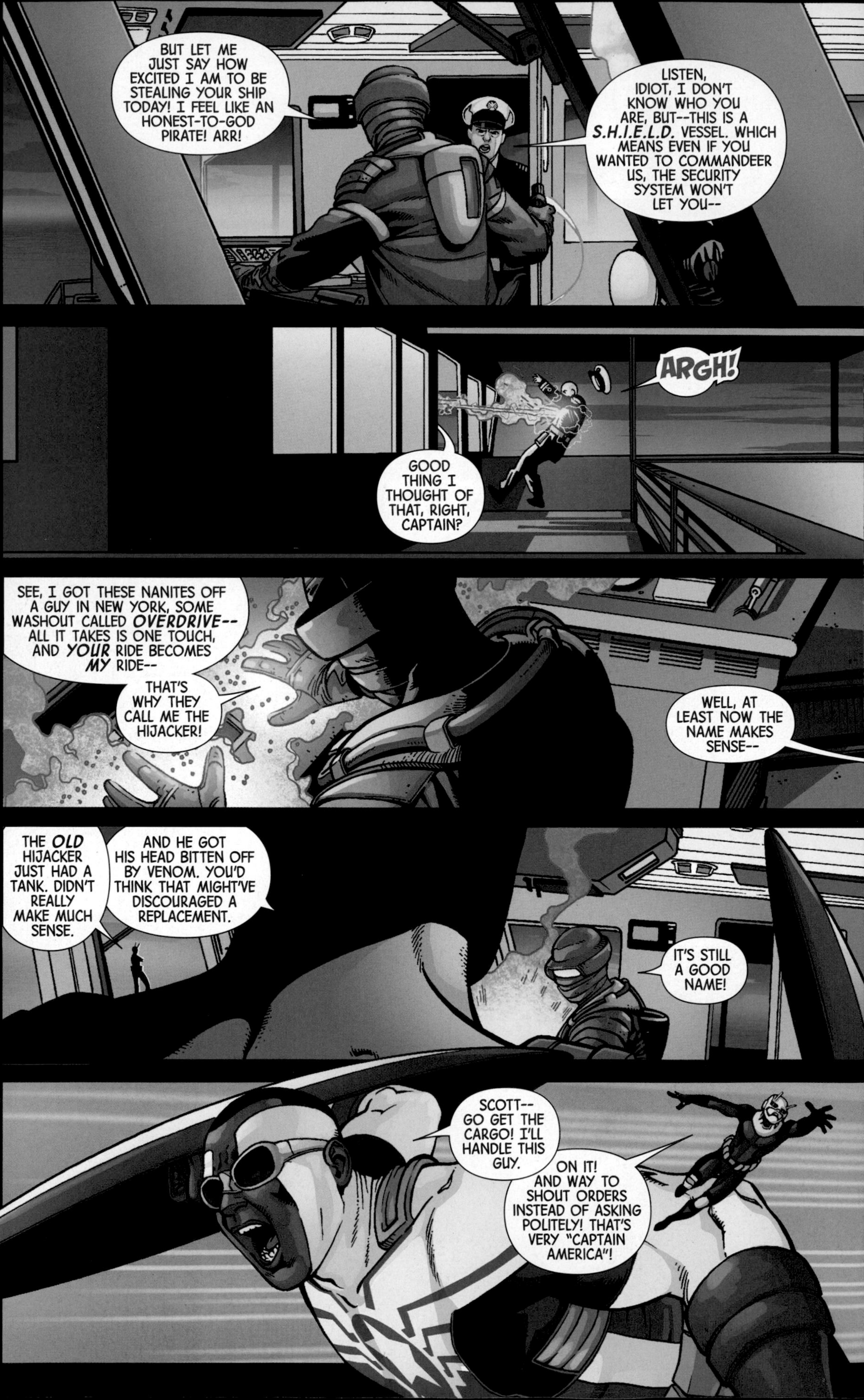

BUT LET ME JUST SAY HOW EXCITED I AM TO BE STEALING YOUR SHIP TODAY! I FEEL LIKE AN HONEST-TO-GOD PIRATE! ARR!
LISTEN, IDIOT, I DON'T KNOW WHO YOU ARE, BUT--THIS IS A *S.H.I.E.L.D.* VESSEL. WHICH MEANS EVEN IF YOU WANTED TO COMMANDEER US, THE SECURITY SYSTEM WON'T LET YOU--
ARGH!
GOOD THING I THOUGHT OF THAT, RIGHT, CAPTAIN?
SEE, I GOT THESE NANITES OFF A GUY IN NEW YORK, SOME WASHOUT CALLED *OVERDRIVE--* ALL IT TAKES IS ONE TOUCH, AND *YOUR* RIDE BECOMES *MY* RIDE--
THAT'S WHY THEY CALL ME THE HIJACKER!
WELL, AT LEAST NOW THE NAME MAKES SENSE--
THE *OLD* HIJACKER JUST HAD A TANK. DIDN'T REALLY MAKE MUCH SENSE.
AND HE GOT HIS HEAD BITTEN OFF BY VENOM. YOU'D THINK THAT MIGHT'VE DISCOURAGED A REPLACEMENT.
IT'S STILL A GOOD NAME!
SCOTT-- GO GET THE CARGO! I'LL HANDLE THIS GUY.
ON IT! AND WAY TO SHOUT ORDERS INSTEAD OF ASKING POLITELY! THAT'S VERY "CAPTAIN AMERICA"!

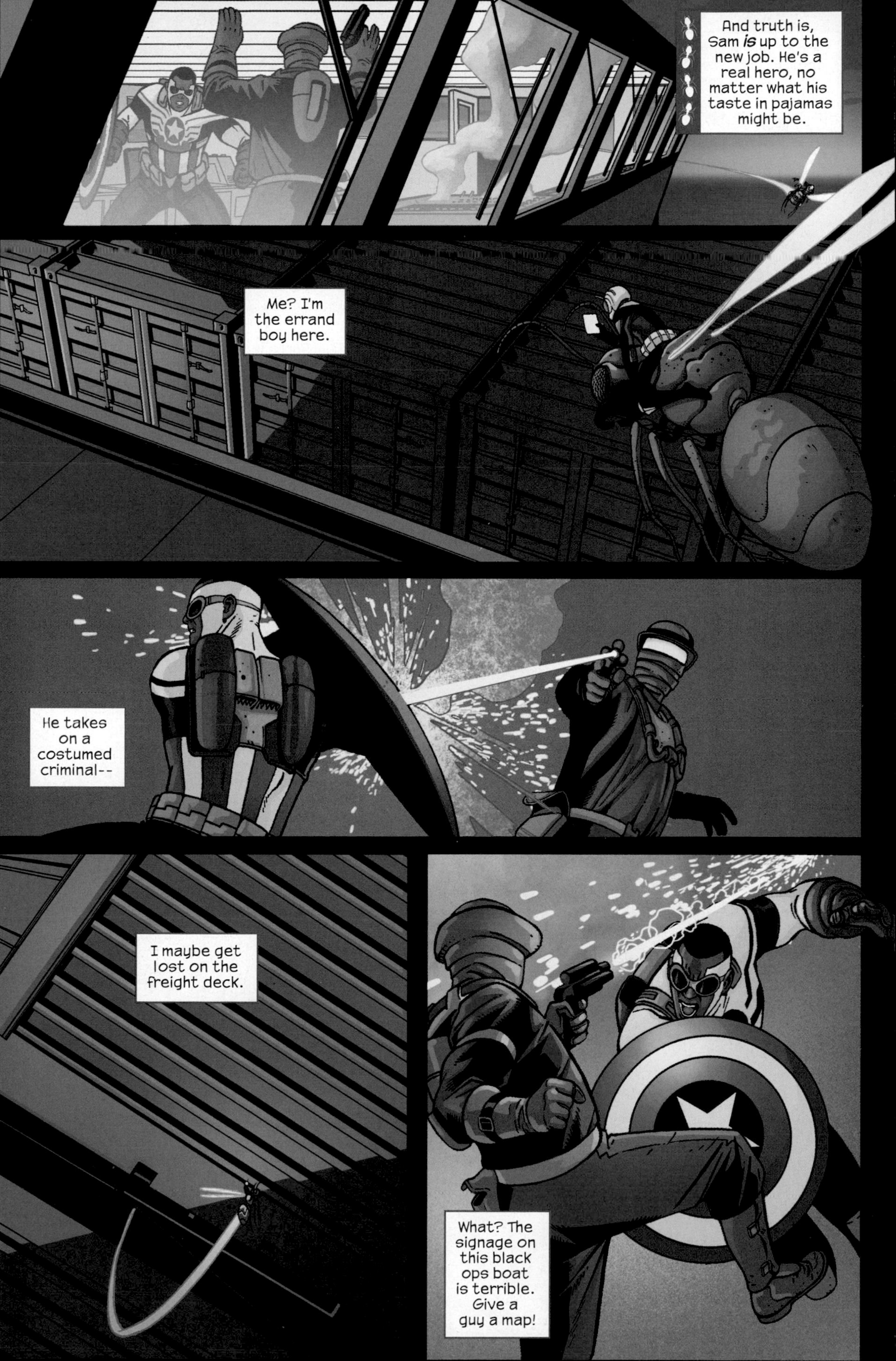
And truth is, Sam *is* up to the new job. He's a real hero, no matter what his taste in pajamas might be.
Me? I'm the errand boy here.
He takes on a costumed criminal--
I maybe get lost on the freight deck.
What? The signage on this black ops boat is terrible. Give a guy a map!

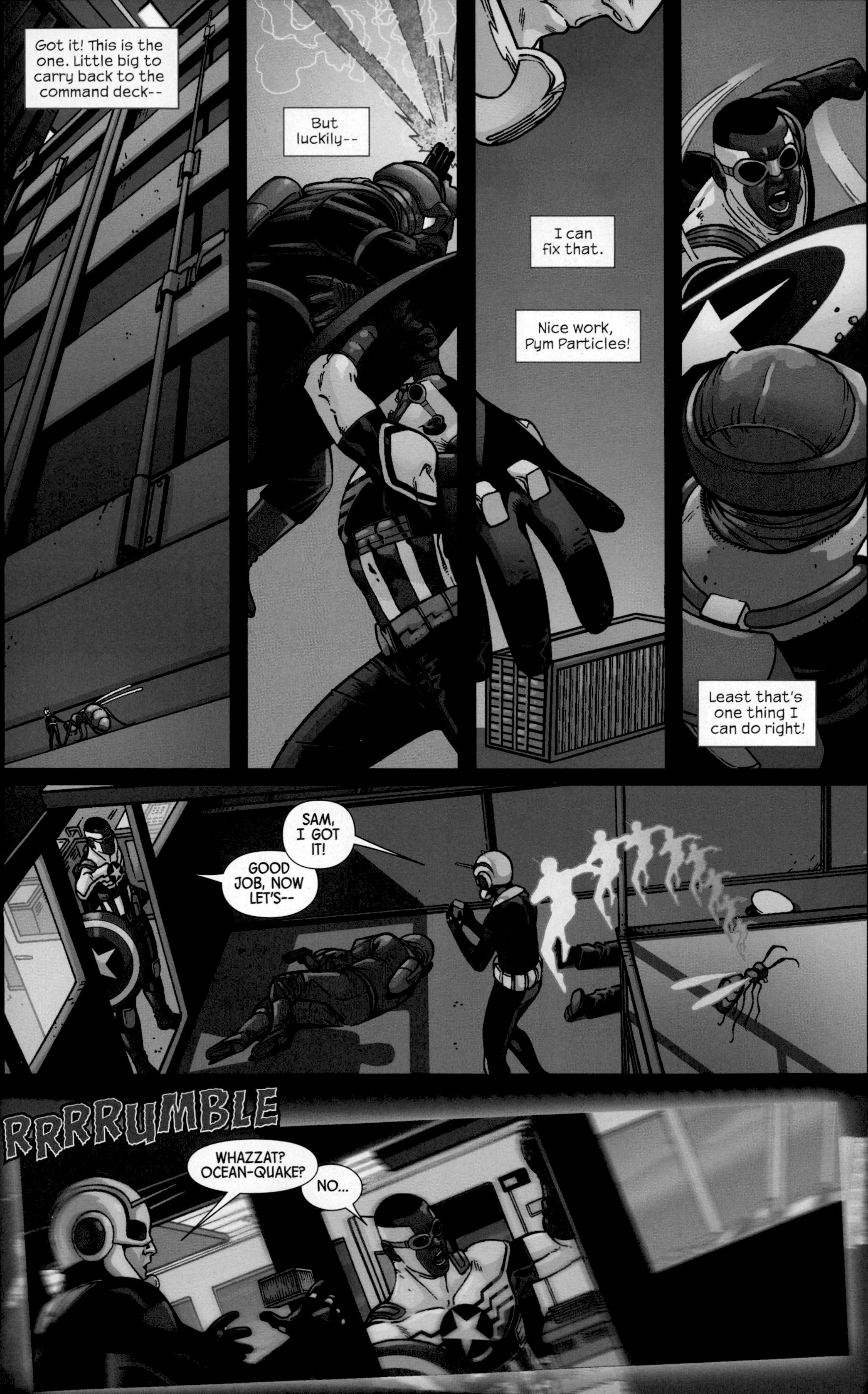
Got it! This is the one. Little big to carry back to the command deck--
But luckily--
I can fix that.
Nice work, Pym Particles!
Least that's one thing I can do right!
SAM, I GOT IT!
GOOD JOB, NOW LET'S--
RRRRUMBLE
WHAZZAT? OCEAN-QUAKE?
NO...

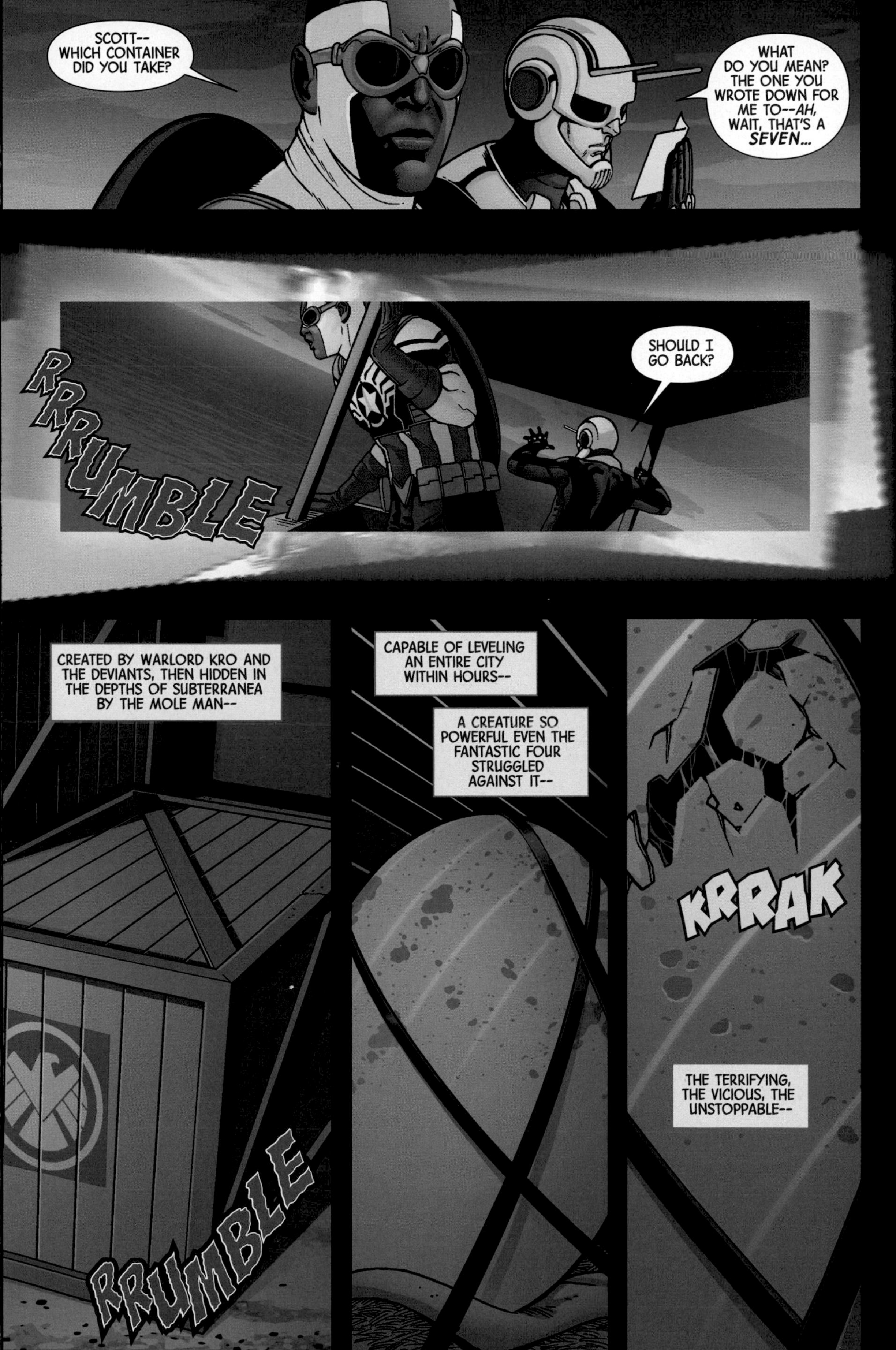
SCOTT-- WHICH CONTAINER DID YOU TAKE?
WHAT DO YOU MEAN? THE ONE YOU WROTE DOWN FOR ME TO--AH, WAIT, THAT'S A SEVEN...
RRRUMBLE
SHOULD I GO BACK?
CREATED BY WARLORD KRO AND THE DEVIANTS, THEN HIDDEN IN THE DEPTHS OF SUBTERRANEA BY THE MOLE MAN--
RRUMBLE
CAPABLE OF LEVELING AN ENTIRE CITY WITHIN HOURS--
A CREATURE SO POWERFUL EVEN THE FANTASTIC FOUR STRUGGLED AGAINST IT--
KRRAK
THE TERRIFYING, THE VICIOUS, THE UNSTOPPABLE--

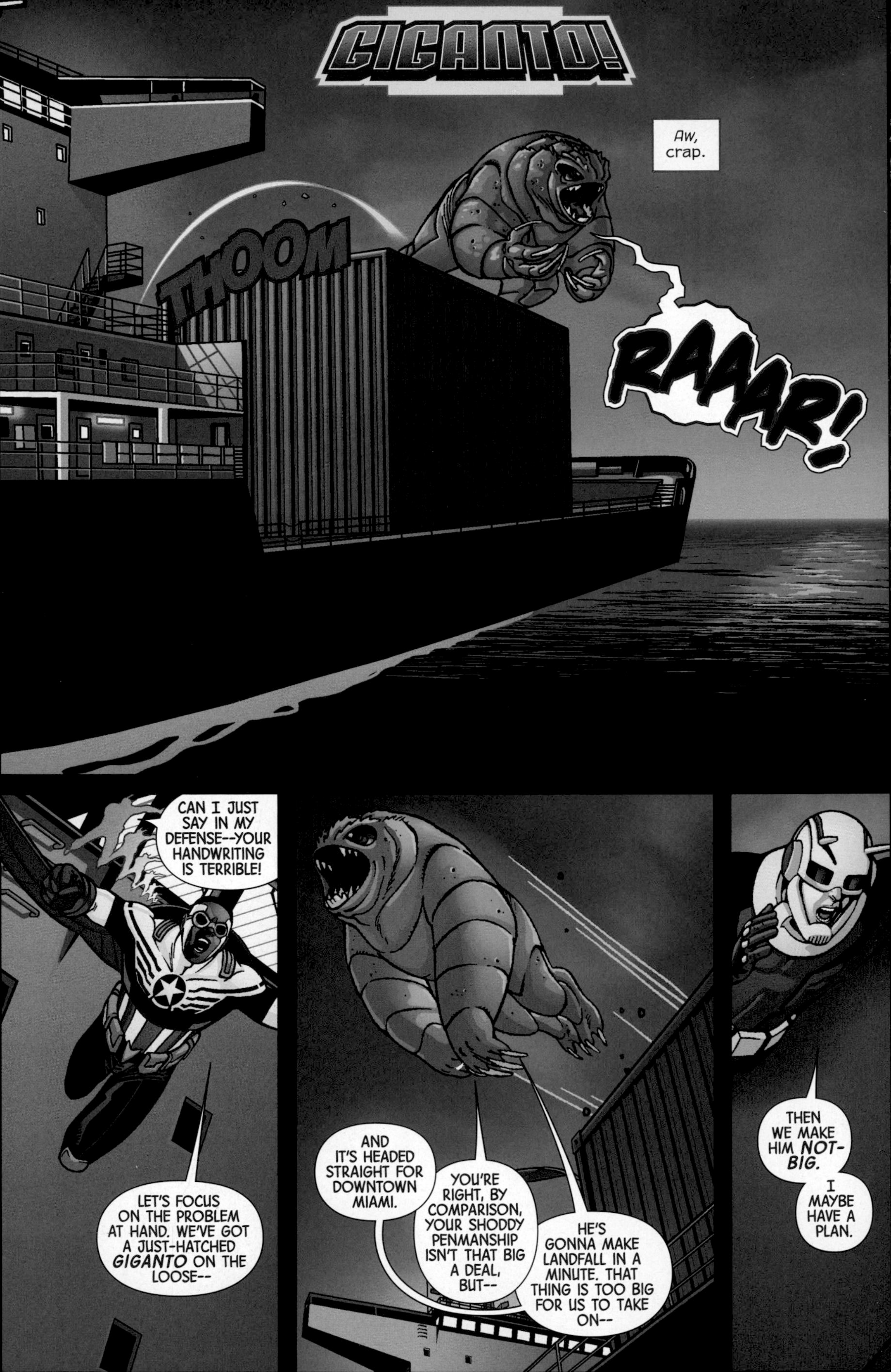
GIGANTO!
Aw, crap.
THOOM
RAAAR!
CAN I JUST SAY IN MY DEFENSE--YOUR HANDWRITING IS TERRIBLE!
LET'S FOCUS ON THE PROBLEM AT HAND. WE'VE GOT A JUST-HATCHED GIGANTO ON THE LOOSE--
AND IT'S HEADED STRAIGHT FOR DOWNTOWN MIAMI.
YOU'RE RIGHT, BY COMPARISON, YOUR SHODDY PENMANSHIP ISN'T THAT BIG A DEAL, BUT--
HE'S GONNA MAKE LANDFALL IN A MINUTE. THAT THING IS TOO BIG FOR US TO TAKE ON--
THEN WE MAKE HIM NOT-BIG.
I MAYBE HAVE A PLAN.

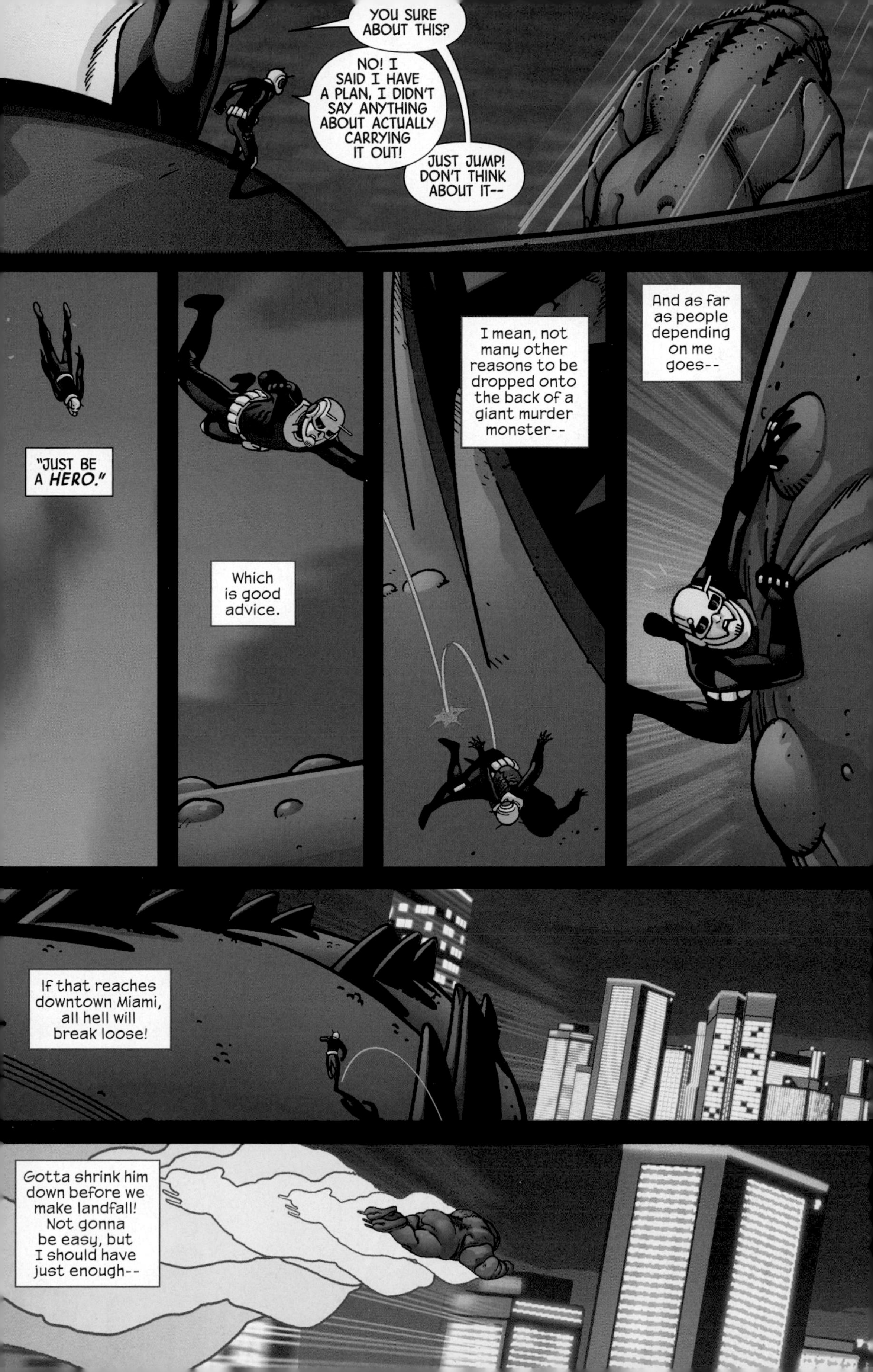
YOU SURE ABOUT THIS?
NO! I SAID I HAVE A PLAN, I DIDN'T SAY ANYTHING ABOUT ACTUALLY CARRYING IT OUT!
JUST JUMP! DON'T THINK ABOUT IT--
"JUST BE A HERO."
Which is good advice.
I mean, not many other reasons to be dropped onto the back of a giant murder monster--
And as far as people depending on me goes--
If that reaches downtown Miami, all hell will break loose!
Gotta shrink him down before we make landfall! Not gonna be easy, but I should have just enough--

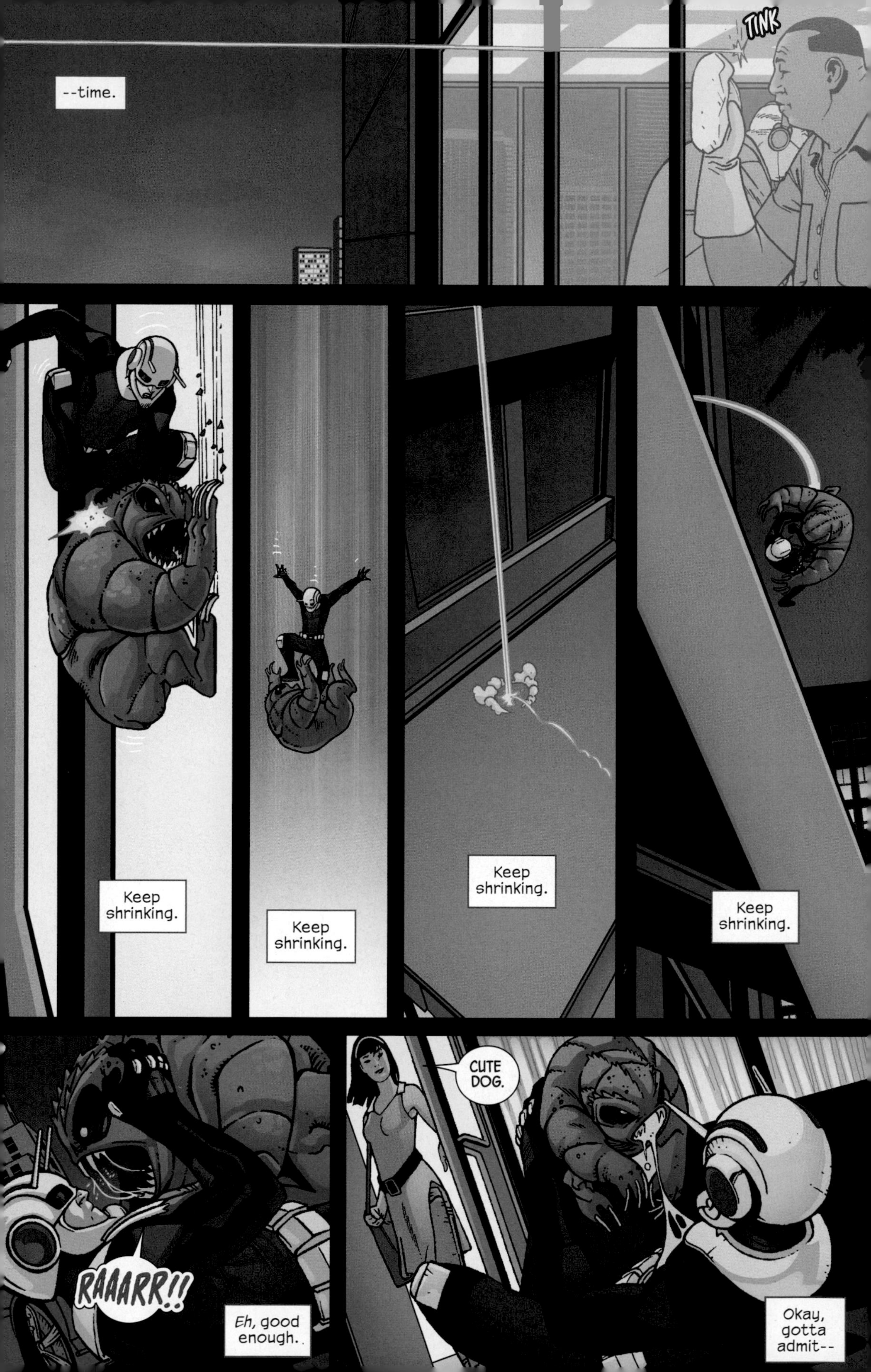
TINK
--time.
Keep shrinking.
Keep shrinking.
Keep shrinking.
Keep shrinking.
RAAARR!!
Eh, good enough.
CUTE DOG.
Okay, gotta admit--

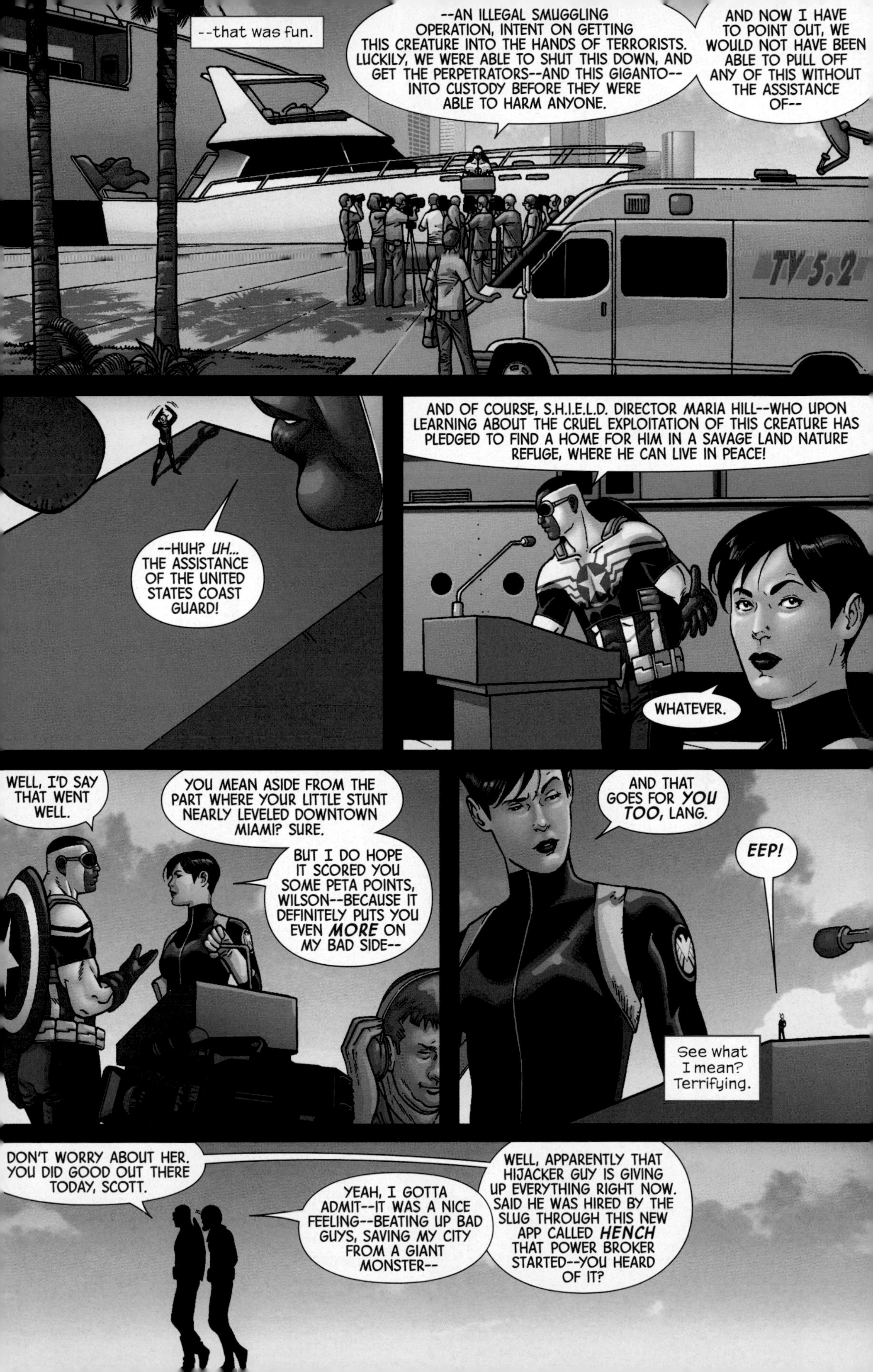
--that was fun.
--AN ILLEGAL SMUGGLING OPERATION, INTENT ON GETTING THIS CREATURE INTO THE HANDS OF TERRORISTS. LUCKILY, WE WERE ABLE TO SHUT THIS DOWN, AND GET THE PERPETRATORS--AND THIS GIGANTO--INTO CUSTODY BEFORE THEY WERE ABLE TO HARM ANYONE.
AND NOW I HAVE TO POINT OUT, WE WOULD NOT HAVE BEEN ABLE TO PULL OFF ANY OF THIS WITHOUT THE ASSISTANCE OF--
TV 5.2
--HUH? UH... THE ASSISTANCE OF THE UNITED STATES COAST GUARD!
AND OF COURSE, S.H.I.E.L.D. DIRECTOR MARIA HILL--WHO UPON LEARNING ABOUT THE CRUEL EXPLOITATION OF THIS CREATURE HAS PLEDGED TO FIND A HOME FOR HIM IN A SAVAGE LAND NATURE REFUGE, WHERE HE CAN LIVE IN PEACE!
WHATEVER.
WELL, I'D SAY THAT WENT WELL.
YOU MEAN ASIDE FROM THE PART WHERE YOUR LITTLE STUNT NEARLY LEVELED DOWNTOWN MIAMI? SURE.
BUT I DO HOPE IT SCORED YOU SOME PETA POINTS, WILSON--BECAUSE IT DEFINITELY PUTS YOU EVEN MORE ON MY BAD SIDE--
AND THAT GOES FOR YOU TOO, LANG.
EEP!
See what I mean? Terrifying.
DON'T WORRY ABOUT HER. YOU DID GOOD OUT THERE TODAY, SCOTT.
YEAH, I GOTTA ADMIT--IT WAS A NICE FEELING--BEATING UP BAD GUYS, SAVING MY CITY FROM A GIANT MONSTER--
WELL, APPARENTLY THAT HIJACKER GUY IS GIVING UP EVERYTHING RIGHT NOW. SAID HE WAS HIRED BY THE SLUG THROUGH THIS NEW APP CALLED HENCH THAT POWER BROKER STARTED--YOU HEARD OF IT?

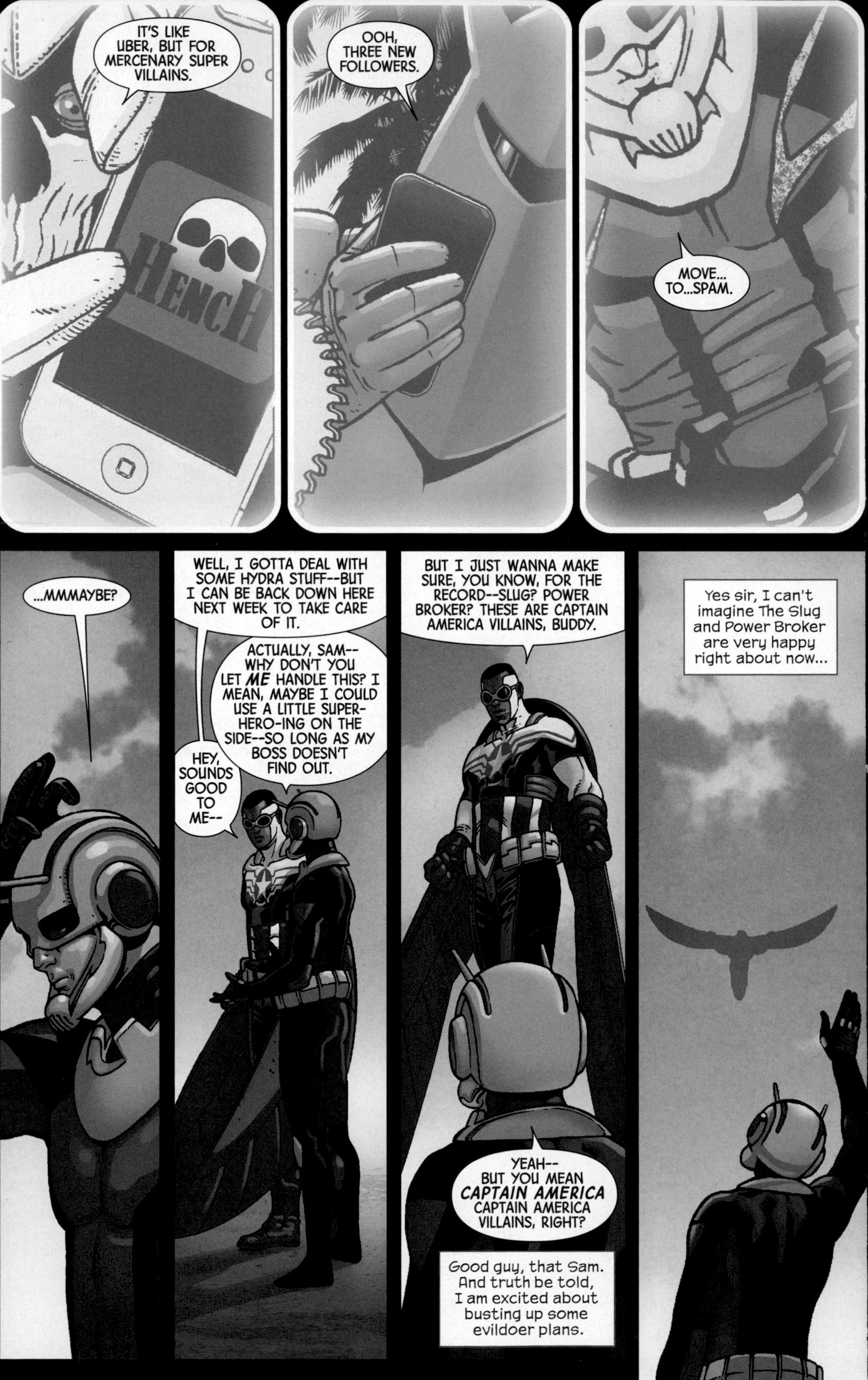
IT'S LIKE UBER, BUT FOR MERCENARY SUPER VILLAINS.
HENCH
OOH, THREE NEW FOLLOWERS.
MOVE... TO...SPAM.
...MMMAYBE?
WELL, I GOTTA DEAL WITH SOME HYDRA STUFF--BUT I CAN BE BACK DOWN HERE NEXT WEEK TO TAKE CARE OF IT.
ACTUALLY, SAM--WHY DON'T YOU LET *ME* HANDLE THIS? I MEAN, MAYBE I COULD USE A LITTLE SUPER-HERO-ING ON THE SIDE--SO LONG AS MY BOSS DOESN'T FIND OUT.
HEY, SOUNDS GOOD TO ME--
BUT I JUST WANNA MAKE SURE, YOU KNOW, FOR THE RECORD--SLUG? POWER BROKER? THESE ARE CAPTAIN AMERICA VILLAINS, BUDDY.
YEAH--BUT YOU MEAN *CAPTAIN AMERICA* CAPTAIN AMERICA VILLAINS, RIGHT?
Good guy, that Sam. And truth be told, I am excited about busting up some evildoer plans.
Yes sir, I can't imagine The Slug and Power Broker are very happy right about now...

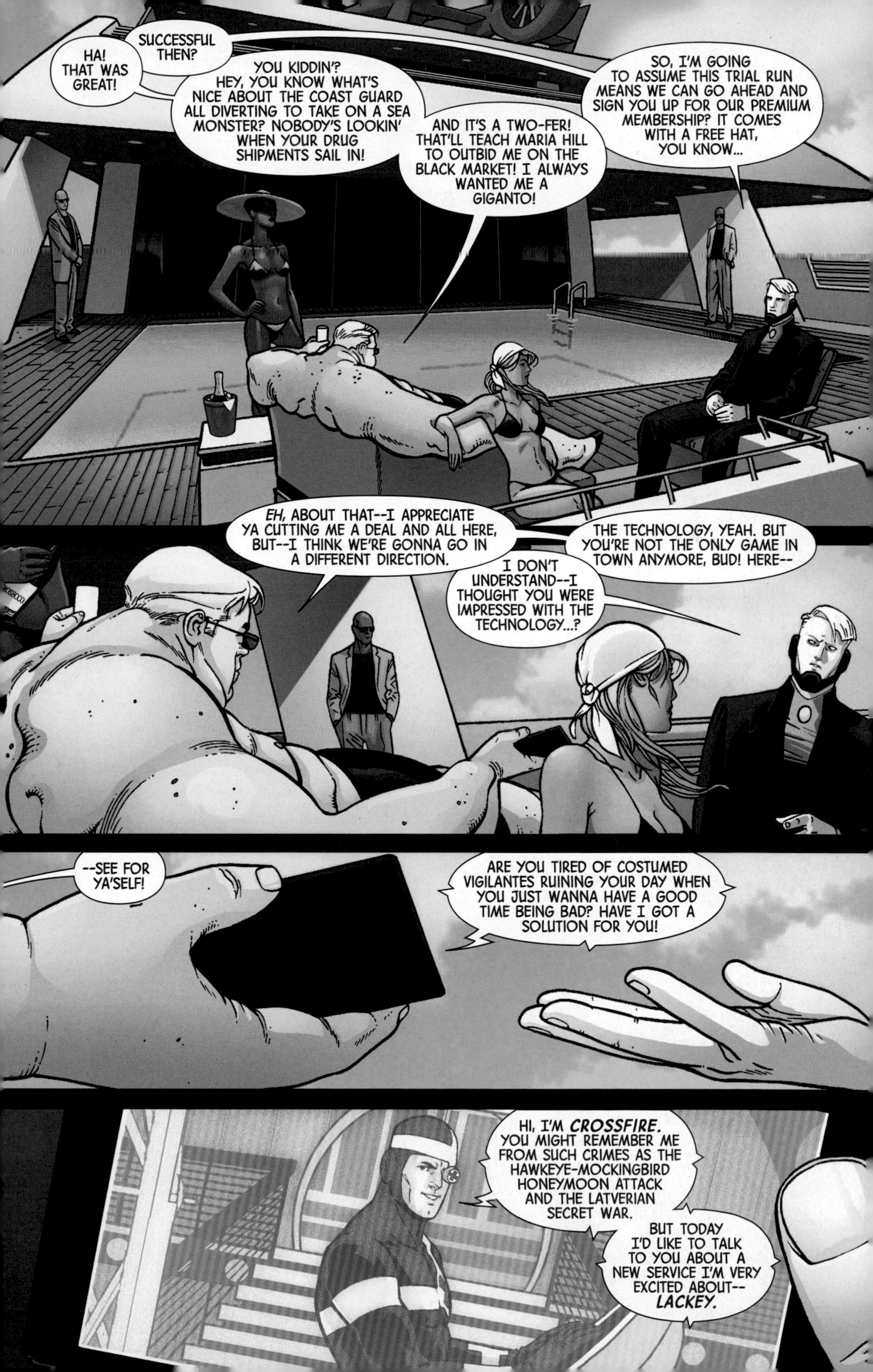
HA! THAT WAS GREAT!
SUCCESSFUL THEN?
YOU KIDDIN'? HEY, YOU KNOW WHAT'S NICE ABOUT THE COAST GUARD ALL DIVERTING TO TAKE ON A SEA MONSTER? NOBODY'S LOOKIN' WHEN YOUR DRUG SHIPMENTS SAIL IN!
AND IT'S A TWO-FER! THAT'LL TEACH MARIA HILL TO OUTBID ME ON THE BLACK MARKET! I ALWAYS WANTED ME A GIGANTO!
SO, I'M GOING TO ASSUME THIS TRIAL RUN MEANS WE CAN GO AHEAD AND SIGN YOU UP FOR OUR PREMIUM MEMBERSHIP? IT COMES WITH A FREE HAT, YOU KNOW...
EH, ABOUT THAT--I APPRECIATE YA CUTTING ME A DEAL AND ALL HERE, BUT--I THINK WE'RE GONNA GO IN A DIFFERENT DIRECTION.
I DON'T UNDERSTAND--I THOUGHT YOU WERE IMPRESSED WITH THE TECHNOLOGY...?
THE TECHNOLOGY, YEAH. BUT YOU'RE NOT THE ONLY GAME IN TOWN ANYMORE, BUD! HERE--
--SEE FOR YA'SELF!
ARE YOU TIRED OF COSTUMED VIGILANTES RUINING YOUR DAY WHEN YOU JUST WANNA HAVE A GOOD TIME BEING BAD? HAVE I GOT A SOLUTION FOR YOU!
HI, I'M CROSSFIRE. YOU MIGHT REMEMBER ME FROM SUCH CRIMES AS THE HAWKEYE-MOCKINGBIRD HONEYMOON ATTACK AND THE LATVERIAN SECRET WAR.
BUT TODAY I'D LIKE TO TALK TO YOU ABOUT A NEW SERVICE I'M VERY EXCITED ABOUT--LACKEY.

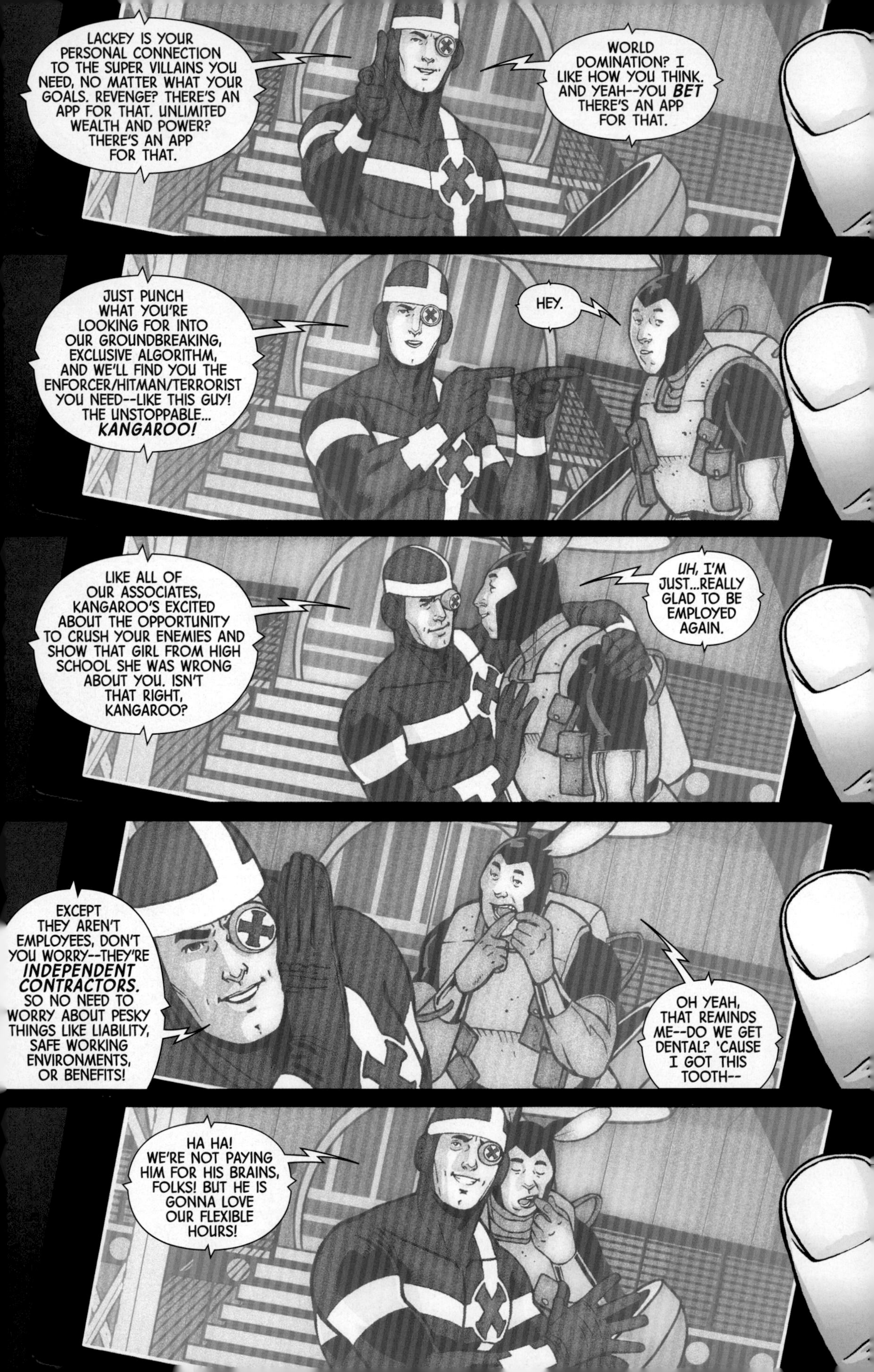
LACKEY IS YOUR PERSONAL CONNECTION TO THE SUPER VILLAINS YOU NEED, NO MATTER WHAT YOUR GOALS. REVENGE? THERE'S AN APP FOR THAT. UNLIMITED WEALTH AND POWER? THERE'S AN APP FOR THAT.
WORLD DOMINATION? I LIKE HOW YOU THINK. AND YEAH--YOU *BET* THERE'S AN APP FOR THAT.
JUST PUNCH WHAT YOU'RE LOOKING FOR INTO OUR GROUNDBREAKING, EXCLUSIVE ALGORITHM, AND WE'LL FIND YOU THE ENFORCER/HITMAN/TERRORIST YOU NEED--LIKE THIS GUY! THE UNSTOPPABLE... *KANGAROO!*
HEY.
LIKE ALL OF OUR ASSOCIATES, KANGAROO'S EXCITED ABOUT THE OPPORTUNITY TO CRUSH YOUR ENEMIES AND SHOW THAT GIRL FROM HIGH SCHOOL SHE WAS WRONG ABOUT YOU. ISN'T THAT RIGHT, KANGAROO?
UH, I'M JUST...REALLY GLAD TO BE EMPLOYED AGAIN.
EXCEPT THEY AREN'T EMPLOYEES, DON'T YOU WORRY--THEY'RE ***INDEPENDENT CONTRACTORS.*** SO NO NEED TO WORRY ABOUT PESKY THINGS LIKE LIABILITY, SAFE WORKING ENVIRONMENTS, OR BENEFITS!
OH YEAH, THAT REMINDS ME--DO WE GET DENTAL? 'CAUSE I GOT THIS TOOTH--
HA HA! WE'RE NOT PAYING HIM FOR HIS BRAINS, FOLKS! BUT HE IS GONNA LOVE OUR FLEXIBLE HOURS!

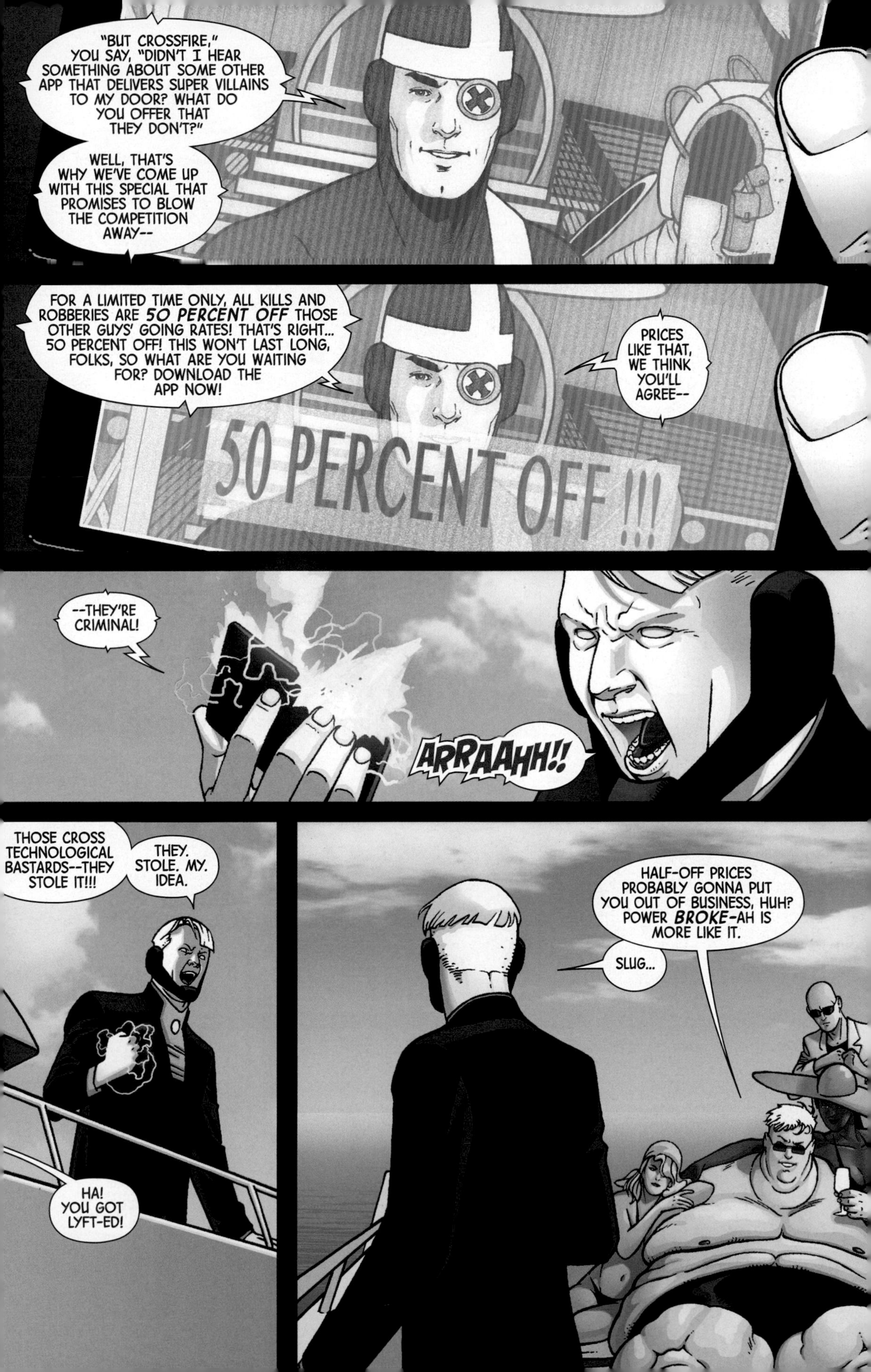
"BUT CROSSFIRE," YOU SAY, "DIDN'T I HEAR SOMETHING ABOUT SOME OTHER APP THAT DELIVERS SUPER VILLAINS TO MY DOOR? WHAT DO YOU OFFER THAT THEY DON'T?"
WELL, THAT'S WHY WE'VE COME UP WITH THIS SPECIAL THAT PROMISES TO BLOW THE COMPETITION AWAY--
FOR A LIMITED TIME ONLY, ALL KILLS AND ROBBERIES ARE *50 PERCENT OFF* THOSE OTHER GUYS' GOING RATES! THAT'S RIGHT... 50 PERCENT OFF! THIS WON'T LAST LONG, FOLKS, SO WHAT ARE YOU WAITING FOR? DOWNLOAD THE APP NOW!
PRICES LIKE THAT, WE THINK YOU'LL AGREE--
50 PERCENT OFF !!!
--THEY'RE CRIMINAL!
ARRAAHH!!
THOSE CROSS TECHNOLOGICAL BASTARDS--THEY STOLE IT!!!
THEY. STOLE. MY. IDEA.
HA! YOU GOT LYFT-ED!
HALF-OFF PRICES PROBABLY GONNA PUT YOU OUT OF BUSINESS, HUH? POWER *BROKE*-AH IS MORE LIKE IT.
SLUG...

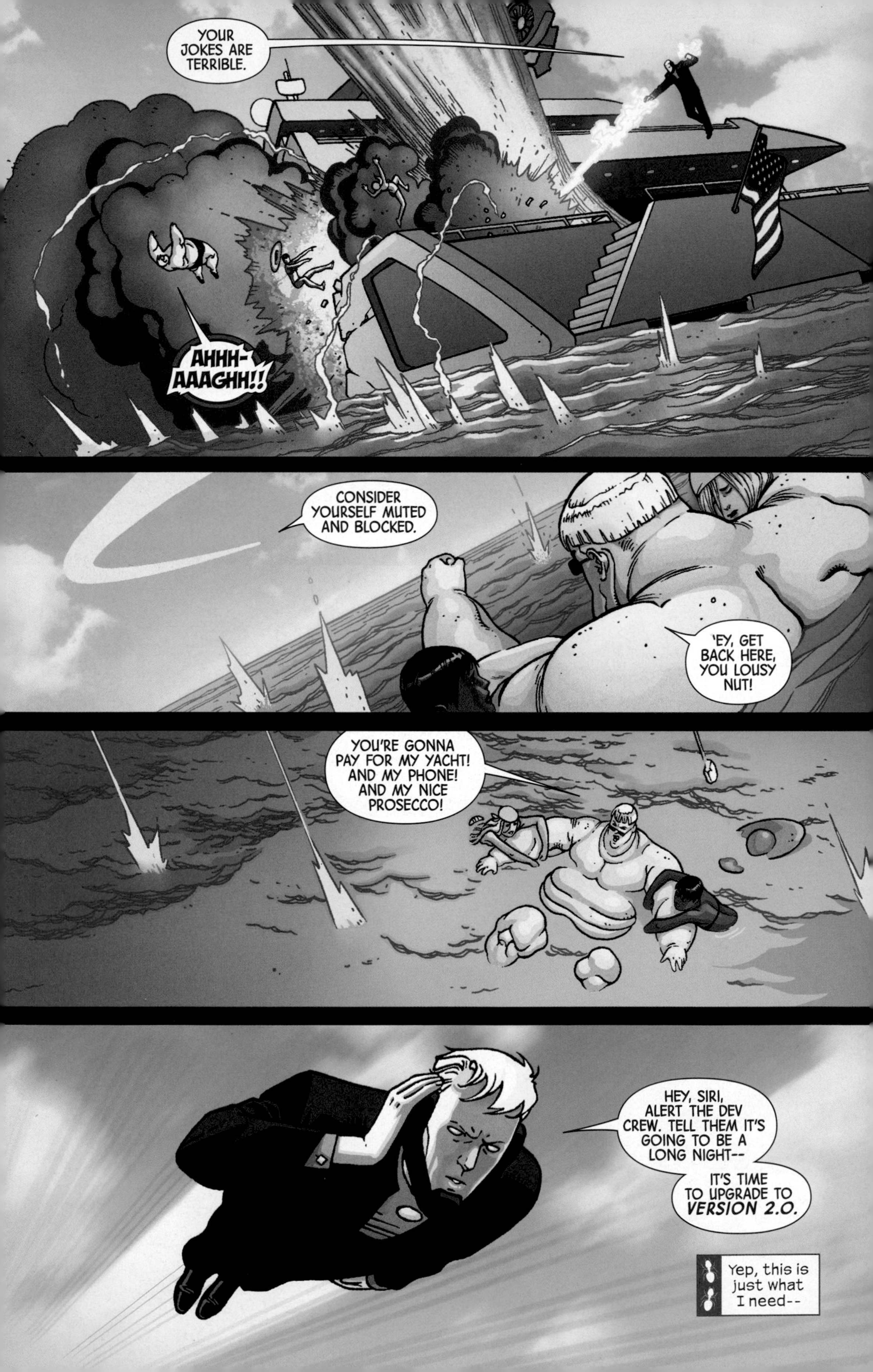
YOUR JOKES ARE TERRIBLE.
AHHH-AAAGHH!!
CONSIDER YOURSELF MUTED AND BLOCKED.
'EY, GET BACK HERE, YOU LOUSY NUT!
YOU'RE GONNA PAY FOR MY YACHT! AND MY PHONE! AND MY NICE PROSECCO!
HEY, SIRI, ALERT THE DEV CREW. TELL THEM IT'S GOING TO BE A LONG NIGHT--
IT'S TIME TO UPGRADE TO *VERSION 2.0.*
Yep, this is just what I need--

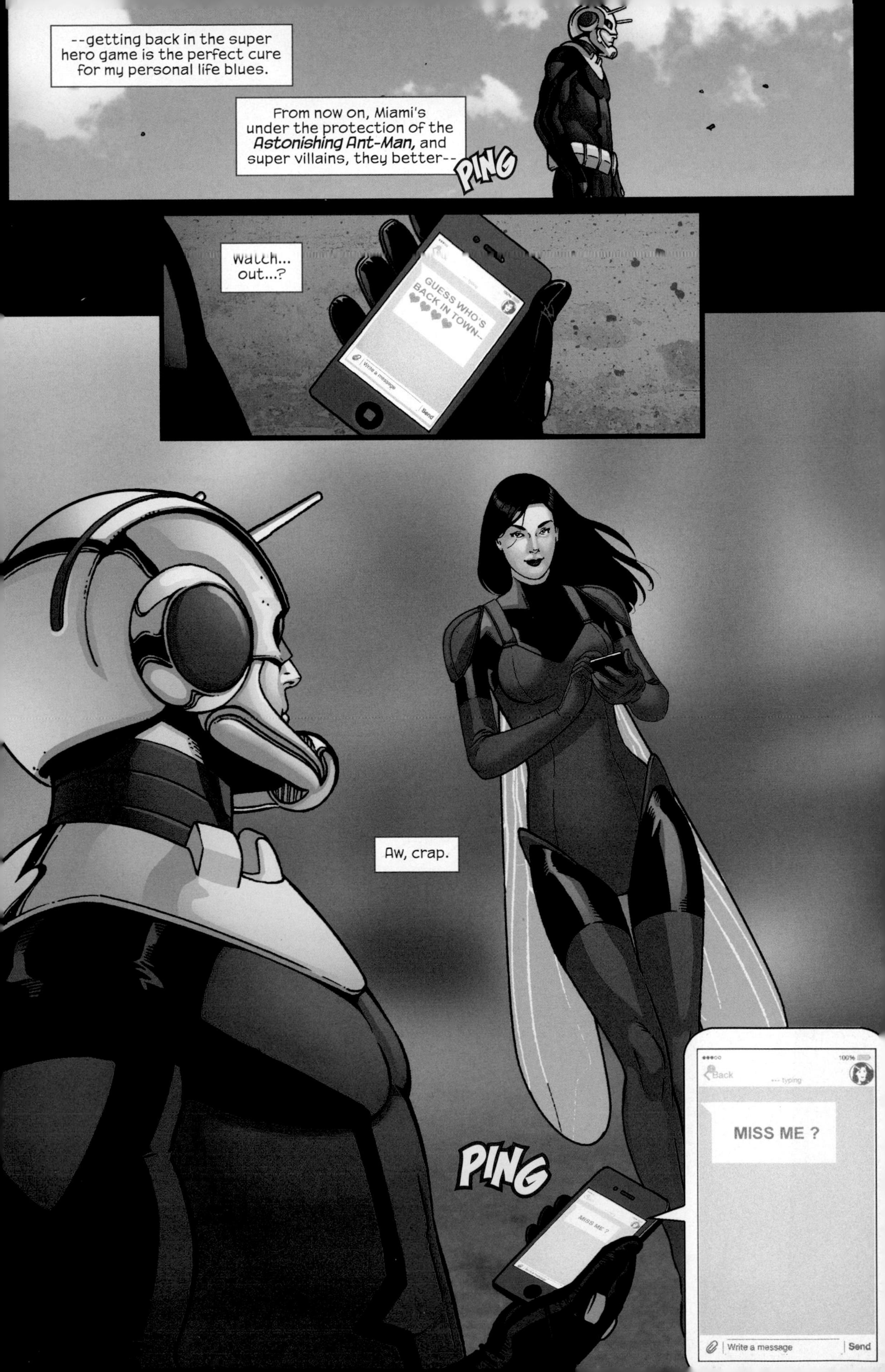
--getting back in the super hero game is the perfect cure for my personal life blues.
From now on, Miami's under the protection of the *Astonishing Ant-Man,* and super villains, they better--
PING
Watch... out...?
GUESS WHO'S BACK IN TOWN--
Write a message
Send
Aw, crap.
PING
MISS ME ?
Back
typing
MISS ME ?
Write a message
Send

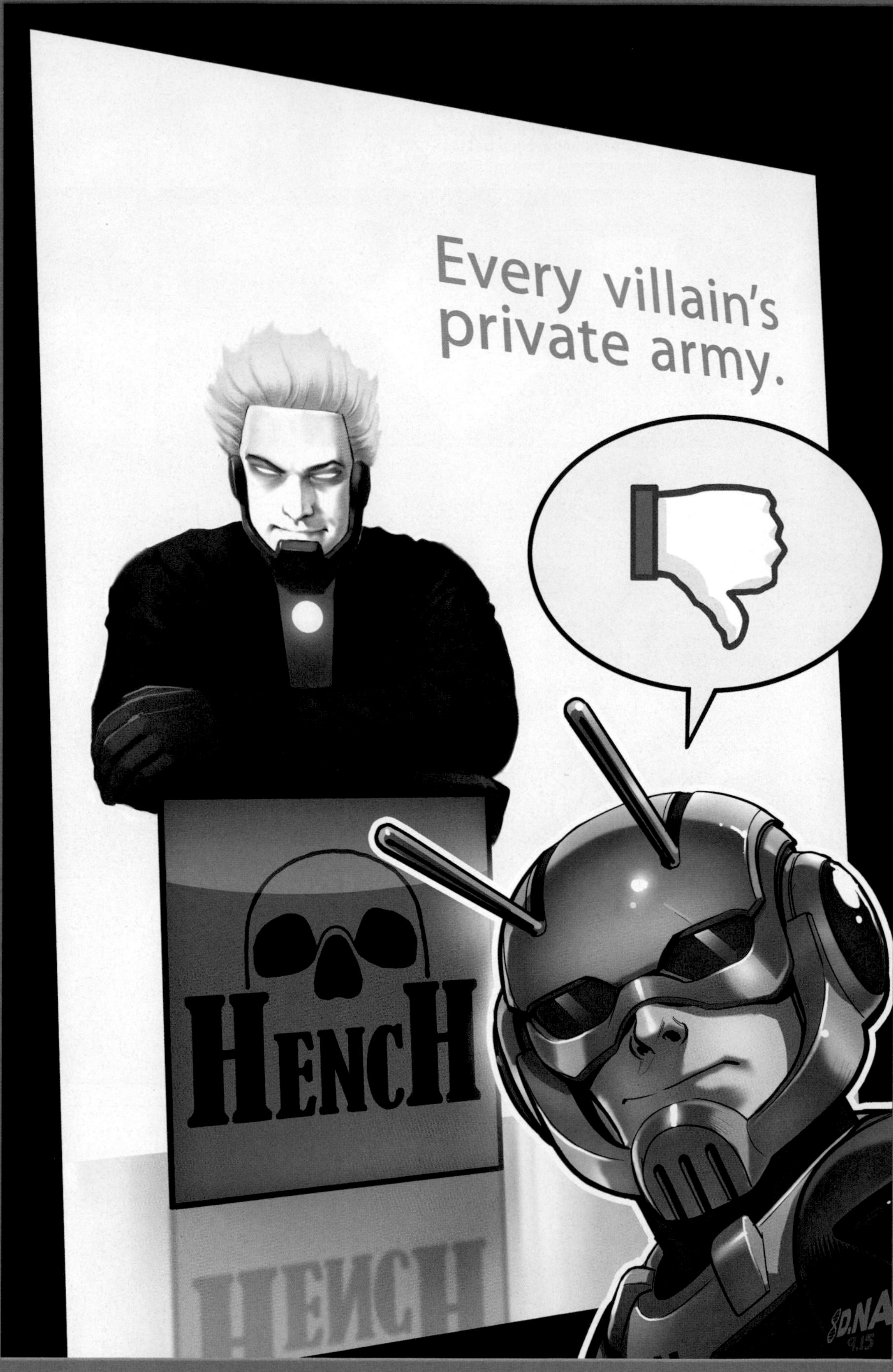
Every villain's private army.
HENCH
HENCH
D.NA 9.15

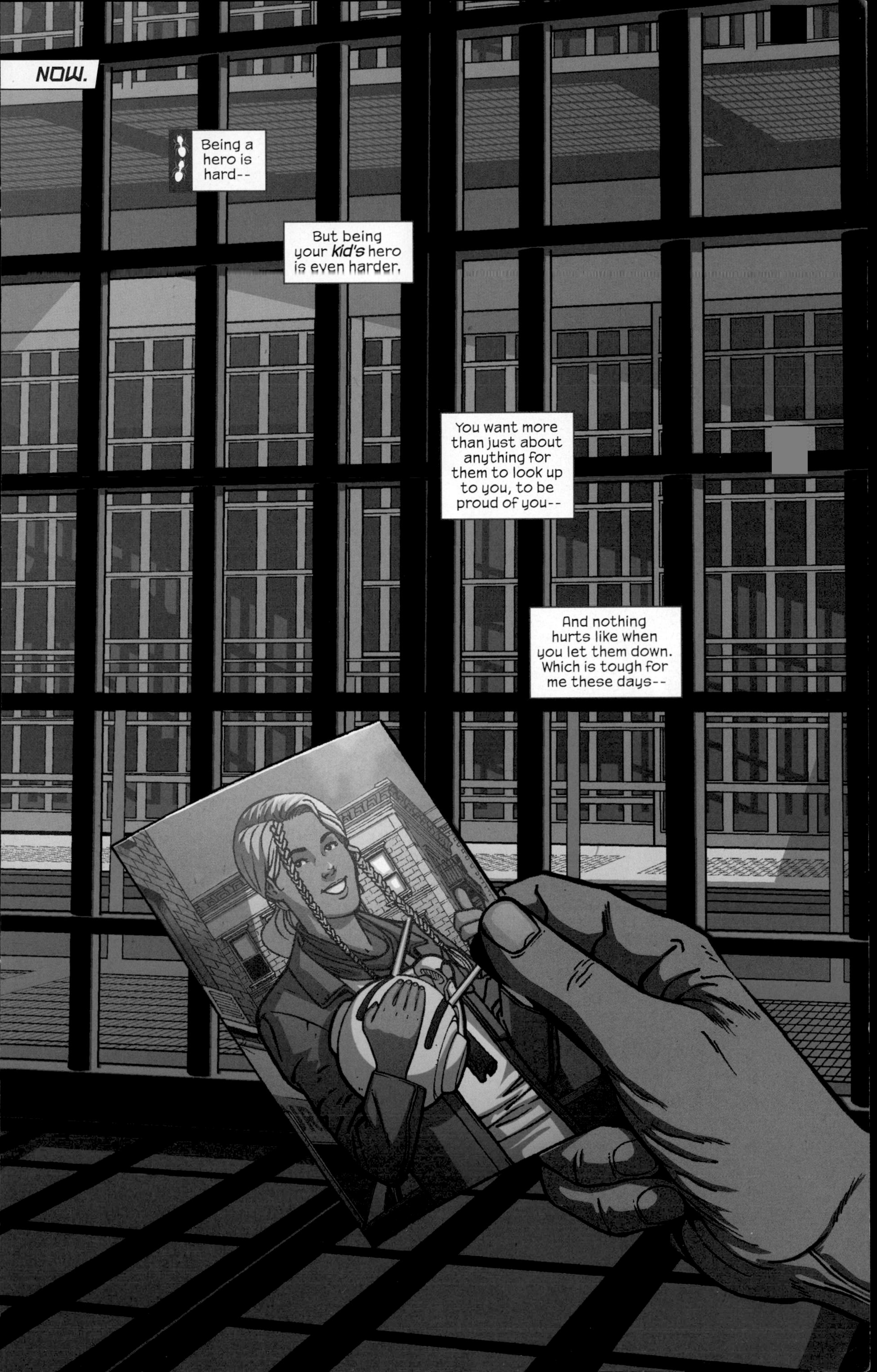
NOW.
Being a hero is hard--
But being your *kid's* hero is even harder.
You want more than just about anything for them to look up to you, to be proud of you--
And nothing hurts like when you let them down. Which is tough for me these days--

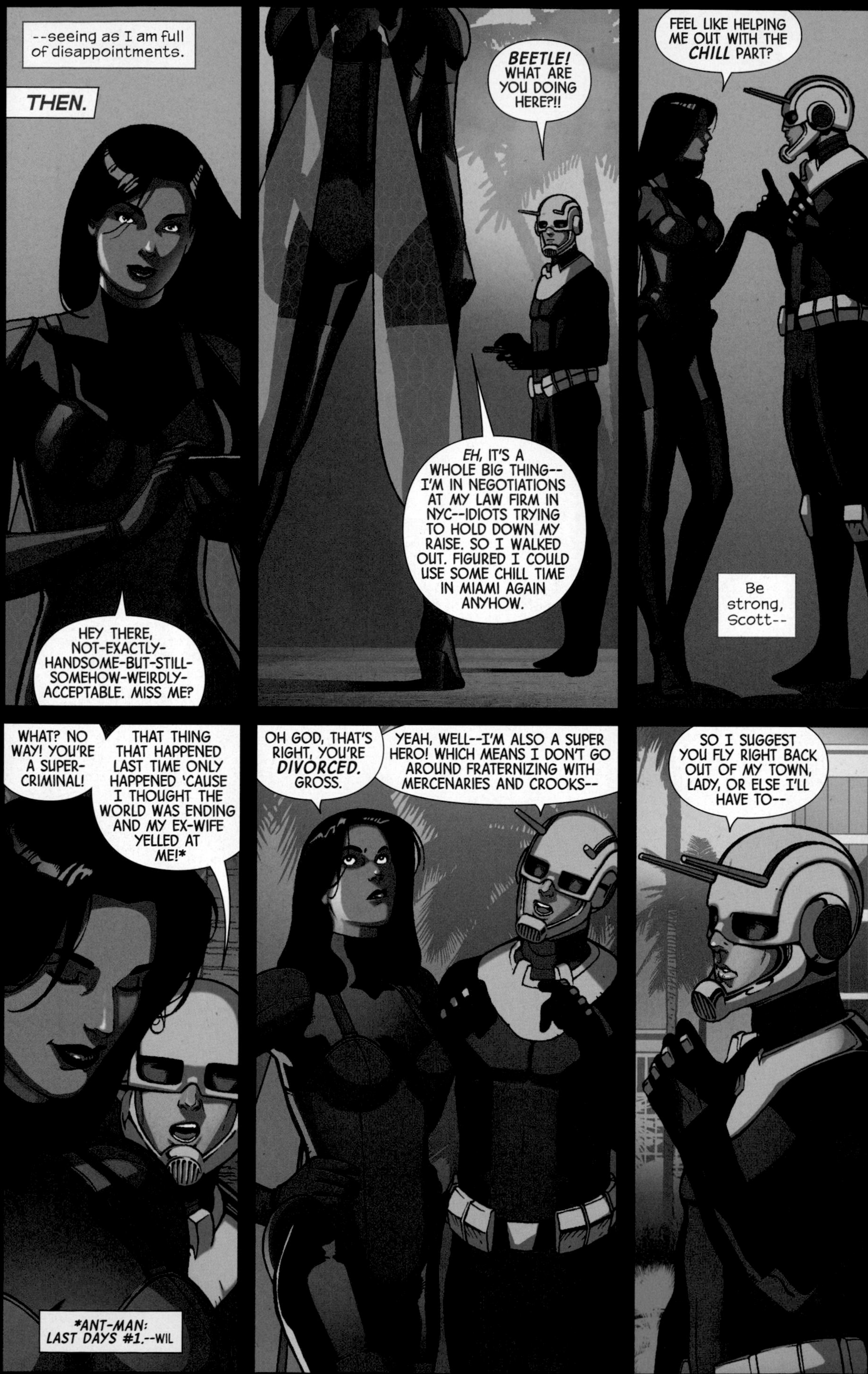

--seeing as I am full of disappointments.
THEN.
HEY THERE, NOT-EXACTLY-HANDSOME-BUT-STILL-SOMEHOW-WEIRDLY-ACCEPTABLE. MISS ME?
BEETLE! WHAT ARE YOU DOING HERE?!!
EH, IT'S A WHOLE BIG THING--I'M IN NEGOTIATIONS AT MY LAW FIRM IN NYC--IDIOTS TRYING TO HOLD DOWN MY RAISE. SO I WALKED OUT. FIGURED I COULD USE SOME CHILL TIME IN MIAMI AGAIN ANYHOW.
FEEL LIKE HELPING ME OUT WITH THE CHILL PART?
Be strong, Scott--
WHAT? NO WAY! YOU'RE A SUPER-CRIMINAL!
THAT THING THAT HAPPENED LAST TIME ONLY HAPPENED 'CAUSE I THOUGHT THE WORLD WAS ENDING AND MY EX-WIFE YELLED AT ME!*
*ANT-MAN: LAST DAYS #1.--WIL
OH GOD, THAT'S RIGHT, YOU'RE DIVORCED. GROSS.
YEAH, WELL--I'M ALSO A SUPER HERO! WHICH MEANS I DON'T GO AROUND FRATERNIZING WITH MERCENARIES AND CROOKS--
SO I SUGGEST YOU FLY RIGHT BACK OUT OF MY TOWN, LADY, OR ELSE I'LL HAVE TO--

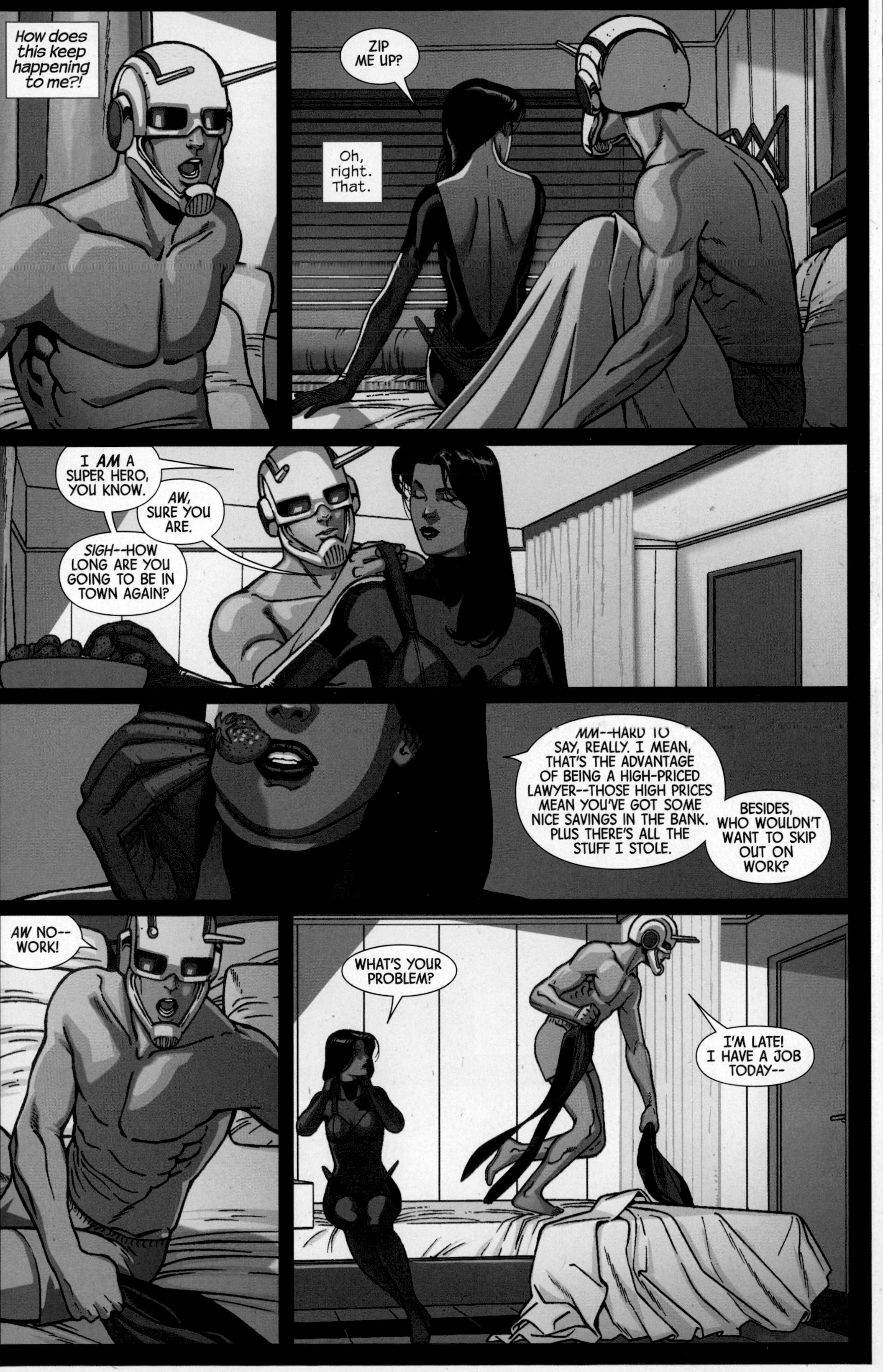
How does this keep happening to me?!
ZIP ME UP?
Oh, right. That.
I AM A SUPER HERO, YOU KNOW.
AW, SURE YOU ARE.
SIGH--HOW LONG ARE YOU GOING TO BE IN TOWN AGAIN?
MM--HARD TO SAY, REALLY. I MEAN, THAT'S THE ADVANTAGE OF BEING A HIGH-PRICED LAWYER--THOSE HIGH PRICES MEAN YOU'VE GOT SOME NICE SAVINGS IN THE BANK. PLUS THERE'S ALL THE STUFF I STOLE.
BESIDES, WHO WOULDN'T WANT TO SKIP OUT ON WORK?
AW NO--WORK!
WHAT'S YOUR PROBLEM?
I'M LATE! I HAVE A JOB TODAY--

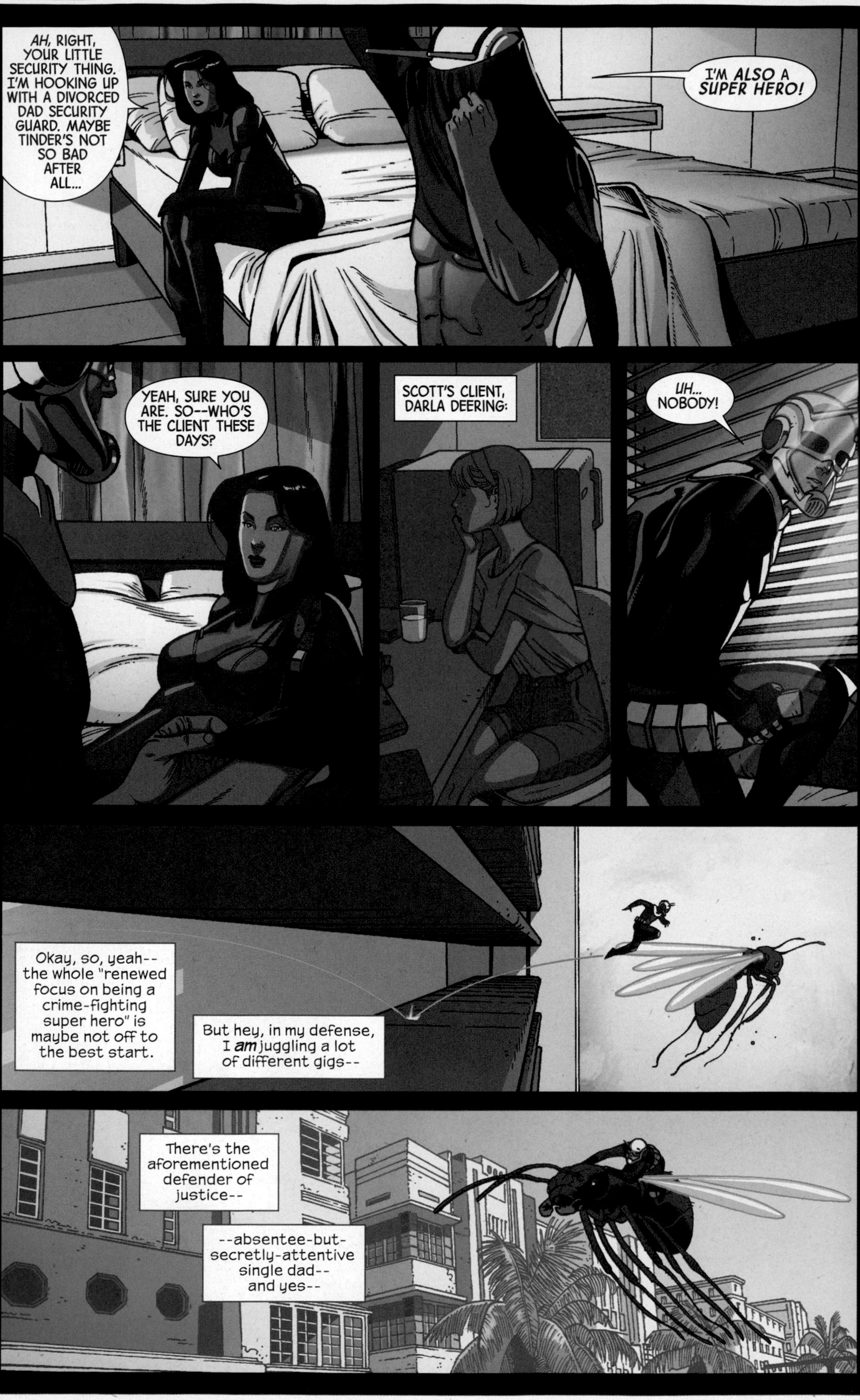
AH, RIGHT, YOUR LITTLE SECURITY THING. I'M HOOKING UP WITH A DIVORCED DAD SECURITY GUARD. MAYBE TINDER'S NOT SO BAD AFTER ALL...
I'M ALSO A SUPER HERO!
YEAH, SURE YOU ARE. SO--WHO'S THE CLIENT THESE DAYS?
SCOTT'S CLIENT, DARLA DEERING:
UH... NOBODY!
Okay, so, yeah--the whole "renewed focus on being a crime-fighting super hero" is maybe not off to the best start.
But hey, in my defense, I am juggling a lot of different gigs--
There's the aforementioned defender of justice--
--absentee-but-secretly-attentive single dad--and yes--

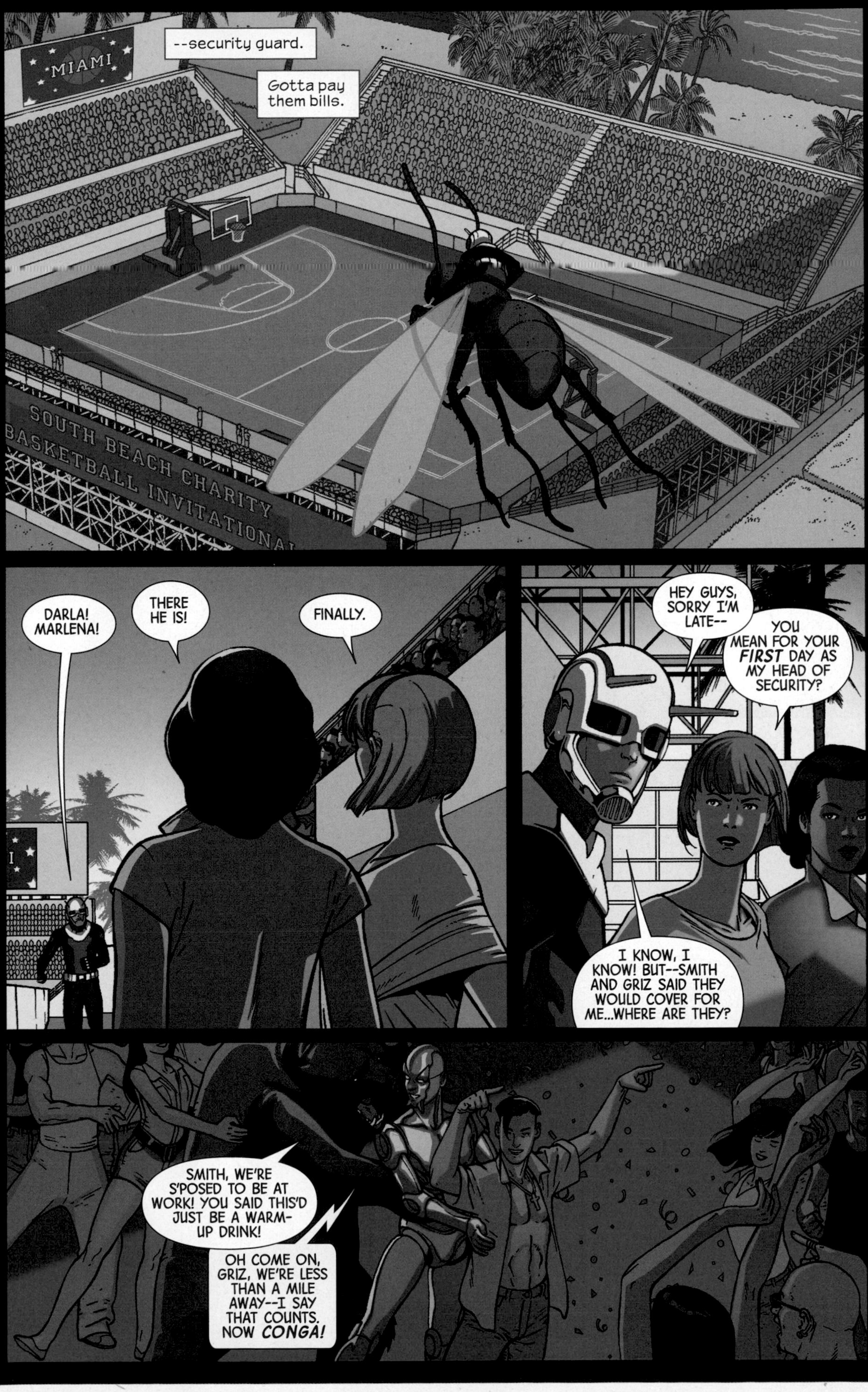
--security guard.
Gotta pay them bills.
MIAMI
SOUTH BEACH CHARITY BASKETBALL INVITATIONAL
DARLA! MARLENA!
THERE HE IS!
FINALLY.
HEY GUYS, SORRY I'M LATE--
YOU MEAN FOR YOUR *FIRST* DAY AS MY HEAD OF SECURITY?
I KNOW, I KNOW! BUT--SMITH AND GRIZ SAID THEY WOULD COVER FOR ME...WHERE ARE THEY?
SMITH, WE'RE S'POSED TO BE AT WORK! YOU SAID THIS'D JUST BE A WARM-UP DRINK!
OH COME ON, GRIZ, WE'RE LESS THAN A MILE AWAY--I SAY THAT COUNTS. NOW *CONGA!*

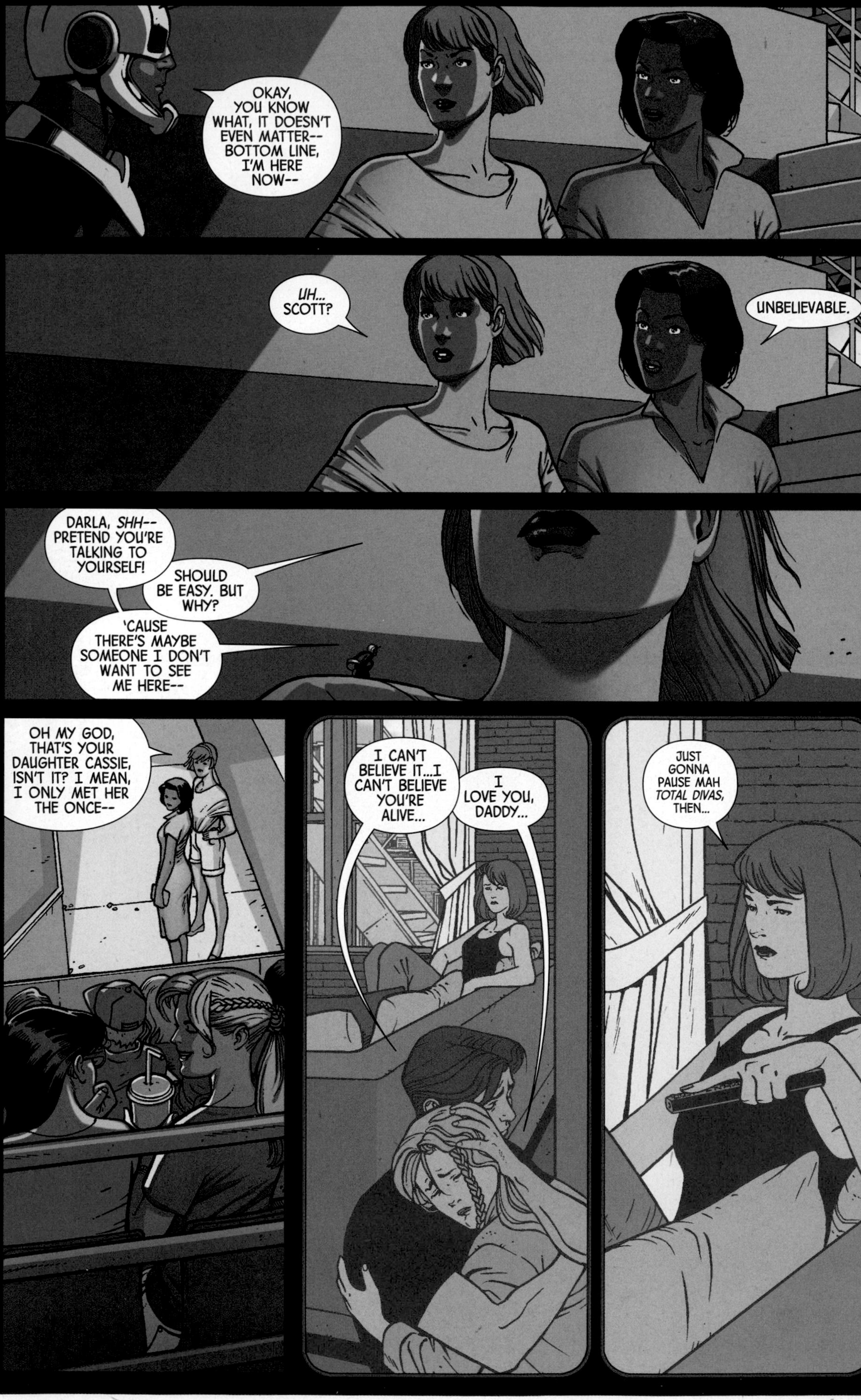
OKAY, YOU KNOW WHAT, IT DOESN'T EVEN MATTER-- BOTTOM LINE, I'M HERE NOW--
UH... SCOTT?
UNBELIEVABLE.
DARLA, SHH-- PRETEND YOU'RE TALKING TO YOURSELF!
SHOULD BE EASY. BUT WHY?
'CAUSE THERE'S MAYBE SOMEONE I DON'T WANT TO SEE ME HERE--
OH MY GOD, THAT'S YOUR DAUGHTER CASSIE, ISN'T IT? I MEAN, I ONLY MET HER THE ONCE--
I CAN'T BELIEVE IT...I CAN'T BELIEVE YOU'RE ALIVE...
I LOVE YOU, DADDY...
JUST GONNA PAUSE MAH TOTAL DIVAS, THEN...

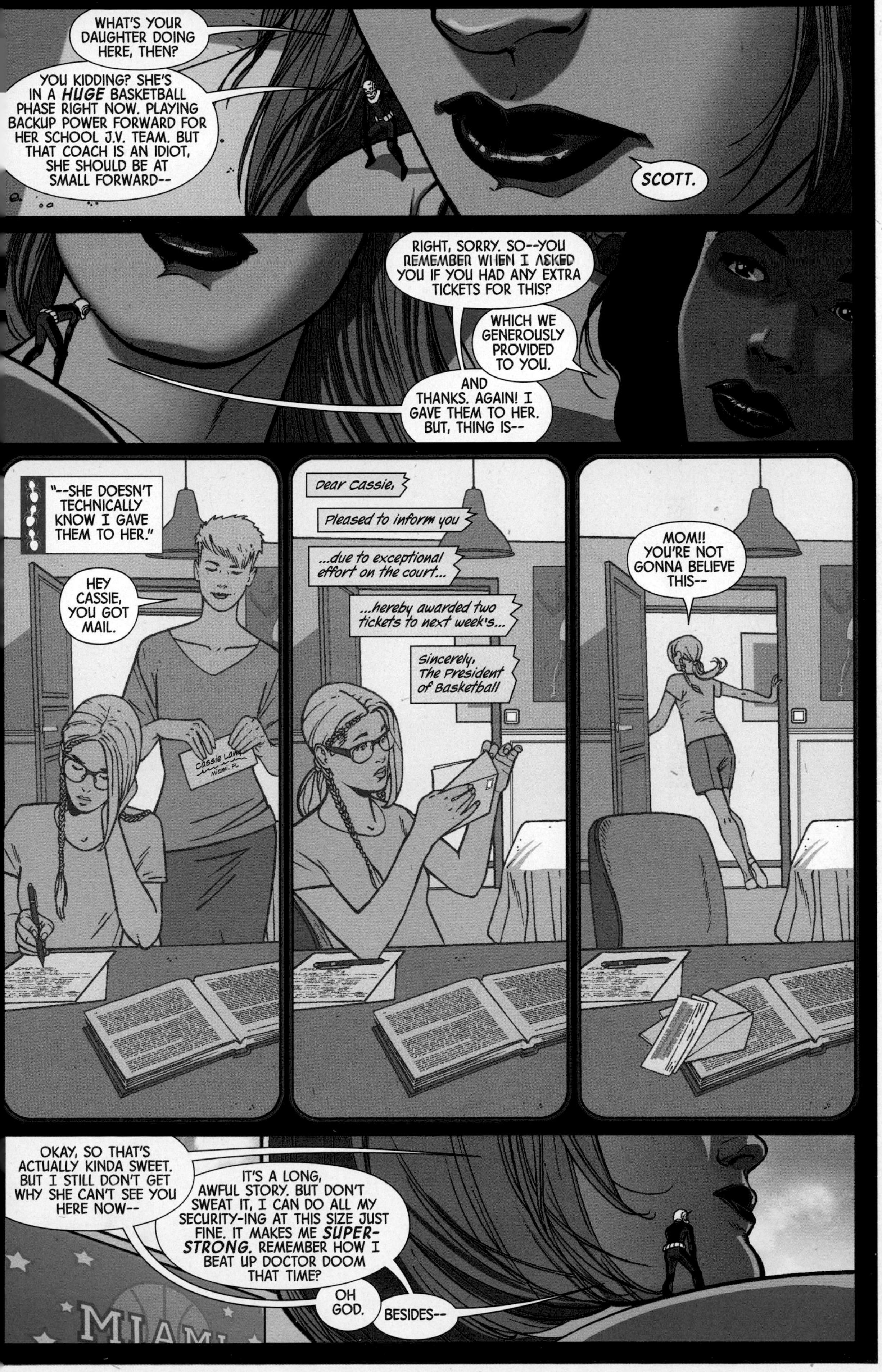
WHAT'S YOUR DAUGHTER DOING HERE, THEN?
YOU KIDDING? SHE'S IN A HUGE BASKETBALL PHASE RIGHT NOW. PLAYING BACKUP POWER FORWARD FOR HER SCHOOL J.V. TEAM. BUT THAT COACH IS AN IDIOT, SHE SHOULD BE AT SMALL FORWARD--
SCOTT.
RIGHT, SORRY. SO--YOU REMEMBER WHEN I ASKED YOU IF YOU HAD ANY EXTRA TICKETS FOR THIS?
WHICH WE GENEROUSLY PROVIDED TO YOU.
AND THANKS. AGAIN! I GAVE THEM TO HER. BUT, THING IS--
"--SHE DOESN'T TECHNICALLY KNOW I GAVE THEM TO HER."
HEY CASSIE, YOU GOT MAIL.
Cassie Lang
Miami, FL
Dear Cassie,
Pleased to inform you
...due to exceptional effort on the court...
...hereby awarded two tickets to next week's...
Sincerely, The President of Basketball
MOM!! YOU'RE NOT GONNA BELIEVE THIS--
OKAY, SO THAT'S ACTUALLY KINDA SWEET. BUT I STILL DON'T GET WHY SHE CAN'T SEE YOU HERE NOW--
IT'S A LONG, AWFUL STORY. BUT DON'T SWEAT IT, I CAN DO ALL MY SECURITY-ING AT THIS SIZE JUST FINE. IT MAKES ME SUPER-STRONG. REMEMBER HOW I BEAT UP DOCTOR DOOM THAT TIME?
OH GOD.
BESIDES--
MIAMI

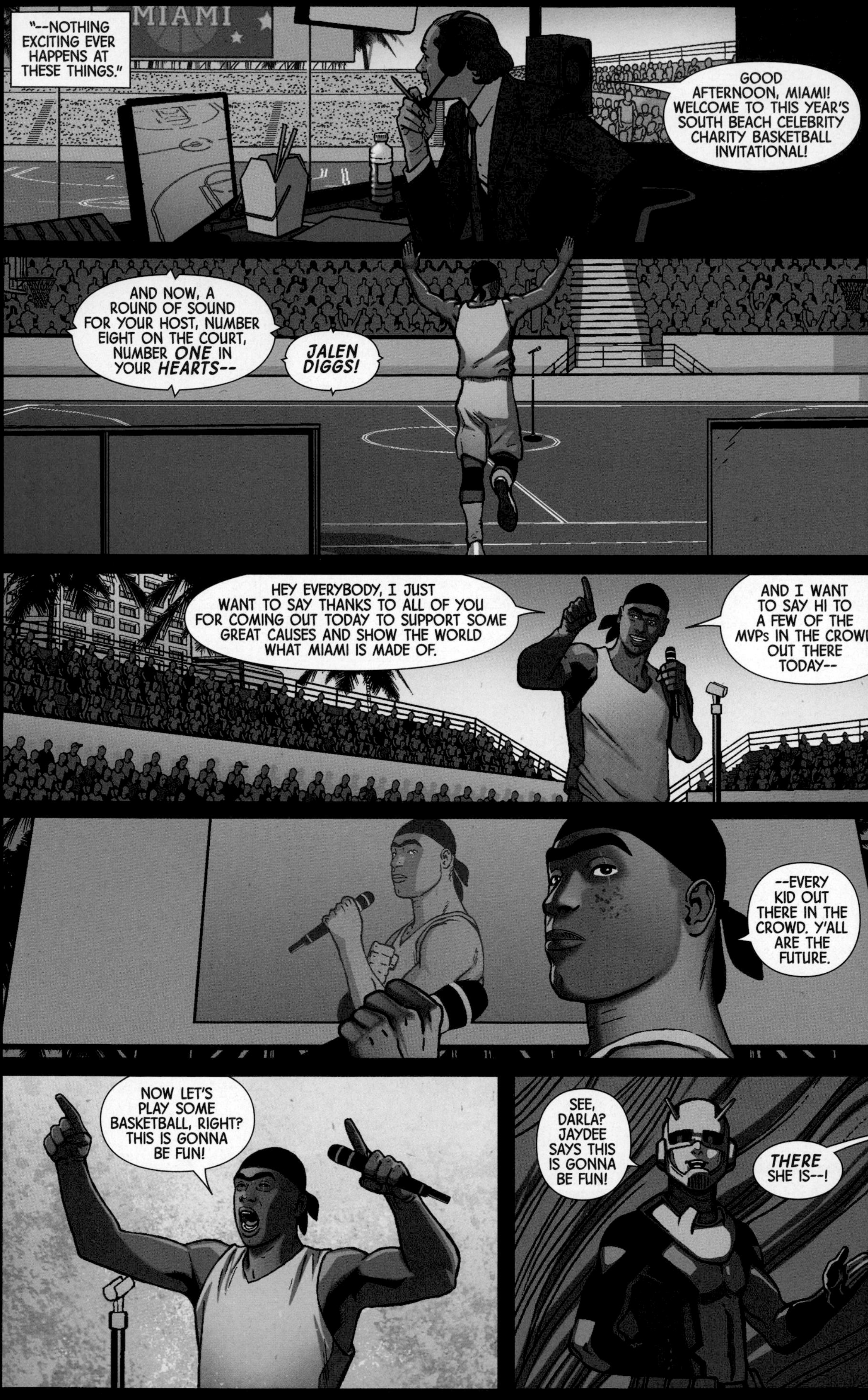

"--NOTHING EXCITING EVER HAPPENS AT THESE THINGS."
MIAMI
GOOD AFTERNOON, MIAMI! WELCOME TO THIS YEAR'S SOUTH BEACH CELEBRITY CHARITY BASKETBALL INVITATIONAL!
AND NOW, A ROUND OF SOUND FOR YOUR HOST, NUMBER EIGHT ON THE COURT, NUMBER ONE IN YOUR HEARTS--
JALEN DIGGS!
HEY EVERYBODY, I JUST WANT TO SAY THANKS TO ALL OF YOU FOR COMING OUT TODAY TO SUPPORT SOME GREAT CAUSES AND SHOW THE WORLD WHAT MIAMI IS MADE OF.
AND I WANT TO SAY HI TO A FEW OF THE MVPs IN THE CROWD OUT THERE TODAY--
--EVERY KID OUT THERE IN THE CROWD. Y'ALL ARE THE FUTURE.
NOW LET'S PLAY SOME BASKETBALL, RIGHT? THIS IS GONNA BE FUN!
SEE, DARLA? JAYDEE SAYS THIS IS GONNA BE FUN!
THERE SHE IS--!

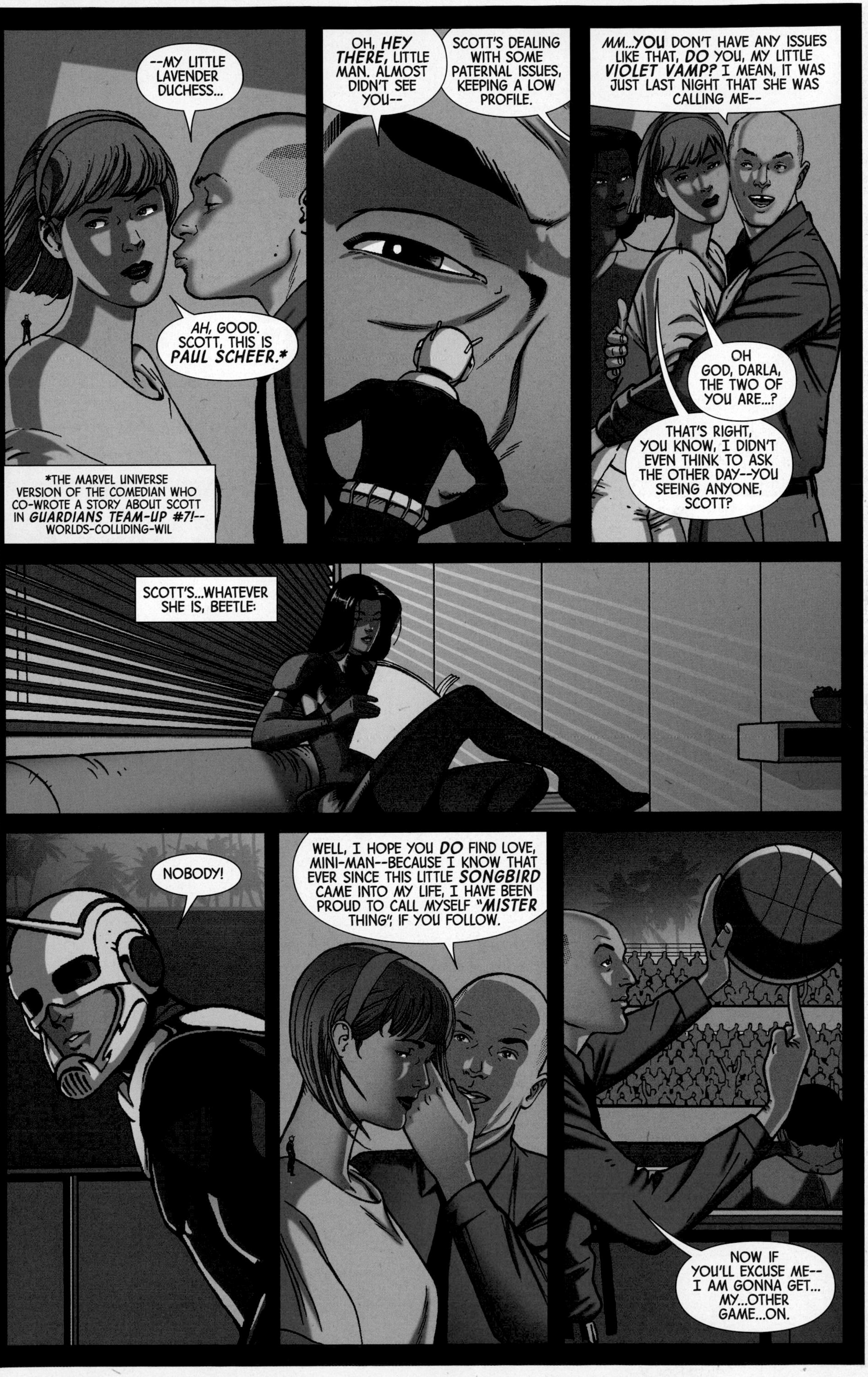
--MY LITTLE LAVENDER DUCHESS...
AH, GOOD. SCOTT, THIS IS PAUL SCHEER.*
*THE MARVEL UNIVERSE VERSION OF THE COMEDIAN WHO CO-WROTE A STORY ABOUT SCOTT IN GUARDIANS TEAM-UP #7!-- WORLDS-COLLIDING-WIL
OH, HEY THERE, LITTLE MAN. ALMOST DIDN'T SEE YOU--
SCOTT'S DEALING WITH SOME PATERNAL ISSUES, KEEPING A LOW PROFILE.
MM...YOU DON'T HAVE ANY ISSUES LIKE THAT, DO YOU, MY LITTLE VIOLET VAMP? I MEAN, IT WAS JUST LAST NIGHT THAT SHE WAS CALLING ME--
OH GOD, DARLA, THE TWO OF YOU ARE...?
THAT'S RIGHT, YOU KNOW, I DIDN'T EVEN THINK TO ASK THE OTHER DAY--YOU SEEING ANYONE, SCOTT?
SCOTT'S...WHATEVER SHE IS, BEETLE:
NOBODY!
WELL, I HOPE YOU DO FIND LOVE, MINI-MAN--BECAUSE I KNOW THAT EVER SINCE THIS LITTLE SONGBIRD CAME INTO MY LIFE, I HAVE BEEN PROUD TO CALL MYSELF "MISTER THING", IF YOU FOLLOW.
NOW IF YOU'LL EXCUSE ME-- I AM GONNA GET... MY...OTHER GAME...ON.

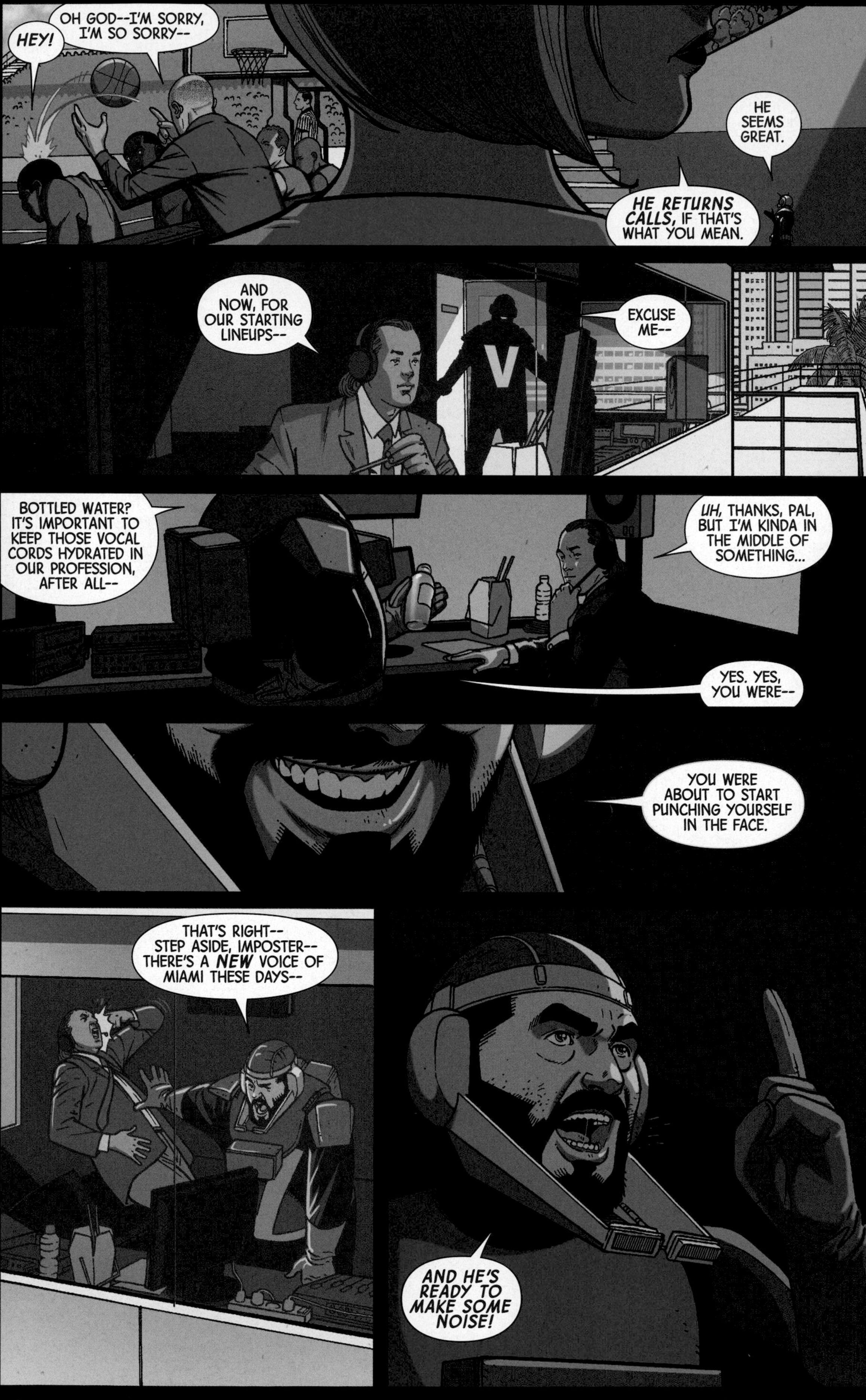
HEY!
OH GOD--I'M SORRY, I'M SO SORRY--
HE SEEMS GREAT.
HE RETURNS CALLS, IF THAT'S WHAT YOU MEAN.
AND NOW, FOR OUR STARTING LINEUPS--
EXCUSE ME--
BOTTLED WATER? IT'S IMPORTANT TO KEEP THOSE VOCAL CORDS HYDRATED IN OUR PROFESSION, AFTER ALL--
UH, THANKS, PAL, BUT I'M KINDA IN THE MIDDLE OF SOMETHING...
YES. YES, YOU WERE--
YOU WERE ABOUT TO START PUNCHING YOURSELF IN THE FACE.
THAT'S RIGHT-- STEP ASIDE, IMPOSTER-- THERE'S A NEW VOICE OF MIAMI THESE DAYS--
AND HE'S READY TO MAKE SOME NOISE!

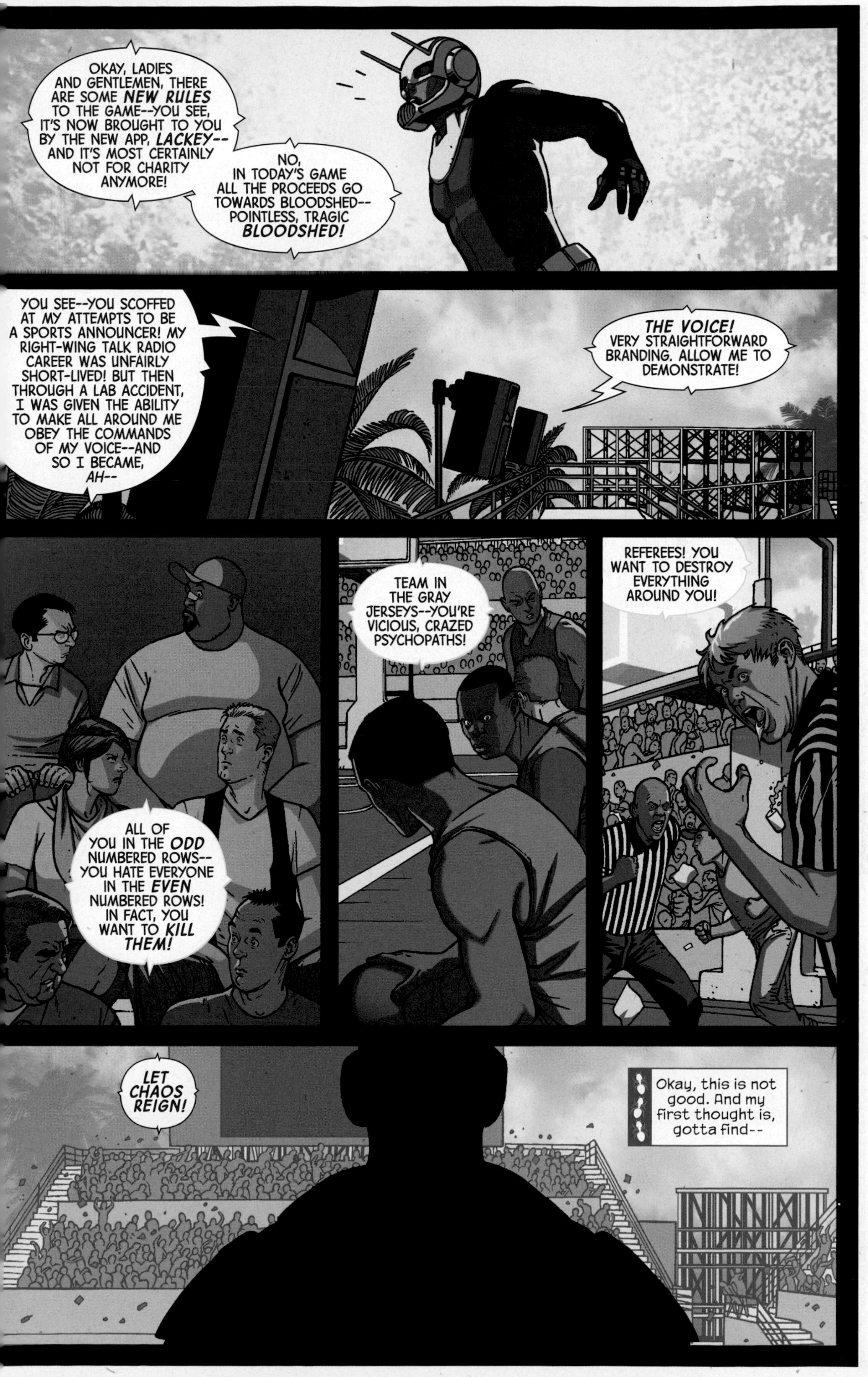
OKAY, LADIES AND GENTLEMEN, THERE ARE SOME NEW RULES TO THE GAME--YOU SEE, IT'S NOW BROUGHT TO YOU BY THE NEW APP, LACKEY--AND IT'S MOST CERTAINLY NOT FOR CHARITY ANYMORE!
NO, IN TODAY'S GAME ALL THE PROCEEDS GO TOWARDS BLOODSHED--POINTLESS, TRAGIC BLOODSHED!
YOU SEE--YOU SCOFFED AT MY ATTEMPTS TO BE A SPORTS ANNOUNCER! MY RIGHT-WING TALK RADIO CAREER WAS UNFAIRLY SHORT-LIVED! BUT THEN THROUGH A LAB ACCIDENT, I WAS GIVEN THE ABILITY TO MAKE ALL AROUND ME OBEY THE COMMANDS OF MY VOICE--AND SO I BECAME, AH--
THE VOICE! VERY STRAIGHTFORWARD BRANDING. ALLOW ME TO DEMONSTRATE!
ALL OF YOU IN THE ODD NUMBERED ROWS--YOU HATE EVERYONE IN THE EVEN NUMBERED ROWS! IN FACT, YOU WANT TO KILL THEM!
TEAM IN THE GRAY JERSEYS--YOU'RE VICIOUS, CRAZED PSYCHOPATHS!
REFEREES! YOU WANT TO DESTROY EVERYTHING AROUND YOU!
LET CHAOS REIGN!
Okay, this is not good. And my first thought is, gotta find--

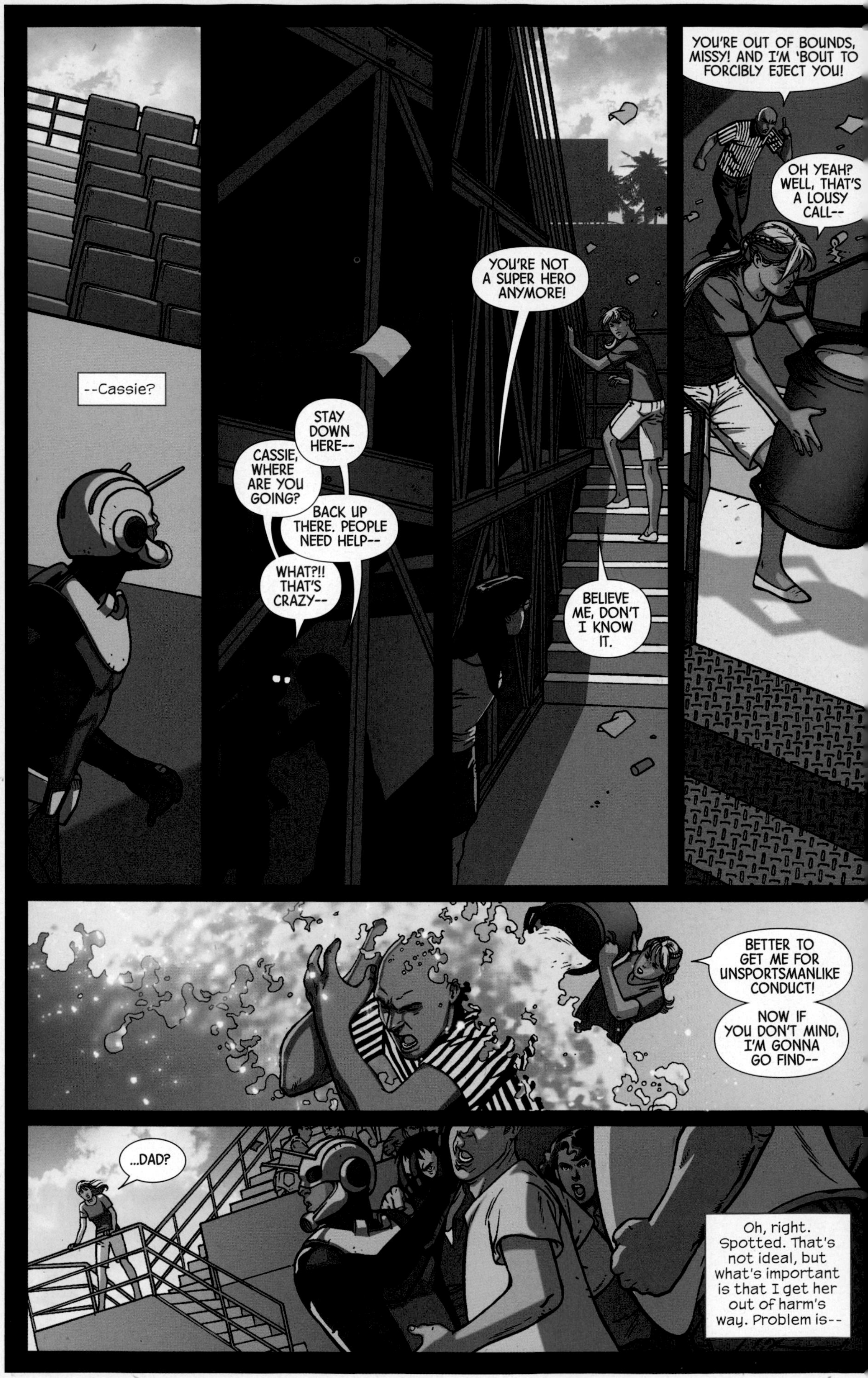
--Cassie?
CASSIE, WHERE ARE YOU GOING?
STAY DOWN HERE--
BACK UP THERE. PEOPLE NEED HELP--
WHAT?!! THAT'S CRAZY--
YOU'RE NOT A SUPER HERO ANYMORE!
BELIEVE ME, DON'T I KNOW IT.
YOU'RE OUT OF BOUNDS, MISSY! AND I'M 'BOUT TO FORCIBLY EJECT YOU!
OH YEAH? WELL, THAT'S A LOUSY CALL--
BETTER TO GET ME FOR UNSPORTSMANLIKE CONDUCT!
NOW IF YOU DON'T MIND, I'M GONNA GO FIND--
...DAD?
Oh, right. Spotted. That's not ideal, but what's important is that I get her out of harm's way. Problem is--

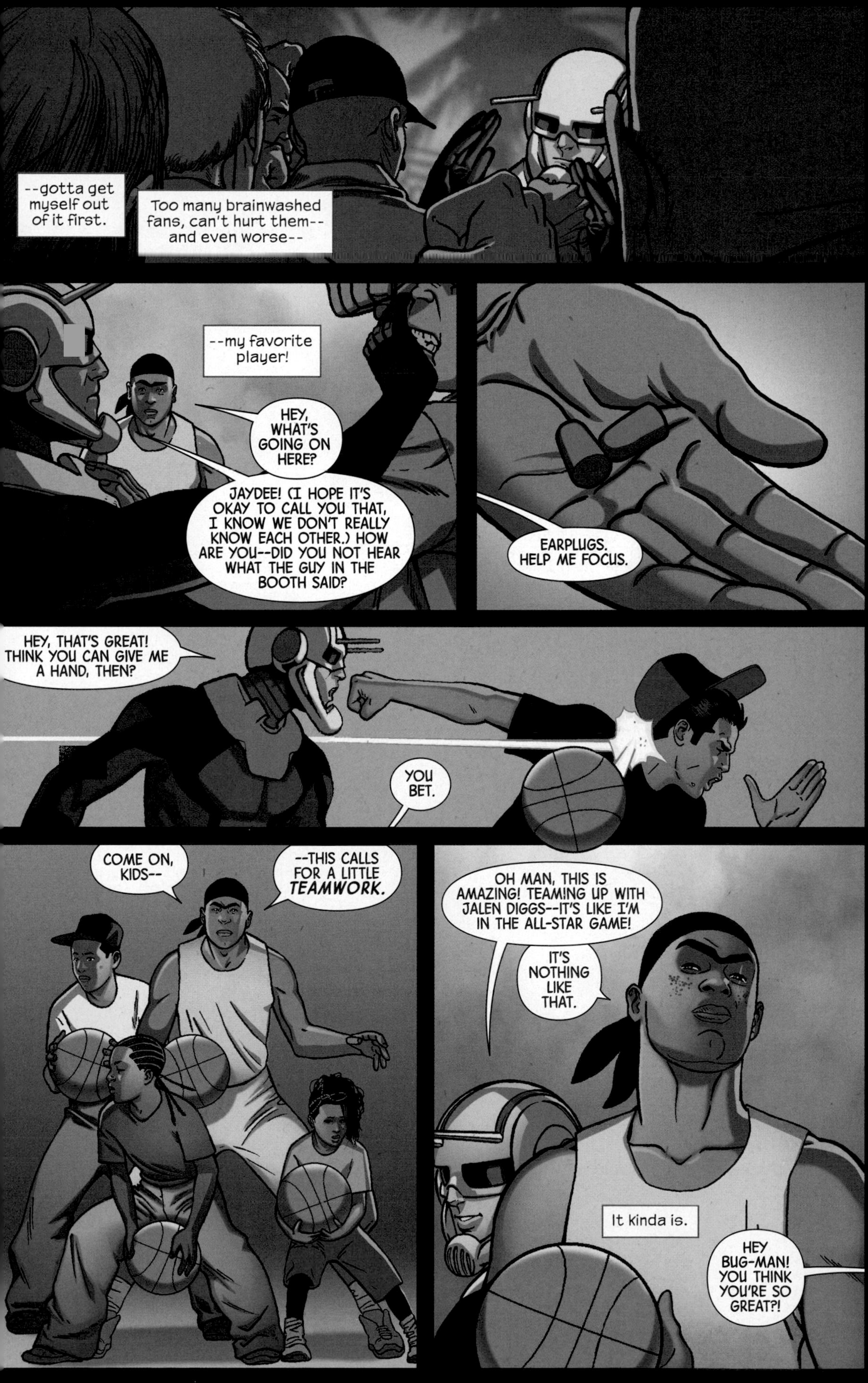
--gotta get myself out of it first.
Too many brainwashed fans, can't hurt them--and even worse--
--my favorite player!
HEY, WHAT'S GOING ON HERE?
JAYDEE! (I HOPE IT'S OKAY TO CALL YOU THAT, I KNOW WE DON'T REALLY KNOW EACH OTHER.) HOW ARE YOU--DID YOU NOT HEAR WHAT THE GUY IN THE BOOTH SAID?
EARPLUGS. HELP ME FOCUS.
HEY, THAT'S GREAT! THINK YOU CAN GIVE ME A HAND, THEN?
YOU BET.
COME ON, KIDS--
--THIS CALLS FOR A LITTLE TEAMWORK.
OH MAN, THIS IS AMAZING! TEAMING UP WITH JALEN DIGGS--IT'S LIKE I'M IN THE ALL-STAR GAME!
IT'S NOTHING LIKE THAT.
It kinda is.
HEY BUG-MAN! YOU THINK YOU'RE SO GREAT?!

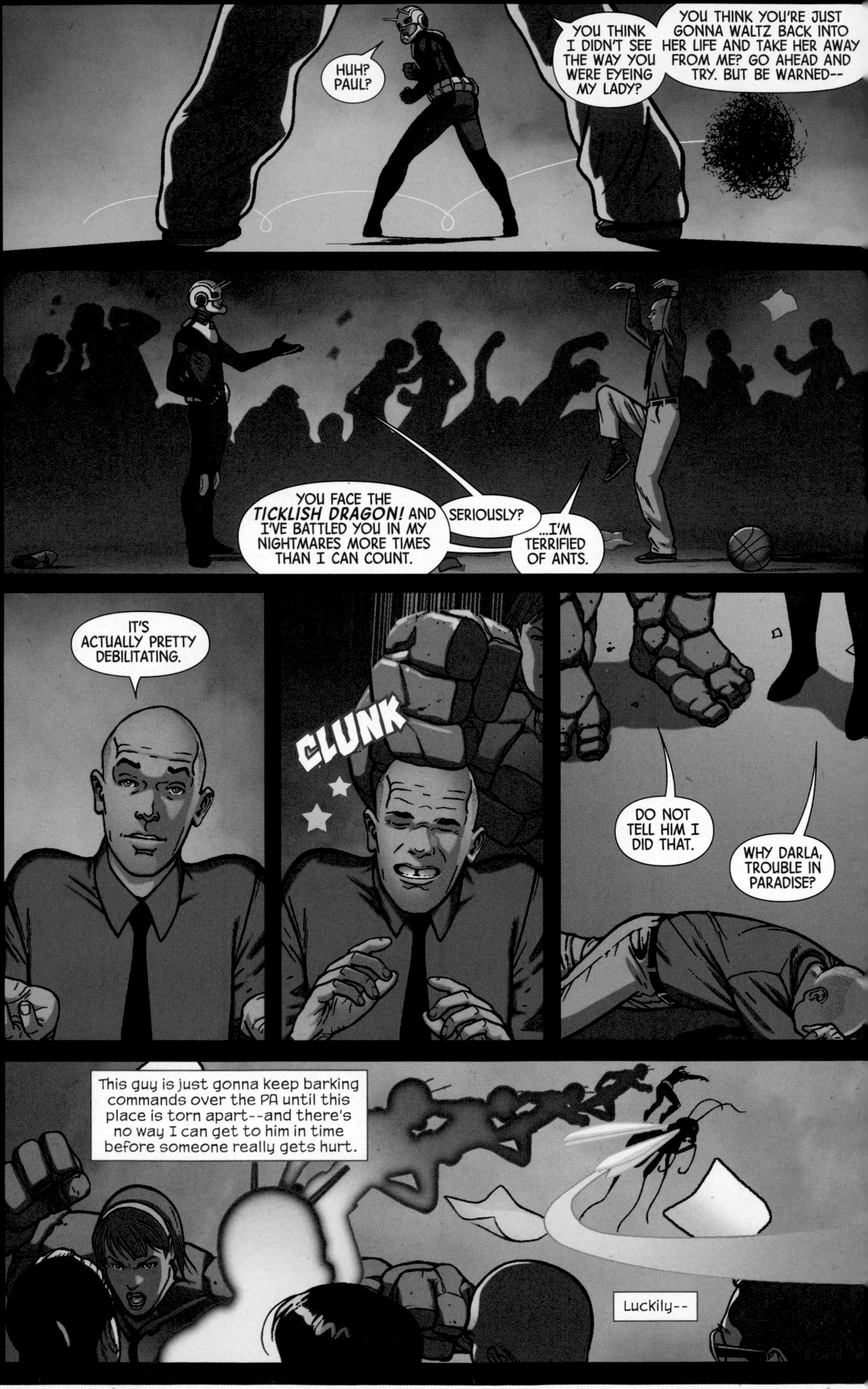
HUH? PAUL?
YOU THINK I DIDN'T SEE THE WAY YOU WERE EYEING MY LADY?
YOU THINK YOU'RE JUST GONNA WALTZ BACK INTO HER LIFE AND TAKE HER AWAY FROM ME? GO AHEAD AND TRY. BUT BE WARNED--
YOU FACE THE TICKLISH DRAGON! AND I'VE BATTLED YOU IN MY NIGHTMARES MORE TIMES THAN I CAN COUNT.
SERIOUSLY?
...I'M TERRIFIED OF ANTS.
IT'S ACTUALLY PRETTY DEBILITATING.
CLUNK
DO NOT TELL HIM I DID THAT.
WHY DARLA, TROUBLE IN PARADISE?
This guy is just gonna keep barking commands over the PA until this place is torn apart--and there's no way I can get to him in time before someone really gets hurt.
Luckily--

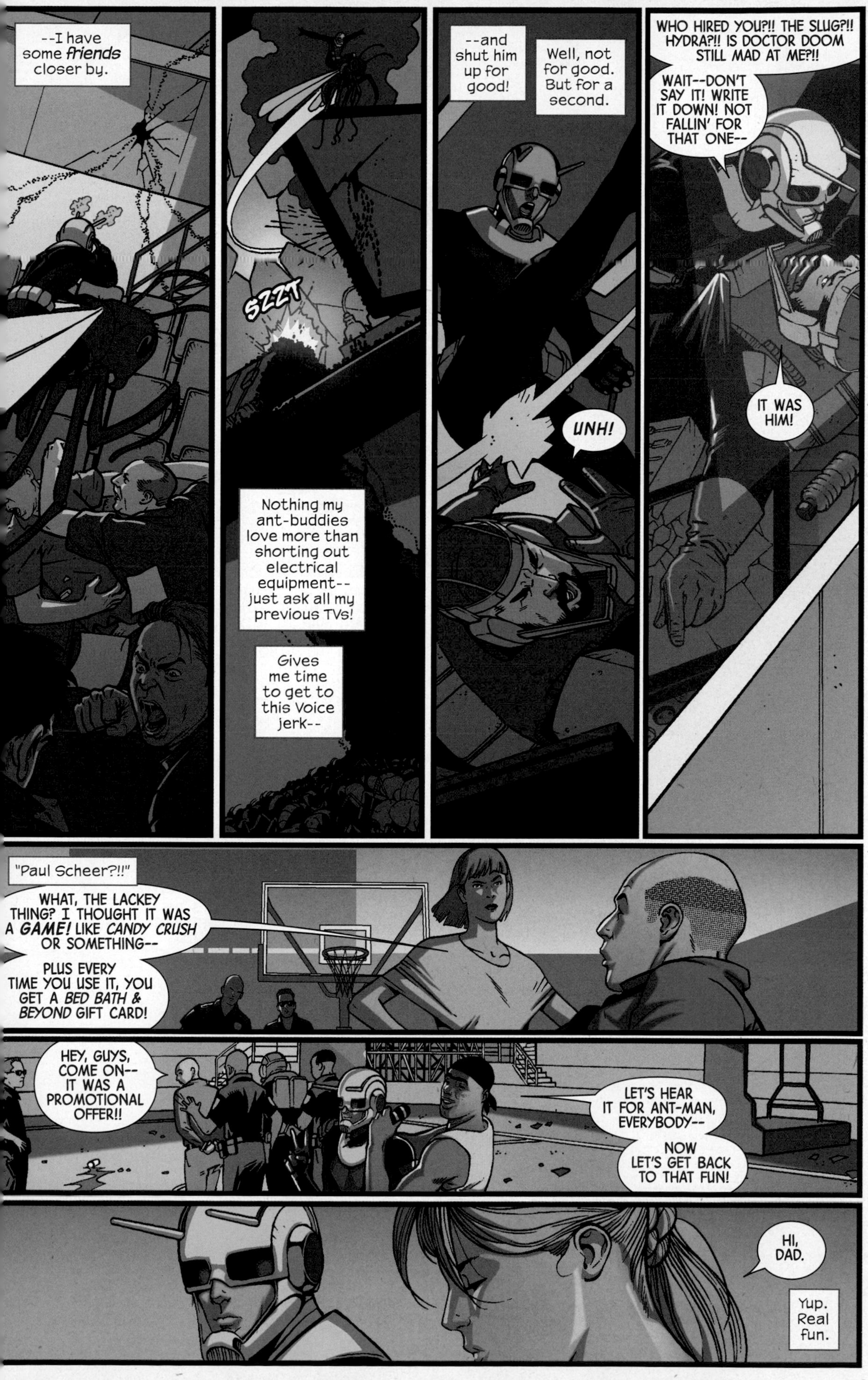
--I have some *friends* closer by.
SZZT
Nothing my ant-buddies love more than shorting out electrical equipment--just ask all my previous TVs!
Gives me time to get to this Voice jerk--
--and shut him up for good!
Well, not for good. But for a second.
UNH!
WHO HIRED YOU?!! THE SLUG?!! HYDRA?!! IS DOCTOR DOOM STILL MAD AT ME?!!
WAIT--DON'T SAY IT! WRITE IT DOWN! NOT FALLIN' FOR THAT ONE--
IT WAS HIM!
"Paul Scheer?!!"
WHAT, THE LACKEY THING? I THOUGHT IT WAS A ***GAME!*** LIKE *CANDY CRUSH* OR SOMETHING--
PLUS EVERY TIME YOU USE IT, YOU GET A *BED BATH & BEYOND* GIFT CARD!
HEY, GUYS, COME ON--IT WAS A PROMOTIONAL OFFER!!
LET'S HEAR IT FOR ANT-MAN, EVERYBODY--
NOW LET'S GET BACK TO THAT FUN!
HI, DAD.
Yup. Real fun.

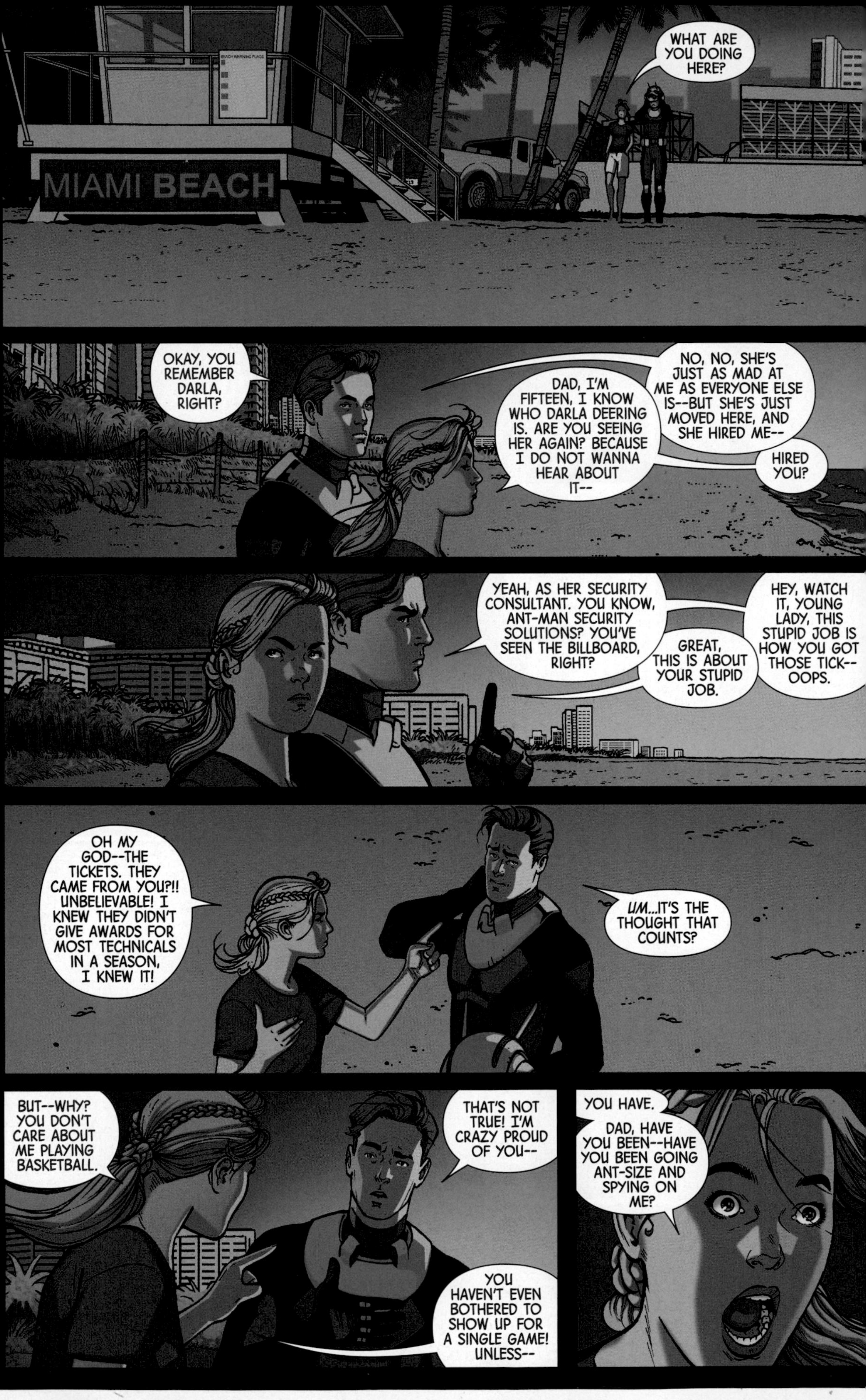
MIAMI BEACH
WHAT ARE YOU DOING HERE?
OKAY, YOU REMEMBER DARLA, RIGHT?
DAD, I'M FIFTEEN, I KNOW WHO DARLA DEERING IS. ARE YOU SEEING HER AGAIN? BECAUSE I DO NOT WANNA HEAR ABOUT IT--
NO, NO, SHE'S JUST AS MAD AT ME AS EVERYONE ELSE IS--BUT SHE'S JUST MOVED HERE, AND SHE HIRED ME--
HIRED YOU?
YEAH, AS HER SECURITY CONSULTANT. YOU KNOW, ANT-MAN SECURITY SOLUTIONS? YOU'VE SEEN THE BILLBOARD, RIGHT?
GREAT, THIS IS ABOUT YOUR STUPID JOB.
HEY, WATCH IT, YOUNG LADY, THIS STUPID JOB IS HOW YOU GOT THOSE TICK-- OOPS.
OH MY GOD--THE TICKETS. THEY CAME FROM YOU?!! UNBELIEVABLE! I KNEW THEY DIDN'T GIVE AWARDS FOR MOST TECHNICALS IN A SEASON, I KNEW IT!
UM...IT'S THE THOUGHT THAT COUNTS?
BUT--WHY? YOU DON'T CARE ABOUT ME PLAYING BASKETBALL.
THAT'S NOT TRUE! I'M CRAZY PROUD OF YOU--
YOU HAVEN'T EVEN BOTHERED TO SHOW UP FOR A SINGLE GAME! UNLESS--
YOU HAVE.
DAD, HAVE YOU BEEN--HAVE YOU BEEN GOING ANT-SIZE AND SPYING ON ME?

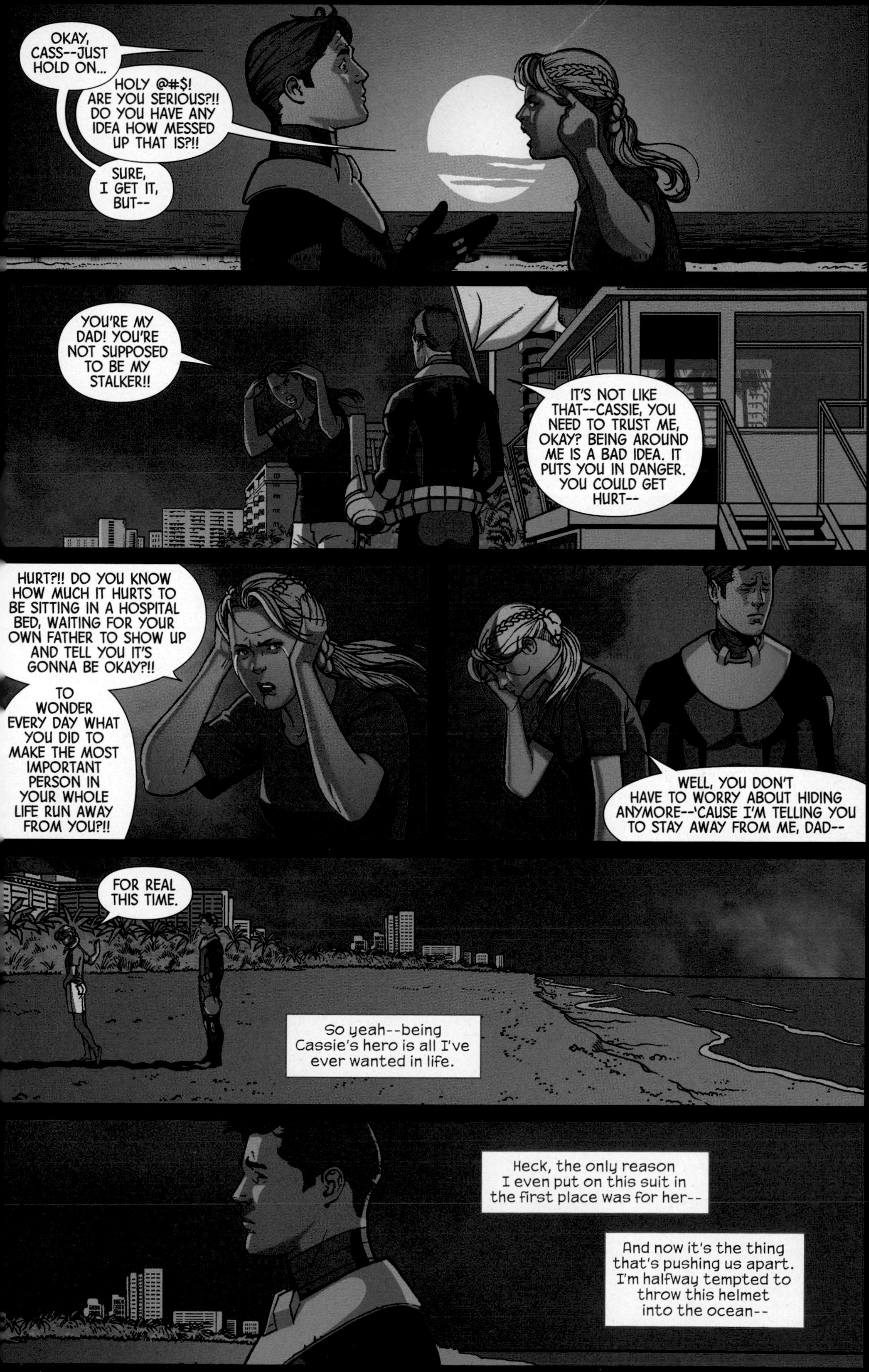

OKAY, CASS--JUST HOLD ON...
HOLY @#$! ARE YOU SERIOUS?!! DO YOU HAVE ANY IDEA HOW MESSED UP THAT IS?!!
SURE, I GET IT, BUT--
YOU'RE MY DAD! YOU'RE NOT SUPPOSED TO BE MY STALKER!!
IT'S NOT LIKE THAT--CASSIE, YOU NEED TO TRUST ME, OKAY? BEING AROUND ME IS A BAD IDEA. IT PUTS YOU IN DANGER. YOU COULD GET HURT--
HURT?!! DO YOU KNOW HOW MUCH IT HURTS TO BE SITTING IN A HOSPITAL BED, WAITING FOR YOUR OWN FATHER TO SHOW UP AND TELL YOU IT'S GONNA BE OKAY?!!
TO WONDER EVERY DAY WHAT YOU DID TO MAKE THE MOST IMPORTANT PERSON IN YOUR WHOLE LIFE RUN AWAY FROM YOU?!!
WELL, YOU DON'T HAVE TO WORRY ABOUT HIDING ANYMORE--'CAUSE I'M TELLING YOU TO STAY AWAY FROM ME, DAD--
FOR REAL THIS TIME.
So yeah--being Cassie's hero is all I've ever wanted in life.
Heck, the only reason I even put on this suit in the first place was for her--
And now it's the thing that's pushing us apart. I'm halfway tempted to throw this helmet into the ocean--

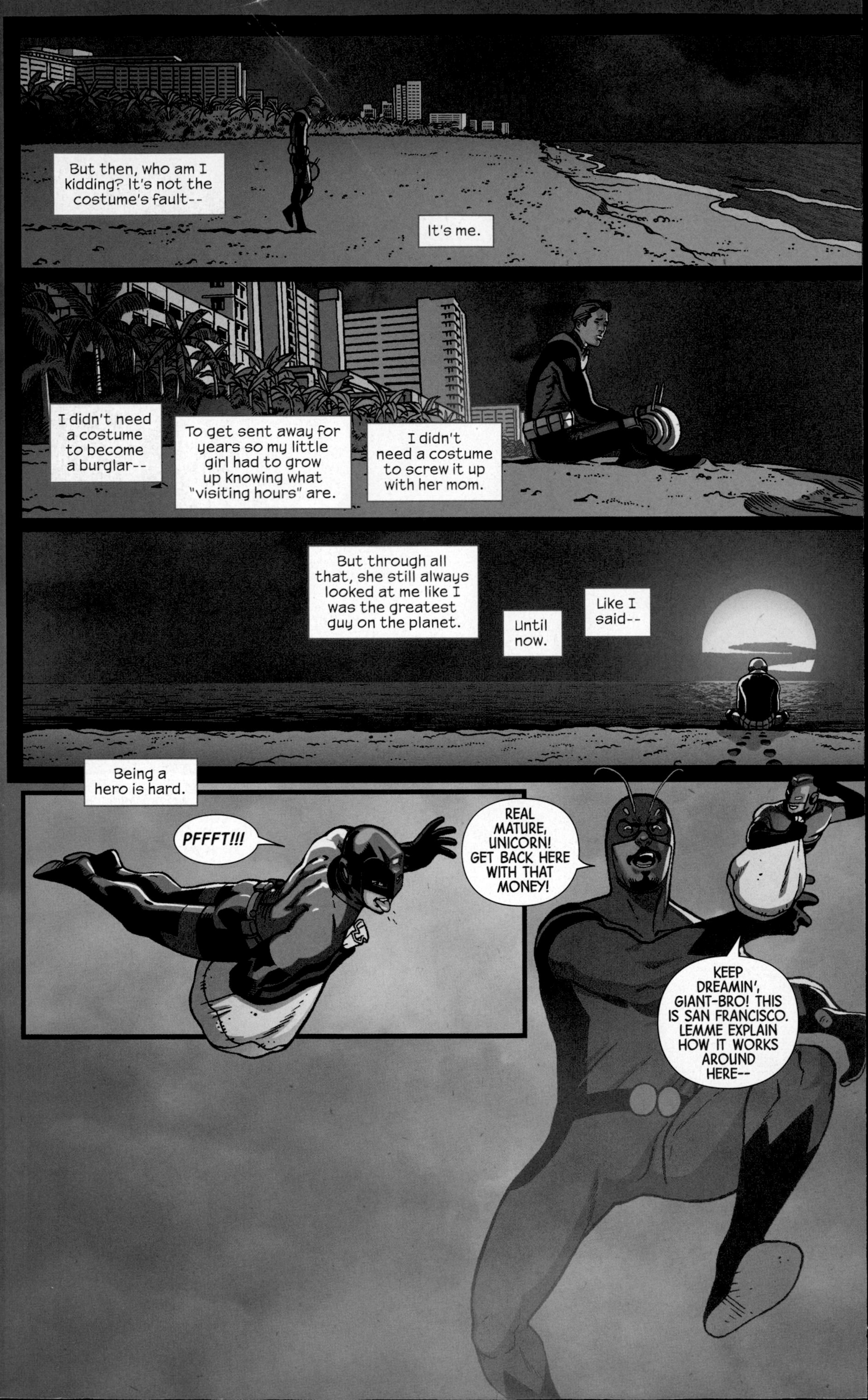
But then, who am I kidding? It's not the costume's fault--
It's me.
I didn't need a costume to become a burglar--
To get sent away for years so my little girl had to grow up knowing what "visiting hours" are.
I didn't need a costume to screw it up with her mom.
But through all that, she still always looked at me like I was the greatest guy on the planet.
Until now.
Like I said--
Being a hero is hard.
PFFFT!!!
REAL MATURE, UNICORN! GET BACK HERE WITH THAT MONEY!
KEEP DREAMIN', GIANT-BRO! THIS IS SAN FRANCISCO. LEMME EXPLAIN HOW IT WORKS AROUND HERE--

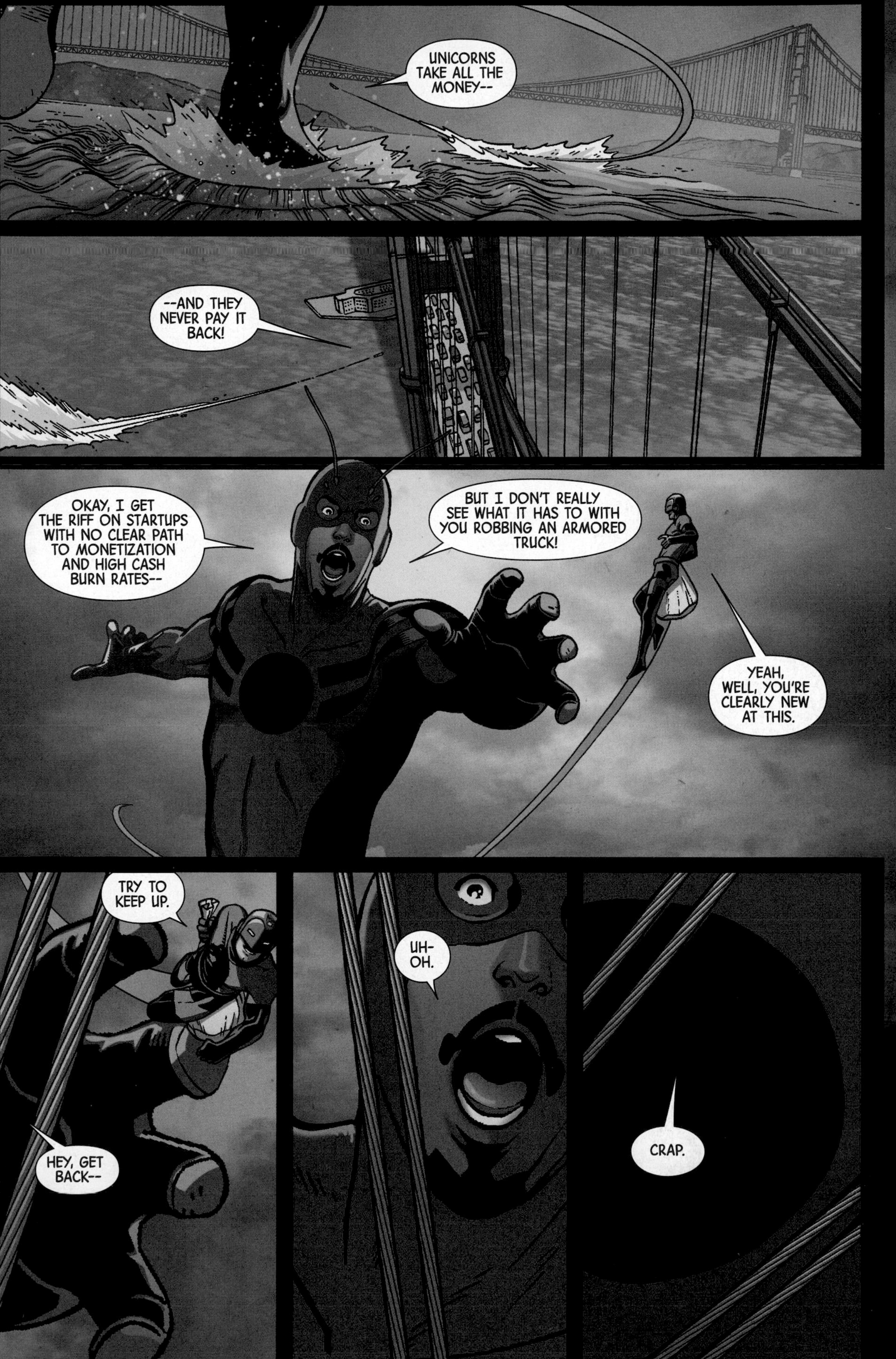
UNICORNS TAKE ALL THE MONEY--
--AND THEY NEVER PAY IT BACK!
OKAY, I GET THE RIFF ON STARTUPS WITH NO CLEAR PATH TO MONETIZATION AND HIGH CASH BURN RATES--
BUT I DON'T REALLY SEE WHAT IT HAS TO WITH YOU ROBBING AN ARMORED TRUCK!
YEAH, WELL, YOU'RE CLEARLY NEW AT THIS.
TRY TO KEEP UP.
HEY, GET BACK--
UH-OH.
CRAP.

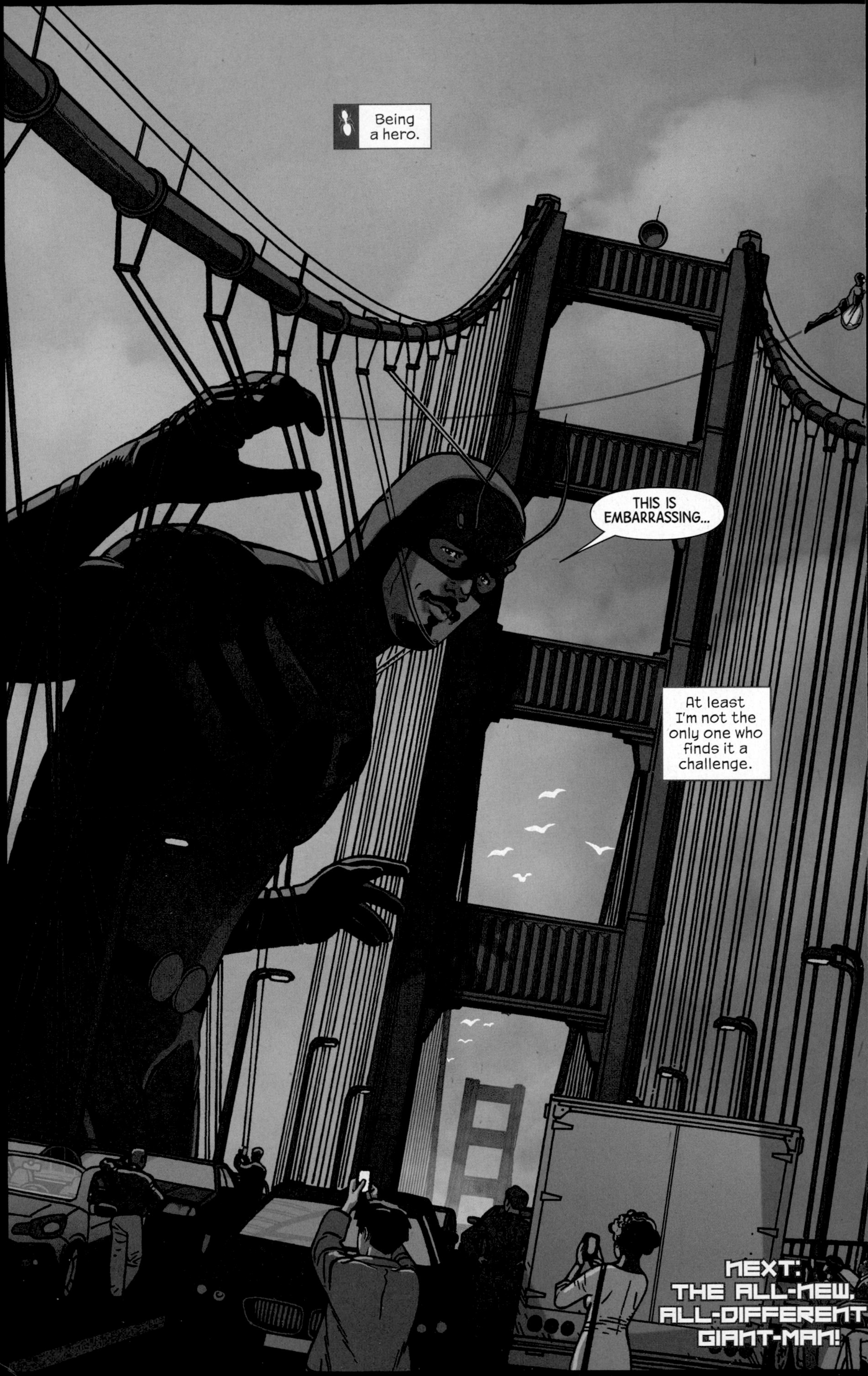
Being a hero.
THIS IS EMBARRASSING...
At least I'm not the only one who finds it a challenge.
NEXT: THE ALL-NEW, ALL-DIFFERENT GIANT-MAN!

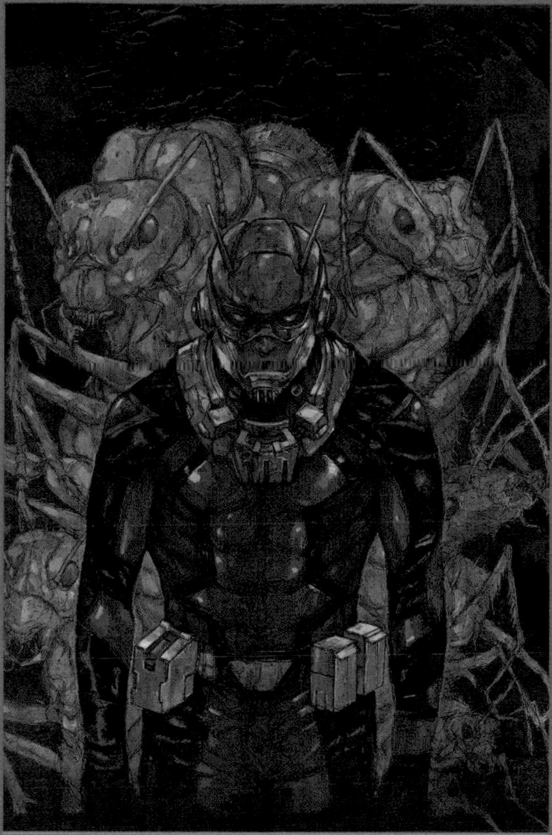

ANT-MAN: LAST DAYS #1 MANGA VARIANT
BY **Q HAYASHIDA**

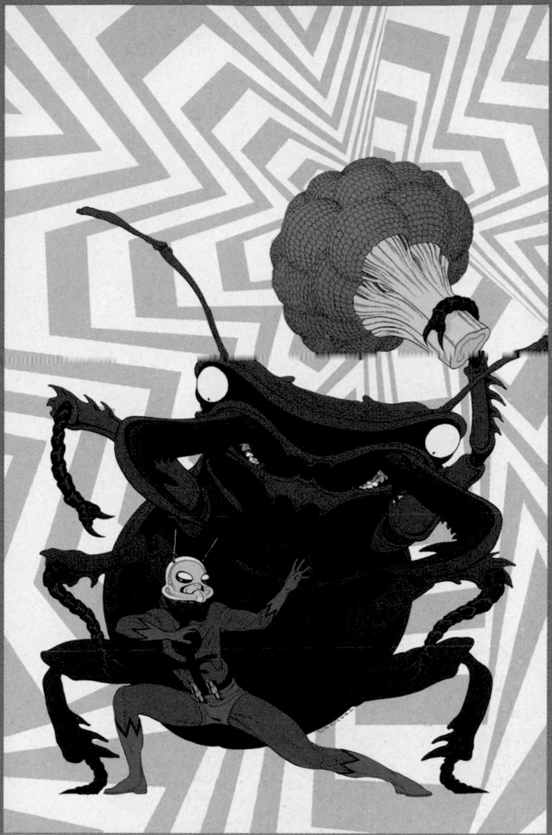

#1 KIRBY MONSTER VARIANT
BY **TRADD MOORE**

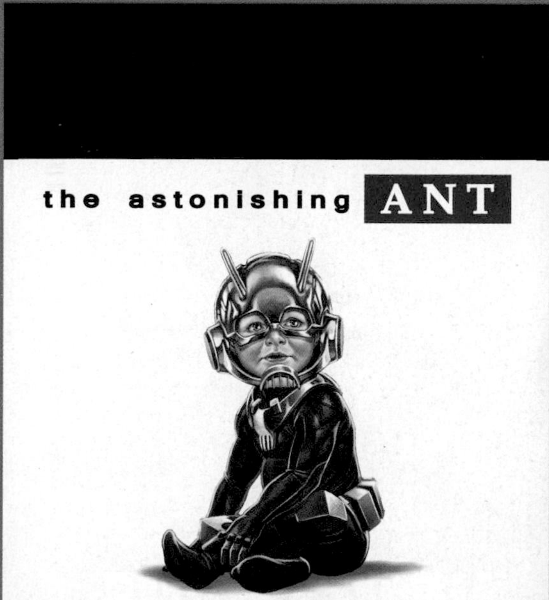

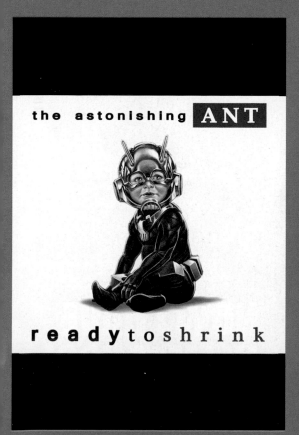

the astonishing ANT
readytoshrink

#1 HIP-HOP VARIANT
BY **MARK BROOKS**

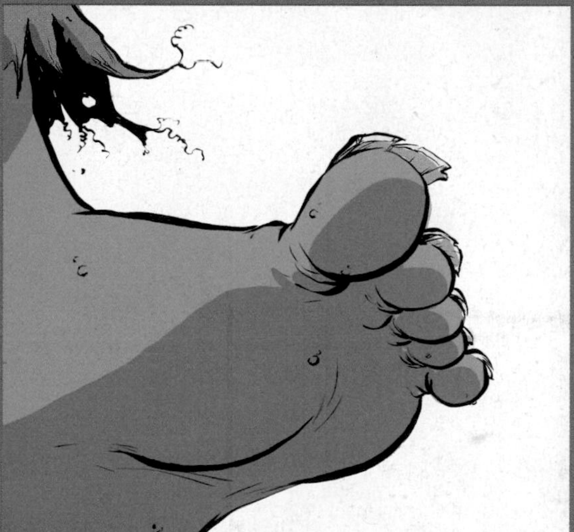

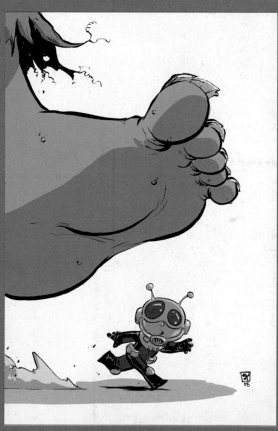

#1 VARIANT
BY **SKOTTIE YOUNG**

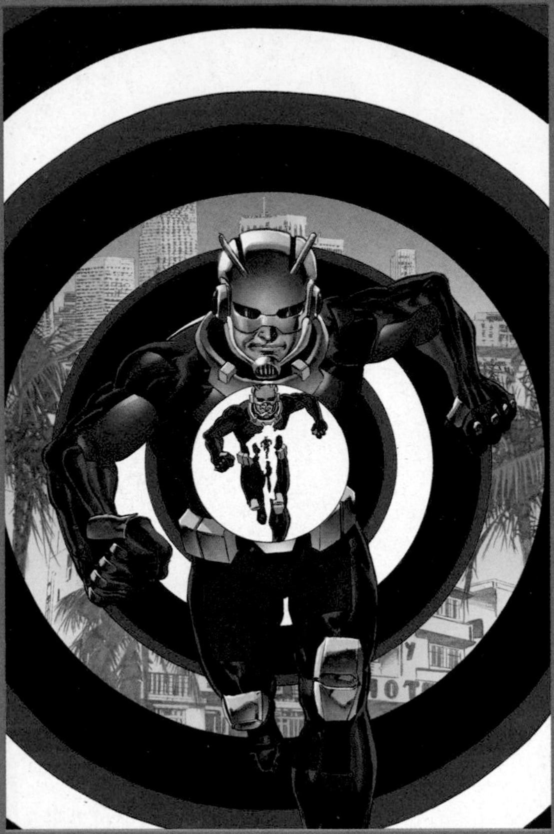

#2 VARIANT
BY **MIKE PERKINS** & **ANDY TROY**

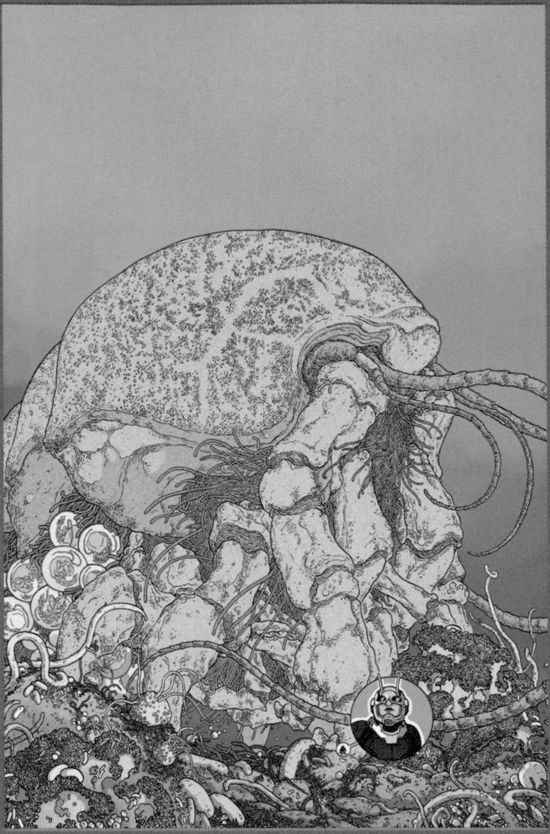

#3 VARIANT
BY **ULISES FARIÑAS**

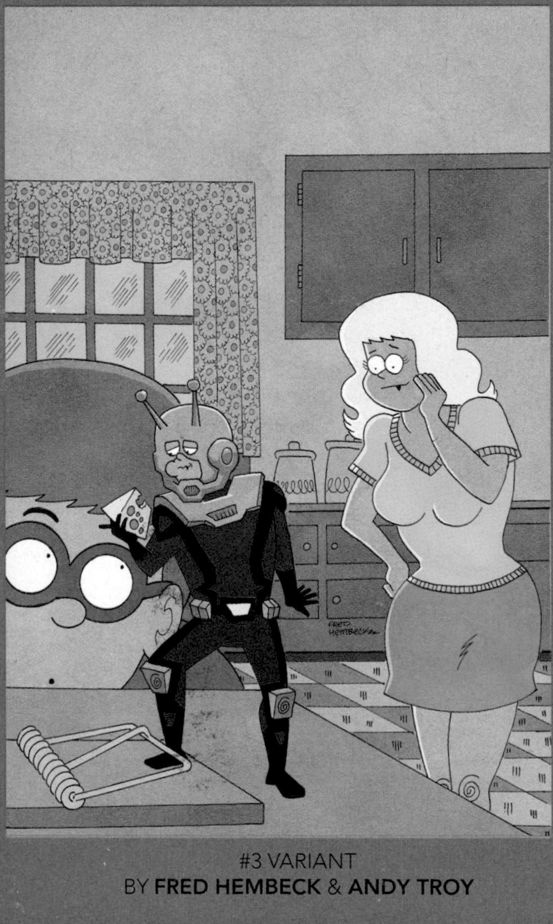

#3 VARIANT
BY **FRED HEMBECK** & **ANDY TROY**

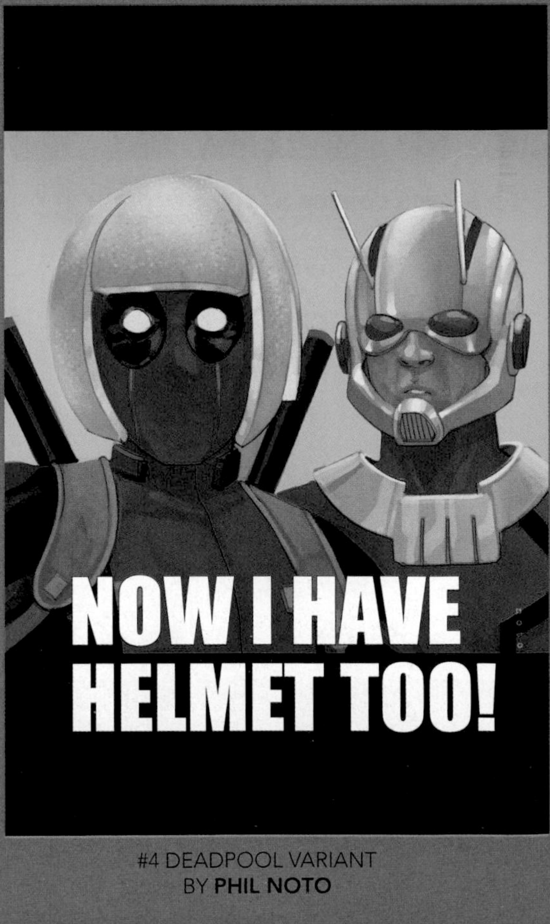
NOW I HAVE
HELMET TOO!

#4 DEADPOOL VARIANT
BY **PHIL NOTO**